Python for DevOps
Learn Ruthlessly Effective Automation

*Noah Gift, Kennedy Behrman,
Alfredo Deza, and Grig Gheorghiu*

Beijing · Boston · Farnham · Sebastopol · Tokyo

Python for DevOps

by Noah Gift, Kennedy Behrman, Alfredo Deza, and Grig Gheorghiu

Published by O'Reilly Media, Inc., 1005 Gravenstein Highway North, Sebastopol, CA 95472.

O'Reilly books may be purchased for educational, business, or sales promotional use. Online editions are also available for most titles (*http://oreilly.com*). For more information, contact our corporate/institutional sales department: 800-998-9938 or *corporate@oreilly.com*.

Acquisitions Editor: Rachel Roumeliotis
Development Editor: Corbin Collins
Production Editor: Christopher Faucher
Copyeditor: nSight, Inc.
Proofreader: Sonia Saruba

Indexer: WordCo Indexing Services, Inc.
Interior Designer: David Futato
Cover Designer: Karen Montgomery
Illustrator: Rebecca Demarest

December 2019:   First Edition

Revision History for the First Release

2019-12-11:   First Release
2020-06-19:   Second Release

See *http://oreilly.com/catalog/errata.csp?isbn=9781492057697* for release details.

978-1-492-05769-7

[LSI]

Table of Contents

Preface

One time Noah was in the ocean, and a wave crashed on top of him and took his breath away as it pulled him deeper into the sea. Just as he started to recover his breath, another wave dropped on top. It extracted much of his remaining energy. It pulled him even deeper into the ocean. Just as he started to recover, yet another wave crashed down on top. The more he would fight the waves and the sea, the more energy was drained. He seriously wondered if he would die at that moment. He couldn't breathe, his body ached, and he was terrified he was going to drown. Being close to death helped him focus on the only thing that could save him, which was conserving his energy and using the waves—not fighting them.

Being in a startup that doesn't practice DevOps is a lot like that day at the beach. There are production fires that burn for months; everything is manual, alerts wake you up for days on end damaging your health. The only escape from this death spiral is the DevOps way.

Do one right thing, then another, until you find clarity. First, set up a build server, start testing your code, and automate manual tasks. Do something; it can be anything, but have a "bias for action." Do that first thing right and make sure it is automated.

A common trap in startups or any company is the search for superheroes. "We need a performance engineer" because they will fix our performance problems. "We need a Chief Revenue Officer" because they will fix all sales problems. "We need DevOps engineers" because they will fix our deployment process.

At one company, Noah had a project that was over a year late, and the web application had been rewritten three times in multiple languages. This next release only needed a "performance engineer" to get it finished. I remember being the only one brave or stupid enough to say, "What is a performance engineer?" This engineer made everything work at scale. He realized at that point that they were looking for a superhero to save them. Superhero hiring syndrome is the best way to pick up on something being very wrong on a new product or a new startup. No employee will save a company unless they first save themselves.

At other companies, Noah heard similar things: "If we could only hire a senior Erlang engineer," or "If we could only hire someone to make us revenue," or "If we could only hire someone to teach us to be financially disciplined," or "If we could only hire a Swift developer," etc. This hire is the last thing your startup or new product needs— it needs to understand what it is doing wrong that only a superhero can save the day.

In the case of the company that wanted to hire a performance engineer, it turned out that the real issue was inadequate technical supervision. The wrong people were in charge (and verbally shouting down the people who could fix it). By removing a poor performer, listening to an existing team member who knew how to fix the problem all along, deleting that job listing, doing one right thing at a time, and inserting qualified engineering management, the issue resolved itself without a superhero hire.

No one will save you at your startup; you and your team have to protect yourselves by creating great teamwork, a great process, and believing in your organization. The solution to the problem isn't a new hire; it is being honest and mindful about the situation you are in, how you got there, and doing one right thing at a time until you work your way out. There is no superhero unless it is you.

Just like being in the ocean in a storm and slowly drowning, no one is going to save you or the company unless it is you. You are the superhero your company needs, and you might discover your coworkers are too.

There is a way out of the chaos, and this book can be your guide. Let's get started.

What Does DevOps Mean to the Authors?

Many abstract concepts in the software industry are hard to define precisely. Cloud Computing, Agile, and Big Data are good examples of topics that can have many definitions depending on whom you talk to. Instead of strictly defining what DevOps is, let's use some phrases that show evidence DevOps is occurring:

- Two-way collaboration between Development and Operation teams.
- Turnaround of Ops tasks in minutes to hours, not days to weeks.
- Strong involvement from developers; otherwise, it's back to Devs versus Ops.
- Operations people need development skills—at least Bash and Python.
- Developer people need operational skills—their responsibilities don't end with writing the code, but with deploying the system to production and monitoring alerts.
- Automation, automation, automation: you can't accurately automate without Dev skills, and you can't correctly automate without Ops skills
- Ideally: self-service for developers, at least in terms of deploying code.

- Can be achieved via CI/CD pipelines.
- GitOps.
- Bidirectional *everything* between Development and Operations (tooling, knowledge, etc.).
- Constant collaboration in design, implementation, deployment—and yes, automation—can't be successful without cooperation.
- If it isn't automated, it's broken.
- Cultural: Hierarchy < Process.
- Microservices > Monolithic.
- The continuous deployment system is the heart and soul of the software team.
- There are no superheroes.
- Continuous delivery isn't an option; it is a mandate.

How to Use This Book

This book is useful in any order. You can randomly open any chapter you like, and you should be able to find something helpful to apply to your job. If you are an experienced Python programmer, you may want to skim Chapter 1. Likewise, if you are interested in war stories, case studies, and interviews, you may want to read the Chapter 16 first.

Conceptual Topics

The content is broken up into several conceptual topics. The first group is Python Foundations, and it covers a brief introduction to the language as well as automating text, writing command-line tools, and automating the file system.

Next up is Operations, which includes useful Linux utilities, package management, build systems, monitoring and instrumentation, and automated testing. These are all essential topics to master to become a competent DevOps practitioner.

Cloud Foundations are in the next section, and there are chapters on Cloud Computing, Infrastructure as Code, Kubernetes, and Serverless. There is currently a crisis in the software industry around finding enough talent trained in the Cloud. Mastering this section will pay immediate dividends to both your salary and your career.

Next up is the Data section. Machine Learning Operations and Data Engineering are both covered from the perspective of DevOps. There is also a full soup to nuts machine learning project walkthrough that takes you through the building, deploying, and operationalizing of a machine learning model using Flask, Sklearn, Docker, and Kubernetes.

The last section is Chapter 16 on case studies, interviews, and DevOps war stories. This chapter makes for good bed time reading.

Python Foundations

- Chapter 1, *Python Essentials for DevOps*
- Chapter 2, *Automating Files and the Filesystem*
- Chapter 3, *Working with the Command Line*

Operations

- Chapter 4, *Useful Linux Utilities*
- Chapter 5, *Package Management*
- Chapter 6, *Continuous Integration and Continuous Deployment*
- Chapter 7, *Monitoring and Logging*
- Chapter 8, *Pytest for DevOps*

Cloud Foundations

- Chapter 9, *Cloud Computing*
- Chapter 10, *Infrastructure as Code*
- Chapter 11, *Container Technologies: Docker and Docker Compose*
- Chapter 12, *Container Orchestration: Kubernetes*
- Chapter 13, *Serverless Technologies*

Data

- Chapter 14, *MLOps and Machine learning Engineering*
- Chapter 15, *Data Engineering*

Case Studies

- Chapter 16, *DevOps War Stories and Interviews*

Conventions Used in This Book

The following typographical conventions are used in this book:

Italic
: Indicates new terms, URLs, email addresses, filenames, and file extensions.

`Constant width`
: Used for program listings, as well as within paragraphs to refer to program elements such as variable or function names, databases, data types, environment variables, statements, and keywords.

`Constant width bold`
: Shows commands or other text that should be typed literally by the user.

`Constant width italic`
: Shows text that should be replaced with user-supplied values or by values determined by context.

 This element signifies a tip or suggestion.

 This element signifies a general note.

 This element indicates a warning or caution.

Using Code Examples

Supplemental material (code examples, exercises, etc.) is available for download at *https://pythondevops.com*. You can also view DevOps content related to the code in the book at the Pragmatic AI Labs YouTube channel (*https://oreil.ly/QIYte*).

If you have a technical question for the authors or a problem using the code examples, please email *technical@pythondevops.com*.

This book is here to help you get your job done. In general, if example code is offered with this book, you may use it in your programs and documentation. You do not need to contact us for permission unless you're reproducing a significant portion of the code. For example, writing a program that uses several chunks of code from this book does not require permission. Selling or distributing examples from O'Reilly books does require permission. Answering a question by citing this book and quoting example code does not require permission. Incorporating a significant amount of example code from this book into your product's documentation does require permission.

We appreciate, but generally do not require, attribution. An attribution usually includes the title, author, publisher, and ISBN. For example: "*Python for DevOps* by Noah Gift, Kennedy Behrman, Alfredo Deza, and Grig Gheorghiu. (O'Reilly). Copyright 2020 Noah Gift, Kennedy Behrman, Alfredo Deza, Grig Gheorghiu, 978-1-492-05769-7."

If you feel your use of code examples falls outside fair use or the permission given above, feel free to contact us at *permissions@oreilly.com*.

O'Reilly Online Learning

 For more than 40 years, *O'Reilly Media* has provided technology and business training, knowledge, and insight to help companies succeed.

Our unique network of experts and innovators share their knowledge and expertise through books, articles, and our online learning platform. O'Reilly's online learning platform gives you on-demand access to live training courses, in-depth learning paths, interactive coding environments, and a vast collection of text and video from O'Reilly and 200+ other publishers. For more information, please visit *http://oreilly.com*.

How to Contact Us

Please address comments and questions concerning this book to the publisher:

O'Reilly Media, Inc.
1005 Gravenstein Highway North
Sebastopol, CA 95472
800-998-9938 (in the United States or Canada)
707-829-0515 (international or local)
707-829-0104 (fax)

We have a web page for this book, where we list errata, examples, and any additional information. You can access this page at *oreil.ly/python-for-devops*.

Email *bookquestions@oreilly.com* to comment or ask technical questions about this book.

For news and more information about our books and courses, see our website at *http://www.oreilly.com*.

Find us on Facebook: *http://facebook.com/oreilly*

Follow us on Twitter: *http://twitter.com/oreillymedia*

Watch us on YouTube: *http://www.youtube.com/oreillymedia*

Acknowledgments

To start off, the authors would like to thank the two main technical reviewers of the book:

Wes Novack is an architect and engineer specializing in public cloud systems and web-scale SaaS applications. He designs, builds, and manages complex systems that enable highly available infrastructure, continuous delivery pipelines, and rapid releases within large, polyglot microservice ecosystems hosted on AWS and GCP. Wes makes extensive use of languages, frameworks, and tools to define Infrastructure as Code, drive automation, and eliminate toil. He is vocal in the tech community by participating in mentorship, workshops, and conferences, and he is also a Pluralsight video course author. Wes is an advocate for the CALMS of DevOps; Culture, Automation, Lean, Measurement, and Sharing. You can find him on Twitter @WesleyTech or visit his personal blog (*https://wesnovack.com*).

Brad Andersen is a software engineer and architect. He has designed and developed software professionally for 30 years. He works as a catalyst for change and innovation; he has assumed leadership and development roles across a spectrum from enterprise organizations to startups. Brad is currently pursuing a master's degree in data science at the University of California, Berkeley. You can find more information on Brad's LinkedIn profile (*https://www.linkedin.com/in/andersen-bradley*).

We would also like to thank Jeremy Yabrow and Colin B. Erdman for chipping in with many great ideas and bits of feedback.

Noah

I would like to thank the coauthors of the book: Grig, Kennedy, and Alfredo. It was incredible working with a team that was this effective.

Kennedy

Thanks to my coauthors, it has been a pleasure to work with you. And thanks for the patience and understanding of my family.

Alfredo

In 2010—nine years ago as of this writing—I landed my first software engineering job. I was 31 years old with no college education and no previous engineering experience. That job meant accepting a reduced salary and no health insurance. I learned a lot, met amazing people, and gained expertise through relentless determination. Throughout those years, it would've been impossible to get here without people opening opportunities and pointing me in the right direction.

Thanks to Chris Benson, who saw that I was hungry for learning and kept finding opportunities to have me around.

Thanks to Alejandro Cadavid, who realized that I could fix things nobody else wanted to fix. You helped me get work when no one (including myself) thought I could be useful.

Carlos Coll got me into programming and didn't let me quit even when I asked him to. Learning to program changed my life, and Carlos had the patience to push me to learn and land my first program in production.

To Joni Benton, for believing in me and helping me land my first full-time job.

Thanks to Jonathan LaCour, an inspiring boss who continues to help me get to a better place. Your advice has always been invaluable to me.

Noah, thanks for your friendship and guidance you are a tremendous source of motivation to me. I always enjoy working together, like that one time when we rebuilt infrastructure from scratch. Your patience and guidance when I had no idea about Python was life-changing.

Lastly, a tremendous thanks to my family. My wife Claudia, who never doubts my ability to learn and improve, and so generous and understanding of the time I spent working toward this book. My children, Efrain, Ignacio, and Alana: I love you all.

Grig

My thanks to all creators of open source software. Without them, our jobs would be so much more bleak and unfulfilling. Also thank you to all who blog and share your knowledge freely. Lastly, I also wish to thank the coauthors of this book. It's been a really fun ride.

## CHAPTER 1

Python Essentials for DevOps

DevOps, the combination of software development with information technology operations, has been a hot field during the last decade. Traditional boundaries among software development, deployment, maintenance, and quality assurance have been broken, enabling more integrated teams. Python has been a popular language both in traditional IT operations and in DevOps due to its combination of flexibility, power, and ease of use.

The Python programming language was publicly released in the early 1990s for use in system administration. It has been a great success in this area and has gained wide adoption. Python is a general-purpose programming language used in just about every domain. The visual effects and the motion picture industries embraced it. More recently, it has become the de facto language of data science and machine learning (ML). It has been used across industries from aviation to bioinformatics. Python has an extensive arsenal of tools to cover the wide-ranging needs of its users. Learning the whole Python Standard Library (the capabilities that come with any Python installation) would be a daunting task. Trying to learn all the third-party packages that enliven the Python ecosystem would be an immense undertaking. The good news is that you don't need to do those things. You can become a powerful DevOps practitioner by learning only a small subset of Python.

In this chapter, we draw on our decades of Python DevOps experience to teach only the elements of the language that you need. These are the parts of Python DevOps that are used daily. They form the essential toolbox to get things done. Once you have these core concepts down, you can add more complicated tools, as you'll see in later chapters.

Installing and Running Python

If you want to try the code in this overview, you need Python 3.7 or later installed (the latest release is 3.8.0 as of this writing) and access to a shell. In macOS X, Windows, and most Linux distributions, you can open the terminal application to access a shell. To see what version of Python you are using, open a shell, and type `python --version`:

```
$ python --version
Python 3.8.0
```

Python installers can be downloaded directly from the Python.org website (*https://www.python.org/downloads*). Alternatively, you can use a package manager such as Apt, RPM, MacPorts, Homebrew, Chocolatey, or many others.

The Python Shell

The simplest way to run Python is to use the built-in interactive interpreter. Just type `python` in a shell. You can then interactively run Python statements. Type `exit()` to exit the shell.

```
$ python
Python 3.8.0 (default, Sep 23 2018, 09:47:03)
[Clang 9.0.0 (clang-900.0.38)] on darwin
Type "help", "copyright", "credits" or "license" for more information.
>>> 1 + 2
3
>>> exit()
```

Python scripts

Python code runs from a file with the *.py* extension:

```
# This is my first Python script
print('Hello world!')
```

Save this code to a file named *hello.py*. To invoke the script, in a shell run `python` followed by the filename:

```
$ python hello.py
Hello world!
```

Python scripts are how most production Python code runs.

IPython

Besides the built-in interactive shell, several third-party interactive shells run Python code. One of the most popular is IPython (*https://ipython.org*). IPython offers *introspection* (the ability to dynamically get information about objects), syntax highlighting, special *magic* commands (which we touch on later in this chapter), and many more features, making it a pleasure to use for exploring Python. To install IPython, use the Python package manager, pip:

```
$ pip install ipython
```

Running is similar to running the built-in interactive shell described in the previous section:

```
$ ipython
Python 3.8.0 (default, Sep 23 2018, 09:47:03)
Type 'copyright', 'credits' or 'license' for more information
IPython 7.5.0 -- An enhanced Interactive Python. Type '?' for help.
In [1]: print('Hello')
Hello

In [2]: exit()
```

Jupyter Notebooks

A spin-off from the iPython project, the Jupyter project allows documents containing text, code, and visualizations. These documents are powerful tools for combining running code, output, and formatted text. Jupyter enables the delivery of documentation along with the code. It has achieved widespread popularity, especially in the data science world. Here is how to install and run Jupyter notebooks:

```
$ pip install jupyter
$ jupyter notebook
```

This command opens a web browser tab showing the current working directory. From here, you can open existing notebooks in the current project or create new ones.

Procedural Programming

If you've been around programming at all, you've probably heard terms like object-oriented programming (OOP) and functional programming. These are different architectural paradigms used to organize programs. One of the most basic paradigms, procedural programming, is an excellent place to start. *Procedural programming* is the issuing of instructions to a computer in an ordered sequence:

```
>>> i = 3
>>> j = i +1
>>> i + j
7
```

As you can see in this example, there are three statements that are executed in order from the first line to the last. Each statement uses the state produced by the previous ones. In this case, the first statement assigns the value 3 to a variable named i. In the second statement, this variable's value is used to assign a value to a variable named j, and in the third statement, the values from both variables are added together. Don't worry about the details of these statements yet; notice that they are executed in order and rely on the state created by the previous statements.

Variables

A variable is a name that points to some value. In the previous example, the variables are i and j . Variables in Python can be assigned to new values:

```
>>> dog_name = 'spot'
>>> dog_name
'spot'
>>> dog_name = 'rex'
>>> dog_name
'rex'
>>> dog_name = 't-' + dog_name
>>> dog_name
't-rex'
>>>
```

Python variables use dynamic typing. In practice, this means that they can be reassigned to values of different types or classes:

```
>>> big = 'large'
>>> big
'large'
>>> big = 1000*1000
>>> big
1000000
>>> big = {}
>>> big
{}
>>>
```

Here the same variable is set to a string, a number, and a dictionary. Variables can be reassigned to values of any type.

Basic Math

Basic math operations such as addition, subtraction, multiplication, and division can all be performed using built-in math operators:

```
>>> 1 + 1
2
>>> 3 - 4
-1
>>> 2*5
10
>>> 2/3
0.6666666666666666
```

Note that a // symbol is for integer division. The symbol ** creates an exponent, and % is the modulo operator:

```
>>> 5/2
2.5
>>> 5//2
2
>>> 3**2
9
>>> 5%2
1
```

Comments

Comments are text ignored by the Python interpreter. They are useful for documentation of code and can be mined by some services to provide standalone documentation. Single-line comments are delineated by prepending with #. A single-line comment can start at the beginning of a line, or at any point thereafter. Everything after the # is part of the comment until a new line break occurs:

```
# This is a comment
1 + 1 # This comment follows a statement
```

Multiline comments are enclosed themselves in blocks beginning and ending with either """ or ''':

```
"""
This statement is a block comment.
It can run for multiple lines
"""

'''
This statement is also a block comment
'''
```

Built-in Functions

Functions are statements grouped as a unit. You invoke a function by typing the function name, followed by parentheses. If the function takes arguments, the arguments appear within the parentheses. Python has many built-in functions. Two of the most widely used built-in functions are print and range.

Print

The print function produces output that a user of a program can view. It is less relevant in interactive environments but is a fundamental tool when writing Python scripts. In the previous example, the argument to the print function is written as output when the script runs:

```
# This is my first Python script
print("Hello world!")

$ python hello.py
Hello world!
```

print can be used to see the value of a variable or to give feedback as to the state of a program. print generally outputs the standard output stream and is visible as program output in a shell.

Range

Though range is a built-in function, it is technically not a function at all. It is a type representing a sequence of numbers. When calling the range() constructor, an object representing a sequence of numbers is returned. Range objects count through a sequence of numbers. The range function takes up to three integer arguments. If only one argument appears, then the sequence is represented by the numbers from zero up to, but not including, that number. If a second argument appears, it represents the starting point, rather than the default of starting from 0. The third argument can be used to specify the step distance, and it defaults to 1.

```
>>> range(10)
range(0, 10)
>>> list(range(10))
[0, 1, 2, 3, 4, 5, 6, 7, 8, 9]
>>> list(range(5, 10))
[5, 6, 7, 8, 9]
>>> list(range(5, 10, 3))
[5, 8]
>>>
```

range maintains a small memory footprint, even over extended sequences, as it only stores the start, stop, and step values. The range function can iterate through long sequences of numbers without performance constraints.

Execution Control

Python has many constructs to control the flow of statement execution. You can group statements you wish to run together as a block of code. These blocks can be run multiple times using for and while loops or only run under certain conditions using if statements, while loops, or try-except blocks. Using these constructs is the first step to taking advantage of the power of programming. Different languages demarcate blocks of code using different conventions. Many languages with syntax similar to the C language (a very influential language used in writing Unix) use curly brackets around a group of statements to define a block. In Python, indentation is used to indicate a block. Statements are grouped by indentation into blocks that execute as a unit.

The Python interpreter does not care if you use tabs or spaces to indent, as long as you are consistent. The Python style guide, PEP-8 (*https://oreil.ly/b5yU4*), however, recommends using four whitespaces for each level of indentation.

if/elif/else

`if/elif/else` statements are common ways to branch between decisions in code. A block directly after an `if` statement runs if that statement evaluates to `True`:

```
>>> i = 45
>>> if i == 45:
...     print('i is 45')
...
...
i is 45
>>>
```

Here we used the == operator, which returns `True` if items are equal and `False` if not. Optionally, this block can follow an `elif` or `else` statement with an accompanying block. In the case of an `elif` statement, this block only executes if the `elif` evaluates to `True`:

```
>>> i = 35
>>> if i == 45:
...     print('i is 45')
... elif i == 35:
...     print('i is 35')
...
...
i is 35
>>>
```

Multiple `elif` loops can append together. If you are familiar with `switch` statements in other languages, this simulates that same behavior of choosing from multiple choices. Adding an `else` statement at the end runs a block if none of the other conditions evaluate as `True`:

```
>>> i = 0
>>> if i == 45:
...     print('i is 45')
... elif i == 35:
...     print('i is 35')
... elif i > 10:
...     print('i is greater than 10')
... elif i%3 == 0:
...     print('i is a multiple of 3')
... else:
...     print('I don't know much about i...')
...
```

```
...
i is a multiple of 3
>>>
```

You can nest if statements, creating blocks containing if statements that only execute if an outer if statement is True:

```
>>> cat = 'spot'
>>> if 's' in cat:
...     print("Found an 's' in a cat")
...     if cat == 'Sheba':
...         print("I found Sheba")
...     else:
...         print("Some other cat")
... else:
...     print(" a cat without 's'")
...
...
Found an 's' in a cat
Some other cat
>>>
```

for Loops

for loops allow you to repeat a block of statements (a code block) once for each
member of a *sequence* (ordered group of items). As you iterate through the sequence,
the current item can be accessed by the code block. One of most common uses of
loops is to iterate through a range object to do a task a set number of times:

```
>>> for i in range(10):
...     x = i*2
...     print(x)
...
...
0
2
4
6
8
10
12
14
16
18
>>>
```

In this example, our block of code is as follows:

```
...     x = i*2
...     print(x)
```

We repeat this code 10 times, each time assigning the variable i to the next number in the sequence of integers from 0–9. for loops can be used to iterate through any of the Python sequence types. You will see these later in this chapter.

continue

The continue statement skips a step in a loop, jumping to the next item in the sequence:

```
>>> for i in range(6):
...     if i == 3:
...         continue
...     print(i)
...
...
0
1
2
4
5
>>>
```

while Loops

while loops repeat a block as long as a condition evaluates to True:

```
>>> count = 0
>>> while count < 3:
...     print(f"The count is {count}")
...     count += 1
...
...
The count is 0
The count is 1
The count is 2
>>>
```

It is essential to define a way for your loop to end. Otherwise, you will be stuck in the loop until your program crashes. One way to handle this is to define your conditional statement such that it eventually evaluates to False. An alternative pattern uses the break statement to exit a loop using a nested conditional:

```
>>> count = 0
>>> while True:
...     print(f"The count is {count}")
...     if count > 5:
...         break
...     count += 1
...
...
The count is 0
```

```
The count is 1
The count is 2
The count is 3
The count is 4
The count is 5
The count is 6
>>>
```

Handling Exceptions

Exceptions are a type of error causing your program to crash if not handled (caught). Catching them with a `try-except` block allows the program to continue. These blocks are created by indenting the block in which the exception might be raised, putting a `try` statement before it and an `except` statement after it, followed by a code block that should run when the error occurs:

```
>>> thinkers = ['Plato', 'PlayDo', 'Gumby']
>>> while True:
...     try:
...         thinker = thinkers.pop()
...         print(thinker)
...     except IndexError as e:
...         print("We tried to pop too many thinkers")
...         print(e)
...         break
...
...
...
Gumby
PlayDo
Plato
We tried to pop too many thinkers
pop from empty list
>>>
```

There are many built-in exceptions, such as `IOError`, `KeyError`, and `ImportError`. Many third-party packages also define their own exception classes. They indicate that something has gone very wrong, so it only pays to catch them if you are confident that the problem won't be fatal to your software. You can specify explicitly which exception type you will catch. Ideally, you should catch the exact exception type (in our example, this was the exception `IndexError`).

Built-in Objects

In this overview, we will not be covering OOP. The Python language, however, comes with quite a few built-in classes.

What Is an Object?

In OOP, data or state and functionality appear together. The essential concepts to understand when working with objects are *class instantiation* (creating objects from classes) and *dot syntax* (the syntax for accessing an object's attributes and methods). A class defines attributes and methods shared by its objects. Think of it as the technical drawing of a car model. The class can then be instantiated to create an instance. The instance, or object, is a single car built based on those drawings.

```
>>> # Define a class for fancy defining fancy cars
>>> class FancyCar():
...     pass
...
>>> type(FancyCar)
<class 'type'>
>>> # Instantiate a fancy car
>>> my_car = FancyCar()
>>> type(my_car)
<class '__main__.FancyCar'>
```

You don't need to worry about creating your own classes at this point. Just understand that each object is an instantiation of a class.

Object Methods and Attributes

Objects store data in attributes. These attributes are variables attached to the object or object class. Objects define functionality in *object methods* (methods defined for all objects in a class) and *class methods* (methods attached to a class and shared by all objects in the class), which are functions attached to the object.

> In Python documentation, functions attached to objects and classes are referred to as methods.

These functions have access to the object's attributes and can modify and use the object's data. To call an object's method or access one of its attributes, we use dot syntax:

```
>>> # Define a class for fancy defining fancy cars
>>> class FancyCar():
...     # Add a class variable
...     wheels = 4
...     # Add a method
...     def driveFast(self):
...         print("Driving so fast")
...
...
```

```
...
>>> # Instantiate a fancy car
>>> my_car = FancyCar()
>>> # Access the class attribute
>>> my_car.wheels
4
>>> # Invoke the method
>>> my_car.driveFast()
Driving so fast
>>>
```

So here our `FancyCar` class defines a method called `driveFast` and an attribute `wheels`. When you instantiate an instance of `FancyCar` named `my_car`, you can access the attribute and invoke the method using the dot syntax.

Sequences

Sequences are a family of built-in types, including the *list, tuple, range, string,* and *binary* types. Sequences represent ordered and finite collections of items.

Sequence operations

There are many operations that work across all of the types of sequences. We cover some of the most commonly used operations here.

You can use the `in` and `not in` operators to test whether or not an item exists in a sequence:

```
>>> 2 in [1,2,3]
True
>>> 'a' not in 'cat'
False
>>> 10 in range(12)
True
>>> 10 not in range(2, 4)
True
```

You can reference the contents of a sequence by using its index number. To access the item at some index, use square brackets with the index number as an argument. The first item indexed is at position 0, the second at 1, and so forth up to the number one less than the number of items:

```
>>> my_sequence = 'Bill Cheatham'
>>> my_sequence[0]
'B'
>>> my_sequence[2]
'l'
>>> my_sequence[12]
'm'
```

Indexing can appear from the end of a sequence rather than from the front using negative numbers. The last item has the index of –1, the second to last has the index of –2, and so forth:

```
>>> my_sequence = "Bill Cheatham"
>>> my_sequence[-1]
'm'
>>> my_sequence[-2]
'a'
>>> my_sequence[-13]
'B'
```

The index of an item results from the index method. By default, it returns the index of the first occurrence of the item, but optional arguments can define a subrange in which to search:

```
>>> my_sequence = "Bill Cheatham"
>>> my_sequence.index('C')
5
>>> my_sequence.index('a')
8
>>> my_sequence.index('a',9, 12)
11
>>> my_sequence[11]
'a'
>>>
```

You can produce a new sequence from a sequence using slicing. A slice appears by invoking a sequence with brackets containing optional start, stop, and step arguments:

```
my_sequence[start:stop:step]
```

start is the index of the first item to use in the new sequence, stop the first index beyond that point, and step, the distance between items. These arguments are all optional and are replaced with default values if omitted. This statement produces a copy of the original sequence. The default value for start is 0, for stop is the length of the sequence, and for step is 1. Note that if the step does not appear, the corresponding : can also be dropped:

```
>>> my_sequence = ['a', 'b', 'c', 'd', 'e', 'f', 'g']
>>> my_sequence[2:5]
['c', 'd', 'e']
>>> my_sequence[:5]
['a', 'b', 'c', 'd', 'e']
>>> my_sequence[3:]
['d', 'e', 'f', 'g']
>>>
```

Negative numbers can be used to index backward:

```
>>> my_sequence[-6:]
['b', 'c', 'd', 'e', 'f', 'g']
>>> my_sequence[3:-1]
['d', 'e', 'f']
>>>
```

Sequences share many operations for getting information about them and their contents. len returns the length of the sequence, min the smallest member, max the largest, and count the number of a particular item. min and max work only on sequences with items that are comparable. Remember that these work with any sequence type:

```
>>> my_sequence = [0, 1, 2, 0, 1, 2, 3, 0, 1, 2, 3, 4]
>>> len(my_sequence)
12
>>> min(my_sequence)
0
>>> max(my_sequence)
4
>>> my_sequence.count(1)
3
>>>
```

Lists

Lists, one of the most commonly used Python data structures, represent an ordered collection of items of any type. The use of square brackets indicates a list syntax.

The function list() can be used to create an empty list or a list based on another finite iterable object (such as another sequence):

```
>>> list()
[]
>>> list(range(10))
[0, 1, 2, 3, 4, 5, 6, 7, 8, 9]
>>> list("Henry Miller")
['H', 'e', 'n', 'r', 'y', ' ', 'M', 'i', 'l', 'l', 'e', 'r']
>>>
```

Lists created by using square brackets directly are the most common form. Items in the list need to be enumerated explicitly in this case. Remember that the items in a list can be of different types:

```
>>> empty = []
>>> empty
[]
>>> nine = [0, 1, 2, 3, 4, 5, 6, 7, 8, 9]
>>> nine
[0, 1, 2, 3, 4, 5, 6, 7, 8, 9]
>>> mixed = [0, 'a', empty, 'WheelHoss']
>>> mixed
```

```
[0, 'a', [], 'WheelHoss']
>>>
```

The most efficient way to add a single item to a list is to append the item to the end of the list. A less efficient method, insert, allows you to insert an item at the index position of your choice:

```
>>> pies = ['cherry', 'apple']
>>> pies
['cherry', 'apple']
>>> pies.append('rhubarb')
>>> pies
['cherry', 'apple', 'rhubarb']
>>> pies.insert(1, 'cream')
>>> pies
['cherry', 'cream', 'apple', 'rhubarb']
>>>
```

The contents of one list can be added to another using the extend method:

```
>>> pies
['cherry', 'cream', 'apple', 'rhubarb']
>>> desserts = ['cookies', 'paste']
>>> desserts
['cookies', 'paste']
>>> desserts.extend(pies)
>>> desserts
['cookies', 'paste', 'cherry', 'cream', 'apple', 'rhubarb']
>>>
```

The most efficient and common way of removing the last item from a list and returning its value is to pop it. An index argument can be supplied to this method, removing and returning the item at that index. This technique is less efficient, as the list needs to be re-indexed:

```
>>> pies
['cherry', 'cream', 'apple', 'rhubarb']
>>> pies.pop()
'rhubarb'
>>> pies
['cherry', 'cream', 'apple']
>>> pies.pop(1)
'cream'
>>> pies
['cherry', 'apple']
```

There is also a remove method, which removes the first occurrence of an item.

```
>>> pies.remove('apple')
>>> pies
['cherry']
>>>
```

One of the most potent and idiomatic Python features, list comprehensions, allows you to use the functionality of a for loop in a single line. Let's look at a simple example, starting with a for loop squaring all of the numbers from 0–9 and appending them to a list:

```
>>> squares = []
>>> for i in range(10):
...     squared = i*i
...     squares.append(squared)
...
...
>>> squares
[0, 1, 4, 9, 16, 25, 36, 49, 64, 81]
>>>
```

In order to replace this with a list comprehension, we do the following:

```
>>> squares = [i*i for i in range(10)]
>>> squares
[0, 1, 4, 9, 16, 25, 36, 49, 64, 81]
>>>
```

Note that the functionality of the inner block is put first, followed by the for statement. You can also add conditionals to list comprehensions, filtering the results:

```
>>> squares = [i*i for i in range(10) if i%2==0]
>>> squares
[0, 4, 16, 36, 64]
>>>
```

Other techniques for list comprehensions include nesting them and using multiple variables, but the more straightforward form shown here is the most common.

Strings

The string sequence type is a collection of ordered characters surrounded by quotation marks. As of Python 3, strings default to using *UTF-8* encoding.

You can create strings either by using the string constructor method, str(), or by directly enclosing the text in quotation marks:

```
>>> str()
''
>>> "some new string!"
'some new string!'
>>> 'or with single quotes'
'or with single quotes'
```

The string constructor can be used to make strings from other objects:

```
>>> my_list = list()
>>> str(my_list)
'[]'
```

You can create multiline strings by using triple quotes around the content:

```
>>> multi_line = """This is a
... multi-line string,
... which includes linebreaks.
... """
>>> print(multi_line)
This is a
multi-line string,
which includes linebreaks.
>>>
```

In addition to the methods shared by all sequences, strings have quite a few methods distinct to their class.

It is relatively common for user text to have trailing or leading whitespace. If someone types " yes " in a form instead of "yes" you usually want to treat them the same. Python strings have a `strip` method just for this case. It returns a string with the whitespace removed from the beginning and end. There are also methods to remove the whitespace from only the right or left side of the string:

```
>>> input = "  I want more   "
>>> input.strip()
'I want more'
>>> input.rstrip()
'  I want more'
>>> input.lstrip()
'I want more   '
```

On the other hand, if you want to add padding to a string, you can use the `ljust` or `rjust` methods. Either one pads with whitespace by default, or takes a character argument:

```
>>> output = 'Barry'
>>> output.ljust(10)
'Barry     '
>>> output.rjust(10, '*')
'*****Barry'
```

Sometimes you want to break a string up into a list of substrings. Perhaps you have a sentence you want to turn into a list of words, or a string of words separated by commas. The `split` method breaks a string into a list of strings. By default, it uses whitespace as the token to make the breaks. An optional argument can be used to add in another character where the split can break:

```
>>> text = "Mary had a little lamb"
>>> text.split()
['Mary', 'had', 'a', 'little', 'lamb']
>>> url = "gt.motomomo.io/v2/api/asset/143"
>>> url.split('/')
['gt.motomomo.io', 'v2', 'api', 'asset', '143']
```

You can easily create a new string from a sequence of strings and join them into a single string. This method inserts a string as a separator between a list of other strings:

```
>>> items = ['cow', 'milk', 'bread', 'butter']
>>> " and ".join(items)
'cow and milk and bread and butter'
```

Changing the case of text is a common occurrence, whether it is making the case uniform for comparison or changing in preparation for user consumption. Python strings have several methods to make this an easy process:

```
>>> name = "bill monroe"
>>> name.capitalize()
'Bill monroe'
>>> name.upper()
'BILL MONROE'
>>> name.title()
'Bill Monroe'
>>> name.swapcase()
'BILL MONROE'
>>> name = "BILL MONROE"
>>> name.lower()
'bill monroe'
```

Python also provides methods to understand a string's content. Whether it's checking the case of the text, or seeing if it represents a number, there are quite a few built-in methods for interrogation. Here are just a few of the most commonly used methods:

```
>>> "William".startswith('W')
True
>>> "William".startswith('Bill')
False
>>> "Molly".endswith('olly')
True
>>> "abc123".isalnum()
True
>>> "abc123".isalpha()
False
>>> "abc".isalnum()
True
>>> "123".isnumeric()
True
>>> "Sandy".istitle()
True
>>> "Sandy".islower()
False
>>> "SANDY".isupper()
True
```

You can insert content into a string and control its format at runtime. Your program can use the values of variables or other calculated content in strings. This approach is used in both creating user-consumed text and for writing software logs.

The older form of string formatting in Python comes from the C language `printf` function. You can use the modulus operator, `%`, to insert formatted values into a string. This technique applies to the form `string % values`, where values can be a single nontuple or a tuple of multiple values. The string itself must have a conversion specifier for each value. The conversion specifier, at a minimum, starts with a `%` and is followed by a character representing the type of value inserted:

```
>>> "%s + %s = %s" % (1, 2, "Three")
'1 + 2 = Three'
>>>
```

Additional format arguments include the conversion specifier. For example, you can control the number of places a float, `%f`, prints:

```
>>> "%.3f" % 1.234567
'1.235'
```

This mechanism for string formatting was the dominant one in Python for years, and you encounter it in legacy code. This approach offers some compelling features, such as sharing syntax with other languages. It also has some pitfalls. In particular, due to the use of a sequence to hold the arguments, errors related to displaying `tuple` and `dict` objects are common. We recommend adopting newer formatting options, such as the string `format` method, template strings, and f-strings, to both avoid these errors and increase the simplicity and readability of your code.

Python 3 introduced a new way of formatting strings using the string method `format`. This way of formatting has been backported to Python 2 as well. This specification uses curly brackets in the string to indicate replacement fields rather than the modulus-based conversion specifiers of the old-style formatting. The insert values become arguments to the string `format` method. The order of the arguments determines their placement order in the target string:

```
>>> '{} comes before {}'.format('first', 'second')
'first comes before second'
>>>
```

You can specify index numbers in the brackets to insert values in an order different than that in the argument list. You can also repeat a value by specifying the same index number in multiple replacement fields:

```
>>> '{1} comes after {0}, but {1} comes before {2}'.format('first',
                                                           'second',
                                                           'third')
'second comes after first, but second comes before third'
>>>
```

An even more powerful feature is that the insert values can be specified by name:

```
>>> '''{country} is an island.
... {country} is off of the coast of
... {continent} in the {ocean}'''.format(ocean='Indian Ocean',
...                                       continent='Africa',
...                                       country='Madagascar')
'Madagascar is an island.
Madagascar is off of the coast of
Africa in the Indian Ocean'
```

Here a `dict` works to supply the key values for name-based replacement fields:

```
>>> values = {'first': 'Bill', 'last': 'Bailey'}
>>> "Won't you come home {first} {last}?".format(**values)
"Won't you come home Bill Bailey?"
```

You can also specify format specification arguments. Here they add left and right padding using > and <. In the second example, we specify a character to use in the padding:

```
>>> text = "|{0:>22}||{0:<22}|"
>>> text.format('0','0')
'|                     0||0                     |'
>>> text = "|{0:<>22}||{0:><22}|"
>>> text.format('0','0')
'|<<<<<<<<<<<<<<<<<<<<<0||0>>>>>>>>>>>>>>>>>>>>>|'
```

Format specifications are done using the format specification mini-language (*https://oreil.ly/ZOFJg*). Our topic also uses another type of language called *f-strings*.

Python f-strings use the same formatting language as the `format` method, but offer a more straightforward and intuitive mechanism for using them. f-strings are prepended with either *f* or *F* before the first quotation mark. Like the `format` string previously described, f-strings use curly braces to demarcate replacement fields. In an f-string, however, the content of the replacement field is an expression. This approach means it can refer to variables defined in the current scope or involve calculations:

```
>>> a = 1
>>> b = 2
>>> f"a is {a}, b is {b}. Adding them results in {a + b}"
'a is 1, b is 2. Adding them results in 3'
```

As in `format` strings, format specifications in f-strings happen within the curly brackets after the value expression and start with a `:`:

```
>>> count = 43
>>> f"|{count:5d}"
'|   43'
```

The value expression can contain nested expressions, referencing variables, and expressions in the construction of the parent expression:

```
>>> padding = 10
>>> f"|{count:{padding}d}"
'|        43'
```

 We highly recommend using f-strings for the majority of your string formatting. They combine the power of the specification mini-language with a simple and intuitive syntax.

Template strings are designed to offer a straightforward string substitution mechanism. These built-in methods work for tasks such as internationalization, where simple word substitutions are necessary. They use $ as a substitution character, with optional curly braces surrounding them. The characters directly following the $ identify the value to be inserted. When the `substitute` method of the string template executes, these names are used to assign values.

 Built-in types and functions are available whenever you run Python code, but to access the broader world of functionality available in the Python ecosystem, you need to use the `import` statement. This approach lets you add functionality from the Python Standard Library or third-party services into your environment. You can selectively import parts of a package by using the `from` keyword:

```
>>> from string import Template
>>> greeting = Template("$hello Mark Anthony")
>>> greeting.substitute(hello="Bonjour")
'Bonjour Mark Anthony'
>>> greeting.substitute(hello="Zdravstvuyte")
'Zdravstvuyte Mark Anthony'
>>> greeting.substitute(hello="Nín hǎo")
'Nín hǎo Mark Anthony'
```

Dicts

Aside from strings and lists, dicts may be the most used of the Python built-in classes. A *dict* is a mapping of keys to values. The lookup of any particular value using a key is highly efficient and fast. The keys can be strings, numbers, custom objects, or any other nonmutable type.

 A *mutable* object is one whose contents can change in place. Lists are a primary example; the contents of the list can change without the list's identity changing. Strings are not mutable. You create a new string each time you change the contents of an existing one.

Dicts are represented as comma–separated key/value pairs surrounded by curly braces. The key/value pairs consist of a key, a colon (:), and then a value.

You can create a dict object using the dict() constructor. With no arguments, it creates an empty dict. It takes a sequence of key/value pairs as an argument as well:

```
>>> map = dict()
>>> type(map)
<class 'dict'>
>>> map
{}
>>> kv_list = [['key-1', 'value-1'], ['key-2', 'value-2']]
>>> dict(kv_list)
{'key-1': 'value-1', 'key-2': 'value-2'}
```

You can also create a *dict* directly using curly braces:

```
>>> map = {'key-1': 'value-1', 'key-2': 'value-2'}
>>> map
{'key-1': 'value-1', 'key-2': 'value-2'}
```

You can access the value associated with a key using square bracket syntax:

```
>>> map['key-1']
'value-1'
>>> map['key-2']
'value-2'
```

You can use the same syntax to set a value. If the key is not in the dict, it adds as a new entry. If it already exists, the value changes to the new value:

```
>>> map
{'key-1': 'value-1', 'key-2': 'value-2'}
>>> map['key-3'] = 'value-3'
>>> map
{'key-1': 'value-1', 'key-2': 'value-2', 'key-3': 'value-3'}
>>> map['key-1'] = 13
>>> map
{'key-1': 13, 'key-2': 'value-2', 'key-3': 'value-3'}
```

If you try to access a key that has not been defined in a dict, a KeyError exception will be thrown:

```
>>> map['key-4']
Traceback (most recent call last):
  File "<input>", line 1, in <module>
    map['key-4']
KeyError: 'key-4'
```

You can check to see if the key exists in a dict using the in syntax we saw with sequences. In the case of dicts, it checks for the existence of keys:

```
>>> if 'key-4' in map:
...     print(map['key-4'])
```

```
... else:
...     print('key-4 not there')
...
...
key-4 not there
```

A more intuitive solution is to use the get() method. If you have not defined a key in a dict, it returns a supplied default value. If you have not supplied a default value, it returns None:

```
>>> map.get('key-4', 'default-value')
'default-value'
```

Use del to remove a key-value pair from a dict:

```
>>> del(map['key-1'])
>>> map
{'key-2': 'value-2', 'key-3': 'value-3'}
```

The keys() method returns a dict_keys object with the dict's keys. The values() method returns an dict_values object, and the items() method returns key-value pairs. This last method is useful for iterating through the contents of a dict:

```
>>> map.keys()
dict_keys(['key-1', 'key-2'])
>>> map.values()
dict_values(['value-1', 'value-2'])
>>> for key, value in map.items():
...     print(f"{key}: {value}")
...
...
key-1: value-1
key-2: value-2
```

Similar to list comprehensions, dict comprehensions are one-line statements returning a dict by iterating through a sequence:

```
>>> letters = 'abcde'
>>> # mapping individual letters to their upper-case representations
>>> cap_map = {x: x.upper() for x in letters}
>>> cap_map['b']
'B'
```

Functions

You have seen some Python built-in functions already. Now move on to writing your own. Remember, a *function* is a mechanism for encapsulating a block of code. You can repeat the behavior of this block in multiple spots without having to duplicate the code. Your code will be better organized, more testable, maintainable, and easier to understand.

Anatomy of a Function

The first line of a function definition starts with the keyword def, followed by the function name, function parameters enclosed in parentheses, and then :. The rest of the function is a code block and is indented:

```
def <FUNCTION NAME>(<PARAMETERS>):
    <CODE BLOCK>
```

If a string using multiline syntax is provided first in the indented block, it acts as documentation. Use these to describe what your function does, how parameters work, and what it can be expected to return. You will find these docstrings are invaluable for communicating with future users of your code. Various programs and services also use them to create documentation. Providing docstrings is considered a best practice and is highly recommended:

```
>>> def my_function():
...     '''This is a doc string.
...
...     It should describe what the function does,
...     what parameters work, and what the
...     function returns.
...     '''
```

Function arguments occur in the parentheses following the function name. They can be either positional or keyword. Positional arguments use the order of the arguments to assign value:

```
>>> def positioned(first, second):
...     """Assignment based on order."""
...     print(f"first: {first}")
...     print(f"second: {second}")
...
...
>>> positioned(1, 2)
first: 1
second: 2
>>>
```

With keyword arguments, assign each argument a default value:

```
>>> def keywords(first=1, second=2):
...     '''Default values assigned'''
...     print(f"first: {first}")
...     print(f"second: {second}")
...
...
```

The default values are used when no values are passed during function invocation. The keyword parameters can be called by name during function invocation, in which case the order will not matter:

```
>>> keywords(0)
first: 0
second: 2
>>> keywords(3,4)
first: 3
second: 4
>>> keywords(second='one', first='two')
first: two
second: one
```

When using keyword parameters, all parameters defined after a keyword parameter must be keyword parameters as well. All functions return a value. The `return` keyword is used to set this value. If not set from a function definition, the function returns None:

```
>>> def no_return():
...     '''No return defined'''
...     pass
...
>>> result = no_return()
>>> print(result)
None
>>> def return_one():
...     '''Returns 1'''
...     return 1
...
>>> result = return_one()
>>> print(result)
1
```

Functions as Objects

Functions are objects. They can be passed around, or stored in data structures. You can define two functions, put them in a list, and then iterate through the list to invoke them:

```
>>> def double(input):
...     '''double input'''
...     return input*2
...
>>> double
<function double at 0x107d34ae8>
>>> type(double)
<class 'function'>
>>> def triple(input):
...     '''Triple input'''
...     return input*3
...
>>> functions = [double, triple]
>>> for function in functions:
...     print(function(3))
...
```

```
. . .
6
9
```

Anonymous Functions

When you need to create a very limited function, you can create an unnamed (anonymous) one using the `lambda` keyword. Generally, you should limit their use to situations where a function expects a small function as a argument. In this example, you take a list of lists and sort it. The default sorting mechanism compares based on the first item of each sublist:

```
>>> items = [[0, 'a', 2], [5, 'b', 0], [2, 'c', 1]]
>>> sorted(items)
[[0, 'a', 2], [2, 'c', 1], [5, 'b', 0]]
```

To sort based on something other than the first entry, you can define a method which returns the item's second entry and pass it into the sorting function's key parameter:

```
>>> def second(item):
...     '''return second entry'''
...     return item[1]
...
>>> sorted(items, key=second)
[[0, 'a', 2], [5, 'b', 0], [2, 'c', 1]]
```

With the `lambda` keyword, you can do the same thing without the full function definition. Lambdas work with the `lambda` keyword followed by a parameter name, a colon, and a return value:

```
lambda <PARAM>: <RETURN EXPRESSION>
```

Sort using lambdas, first using the second entry and then using the third:

```
>>> sorted(items, key=lambda item: item[1])
[[0, 'a', 2], [5, 'b', 0], [2, 'c', 1]]
>>> sorted(items, key=lambda item: item[2])
[[5, 'b', 0], [2, 'c', 1], [0, 'a', 2]]
```

Be cautious of using lambdas more generally, as they can create code that is poorly documented and confusing to read if used in place of general functions.

Using Regular Expressions

The need to match patterns in strings comes up again and again. You could be looking for an identifier in a log file or checking user input for keywords or a myriad of other cases. You have already seen simple pattern matching using the `in` operation for sequences, or the string `.endswith` and `.startswith` methods. To do more sophisticated matching, you need a more powerful tool. Regular expressions, often referred to as regex, are the answer. Regular expressions use a string of characters to define search patterns. The Python `re` package offers regular expression operations similar to those found in Perl. The `re` module uses backslashes (\) to delineate special characters used in matching. To avoid confusion with regular string escape sequences, raw strings are recommended when defining regular expression patterns. Raw strings are prepended with an *r* before the first quotation mark.

Python strings have several escape sequences. Among the most common are line-feed \n and tab \t.

Searching

Let say you have a cc list from an email as a text and you want to understand more about who is in this list:

```
In [1]: cc_list = '''Ezra Koenig <ekoenig@vpwk.com>,
   ...: Rostam Batmanglij <rostam@vpwk.com>,
   ...: Chris Tomson <ctomson@vpwk.com,
   ...: Bobbi Baio <bbaio@vpwk.com'''
```

If you want to know whether a name is in this text, you could use the `in` sequence membership syntax:

```
In [2]: 'Rostam' in cc_list
Out[2]: True
```

To get similar behavior, you can use the `re.search` function, which returns a `re.Match` object only if there is a match:

```
In [3]: import re
```

```
In [4]: re.search(r'Rostam', cc_list)
Out[4]: <re.Match object; span=(32, 38), match='Rostam'>
```

You can use this as a condition to test for membership:

```
>>> if re.search(r'Rostam', cc_list):
...     print('Found Rostam')
...
...
Found Rostam
```

Character Sets

So far `re` hasn't given you anything you couldn't get using the `in` operator. However, what if you are looking for a person in a text, but you can't remember if the name is *Bobbi* or *Robby*?

With regular expressions, you can use groups of characters, any one of which could appear in a spot. These are called character sets. The characters from which a match should be chosen are enclosed by square brackets in the regular expression definition. You can match on *B* or *R*, followed by *obb*, and either *i* or *y*:

```
In [5]: re.search('[RB]obb[yi]', ',obbi')
Out[5]: <re.Match object; span=(0, 5), match=',obbi'>
```

You can put comma-separated individual characters in a character set or use ranges. The range *A–Z* includes all the capitalized letters; the range *0–9* includes the digits from zero to nine:

```
In [6]: re.search(r'Chr[a-z][a-z]', cc_list)
Out [6]: <re.Match object; span=(69, 74), match='Chris'>
```

The + after an item in a regular expression matches one or more of that item. A number in brackets matches an exact number of characters:

```
In [7]: re.search(r'[A-Za-z]+', cc_list)
Out [7]: <re.Match object; span=(0, 4), match='Ezra'>
In [8]: re.search(r'[A-Za-z]{6}', cc_list)
Out [8]: <re.Match object; span=(5, 11), match='Koenig'>
```

We can construct a match using a combination of character sets and other characters to make a naive match of an email address. The . character has a special meaning. It is a wildcard and matches any character. To match against the actual . character, you must escape it using a backslash:

```
In [9]: re.search(r'[A-Za-z]+@[a-z]+\.[a-z]+', cc_list)
Out[9]: <re.Match object; span=(13, 29), match='ekoenig@vpwk.com'>
```

This example is just a demonstration of character sets. It does not represent the full complexity of a production-ready regular expressions for emails.

Character Classes

In addition to character sets, Python's re offers character classes. These are premade character sets. Some commonly used ones are \w, which is equivalent to [a-zA-Z0-9_] and \d, which is equivalent to [0-9]. You can use the + modifier to match for multiple characters:

```
>>> re.search(r'\w+', cc_list)
<re.Match object; span=(0, 4), match='Ezra'>
```

And you can replace our primative email matcher with \w:

```
>>> re.search(r'\w+\@\w+\.\w+', cc_list)
<re.Match object; span=(13, 29), match='ekoenig@vpwk.com'>
```

Groups

You can use parentheses to define groups in a match. These groups can be accessed from the match object. They are numbered in the order they appear, with the zero group being the full match:

```
>>> re.search(r'(\w+)\@(\w+)\.(\w+)', cc_list)
<re.Match object; span=(13, 29), match='ekoenig@vpwk.com'>
>>> matched = re.search(r'(\w+)\@(\w+)\.(\w+)', cc_list)
>>> matched.group(0)
'ekoenig@vpwk.com'
>>> matched.group(1)
'ekoenig'
>>> matched.group(2)
'vpwk'
>>> matched.group(3)
'com'
```

Named Groups

You can also supply names for the groups by adding ?P<NAME> in the group definition. Then you can access the groups by name instead of number:

```
>>> matched = re.search(r'(?P<name>\w+)\@(?P<SLD>\w+)\.(?P<TLD>\w+)', cc_list)
>>> matched.group('name')
'ekoenig'
>>> print(f'''name: {matched.group("name")}
... Secondary Level Domain: {matched.group("SLD")}
... Top Level Domain: {matched.group("TLD")}''')
name: ekoenig
Secondary Level Domain: vpwk
Top Level Domain: com
```

Find All

Up until now, we have demonstrated returning just the first match found. We can also use findall to return all of the matches as a list of strings:

```
>>> matched = re.findall(r'\w+\@\w+\.\w+', cc_list)
>>> matched
['ekoenig@vpwk.com', 'rostam@vpwk.com', 'ctomson@vpwk.com', 'cbaio@vpwk.com']
>>> matched = re.findall(r'(\w+)\@(\w+)\.(\w+)', cc_list)
>>> matched
[('ekoenig', 'vpwk', 'com'), ('rostam', 'vpwk', 'com'),
 ('ctomson', 'vpwk', 'com'), ('cbaio', 'vpwk', 'com')]
>>> names = [x[0] for x in matched]
>>> names
['ekoenig', 'rostam', 'ctomson', 'cbaio']
```

Find Iterator

When dealing with large texts, such as logs, it is useful to not process the text all at once. You can produce an *iterator* object using the `finditer` method. This object processes text until it finds a match and then stops. Passing it to the `next` function returns the current match and continues processing until finding the next match. In this way, you can deal with each match individually without devoting resources to process all of the input at once:

```
>>> matched = re.finditer(r'\w+\@\w+\.\w+', cc_list)
>>> matched
<callable_iterator object at 0x108e68748>
>>> next(matched)
<re.Match object; span=(13, 29), match='ekoenig@vpwk.com'>
>>> next(matched)
<re.Match object; span=(51, 66), match='rostam@vpwk.com'>
>>> next(matched)
<re.Match object; span=(83, 99), match='ctomson@vpwk.com'>
```

The iterator object, `matched`, can be used in a `for` loop as well:

```
>>> matched = re.finditer("(?P<name>\w+)\@(?P<SLD>\w+)\.(?P<TLD>\w+)", cc_list)
>>> for m in matched:
...     print(m.groupdict())
...
...
{'name': 'ekoenig', 'SLD': 'vpwk', 'TLD': 'com'}
{'name': 'rostam', 'SLD': 'vpwk', 'TLD': 'com'}
{'name': 'ctomson', 'SLD': 'vpwk', 'TLD': 'com'}
{'name': 'cbaio', 'SLD': 'vpwk', 'TLD': 'com'}
```

Substitution

Besides searching and matching, regexes can be used to substitute part or all of a string:

```
>>> re.sub("\d", "#", "The passcode you entered was  09876")
'The passcode you entered was  #####'
>>> users = re.sub("(?P<name>\w+)\@(?P<SLD>\w+)\.(?P<TLD>\w+)",
...                 "\g<TLD>.\g<SLD>.\g<name>", cc_list)
>>> print(users)
Ezra Koenig <com.vpwk.ekoenig>,
Rostam Batmanglij <com.vpwk.rostam>,
Chris Tomson <com.vpwk.ctomson,
Chris Baio <com.vpwk.cbaio
```

Compiling

All of the examples so far have called methods on the `re` module directly. This is adequate for many cases, but if the same match is going to happen many times, performance gains can be had by compiling the regular expression into an object. This object can be reused for matches without recompiling:

```
>>> regex = re.compile(r'\w+\@\w+\.\w+')
>>> regex.search(cc_list)
<re.Match object; span=(13, 29), match='ekoenig@vpwk.com'>
```

Regular expressions offer many more features than we have dealt with here. Indeed many books have been written on their use, but you should now be prepared for most basic cases.

Lazy Evaluation

Lazy evaluation is the idea that, especially when dealing with large amounts of data, you do not want process all of the data before using the results. You have already seen this with the range type, where the memory footprint is the same, even for one representing a large group of numbers.

Generators

You can use generators in a similar way as range objects. They perform some operation on data in chunks as requested. They pause their state in between calls. This means that you can store variables that are needed to calculate output, and they are accessed every time the generator is called.

To write a generator function, use the yield keyword rather than a return statement. Every time the generator is called, it returns the value specified by yield and then pauses its state until it is next called. Let's write a generator that simply counts, returning each subsequent number:

```
>>> def count():
...     n = 0
...     while True:
...         n += 1
...         yield n
...
...
>>> counter = count()
>>> counter
<generator object count at 0x10e8509a8>
>>> next(counter)
1
>>> next(counter)
2
>>> next(counter)
3
```

Note that the generator keeps track of its state, and hence the variable n in each call to the generator reflects the value previously set. Let's implement a Fibonacci generator:

```
>>> def fib():
...     first = 0
...     last = 1
...     while True:
...         first, last = last, first + last
...         yield first
...
>>> f = fib()
>>> next(f)
1
>>> next(f)
1
>>> next(f)
2
>>> next(f)
3
```

We can also iterate using the generator in a for loop:

```
>>> f = fib()
>>> for x in f:
...     print(x)
...     if x > 12:
...         break
...
1
1
2
3
5
8
13
```

Generator Comprehensions

We can use generator comprehensions to create one-line generators. They are created using a syntax similar to list comprehensions, but parentheses are used rather than square brackets:

```
>>> list_o_nums = [x for x in range(100)]
>>> gen_o_nums = (x for x in range(100))
>>> list_o_nums
[0, 1, 2, 3, ...  97, 98, 99]
>>> gen_o_nums
<generator object <genexpr> at 0x10ea14408>
```

Even with this small example, we can see the difference in memory used by using the sys.getsizeof method, which returns the size of an object, in bytes:

```
>>> import sys
>>> sys.getsizeof(list_o_nums)
912
```

```
>>> sys.getsizeof(gen_o_nums)
120
```

More IPython Features

You saw some of IPython's features at the beginning of the chapter. Now let's look at some more advanced features, such as running shell commands from within the IPython interpreter and using magic functions.

Using IPython to Run Unix Shell Commands

You can use IPython to run shell commands. This is one of the most compelling reasons to perform DevOps actions in the IPython shell. Let's take a look at a very simple example where the ! character, which IPython uses to identify shell commands, is put in front of the command ls:

```
In [3]: var_ls = !ls -l
In [4]: type(var_ls)
Out[4]: IPython.utils.text.SList
```

The output of the command is assigned to a Python variable var_ls. The type of this variable is IPython.utils.text.SList. The SList type converts a regular shell command into an object that has three main methods: fields, grep, and sort. Here is an example in action using the Unix df command. The sort method can interpret the whitespace from this Unix command and then sort the third column by size:

```
In [6]: df = !df
In [7]: df.sort(3, nums = True)
```

Let's take a look at SList and .grep next. Here is an example that searches for what commands with kill as part of their names are installed in the */usr/bin* directory:

```
In [10]: ls = !ls -l /usr/bin
In [11]: ls.grep("kill")
Out[11]:
['-rwxr-xr-x   1 root    wheel        1621 Aug 20  2018 kill.d',
 '-rwxr-xr-x   1 root    wheel       23984 Mar 20 23:10 killall',
 '-rwxr-xr-x   1 root    wheel       30512 Mar 20 23:10 pkill']
```

The key take away here is that IPython is a dream environment for hacking around with little shell scripts.

Using IPython magic commands

If you get in the habit of using IPython, you should also get in the habit of using built-in magic commands. They are essentially shortcuts that pack a big punch. Magic commands are indicated by prepending them with %%. Here is an example of how to write inline Bash inside of IPython. Note, this is just a small command, but it could be an entire Bash script:

```
In [13]: %%bash
   ...: uname -a
   ...:
   ...:
Darwin nogibjj.local 18.5.0 Darwin Kernel Version 18.5.0: Mon Mar ...
```

The %%writefile is pretty tricky because you can write and test Python or Bash scripts on the fly, using IPython to execute them. That's not a bad party trick at all:

```
In [16]: %%writefile print_time.py
   ...: #!/usr/bin/env python
   ...: import datetime
   ...: print(datetime.datetime.now().time())
   ...:
   ...:
   ...:
Writing print_time.py

In [17]: cat print_time.py
#!/usr/bin/env python
import datetime
print(datetime.datetime.now().time())

In [18]: !python print_time.py
19:06:00.594914
```

Another very useful command, %who, will show you what is loaded into memory. It comes in quite handy when you have been working in a terminal that has been running for a long time:

```
In [20]: %who
df      ls     var_ls
```

Exercises

- Write a Python function that takes a name as an argument and prints that name.

- Write a Python function that takes a string as an argument and prints whether it is upper- or lowercase.

- Write a list comprehension that results in a list of every letter in the word *smogtether* capitalized.

- Write a generator that alternates between returning *Even* and *Odd*.

## CHAPTER 2

Automating Files and the Filesystem

One of Python's most powerful features is its ability to manipulate text and files. In the DevOps world, you are continually parsing, searching, and changing the text in files, whether you're searching application logs or propagating configuration files. Files are a means of persisting the state of your data, code, and configuration; they are how you look back at what happened in logs and how you control what happens with configuration. With Python, you can create, read, and change files and text in the code that you can use repeatedly. Automating these tasks is indeed one aspect of modern DevOps that separates it from traditional system administration. Rather than keeping a set of instructions that you have to follow manually, you can write code. This diminishes your chances of missing steps or doing them out of order. If you are confident that your system uses the same steps every time you run it, you can have greater understanding and confidence in the process.

Reading and Writing Files

You can use the open function to create a file object that can read and write files. It takes two arguments, the path of the file and the mode (mode optionally defaults to reading). You use the mode to indicate, among other things, if you want to read or write a file and if it is text or binary data. You can open a text file using the mode r to read its contents. The file object has a read method that returns the contents of the file as a string:

```
In [1]: file_path = 'bookofdreams.txt'
In [2]: open_file = open(file_path, 'r')
In [3]: text = open_file.read()
In [4]: len(text)
Out[4]: 476909

In [5]: text[56]
```

```
Out[5]: 's'

In [6]: open_file
Out[6]: <_io.TextIOWrapper name='bookofdreams.txt' mode='r' encoding='UTF-8'>

In [7]: open_file.close()
```

 It is a good practice to close a file when you finish with it. Python closes a file when it is out of scope, but until then the file consumes resources and may prevent other processes from opening it.

You can also read a file using the readlines method. This method reads the file and splits its contents on newline characters. It returns a list of strings. Each string is one line of the original text:

```
In [8]: open_file = open(file_path, 'r')
In [9]: text = open_file.readlines()
In [10]: len(text)
Out[10]: 8796

In [11]: text[100]
Out[11]: 'science, when it admits the possibility of occasional hallucinations\n'

In [12]: open_file.close()
```

A handy way of opening files is to use with statements. You do not need to close a file explicitly in this case. Python closes it and releases the file resource at the end of the indented block:

```
In [13]: with open(file_path, 'r') as open_file:
   ...:     text = open_file.readlines()
   ...:

In [14]: text[101]
Out[14]: 'in the sane and healthy, also admits, of course, the existence of\n'

In [15]: open_file.closed
Out[15]: True
```

Different operating systems use different escaped characters to represent line endings. Unix systems use \n and Windows systems use \r\n. Python converts these to \n when you open a file as text. If you are opening a binary file, such as a *.jpeg* image, you are likely to corrupt the data by this conversion if you open it as text. You can, however, read binary files by appending a *b* to mode:

```
In [15]: file_path = 'bookofdreamsghos00lang.pdf'
In [16]: with open(file_path, 'rb') as open_file:
   ...:     btext = open_file.read()
   ...:
```

```
In [17]: btext[0]
Out[17]: 37

In [18]: btext[:25]
Out[18]: b'%PDF-1.5\n%\xec\xf5\xf2\xe1\xe4\xef\xe3\xf5\xed\xe5\xee\xf4\n18'
```

Adding this opens the file without any line-ending conversion.

To write to a file, use the write mode, represented as the argument w. The tool direnv is used to automatically set up some development environments. You can define environment variables and application runtimes in a file named *.envrc*; direnv uses it to set these things up when you enter the directory with the file. You can set the environment variable STAGE to PROD and TABLE_ID to token-storage-1234 in such a file in Python by using open with the write flag:

```
In [19]: text = '''export STAGE=PROD
    ...: export TABLE_ID=token-storage-1234'''

In [20]: with open('.envrc', 'w') as opened_file:
    ...:     opened_file.write(text)
    ...:

In [21]: !cat .envrc
export STAGE=PROD
export TABLE_ID=token-storage-1234
```

 Be warned that pathlib's write method will overwrite a file if it already exists.

The open function creates a file if it does not already exist and overwrites if it does. If you want to keep existing contents and only append the file, use the append flag a. This flag appends new text to the end of the file while keeping the original content. If you are writing nontext content, such as the contents of a *.jpeg* file, you are likely to corrupt it if you use either the w or a flag. This corruption is likely as Python converts line endings to platform-specific ones when it writes text data. To write binary data, you can safely use wb or ab.

Chapter 3 covers pathlib in depth. Two useful features are convenience functions for reading and writing files. pathlib handles the file object behind the scenes. The following allows you to read text from a file:

```
In [35]: import pathlib

In [36]: path = pathlib.Path(
            "/Users/kbehrman/projects/autoscaler/check_pending.py")
```

```
In [37]: path.read_text()
```

To read binary data, use the `path.read_bytes` method.

When you want to overwrite a file or write a new file, there are methods for writing text and for writing binary data:

```
In [38]: path = pathlib.Path("/Users/kbehrman/sp.config")

In [39]: path.write_text("LOG:DEBUG")
Out[39]: 9

In [40]: path = pathlib.Path("/Users/kbehrman/sp")
Out[41]: 8
```

Reading and writing using the file object's `read` and `write` functions is usually adequate for unstructured text, but what if you are dealing with more complex data? The Javascript Object Notation (JSON) format is widely used to store simple structured data in modern web services. It uses two data structures: a mapping of key-value pairs similar to a Python `dict` and a list of items somewhat similar to a Python `list`. It defines data types for numbers, strings, *booleans* (which hold true/false values), and *nulls* (empty values). The AWS Identity and Access Management (IAM) web service allows you to control access to AWS resources. It uses JSON files to define access policies, as in this sample file:

```
{
    "Version": "2012-10-17",
    "Statement": {
        "Effect": "Allow",
        "Action": "service-prefix:action-name",
        "Resource": "*",
        "Condition": {
            "DateGreaterThan": {"aws:CurrentTime": "2017-07-01T00:00:00Z"},
            "DateLessThan": {"aws:CurrentTime": "2017-12-31T23:59:59Z"}
        }
    }
}
```

You could use the standard file object `read` or `readlines` methods to get the data from such a file:

```
In [8]: with open('service-policy.json', 'r') as opened_file:
   ...:     policy = opened_file.readlines()
   ...:
   ...:
```

The result would not be immediately usable, as it would be a single string or list of strings, depending on your chosen read method:

```
In [9]: print(policy)
['{\n',
 '    "Version": "2012-10-17",
\n',
 '    "Statement": {\n',
 '        "Effect": "Allow",
\n',
 '        "Action": "service-prefix:action-name",
\n',
 '        "Resource": "*",
\n',
 '        "Condition": {\n',
 '            "DateGreaterThan": {"aws:CurrentTime": "2017-07-01T00:00:00Z"},
\n',
 '            "DateLessThan": {"aws:CurrentTime": "2017-12-31T23:59:59Z"}\n',
 '        }\n',
 '    }\n',
 '}\n']
```

You would then need to parse this string (or strings) into data structures and types that match the original, which may be a great deal of work. A far better way is to use the json module:

```
In [10]: import json

In [11]: with open('service-policy.json', 'r') as opened_file:
    ...:     policy = json.load(opened_file)
    ...:
    ...:
    ...:
    ...:
```

This module parses the JSON format for you, returning the data in appropriate Python data structures:

```
In [13]: from pprint import pprint

In [14]: pprint(policy)
{'Statement': {'Action': 'service-prefix:action-name',
               'Condition': {'DateGreaterThan':
                                 {'aws:CurrentTime': '2017-07-01T00:00:00Z'},
                             'DateLessThan':
                                 {'aws:CurrentTime': '2017-12-31T23:59:59Z'}},
               'Effect': 'Allow',
               'Resource': '*'},
 'Version': '2012-10-17'}
```

The pprint module automatically formats Python objects for printing. Its output is often more easily read and is a handy way of looking at nested data structures.

Now you can use the data with the original file structure. For example, here is how you would change the resource whose access this policy controls to S3:

```
In [15]: policy['Statement']['Resource'] = 'S3'
```

```
In [16]: pprint(policy)
{'Statement': {'Action': 'service-prefix:action-name',
               'Condition': {'DateGreaterThan':
                                   {'aws:CurrentTime': '2017-07-01T00:00:00Z'},
                             'DateLessThan':
                                   {'aws:CurrentTime': '2017-12-31T23:59:59Z'}},
               'Effect': 'Allow',
               'Resource': 'S3'},
 'Version': '2012-10-17'}
```

You can write a Python dictionary as a JSON file by using the `json.dump` method. This is how you would update the policy file you just modified:

```
In [17]: with open('service-policy.json', 'w') as opened_file:
    ...:         policy = json.dump(policy, opened_file)
    ...:
    ...:
    ...:
```

Another language commonly used in configuration files is *YAML* ("YAML Ain't Markup Language"). It is a superset of JSON, but has a more compact format, using whitespace similar to how Python uses it.

Ansible is a tool used to automate software configuration, management, and deployment. Ansible uses files, referred to as *playbooks*, to define actions you want to automate. These playbooks use the YAML format:

```
---
- hosts: webservers
  vars:
    http_port: 80
    max_clients: 200
  remote_user: root
  tasks:
  - name: ensure apache is at the latest version
    yum:
      name: httpd
      state: latest
...
```

The most commonly used library for parsing YAML files in Python is PyYAML. It is not in the Python Standard Library, but you can install it using `pip`:

```
$ pip install PyYAML
```

Once installed, you can use PyYAML to import and export YAML data much as you did with JSON:

```
In [18]: import yaml

In [19]: with open('verify-apache.yml', 'r') as opened_file:
    ...:     verify_apache = yaml.safe_load(opened_file)
    ...:
```

The data loads as familiar Python data structures (a list containing a dict):

```
In [20]: pprint(verify_apache)
[{'handlers': [{'name': 'restart apache',
                'service': {'name': 'httpd', 'state': 'restarted'}}],
  'hosts': 'webservers',
  'remote_user': 'root',
  'tasks': [{'name': 'ensure apache is at the latest version',
             'yum': {'name': 'httpd', 'state': 'latest'}},
            {'name': 'write the apache config file',
             'notify': ['restart apache'],
             'template': {'dest': '/etc/httpd.conf', 'src': '/srv/httpd.j2'}},
            {'name': 'ensure apache is running',
             'service': {'name': 'httpd', 'state': 'started'}}],
  'vars': {'http_port': 80, 'max_clients': 200}}]
```

You can also save Python data to a file in YAML format:

```
In [22]: with open('verify-apache.yml', 'w') as opened_file:
    ...:     yaml.dump(verify_apache, opened_file)
    ...:
    ...:
    ...:
```

Another language widely used for representing structured data is Extensible Markup Language (XML). It consists of hierarchical documents of tagged elements. Historically, many web systems used XML to transport data. One such use is for Real Simple Syndication (RSS) feeds. RSS feeds are used to track and notify users of updates to websites and have been used to track the publication of articles from various sources. RSS feeds use XML-formatted pages. Python offers the xml library for dealing with XML documents. It maps the XML documents' hierarchical structure to a tree-like data structure. The nodes of the tree are elements, and a parent-child relationship is used to model the hierarchy. The top parent node is referred to as the root element. To parse an RSS XML document and get its root:

```
In [1]: import xml.etree.ElementTree as ET
In [2]: tree = ET.parse('http_feeds.feedburner.com_oreilly_radar_atom.xml')

In [3]: root = tree.getroot()

In [4]: root
Out[4]: <Element '{http://www.w3.org/2005/Atom}feed' at 0x11292c958>
```

You can walk down the tree by iterating over the child nodes:

```
In [5]: for child in root:
   ...:     print(child.tag, child.attrib)
   ...:
{http://www.w3.org/2005/Atom}title {}
{http://www.w3.org/2005/Atom}id {}
{http://www.w3.org/2005/Atom}updated {}
{http://www.w3.org/2005/Atom}subtitle {}
{http://www.w3.org/2005/Atom}link {'href': 'https://www.oreilly.com'}
{http://www.w3.org/2005/Atom}link {'rel': 'hub',
                                   'href': 'http://pubsubhubbub.appspot.com/'}
{http://www.w3.org/2003/01/geo/wgs84_pos#}long {}
{http://rssnamespace.org/feedburner/ext/1.0}emailServiceId {}
...
```

XML allows for *namespacing* (using tags to group data). XML prepends tags with namespaces enclosed in brackets. If you know the structure of the hierarchy, you can search for elements by using their paths. You can supply a dictionary that defines namespaces as a convenience:

```
In [108]: ns = {'default':'http://www.w3.org/2005/Atom'}
In [106]: authors = root.findall("default:entry/default:author/default:name", ns)

In [107]: for author in authors:
    ...:     print(author.text)
    ...:
Nat Torkington
VM Brasseur
Adam Jacob
Roger Magoulas
Pete Skomoroch
Adrian Cockcroft
Ben Lorica
Nat Torkington
Alison McCauley
Tiffani Bell
Arun Gupta
```

You may find yourself dealing with data stored as comma-separated values (CSV). This format is common for spreadsheet data. You can use the Python csv module to read these easily:

```
In [16]: import csv
In [17]: file_path = '/Users/kbehrman/Downloads/registered_user_count_ytd.csv'

In [18]: with open(file_path, newline='') as csv_file:
    ...:     off_reader = csv.reader(csv_file, delimiter=',')
    ...:     for _ in range(5):
    ...:         print(next(off_reader))
    ...:
['Date', 'PreviousUserCount', 'UserCountTotal', 'UserCountDay']
```

```
['2014-01-02', '61', '5336', '5275']
['2014-01-03', '42', '5378', '5336']
['2014-01-04', '26', '5404', '5378']
['2014-01-05', '65', '5469', '5404']
```

The csv reader object iterates through the *.csv* file one line at a time, allowing you to process the data one row at a time. Processing a file this way is especially useful for large *.csv* files that you do not want to read into memory all at once. Of course, if you need to do multiple row calculations across columns and the file is not overly large, you should load it all at once.

The Pandas package is a mainstay in the data science world. It includes a data structure, the pandas.DataFrame, which acts like a data table, similar to a very powerful spreadsheet. If you have table-like data on which you want to do statistical analysis or that you want to manipulate by rows and columns, DataFrames is the tool for you. It is a third-party library, so you need to install it with pip. You can use a variety of methods to load data into the DataFrames; one of the most common is from a *.csv* file:

```
In [54]: import pandas as pd

In [55]: df = pd.read_csv('sample-data.csv')

In [56]: type(df)
Out[56]: pandas.core.frame.DataFrame
```

You can take a look at the top rows of your DataFrame using the head method:

```
In [57]: df.head(3)
Out[57]:
     Attributes      open       high        low      close     volume
0       Symbols         F          F          F          F          F
1          date       NaN        NaN        NaN        NaN        NaN
2    2018-01-02   11.3007    11.4271    11.2827    11.4271   20773320
```

You can get a statistical insight using the describe method:

```
In [58]: df.describe()
Out[58]:
        Attributes      open     high    low    close     volume
count          357       356      356    356      356        356
unique         357       290      288    297      288        356
top     2018-10-18    10.402   8.3363   10.2   9.8111   36298597
freq             1         5        4      3        4          1
```

Alternatively, you can view a single column of data by using its name in square brackets:

```
In [59]: df['close']
Out[59]:
0              F
1            NaN
```

```
2       11.4271
3       11.5174
4       11.7159
          ...
352      9.83
353      9.78
354      9.71
355      9.74
356      9.52
Name: close, Length: 357, dtype: object
```

Pandas has many more methods for analyzing and manipulating table-like data, and there are many books on its use. It is a tool you should be aware of if you have the need to do data analysis.

Using Regular Expressions to Search Text

The Apache HTTP server is an open source web server widely used to serve web content. The web server can be configured to save log files in different formats. One widely used format is the Common Log Format (CLF). A variety of log analysis tools can understand this format. Below is the layout of this format:

```
<IP Address> <Client Id> <User Id> <Time> <Request> <Status> <Size>
```

What follows is an example line from a log in this format:

```
127.0.0.1 - swills [13/Nov/2019:14:43:30 -0800] "GET /assets/234 HTTP/1.0" 200 2326
```

Chapter 1 introduced you to regular expressions and the Python re module, so let's use it to pull information from a log in the common log format. One trick to constructing regular expressions is to do it in sections. Doing so enables you to get each subexpression working without the complication of debugging the whole expression. You can create a regular expression using named groups to pull out the IP address from a line:

```
In[1]: line = '127.0.0.1 - rj [13/Nov/2019:14:34:30 -0000] "GET HTTP/1.0" 200'

In [2]: re.search(r'(?P<IP>\d+\.\d+\.\d+\.\d+)', line)
Out[2]: <re.Match object; span=(0, 9), match='127.0.0.1'>

In [3]: m = re.search(r'(?P<IP>\d+\.\d+\.\d+\.\d+)', line)

In [4]: m.group('IP')
Out[4]: '127.0.0.1'
```

You can also create a regular expression to get the time:

```
In [5]: r = r'\[(?P<Time>\d\d/\w{3}/\d{4}:\d{2}:\d{2}:\d{2})\]'

In [6]: m = re.search(r, line)
```

```
In [7]: m.group('Time')
Out[7]: '13/Nov/2019:14:43:30'
```

You can grab multiple elements, as has been done here: the IP, user, time, and request:

```
In [8]:  r = r'(?P<IP>\d+\.\d+\.\d+\.\d+)'

In [9]: r += r' - (?P<User>\w+) '

In [10]: r += r'\[(?P<Time>\d\d/\w{3}/\d{4}:\d{2}:\d{2}:\d{2})\]'

In [11]: r += r' (?P<Request>".+")'

In [12]:  m = re.search(r, line)

In [13]: m.group('IP')
Out[13]: '127.0.0.1'

In [14]: m.group('User')
Out[14]: 'rj'

In [15]: m.group('Time')
Out[15]: '13/Nov/2019:14:43:30'

In [16]: m.group('Request')
Out[16]: '"GET HTTP/1.0"'
```

Parsing a single line of a log is interesting but not terribly useful. However, you can use this regular expression as a basis for designing one to pull information from the whole log. Let's say you want to pull all of the IP addresses for GET requests that happened on November 8, 2019. Using the preceding expression, you make modifications based on the specifics of your request:

```
In [62]: r = r'(?P<IP>\d+\.\d+\.\d+\.\d+)'
In [63]: r += r'- (?P<User>\w+)'
In [64]: r += r'\[(?P<Time>08/Nov/\d{4}:\d{2}:\d{2}:\d{2} [-+]\d{4})\]'
In [65]: r += r' (?P<Request>"GET .+")'
```

Use the `finditer` method to process the log, printing the IP addresses of the matching lines:

```
In [66]: matched = re.finditer(r, access_log)

In [67]: for m in matched:
    ...:     print(m.group('IP'))
    ...:
127.0.0.1
342.3.2.33
```

There is a lot that you can do with regular expressions and texts of all sorts. If they do not daunt you, you will find them one of the most powerful tools in dealing with text.

Dealing with Large Files

There are times that you need to process very large files. If the files contain data that can be processed one line at a time, the task is easy with Python. Rather than loading the whole file into memory as you have done up until now, you can read one line at a time, process the line, and then move to the next. The lines are removed from memory automatically by Python's garbage collector, freeing up memory.

 Python automatically allocates and frees memory. Garbage collection is one means of doing this. The Python garbage collector can be controlled using the gc package, though this is rarely needed.

The fact that operating systems use alternate line endings can be a hassle when reading a file created on a different OS. Windows-created files have \r characters in addition to \n. These show up as part of the text on a Linux-based system. If you have a large file and you want to correct the line endings to fit your current OS, you can open the file, read one line at a time, and save it to a new file. Python handles the line-ending translation for you:

```
In [23]: with open('big-data.txt', 'r') as source_file:
    ...:     with open('big-data-corrected.txt', 'w') as target_file:
    ...:         for line in source_file:
    ...:             target_file.write(line)
    ...:
```

Notice that you can nest the with statements to open two files at once and loop through the source file object one line at a time. You can define a generator function to handle this, especially if you need to parse multiple files a single line at a time:

```
In [46]: def line_reader(file_path):
    ...:     with open(file_path, 'r') as source_file:
    ...:         for line in source_file:
    ...:             yield line
    ...:

In [47]: reader = line_reader('big-data.txt')

In [48]: with open('big-data-corrected.txt', 'w') as target_file:
    ...:     for line in reader:
    ...:         target_file.write(line)
    ...:
```

If you do not or cannot use line endings as a means of breaking up your data, as in the case of a large binary file, you can read your data in chunks. You pass the number of bytes read in each chunk to the file objects read method. When there is nothing left to read, the expression returns an empty string:

```
In [27]: with open('bb141548a754113e.jpg', 'rb') as source_file:
    ...:     while True:
    ...:         chunk = source_file.read(1024)
    ...:         if chunk:
    ...:             process_data(chunk)
    ...:         else:
    ...:             break
    ...:
```

Encrypting Text

There are many times you need to encrypt text to ensure security. In addition to Python's built-in package `hashlib`, there is a widely used third-party package called `cryptography`. Let's take a look at both.

Hashing with Hashlib

To be secure, user passwords must be stored encrypted. A common way to handle this is to use a one-way function to encrypt the password into a bit string, which is very hard to reverse engineer. Functions that do this are called *hash functions*. In addition to obscuring passwords, hash functions ensure that documents sent over the web are unchanged during transmission. You run the hash function on the document and send the result along with the document. The recipient can then confirm that the value is the same when they hash the document. The `hashlib` includes secure algorithms for doing this, including *SHA1*, *SHA224*, *SHA384*, *SHA512*, and RSA's *MD5*. This is how you would hash a password using the MD5 algorithm:

```
In [62]: import hashlib

In [63]: secret = "This is the password or document text"

In [64]: bsecret = secret.encode()

In [65]: m = hashlib.md5()

In [66]: m.update(bsecret)

In [67]: m.digest()
Out[67]: b' \xf5\x06\xe6\xfc\x1c\xbe\x86\xddj\x96C\x10\x0f5E'
```

Notice that if your password or document is a string, you need to turn it into a binary string by using the encode method.

Encryption with Cryptography

The `cryptography` library is a popular choice for handling encryption problems in Python. It is a third-party package, so you must install it with `pip`. *Symmetric key encryption* is a group of encryption algorithms based on shared keys. These algorithms include Advanced Encryption Algorithm (AES), Blowfish, Data Encryption Standard (DES), Serpent, and Twofish. A shared key is similar to a password that is used to both encrypt and decrypt text. The fact that both the creator and the reader of an encrypted file need to share the key is a drawback when compared to *asymmetric key encryption*, which we will touch on later. However, symmetric key encryption is faster and more straightforward, and so is appropriate for encrypting large files. Fernet is an implementation of the popular AES algorithm. You first need to generate a key:

```
In [1]: from cryptography.fernet import Fernet

In [2]: key = Fernet.generate_key()

In [3]: key
Out[3]: b'q-fEOs2JIRINDR8toMG7zhQvVhvf5BRPx3mj5Atk5B8='
```

You need to store this key securely, as you need it to decrypt. Keep in mind that anyone who has access to it is also able to decrypt your files. If you choose to save the key to a file, use the binary data type. The next step is to encrypt the data using the Fernet object:

```
In [4]: f = Fernet(key)

In [5]: message = b"Secrets go here"


In [6]: encrypted = f.encrypt(message)

In [7]: encrypted
Out[7]: b'gAAAAABdPyg4 ... plhkpVkC8ezOHaOLIA=='
```

You can decrypt the data using a Fernet object created with the same key:

```
In [1]: f = Fernet(key)

In [2]: f.decrypt(encrypted)
Out[2]: b'Secrets go here'
```

Asymmetric key encryption uses a pair of keys, one public and one private. The public key is designed to be widely shared, while a single user holds the private one. The only way you can decrypt messages that have been encrypted using your public key is by using your private key. This style of encryption is widely used to pass information confidentially both on local networks and across the internet. One very popular asymmetric key algorithm is Rivest-Shamir-Adleman (RSA), which is widely used for communication across networks. The cryptography library offers the ability to create public/private key pairs:

```
In [1]: from cryptography.hazmat.backends import default_backend

In [2]: from cryptography.hazmat.primitives.asymmetric import rsa
```

```
In [3]: private_key = rsa.generate_private_key(public_exponent=65537,
                                               key_size=4096,
                                               backend=default_backend())

In [4]: private_key
Out[4]: <cryptography.hazmat.backends.openssl.rsa._RSAPrivateKey at 0x10d377c18>

In [5]: public_key = private_key.public_key

In [6]: public_key = private_key.public_key()

In [7]: public_key
Out[7]: <cryptography.hazmat.backends.openssl.rsa._RSAPublicKey at 0x10da642b0>
```

You can then use the public key to encrypt:

```
In [8]: message = b"More secrets go here"

In [9]: from cryptography.hazmat.primitives.asymmetric import padding
In [11]: from cryptography.hazmat.primitives import hashes

In [12]: encrypted = public_key.encrypt(message,
    ...:     padding.OAEP(mgf=padding.MGF1(algorithm=hashes.SHA256()),
    ...:     algorithm=hashes.SHA256(),
    ...:     label=None))
```

You can use the private key to decrypt messages:

```
In [13]: decrypted = private_key.decrypt(encrypted,
    ...:     padding.OAEP(mgf=padding.MGF1(algorithm=hashes.SHA256()),
    ...:     algorithm=hashes.SHA256(),
    ...:     label=None))

In [14]: decrypted
Out[14]: b'More secrets go here'
```

The os Module

The os module is one of the most used modules in Python. This module handles many low-level operating system calls and attempts to offer a consistent interface across multiple operating systems, which is important if you think your application might run on both Windows and Unix-based systems. It does offer some operating-specific features (os.O_TEXT for Windows and os.O_CLOEXEC on Linux) that are not available across platforms. Use these only if you are confident that your application does not need to be portable across operating systems. Example 2-1 shows some of the most useful additional methods of the os module.

Example 2-1. More os methods

```
In [1]: os.listdir('.') ❶
Out[1]: ['__init__.py', 'os_path_example.py']

In [2]: os.rename('_crud_handler', 'crud_handler') ❷

In [3]: os.chmod('my_script.py', 0o777) ❸

In [4]: os.mkdir('/tmp/holding') ❹

In [5]: os.makedirs('/Users/kbehrman/tmp/scripts/devops') ❺

In [6]: os.remove('my_script.py') ❻

In [7]: os.rmdir('/tmp/holding') ❼

In [8]: os.removedirs('/Users/kbehrman/tmp/scripts/devops') ❽

In [9]: os.stat('crud_handler') ❾
Out[9]: os.stat_result(st_mode=16877,
                       st_ino=4359290300,
                       st_dev=16777220,
                       st_nlink=18,
                       st_uid=501,
                       st_gid=20,
                       st_size=576,
                       st_atime=1544115987,
                       st_mtime=1541955837,
                       st_ctime=1567266289)
```

❶ List the contents of a directory.

❷ Rename a file or directory.

❸ Change the permission settings of a file or directory.

❹ Create a directory.

❺ Recursively create a directory path.

❻ Delete a file.

❼ Delete a single directory.

❽ Delete a tree of directories, starting with the leaf directory and working up the tree. The operation stops with the first nonempty directory.

⑨ Get stats about the file or directory. These stats include st_mode, the file type and permissions, and st_atime, the time the item was last accessed.

Managing Files and Directories Using os.path

In Python, you can use strings (binary or otherwise) to represent paths. The os.path module offers a plethora of path-related methods for creating and manipulating paths as strings. As previously mentioned, the os module tries to offer cross-platform behaviors, and the os.path submodule is no exception. This module interprets paths based on the current operating system, using forward slashes to separate directories in Unix-like systems and backward slashes in Windows. Your program can construct paths on the fly that work on the current system, whichever it is. The ability to easily split and join paths is probably the most used functionality of os.path. The three methods used to split paths are split, basename, and dirname:

```
In [1]: import os

In [2]: cur_dir = os.getcwd() ❶

In [3]: cur_dir
Out[3]: '/Users/kbehrman/Google-Drive/projects/python-devops/samples/chapter4'

In [4]: os.path.split(cur_dir) ❷
Out[4]: ('/Users/kbehrman/Google-Drive/projects/python-devops/samples',
          'chapter4')

In [5]: os.path.dirname(cur_dir) ❸
Out[5]: '/Users/kbehrman/Google-Drive/projects/python-devops/samples'

In [6]: os.path.basename(cur_dir) ❹
Out[6]: 'chapter4'
```

❶ Get the current working directory.

❷ os.path.split splits the leaf level of the path from the parent path.

❸ os.path.dirname returns the parent path.

❹ os.path.basename returns the leaf name.

You can easily use os.path.dirname to walk up a directory tree:

```
In [7]: while os.path.basename(cur_dir):
   ...:     cur_dir = os.path.dirname(cur_dir)
   ...:     print(cur_dir)
   ...:
/Users/kbehrman/projects/python-devops/samples
/Users/kbehrman/projects/python-devops
```

```
/Users/kbehrman/projects
/Users/kbehrman
/Users
/
```

Using files to configure an application at runtime is a common practice; files in Unix-like systems are named by convention as dotfiles ending with *rc*. Vim's *.vimrc* file and the Bash shell's *.bashrc* are two common examples. You can store these files in different locations. Often programs will define a hierarchy of locations to check. For example, your tool might look first for an environment variable that defines which *rc* file to use, and in its absence, check the working directory, and then the user's home directory. In Example 2-2 we try to locate an *rc* file in these locations. We use the *file* variable that Python automatically sets when Python code runs from a file. This variable is populated with a path relative to the current working directory, not an absolute or full path. Python does not automatically expand paths, as is common in Unix-like systems, so we must expand this path before we use it to construct the path to check our *rc* file. Similarly, Python does not automatically expand environment variables in paths, so we must expand these explicitly.

Example 2-2. find_rc method

```python
def find_rc(rc_name=".examplerc"):

    # Check for Env variable
    var_name = "EXAMPLERC_DIR"
    if var_name in os.environ:                                    ❶
        var_path = os.path.join(f"${var_name}", rc_name)          ❷
        config_path = os.path.expandvars(var_path)                ❸
        print(f"Checking {config_path}")
        if os.path.exists(config_path):                           ❹
            return config_path

    # Check the current working directory
    config_path = os.path.join(os.getcwd(), rc_name)              ❺
    print(f"Checking {config_path}")
    if os.path.exists(config_path):
        return config_path

    # Check user home directory
    home_dir = os.path.expanduser("~/")                           ❻
    config_path = os.path.join(home_dir, rc_name)
    print(f"Checking {config_path}")
    if os.path.exists(config_path):
        return config_path

    # Check Directory of This File
    file_path = os.path.abspath(__file__)                         ❼
    parent_path = os.path.dirname(file_path)                      ❽
```

```
config_path = os.path.join(parent_path, rc_name)
print(f"Checking {config_path}")
if os.path.exists(config_path):
    return config_path

print(f"File {rc_name} has not been found")
```

❶ Check whether the environment variable exists in the current environment.

❷ Use join to construct a path with the environment variable name. This will look something like $EXAMPLERC_DIR/.examplerc.

❸ Expand the environment variable to insert its value into the path.

❹ Check to see if the file exists.

❺ Construct a path using the current working directory.

❻ Use the expanduser function to get the path to the user's home directory.

❼ Expand the relative path stored in *file* to an absolute path.

❽ Use dirname to get the path to the directory holding the current file.

The path submodule also offers ways to interrogate stats about a path. You can determine if a path is a file, a directory, a link, or a mount. You can get stats such as it's size or time of last access or modification. In Example 2-3 we use path to walk down a directory tree and report on the size and last access time of all files therein.

Example 2-3. os_path_walk.py

```
#!/usr/bin/env python

import fire
import os

def walk_path(parent_path):
    print(f"Checking: {parent_path}")
    childs = os.listdir(parent_path) ❶

    for child in childs:
        child_path = os.path.join(parent_path, child) ❷
        if os.path.isfile(child_path): ❸
            last_access = os.path.getatime(child_path) ❹
            size = os.path.getsize(child_path) ❺
            print(f"File: {child_path}")
            print(f"\tlast accessed: {last_access}")
```

```
        print(f"\tsize: {size}")
    elif os.path.isdir(child_path):  ❻
        walk_path(child_path)  ❼

if __name__ == '__main__':
    fire.Fire()
```

❶ os.listdir returns the contents of a directory.

❷ Construct the full path of an item in the parent directory.

❸ Check to see if the path represents a file.

❹ Get the last time the file was accessed.

❺ Get the size of the file.

❻ Check if the path represents a directory.

❼ Check the tree from this directory down.

You could use a script like this to identify large files or files that have not been accessed and then report, move, or delete them.

Walking Directory Trees Using os.walk

The os module offers a convenience function for walking directory trees called os.walk. This function returns a generator that in turn returns a tuple for each iteration. The tuple consists of the current path, a list of directories, and a list of files. In Example 2-4 we rewrite our walk_path function from Example 2-3 to use os.walk. As you can see in this example, with os.walk you don't need to test which paths are files or recall the function with every subdirectory.

Example 2-4. Rewrite walk_path

```
def walk_path(parent_path):
    for parent_path, directories, files in os.walk(parent_path):
        print(f"Checking: {parent_path}")
        for file_name in files:
            file_path = os.path.join(parent_path, file_name)
            last_access = os.path.getatime(file_path)
            size = os.path.getsize(file_path)
            print(f"File: {file_path}")
            print(f"\tlast accessed: {last_access}")
            print(f"\tsize: {size}")
```

Paths as Objects with Pathlib

The `pathlib` library represents paths as objects rather than strings. In Example 2-5 we rewrite Example 2-2 using `pathlib` rather than `os.path`.

Example 2-5. rewrite find_rc

```
def find_rc(rc_name=".examplerc"):

    # Check for Env variable
    var_name = "EXAMPLERC_DIR"
    example_dir = os.environ.get(var_name)  ❶
    if example_dir:
        dir_path = pathlib.Path(example_dir)  ❷
        config_path = dir_path / rc_name  ❸
        print(f"Checking {config_path}")
        if config_path.exists():  ❹
            return config_path.as_postix()  ❺

    # Check the current working directory
    config_path = pathlib.Path.cwd() / rc_name  ❻
    print(f"Checking {config_path}")
    if config_path.exists():
        return config_path.as_postix()

    # Check user home directory
    config_path = pathlib.Path.home() / rc_name  ❼
    print(f"Checking {config_path}")
    if config_path.exists():
        return config_path.as_postix()

    # Check Directory of This File
    file_path = pathlib.Path(__file__).resolve()  ❽
    parent_path = file_path.parent  ❾
    config_path = parent_path / rc_name
    print(f"Checking {config_path}")
    if config_path.exists():
        return config_path.as_postix()

    print(f"File {rc_name} has not been found")
```

❶ As of this writing, `pathlib` does not expand environment variables. Instead you grab the value of the variable from `os.environ`.

❷ This creates a `pathlib.Path` object appropriate for the currently running operating system.

❸   You can construct new `pathlib.Path` objects by following a parent path with forward slashes and strings.

❹   The `pathlib.Path` object itself has an `exists` method.

❺   Call `as_postix` to return the path as a string. Depending on your use case, you can return the `pathlib.Path` object itself.

❻   The class method `pathlib.Path.cwd` returns a `pathlib.Path` object for the current working directory. This object is used immediately here to create the config_path by joining it with the string rc_name.

❼   The class method `pathlib.Path.home` returns a `pathlib.Path` object for the current user's home directory.

❽   Create a `pathlib.Path` object using the relative path stored in *file* and then call its `resolve` method to get the absolute path.

❾   This returns a parent `pathlib.Path` object directly from the object itself.

Working with the Command Line

The command line is where the rubber hits the road. Although there are many powerful tools with graphical interfaces, the command line is still home for DevOps work. Interacting with your shell environment from within Python and creating Python command-line tools are both necessary when using Python for DevOps.

Working with the Shell

Python offers tools for interacting with systems and shells. You should become familiar with the sys, os, and subprocess modules, as all are essential tools.

Talking to the Interpreter with the sys Module

The sys module offers access to variables and methods closely tied to the Python interpreter.

There are two dominant ways to interpret bytes during reading. The first, *little endian*, interprets each subsequent byte as having higher significance (representing a larger digit). The other, *big endian*, assumes the first byte has the greatest significance and moves down from there.

You can use the sys.byteorder attribute to see the byte order of your current architecture:

```
In [1]: import sys

In [2]: sys.byteorder
Out[2]: 'little'
```

You can use `sys.getsizeof` to see the size of Python objects. This is useful if you are dealing with limited memory:

```
In [3]: sys.getsizeof(1)
Out[3]: 28
```

If you want to perform different behaviors, depending on the underlying operating system, you can use `sys.platform` to check:

```
In [5]: sys.platform
Out[5]: 'darwin'
```

A more common situation is that you want to use a language feature or module that is only available in specific versions of Python. You can use the `sys.version_info` to control behavior based on the running Python interpreter. Here we print different messages for Python 3.7, a Python version 3 that is below 3.7, and Python versions lower than 3:

```
if sys.version_info.major < 3:
    print("You need to update your Python version")
elif sys.version_info.minor < 7:
    print("You are not running the latest version of Python")
else:
    print("All is good.")
```

We cover more `sys` usage later in this chapter when we write command-line tools.

Dealing with the Operating System Using the os Module

You have seen the os module used in Chapter 2 for dealing with the filesystem. It also has a grab bag of various attributes and functions related to dealing with the operating system. In Example 3-1 we demonstrate some of them.

Example 3-1. os module examples

```
In [1]: import os

In [2]: os.getcwd()  ❶
Out[2]: '/Users/kbehrman/Google-Drive/projects/python-devops'

In [3]: os.chdir('/tmp')  ❷

In [4]: os.getcwd()
Out[4]: '/private/tmp'

In [5]: os.environ.get('LOGLEVEL')  ❸

In [6]: os.environ['LOGLEVEL'] = 'DEBUG'  ❹

In [7]: os.environ.get('LOGLEVEL')
```

```
Out[7]: 'DEBUG'

In [8]: os.getlogin() ❺
Out[8]: 'kbehrman'
```

❶ Get the current working directory.

❷ Change the current working directory.

❸ The os.environ holds the environment variables that were set when the os module was loaded.

❹ This is the setting and environment variable. This setting exists for subprocesses spawned from this code.

❺ This is the login of the user in the terminal that spawned this process.

The most common usage of the os module is to get settings from environment variables. These could be the level to set your logging, or secrets such as API keys.

Spawn Processes with the subprocess Module

There are many instances when you need to run applications outside of Python from within your Python code. This could be built-in shell commands, Bash scripts, or any other command-line application. To do this, you spawn a new *process* (instance of the application). The subprocess module is the right choice when you want to spawn a process and run commands within it. With subprocess, you can run your favorite shell command or other command-line software and collect its output from within Python. For the majority of use cases, you should use the subprocess.run function to spawn processes:

```
In [1]: cp = subprocess.run(['ls','-l'],
                            capture_output=True,
                            universal_newlines=True)

In [2]: cp.stdout
Out[2]: 'total 96
        -rw-r--r--  1 kbehrman  staff     0 Apr 12 08:48 __init__.py
        drwxr-xr-x  5 kbehrman  staff   160 Aug 18 15:47 __pycache__
        -rw-r--r--  1 kbehrman  staff   123 Aug 13 12:13 always_say_it.py
        -rwxr-xr-x  1 kbehrman  staff  1409 Aug  8 15:36 argparse_example.py
        -rwxr-xr-x  1 kbehrman  staff   734 Aug 12 09:36 click_example.py
        -rwxr-xr-x  1 kbehrman  staff   538 Aug 13 10:41 fire_example.py
        -rw-r--r--  1 kbehrman  staff    41 Aug 18 15:17 foo_plugin_a.py
        -rw-r--r--  1 kbehrman  staff    41 Aug 18 15:47 foo_plugin_b.py
        -rwxr-xr-x  1 kbehrman  staff   335 Aug 10 12:36 simple_click.py
        -rwxr-xr-x  1 kbehrman  staff   256 Aug 13 09:21 simple_fire.py
        -rwxr-xr-x  1 kbehrman  staff   509 Aug  8 10:27 simple_parse.py
```

```
-rwxr-xr-x  1 kbehrman  staff   502 Aug 18 15:11 simple_plugins.py
-rwxr-xr-x  1 kbehrman  staff   850 Aug  6 14:44 sys_argv.py
-rw-r--r--  1 kbehrman  staff   182 Aug 18 16:24 sys_example.py
```

The subprocess.run function returns a CompletedProcess instance once the process completes. In this case, we run the shell command ls with the argument -l to see the contents of the current directory. We set it to capture stdout and stderr with the capture_output parameter. We then access the results using cp.stdout. If we run our ls command on a nonexistent directory, causing it to return an error, we can see the output in cp.stderr:

```
In [3]: cp = subprocess.run(['ls','/doesnotexist'],
                            capture_output=True,
                            universal_newlines=True)

In [3]: cp.stderr
Out[3]: 'ls: /doesnotexist: No such file or directory\n'
```

You can better integrate the handling of errors by using the check parameter. This raises an exception if the subprocess reports an error:

```
In [23]: cp = subprocess.run(['ls', '/doesnotexist'],
                            capture_output=True,
                            universal_newlines=True,
                            check=True)
---------------------------------------------------------------------------
CalledProcessError                        Traceback (most recent call last)
<ipython-input-23-c0ac49c40fee> in <module>
----> 1 cp = subprocess.run(['ls', '/doesnotexist'],
                            capture_output=True,
                            universal_newlines=True,
                            check=True)

~/.pyenv/versions/3.7.0/lib/python3.7/subprocess.py ...
    466         if check and retcode:
    467             raise CalledProcessError(retcode, process.args,
--> 468                                      output=stdout, stderr=stderr)
    469     return CompletedProcess(process.args, retcode, stdout, stderr)
    470

CalledProcessError: Command '['ls', '/doesnotexist']' returned non-zero exit
```

In this way, you don't have to check stderr for failures. You can treat errors from your subprocess much as you would other Python exceptions.

Creating Command-Line Tools

The simplest way to invoke a Python script on the command line is to invoke it using Python. When you construct a Python script, any statements at the top level (not nested in code blocks) run whenever the script is invoked or imported. If you have a function you want to run whenever your code is loaded, you can invoke it at the top level:

```python
def say_it():
    greeting = 'Hello'
    target = 'Joe'
    message = f'{greeting} {target}'
    print(message)

say_it()
```

This function runs whenever the script runs on the command line:

```
$ python always_say_it.py

Hello Joe
```

Also, when the file is imported:

```
In [1]: import always_say_it
Hello Joe
```

This should only be done with the most straightforward scripts, however. A significant downside to this approach is that if you want to import your module into other Python modules, the code runs during import instead of waiting to be invoked by the calling module. Someone who is importing your module usually wants control over when its contents are invoked. You can add functionality that only happens when called from the command line by using the global *name* variable. You have seen that this variable reports the name of the module during import. If the module is called directly on the command line, this sets it to the string *main*. The convention for modules running on the command line is to end with a block testing for this and run command-line specific code from this block. To modify the script to run a function automatically only when invoked on the command line, but not during import, put the function invocation into the block after the test:

```python
def say_it():
    greeting = 'Hello'
    target = 'Joe'
    message = f'{greeting} {target}'
    print(message)

if __name__ == '__main__':
    say_it()
```

When you import this function, this block does not run, as the __name__ variable reflects the module path as imported. It runs when the module is run directly, however:

```
$ python say_it.py

Hello Joe
```

Making Your Shell Script Executable

To eliminate the need to explicitly call type python on the command line when you run your script, you can add the line #!/usr/bin/env python to the top of your file:

```python
#!/usr/bin/env python

def say_it():
    greeting = 'Hello'
    target = 'Joe'
    message = f'{greeting} {target}'
    print(message)

if __name__ == '__main__':
    say_it()
```

Then make the file executable using chmod (a command-line tool for setting permissions):

```
chmod +x say_it.py`
```

You can then call it in a shell without directly invoking Python:

```
$ ./say_it.py

Hello Joe
```

The first step in creating command-line tools is separating code that should only run when invoked on the command line. The next step is to accept command-line arguments. Unless your tool only does one thing, you need to accept commands to know what to do. Also, command-line tools that do more than the simplest tasks accept optional flags to configure their workings. Remember that these commands and flags are the *user interface* (UI) for anyone using your tools. You need to consider how easy they are to use and understand. Providing documentation is an essential part of making your code understandable.

Using sys.argv

The simplest and most basic way to process arguments from the command line is to use the argv attribute of the sys module. This attribute is a list of arguments passed to a Python script at runtime. If the script runs on the command line, the first argument is the name of the script. The rest of the items in the list are any remaining command-line arguments, represented as strings:

```python
#!/usr/bin/env python
"""
Simple command-line tool using sys.argv
"""

import sys

if __name__ == '__main__':
    print(f"The first argument:  '{sys.argv[0]}'")
    print(f"The second argument: '{sys.argv[1]}'")
    print(f"The third argument:  '{sys.argv[2]}'")
    print(f"The fourth argument: '{sys.argv[3]}'")
```

Run it on the command line and see the arguments:

```
$ ./sys_argv.py --a-flag some-value 13

The first argument:  './sys_argv.py'
The second argument: '--a-flag'
The third argument:  'some-value'
The fourth argument: '13'
```

You can use these arguments to write your own argument parser. To see what this might look like, check out Example 3-2.

Example 3-2. Parsing with sys.argv

```python
#!/usr/bin/env python
"""
Simple command-line tool using sys.argv
"""

import sys

def say_it(greeting, target):
    message = f'{greeting} {target}'
    print(message)

if __name__ == '__main__':  ❶
    greeting = 'Hello'  ❷
    target = 'Joe'

    if '--help' in sys.argv:  ❸
        help_message = f"Usage: {sys.argv[0]} --name <NAME> --greeting <GREETING>"
        print(help_message)
        sys.exit()  ❹

    if '--name' in sys.argv:
        # Get position after name flag
        name_index = sys.argv.index('--name') + 1  ❺
```

```
    if name_index < len(sys.argv):  ❻
        name = sys.argv[name_index]

if '--greeting' in sys.argv:
    # Get position after greeting flag
    greeting_index = sys.argv.index('--greeting') + 1
    if greeting_index < len(sys.argv):
        greeting = sys.argv[greeting_index]

say_it(greeting, name)  ❼
```

❶ Here we test to see if we are running from the command line.

❷ Default values are set in these two lines.

❸ Check if the string --help is in the list of arguments.

❹ Exit the program after printing the help message.

❺ We need the position of the value after the flag, which should be the associated value.

❻ Test that the arguments list is long enough. It will not be if the flag was provided without a value.

❼ Call the function with the values as modified by the arguments.

Example 3-2 goes far enough to print out a simple help message and accept arguments to the function:

```
$ ./sys_argv.py --help
Usage: ./sys_argv.py --name <NAME> --greeting <GREETING>

$ ./sys_argv.py --name Sally --greeting Bonjour
Bonjour Sally
```

This approach is fraught with complication and potential bugs. Example 3-2 fails to handle many situations. If a user misspells or miscapitalizes a flag, the flag is ignored with no useful feedback. If they use commands that are not supported or try to use more than one value with a flag, once again the error is ignored. You should be aware of the argv parsing approach, but do not use it for any production code unless you specifically set out to write an argument parser. Luckily there are modules and packages designed for the creation of command-line tools. These packages provide frameworks to design the user interface for your module when running in a shell. Three popular solutions are *argparse*, *click*, and *python-fire*. All three include ways to design required arguments, optional flags, and means to display help documentation. The first, argparse, is part of the Python standard library, and the other two are third-party packages that need to be installed separately (using pip).

Using argparse

argparse abstracts away many of the details of parsing arguments. With it, you design your command-line user interface in detail, defining commands and flags along with their help messages. It uses the idea of parser objects, to which you attach commands and flags. The parser then parses the arguments, and you use the results to call your code. You construct your interface using ArgumentParser objects that parse user input for you:

```python
if __name__ == '__main__':
    parser = argparse.ArgumentParser(description='Maritime control')
```

You add position-based commands or optional flags to the parser using the add_argu ment method (see Example 3-3). The first argument to this method is the name of the new argument (command or flag). If the name begins with a dash, it is treated as an optional flag argument; otherwise it is treated as a position-dependent command. The parser creates a parsed-arguments object, with the arguments as attributes that you can then use to access input. Example 3-3 is a simple program that echoes a users input and shows the basics of how argparse works.

Example 3-3. simple_parse.py

```python
#!/usr/bin/env python
"""
Command-line tool using argparse
"""

import argparse


if __name__ == '__main__':
    parser = argparse.ArgumentParser(description='Echo your input')  ❶
    parser.add_argument('message',                                   ❷
                        help='Message to echo')

    parser.add_argument('--twice', '-t',                             ❸
                        help='Do it twice',
                        action='store_true')                         ❹

    args = parser.parse_args()  ❺

    print(args.message)    ❻
    if args.twice:
        print(args.message)
```

❶ Create the parser object, with its documentation message.

❷ Add a position-based command with its help message.

❸ Add an optional argument.   ˙

❹ Store the optional argument as a boolean value.

❺ Use the parser to parse the arguments.

❻ Access the argument values by name. The optional argument's name has the --
removed.

When you run it with the `--twice` flag, the input message prints twice:

```
$ ./simple_parse.py hello --twice
hello
hello
```

`argparse` automatically sets up help and usage messages based on the help and
description text you supply:

```
$ ./simple_parse.py  --help
usage: simple_parse.py [-h] [--twice] message

Echo your input

positional arguments:
  message      Message to echo

optional arguments:
  -h, --help   show this help message and exit
  --twice, -t  Do it twice
```

Many command-line tools use nested levels of commands to group command areas
of control. Think of `git`. It has top-level commands, such as `git stash`, which have
separate commands under them, such as `git stash pop`. With `argparse`, you create
subcommands by creating subparsers under your main parser. You can create a hierarchy of commands using subparsers. In Example 3-4, we implement a maritime
application that has commands for ships and sailors. Two subparsers are added to the
main parser; each subparser has its own commands.

Example 3-4. argparse_example.py

```
#!/usr/bin/env python
"""
Command-line tool using argparse
"""

import argparse
```

```python
def sail():
    ship_name = 'Your ship'
    print(f"{ship_name} is setting sail")

def list_ships():
    ships = ['John B', 'Yankee Clipper', 'Pequod']
    print(f"Ships: {','.join(ships)}")

def greet(greeting, name):
    message = f'{greeting} {name}'
    print(message)

if __name__ == '__main__':
    parser = argparse.ArgumentParser(description='Maritime control')  ❶

    parser.add_argument('--twice', '-t',   ❷
                        help='Do it twice',
                        action='store_true')

    subparsers = parser.add_subparsers(dest='func')  ❸

    ship_parser =  subparsers.add_parser('ships',   ❹
                                        help='Ship related commands')
    ship_parser.add_argument('command',  ❺
                            choices=['list', 'sail'])

    sailor_parser = subparsers.add_parser('sailors',  ❻
                                        help='Talk to a sailor')
    sailor_parser.add_argument('name',  ❼
                            help='Sailors name')
    sailor_parser.add_argument('--greeting', '-g',
                            help='Greeting',
                            default='Ahoy there')

    args = parser.parse_args()
    if args.func == 'sailors':  ❽
        greet(args.greeting, args.name)
    elif args.command == 'list':
        list_ships()
    else:
        sail()
```

❶ Create the top-level parser.

❷ Add a top-level argument that can be used along with any command under this parser's hierarchy.

❸ Create a subparser object to hold the subparsers. The dest is the name of the attribute used to choose a subparser.

❹ Add a subparser for *ships*.

❺ Add a command to the *ships* subparser. The `choices` parameter gives a list of possible choices for the command.

❻ Add a subparser for *sailors*.

❼ Add a required positional argument to the *sailors* subparser.

❽ Check which subparser is used by checking the `func` value.

Example 3-4 has one top-level optional argument (`twice`) and two subparsers. Each subparser has its own commands and flags. `argparse` automatically creates a hierarchy of help messages and displays them with the `--help` flag. The top-level help commands, including the subparsers and the top-level `twice` argument, are documented:

```
$ ./argparse_example.py --help
usage: argparse_example.py [-h] [--twice] {ships,sailors} ...

Maritime control

positional arguments:
  {ships,sailors}
    ships         Ship related commands
    sailors       Talk to a sailor

optional arguments:
  -h, --help      show this help message and exit
  --twice, -t     Do it twice
```

You can dig into the subcommands (subparsers) by using the `help` flag after the command:

```
$ ./argparse_example.py ships --help
usage: argparse_example.py ships [-h] {list,sail}

positional arguments:
  {list,sail}

optional arguments:
  -h, --help   show this help message and exit
```

As you can see, `argparse` gives you a lot of control over your command-line interface. You can design a multilayered interface with built-in documentation with many options to fine-tune your design. Doing so takes a lot of work on your part, however, so let's look at some easier options.

Using click

The `click` package was first developed to work with web framework `flask`. It uses Python *function decorators* to bind the command-line interface directly with your functions. Unlike `argparse`, `click` interweaves your interface decisions directly with the rest of your code.

Function Decorators

Python decorators are a special syntax for functions which take other functions as arguments. Python functions are objects, so any function can take a function as an argument. The decorator syntax provides a clean and easy way to do this. The basic format of a decorator is:

```
In [2]: def some_decorator(wrapped_function):
   ...:     def wrapper():
   ...:         print('Do something before calling wrapped function')
   ...:         wrapped_function()
   ...:         print('Do something after calling wrapped function')
   ...:     return wrapper
   ...:
```

You can define a function and pass it as an argument to this function:

```
In [3]: def foobat():
   ...:     print('foobat')
   ...:
```

```
In [4]: f = some_decorator(foobat)
```

```
In [5]: f()
Do something before calling wrapped function
foobat
Do something after calling wrapped function
```

The decorator syntax simplifies this by indicating which function should be wrapped by *decorating* it with `@decorator_name`. Here is an example using the decorator syntax with our `some_decorator` function:

```
In [6]: @some_decorator
   ...: def batfoo():
   ...:     print('batfoo')
   ...:
```

```
In [7]: batfoo()
Do something before calling wrapped function
batfoo
Do something after calling wrapped function
```

Now you call your wrapped function using its name rather than the decorator name. Pre-built functions intended as decorators are offered both as part of the Python Standard Library (staticMethod, classMethod) and as part of third-party packages, such as Flask and Click.

This means that you tie your flags and options directly to the parameters of the functions that they expose. You can create a simple command-line tool from your functions using click's command and option functions as decorators before your function:

```python
#!/usr/bin/env python
"""
Simple Click example
"""

import click


@click.command()
@click.option('--greeting', default='Hiya', help='How do you want to greet?')
@click.option('--name', default='Tammy', help='Who do you want to greet?')
def greet(greeting, name):
    print(f"{greeting} {name}")


if __name__ == '__main__':
    greet()
```

click.command indicates that a function should be exposed to command-line access. click.option adds an argument to the command-line, automatically linking it to the function parameter of the same name (--greeting to greet and --name to name). click does some work behind the scenes so that we can call our greet method in our main block without parameters that are covered by the options decorators.

These decorators handle parsing command-line arguments and automatically produce help messages:

```
$ ./simple_click.py --greeting Privet --name Peggy
Privet Peggy

$ ./simple_click.py --help
Usage: simple_click.py [OPTIONS]

Options:
  --greeting TEXT  How do you want to greet?
  --name TEXT      Who do you want to greet?
  --help           Show this message and exit.
```

You can see that with click you can expose your functions for command-line use with much less code than argparse. You can concentrate on the business logic of your code rather than designing the interface.

Now let's look at a more complicated example with nested commands. Commands are nested by using `click.group` creating functions that represent the groups. In Example 3-5 we nest commands with `argparse`, using an interface that is very similar to the one from Example 3-4.

Example 3-5. click_example.py

```python
#!/usr/bin/env python
"""
Command-line tool using click
"""
import click

@click.group()  ❶
def cli():  ❷
    pass

@click.group(help='Ship related commands')  ❸
def ships():
    pass

cli.add_command(ships)  ❹

@ships.command(help='Sail a ship')  ❺
def sail():
    ship_name = 'Your ship'
    print(f"{ship_name} is setting sail")

@ships.command(help='List all of the ships')
def list_ships():
    ships = ['John B', 'Yankee Clipper', 'Pequod']
    print(f"Ships: {','.join(ships)}")

@cli.command(help='Talk to a sailor')  ❻
@click.option('--greeting', default='Ahoy there', help='Greeting for sailor')
@click.argument('name')
def sailors(greeting, name):
    message = f'{greeting} {name}'
    print(message)

if __name__ == '__main__':
    cli()  ❼
```

❶ Create a top-level group under which other groups and commands will reside.

❷ Create a function to act as the top-level group. The `click.group` method transforms the function into a group.

❸ Create a group to hold the `ships` commands.

❹ Add the `ships` group as a command to the top-level group. Note that the `cli` function is now a group with an `add_command` method.

❺ Add a command to the `ships` group. Notice that `ships.command` is used instead of `click.command`.

❻ Add a command to the `cli` group.

❼ Call the top-level group.

The top-level help messages generated by `click` look like this:

```
./click_example.py --help
Usage: click_example.py [OPTIONS] COMMAND [ARGS]...

Options:
  --help  Show this message and exit.

Commands:
  sailors  Talk to a sailor
  ships    Ship related commands
```

You can dig into the help for a subgroup like this:

```
$ ./click_example.py ships --help
Usage: click_example.py ships [OPTIONS] COMMAND [ARGS]...

  Ship related commands

Options:
  --help  Show this message and exit.

Commands:
  list-ships  List all of the ships
  sail        Sail a ship
```

If you compare Example 3-4 and Example 3-5, you will see some of the differences between using `argparse` and `click`. The `click` approach certainly requires less code, almost half in these examples. The user interface (UI) code is interspersed throughout the whole program; it is especially important when creating functions that solely act as groups. If you have a complex program, with a complex interface, you should try as best as possible to isolate different functionality. By doing so, you make individual pieces easier to test and debug. In such a case, you might choose `argparse` to keep your interface code separate.

Defining Classes

A class definition starts with the keyword class followed by the class name and parentheses:

```
In [1]: class MyClass():
```

Attributes and method definitions follow in the indented code block. All methods of a class recieve as their first parameter a copy of the instantiated class object. By convention this is refered to as self:

```
In [1]: class MyClass():
   ...:     def some_method(self):
   ...:         print(f"Say hi to {self}")
   ...:

In [2]: myObject = MyClass()

In [3]: myObject.some_method()
Say hi to <__main__.MyClass object at 0x1056f4160>
```

Every class has an *init* method. When the class is instantiated, this method is called. If you do not define this method, it gets a default one, inherited from the Python base object class:

```
In [4]: MyClass.__init__
Out[4]: <slot wrapper '__init__' of 'object' objects>
```

Generally you define an object's attributes in the *init* method:

```
In [5]: class MyOtherClass():
   ...:     def __init__(self, name):
   ...:         self.name = name
   ...:

In [6]: myOtherObject = MyOtherClass('Sammy')

In [7]: myOtherObject.name
Out[7]: 'Sammy'
```

fire

Now, let's take a step farther down the road of making a command-line tool with minimal UI code. The fire package uses introspection of your code to create interfaces automatically. If you have a simple function you want to expose, you call fire.Fire with it as an argument:

```
#!/usr/bin/env python
"""
```

```
Simple fire example
"""

import fire

def greet(greeting='Hiya', name='Tammy'):
    print(f"{greeting} {name}")

if __name__ == '__main__':
    fire.Fire(greet)
```

fire then creates the UI based on the method's name and arguments:

```
$ ./simple_fire.py --help

NAME
    simple_fire.py

SYNOPSIS
    simple_fire.py <flags>

FLAGS
    --greeting=GREETING
    --name=NAME
```

In simple cases, you can expose multiple methods automatically by invoking fire with no arguments:

```
#!/usr/bin/env python
"""
Simple fire example
"""

import fire

def greet(greeting='Hiya', name='Tammy'):
    print(f"{greeting} {name}")

def goodbye(goodbye='Bye', name='Tammy'):
    print(f"{goodbye} {name}")

if __name__ == '__main__':
    fire.Fire()
```

fire creates a command from each function and documents automatically:

```
$ ./simple_fire.py --help
INFO: Showing help with the command 'simple_fire.py -- --help'.

NAME
    simple_fire.py

SYNOPSIS
    simple_fire.py GROUP | COMMAND

GROUPS
```

```
    GROUP is one of the following:

        fire
            The Python fire module.

    COMMANDS
        COMMAND is one of the following:

        greet

        goodbye
    (END)
```

This is really convenient if you are trying to understand someone else's code or debug your own. With one line of additional code, you can interact with all of a module's functions from the command-line. That is powerful. Because fire uses the structure of your program itself to determine the interface, it is even more tied to your non-interface code than argparse or click. To mimic our nest command interface, you need to define classes with the structure of the interface you want to expose. To see an approach to this, check out Example 3-6.

Example 3-6. fire_example.py

```python
#!/usr/bin/env python
"""
Command-line tool using fire
"""
import fire

class Ships(): ❶
    def sail(self):
        ship_name = 'Your ship'
        print(f"{ship_name} is setting sail")

    def list(self):
        ships = ['John B', 'Yankee Clipper', 'Pequod']
        print(f"Ships: {','.join(ships)}")

def sailors(greeting, name): ❷
    message = f'{greeting} {name}'
    print(message)

class Cli(): ❸

    def __init__(self):
        self.sailors = sailors
        self.ships = Ships()

if __name__ == '__main__':
    fire.Fire(Cli) ❹
```

❶ Define a class for the ships commands.

❷ `sailors` has no subcommands, so it can be defined as a function.

❸ Define a class to act as the top group. Add the `sailors` function and the `Ships` as attributes of the class.

❹ Call `fire.Fire` on the class acting as the top-level group.

The automatically generated documentation at the top level represents the `Ships` class as a group, and the `sailors` command as a command:

```
$ ./fire_example.py

NAME
    fire_example.py

SYNOPSIS
    fire_example.py GROUP | COMMAND

GROUPS
    GROUP is one of the following:

     ships

COMMANDS
    COMMAND is one of the following:

     sailors
(END)
```

The documentation for the `ships` group shows the commands representing the methods attached to the `Ships` class:

```
$ ./fire_example.py ships --help
INFO: Showing help with the command 'fire_example.py ships -- --help'.

NAME
    fire_example.py ships

SYNOPSIS
    fire_example.py ships COMMAND

COMMANDS
    COMMAND is one of the following:

     list

     sail
(END)
```

The parameters for the `sailors` function are turned into positional arguments:

```
$ ./fire_example.py sailors --help
INFO: Showing help with the command 'fire_example.py sailors -- --help'.

NAME
    fire_example.py sailors

SYNOPSIS
    fire_example.py sailors GREETING NAME

POSITIONAL ARGUMENTS
    GREETING
    NAME

NOTES
    You can also use flags syntax for POSITIONAL ARGUMENTS
(END)
```

You can call the commands and subcommands as expected:

```
$ ./fire_example.py ships sail
Your ship is setting sail
$ ./fire_example.py ships list
Ships: John B,Yankee Clipper,Pequod
$ ./fire_example.py sailors Hiya Karl
Hiya Karl
```

An exciting feature of `fire` is the ability to enter an interactive mode easily. By using the `--interactive` flag, `fire` opens an IPython shell with the object and functions of your script available:

```
$ ./fire_example.py sailors Hiya Karl -- --interactive
Hiya Karl
Fire is starting a Python REPL with the following objects:
Modules: fire
Objects: Cli, Ships, component, fire_example.py, result, sailors, self, trace

Python 3.7.0 (default, Sep 23 2018, 09:47:03)
Type 'copyright', 'credits' or 'license' for more information
IPython 7.5.0 -- An enhanced Interactive Python. Type '?' for help.
--------------------------------------------------------------------
In [1]: sailors
Out[1]: <function __main__.sailors(greeting, name)>

In [2]: sailors('hello', 'fred')
hello fred
```

Here we run the maritime program's `sailors` command in interactive mode. An IPython shell opens, and you have access to the `sailors` function. This interactive mode, in combination with the ease of exposing objects with `fire`, makes it the right tool both for debugging and introducing yourself to new code.

You have now run the gamut in command-line tool building libraries, from the very hands-on argparse, to the less verbose click, and lastly to the minimal fire. So which one should you use? We recommend click for most use cases. It balances ease and control. In the case of complex interfaces where you want to separate the UI code from business logic, argparse is the way to go. Moreover, if you need to access code that does not have a command-line interface quickly, fire is right for you.

Implementing Plug-ins

Once you've implemented your application's command-line user interface, you might want to consider a plug-in system. Plug-ins are pieces of code supplied by the user of your program to extend functionality. Plug-in systems are used in all sorts of applications, from large applications like Autodesk's Maya to minimal web frameworks like Flask. You could write a tool that handles walking a filesystem and allows a user to provide plug-ins to operate on its contents. A key part of any plug-in system is plug-in discover. Your program needs to know what plug-ins are available to load and run. In Example 3-7, we write a simple application that discovers and runs plug-ins. It uses a user-supplied prefix to search for, load, and run plug-ins.

Example 3-7. simple_plugins.py

```python
#!/usr/bin/env python
import fire
import pkgutil
import importlib

def find_and_run_plugins(plugin_prefix):
    plugins = {}

    # Discover and Load Plugins
    print(f"Discovering plugins with prefix: {plugin_prefix}")
    for _, name, _ in  pkgutil.iter_modules():  ❶
        if name.startswith(plugin_prefix):  ❷
            module = importlib.import_module(name)  ❸
            plugins[name] = module

    # Run Plugins
    for name, module in plugins.items():
        print(f"Running plugin {name}")
        module.run()  ❹

if __name__ == '__main__':
    fire.Fire()
```

❶ pkgutil.iter_modules returns all modules available in the current sys.path.

❷ Check if the module uses our plug-in prefix.

❸ Use `importlib` to load the module, saving it in a `dict` for later use.

❹ Call the `run` method on the plug-in.

Writing supplying plug-ins to Example 3-7 is as simple as supplying modules whose names use a shared prefix and whose functionality is accessed using a method named `run`. If you write two files using the prefix `foo_plugin` with individual run methods:

```
def run():
    print("Running plugin A")

def run():
    print("Running plugin B")
```

You can discover and run them with our plugin application:

```
$ ./simple_plugins.py find_and_run_plugins foo_plugin
Running plugin foo_plugin_a
Running plugin A
Running plugin foo_plugin_b
Running plugin B
```

You can easily extend this simple example to create plug-in systems for your applications.

Case Study: Turbocharging Python with Command-Line Tools

It's as good a time as ever to be writing code these days; a little bit of code goes a long way. Just a single function is capable of performing incredible things. Thanks to GPUs, machine learning, the cloud, and Python, it's easy to create "turbocharged" command-line tools. Think of it as upgrading your code from using a basic internal combustion engine to a jet engine. What's the basic recipe for the upgrade? One function, a sprinkle of powerful logic, and, finally, a decorator to route it to the command line.

Writing and maintaining traditional GUI applications—web or desktop—is a Sisyphean task at best. It all starts with the best of intentions, but can quickly turn into a soul crushing, time-consuming ordeal where you end up asking yourself why you thought becoming a programmer was a good idea in the first place. Why did you run that web framework setup utility that essentially automated a 1970s technology—the relational database—into series of Python files? The old Ford Pinto with the exploding rear gas tank has newer technology than your web framework. There has got to be a better way to make a living.

The answer is simple: stop writing web applications and start writing jet-powered command-line tools instead. The turbocharged command-line tools discussed in the following sections are focused on fast results vis-à-vis minimal lines of code. They can do things like learn from data (machine learning), make your code run two thousand times faster, and best of all, generate colored terminal output.

Here are the raw ingredients that will be used to make several solutions:

- Click framework
- Python CUDA framework
- Numba framework
- Scikit-learn machine learning framework

Using the Numba Just-in-Time (JIT) Compiler

Python has a reputation for slow performance because it's fundamentally a scripting language. One way to get around this problem is to use the Numba Just-in-Time (JIT) compiler. Let's take a look at what that code looks like. You can also access the full example in GitHub (*https://oreil.ly/9zFJh*).

First, use a timing decorator to get a grasp on the runtime of your functions:

```
def timing(f):
    @wraps(f)
    def wrap(*args, **kwargs):
        ts = time()
        result = f(*args, **kwargs)
        te = time()
        print(f"fun: {f.__name__}, args: [{args}, {kwargs}] took: {te-ts} sec")
        return result
    return wrap
```

Next, add a numba.jit decorator with the nopython keyword argument and set it to True. This will ensure that the code will be run by JIT instead of regular Python.

```
@timing
@numba.jit(nopython=True)
def expmean_jit(rea):
    """Perform multiple mean calculations"""

    val = rea.mean() ** 2
    return val
```

When you run it, you can see both a jit as well as a regular version being run via the command-line tool:

```
$ python nuclearcli.py jit-test
Running NO JIT
```

```
func:'expmean' args:[(array([[1.0000e+00, 4.2080e+05, 2350e+05, ...,
                              1.0543e+06, 1.0485e+06, 1.0444e+06],
        [2.0000e+00, 5.4240e+05, 5.4670e+05, ...,
                1.5158e+06, 1.5199e+06, 1.5253e+06],
        [3.0000e+00, 7.0900e+04, 7.1200e+04, ...,
                1.1380e+05, 1.1350e+05, 1.1330e+05],
        ...,
        [1.5277e+04, 9.8900e+04, 9.8100e+04, ...,
                2.1980e+05, 2.2000e+05, 2.2040e+05],
        [1.5280e+04, 8.6700e+04, 8.7500e+04, ...,
                1.9070e+05, 1.9230e+05, 1.9360e+05],
        [1.5281e+04, 2.5350e+05, 2.5400e+05, ..., 7.8360e+05, 7.7950e+05,
         7.7420e+05]], dtype=float32),), {}] took: 0.0007 sec
$ python nuclearcli.py jit-test --jit
Running with JIT
func:'expmean_jit' args:[(array([[1.0000e+00, 4.2080e+05, 4.2350e+05, ...,
                              0543e+06, 1.0485e+06, 1.0444e+06],
        [2.0000e+00, 5.4240e+05, 5.4670e+05, ..., 1.5158e+06, 1.5199e+06,
         1.5253e+06],
        [3.0000e+00, 7.0900e+04, 7.1200e+04, ..., 1.1380e+05, 1.1350e+05,
         1.1330e+05],
        ...,
        [1.5277e+04, 9.8900e+04, 9.8100e+04, ..., 2.1980e+05, 2.2000e+05,
         2.2040e+05],
        [1.5280e+04, 8.6700e+04, 8.7500e+04, ..., 1.9070e+05, 1.9230e+05,
         1.9360e+05],
        [1.5281e+04, 2.5350e+05, 2.5400e+05, ..., 7.8360e+05, 7.7950e+05,
@click.option('--jit/--no-jit', default=False)
         7.7420e+05]], dtype=float32),), {}] took: 0.2180 sec
```

How does that work? Just a few lines of code allow for this simple toggle:

```
@cli.command()
def jit_test(jit):
    rea = real_estate_array()
    if jit:
        click.echo(click.style('Running with JIT', fg='green'))
        expmean_jit(rea)
    else:
        click.echo(click.style('Running NO JIT', fg='red'))
        expmean(rea)
```

In some cases, a JIT version could make code run thousands of times faster, but benchmarking is key. Another item to point out is this line:

```
click.echo(click.style('Running with JIT', fg='green'))
```

This script allows for colored terminal output, which can be very helpful when creating sophisticated tools.

Using the GPU with CUDA Python

Another way to turbocharge your code is to run it straight on a GPU. This example requires you run it on a machine with a CUDA enabled. Here's what that code looks like:

```python
@cli.command()
def cuda_operation():
    """Performs Vectorized Operations on GPU"""

    x = real_estate_array()
    y = real_estate_array()

    print("Moving calculations to GPU memory")
    x_device = cuda.to_device(x)
    y_device = cuda.to_device(y)
    out_device = cuda.device_array(
        shape=(x_device.shape[0],x_device.shape[1]), dtype=np.float32)
    print(x_device)
    print(x_device.shape)
    print(x_device.dtype)

    print("Calculating on GPU")
    add_ufunc(x_device,y_device, out=out_device)

    out_host = out_device.copy_to_host()
    print(f"Calculations from GPU {out_host}")
```

It's useful to point out that if the Numpy array is first moved to the GPU, then a vectorized function does the work on the GPU. After that work is completed, the data is moved from the GPU. By using a GPU, there could be a monumental improvement to the code, depending on what it's running. The output from the command-line tool is shown here:

```
$ python nuclearcli.py cuda-operation
Moving calculations to GPU memory
<numba.cuda.cudadrv.devicearray.DeviceNDArray object at 0x7f01bf6ccac8>
(10015, 259)
float32
Calculating on GPU
Calculcations from GPU [
 [2.0000e+00 8.4160e+05 8.4700e+05 ... 2.1086e+06 2.0970e+06 2.0888e+06]
 [4.0000e+00 1.0848e+06 1.0934e+06 ... 3.0316e+06 3.0398e+06 3.0506e+06]
 [6.0000e+00 1.4180e+05 1.4240e+05 ... 2.2760e+05 2.2700e+05 2.2660e+05]
 ...
 [3.0554e+04 1.9780e+05 1.9620e+05 ... 4.3960e+05 4.4000e+05 4.4080e+05]
 [3.0560e+04 1.7340e+05 1.7500e+05 ... 3.8140e+05 3.8460e+05 3.8720e+05]
 [3.0562e+04 5.0700e+05 5.0800e+05 ... 1.5672e+06 1.5590e+06 1.5484e+06]
]
```

Running True Multicore Multithreaded Python Using Numba

One common performance problem with Python is the lack of true, multithreaded performance. This also can be fixed with Numba. Here's an example of some basic operations:

```
@timing
@numba.jit(parallel=True)
def add_sum_threaded(rea):
    """Use all the cores"""

    x,_ = rea.shape
    total = 0
    for _ in numba.prange(x):
        total += rea.sum()
        print(total)

@timing
def add_sum(rea):
    """traditional for loop"""

    x,_ = rea.shape
    total = 0
    for _ in numba.prange(x):
        total += rea.sum()
        print(total)

@cli.command()
@click.option('--threads/--no-jit', default=False)
def thread_test(threads):
    rea = real_estate_array()
    if threads:
        click.echo(click.style('Running with multicore threads', fg='green'))
        add_sum_threaded(rea)
    else:
        click.echo(click.style('Running NO THREADS', fg='red'))
        add_sum(rea)
```

Note that the key difference between the parallel version is that it uses `@numba.jit(parallel=True)` and `numba.prange` to spawn threads for iteration. As you can see in Figure 3-1, all of the CPUs are maxed out on the machine, but when almost the exact same code is run without the parallelization, it only uses a core.

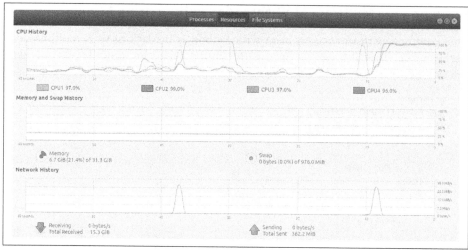

Figure 3-1. Using all of the cores

```
$ python nuclearcli.py thread-test
$ python nuclearcli.py thread-test --threads
```

KMeans Clustering

Another powerful thing that can be accomplished with a command-line tool is machine learning. In the example below, a KMeans clustering function is created with just a few lines of code. This clusters a Pandas DataFrame into a default of three clusters:

```
def kmeans_cluster_housing(clusters=3):
    """Kmeans cluster a dataframe"""
    url = "https://raw.githubusercontent.com/noahgift/\
            socialpowernba/master/data/nba_2017_att_val_elo_win_housing.csv"
    val_housing_win_df =pd.read_csv(url)
    numerical_df =(
        val_housing_win_df.loc[:,["TOTAL_ATTENDANCE_MILLIONS", "ELO",
        "VALUE_MILLIONS", "MEDIAN_HOME_PRICE_COUNTY_MILLIONS"]]
    )
    #scale data
    scaler = MinMaxScaler()
    scaler.fit(numerical_df)
    scaler.transform(numerical_df)
    #cluster data
    k_means = KMeans(n_clusters=clusters)
    kmeans = k_means.fit(scaler.transform(numerical_df))
    val_housing_win_df['cluster'] = kmeans.labels_
    return val_housing_win_df
```

The cluster number can be changed by passing in another number (as shown below) using click:

```
@cli.command()
@click.option("--num", default=3, help="number of clusters")
def cluster(num):
    df = kmeans_cluster_housing(clusters=num)
    click.echo("Clustered DataFrame")
    click.echo(df.head())
```

Finally, the output of the Pandas DataFrame with the cluster assignment is shown next. Note that it now has cluster assignment as a column:

```
$ python -W nuclearcli.py cluster

Clustered DataFrame
              TEAM   GMS   ...        COUNTY   cluster
0    Chicago Bulls    41   ...          Cook         0
1  Dallas Mavericks   41   ...        Dallas         0
2  Sacramento Kings   41   ...     Sacremento         1
3       Miami Heat    41   ...    Miami-Dade         0
4   Toronto Raptors   41   ...   York-County         0

[5 rows x 12 columns]

$ python -W nuclearcli.py cluster --num 2

Clustered DataFrame
              TEAM   GMS   ...        COUNTY   cluster
0    Chicago Bulls    41   ...          Cook         1
1  Dallas Mavericks   41   ...        Dallas         1
2  Sacramento Kings   41   ...     Sacremento         0
3       Miami Heat    41   ...    Miami-Dade         1
4   Toronto Raptors   41   ...   York-County         1

[5 rows x 12 columns]
```

Exercises

- Use sys to write a script that prints *command line* only when run from the command line.

- Use click to create a command-line tool that takes a name as an argument and prints it if it does not begin with a *p*.

- Use fire to access methods in an existing Python script from the command line.

Useful Linux Utilities

The command line and its tooling were one of the main reasons Alfredo felt attached to Linux servers when he started his career. One of his first jobs as a system administrator in a medium-sized company involved taking care of everything that was Linux-related. The small IT department was focused on the Windows servers and desktops, and they thoroughly disliked using the command line. At one point, the IT manager told him that he understood graphical user interfaces (GUIs), installing utilities, and tooling in general to solve problems: *"I am not a coder, if it doesn't exist as a GUI, I can't use it,"* he said.

Alfredo was hired as a contractor to help out with the few Linux servers the company had. At the time, Subversion (SVN) was all the rage for version control (*https://subversion.apache.org*), and the developers depended on this single SVN server to push their work. Instead of using the centralized identity server, provided by two *domain controllers*, it used a text-based authentication system that mapped a user to a hash representing the password. This meant that usernames didn't necessarily map to those in the domain controller and that passwords could be anything. Often, a developer would ask to reset the password, and someone had to edit this text file with the hash. A project manager asked Alfredo to integrate the SVN authentication with the domain controller (Microsoft's Active Directory). The first question he asked was why hadn't the IT department done this already? *"They say it is not possible, but Alfredo, this is a lie, SVN can integrate with Active Directory."*

He had never used an authentication service like Active Directory and barely understood SVN, but he was determined to make this work. Alfredo set out to read all about SVN and Active Directory, tinkered his way around a virtual machine with an SVN server running, and tried to get this authentication to work. It took about two weeks to read up on all the pieces involved and to get it to work. He succeeded in the end and was able to get this system into production. This felt incredibly powerful; he had acquired unique knowledge and was now ready to be fully in charge of this system. The IT manager, as well as the rest of the department, were ecstatic. Alfredo tried to share this newly acquired knowledge with others and was always met with an excuse: *"no time," "too busy," "other priorities,"* and *"perhaps some other time—maybe next week."*

An apt description for technologists is: *knowledge workers.* Your curiosity and a never-ending pursuit of knowledge will continue to make you, and the environments you work on, much better. Don't ever let a coworker (or a whole IT department, as in Alfredo's case) be a deterrent for improving systems. If there is an opportunity to learn something new, jump on it! The worst that can happen is that you have acquired knowledge that perhaps won't be used often, but on the other hand, might change your professional career.

Linux does have desktop environments, but its real power comes from understanding and using the command line, and ultimately, by extending it. When there are no premade tools to solve a problem, seasoned DevOps people will craft their own. This notion of being able to come up with solutions by putting together the core pieces is incredibly powerful, and is what ultimately happened at that job where it felt productive to complete tasks without having to install off-the-shelf software to fix things.

This chapter will go through some common patterns in the shell and will include some useful Python commands that should enhance the ability to interact with a machine. We find that creating aliases and *one-liners* is the most fun one can have at work, and sometimes they are so useful that they end up as plug-ins or standalone pieces of software.

Disk Utilities

There are several different utilities that you can use to get information about devices in a system. A lot of them have feature overlap, and some have an interactive session to deal with disk operations, such as `fdisk` and `parted`.

It is *crucial* to have a good grasp on disk utilities, not only to retrieve information and manipulate partitions, but also to accurately measure performance. Performance, in particular, is one of the tough things to accomplish correctly. The best answer to the question *How do I measure the performance of a device?* is *It depends*, because it is difficult to do for the specific metric one is looking for.

Measuring Performance

If we had to work in an isolated environment with a server that doesn't have access to the internet or that we don't control and therefore can't install packages, we would have to say that the `dd` tool (which should be readily available on all major Linux distributions) would help provide some answers. If at all possible, pair it with `iostat` to isolate the command that hammers the device versus the one that gets the report.

As a seasoned performance engineer once said, it depends on what is measured and how. For example `dd` is single threaded and has limitations, such as being unable to do multiple random reads and writes; it also measures throughput and not input/output operations per second (IOPS). What are you measuring? Throughput or IOPS?

 A word of warning on these examples. They can destroy your system, don't follow them blindly, and make sure to use devices that can get erased.

This simple one-liner will run `dd` to get some numbers of a brand-new device (*/dev/sdc* in this case):

```
$ dd if=/dev/zero of=/dev/sdc count=10 bs=100M
10+0 records in
10+0 records out
1048576000 bytes (1.0 GB, 1000 MiB) copied, 1.01127 s, 1.0 GB/s
```

It writes 10 records of 100 megabytes at a rate of 1 GB/s. This is throughput. An easy way to get IOPS with `dd` is to use `iostat`. In this example, `iostat` runs only on the device getting hammered with `dd`, with the -d flag only to give the device information, and with an interval of one second:

```
$ iostat -d /dev/sdc 1
```

Device	tps	kB_read/s	kB_wrtn/s	kB_read	kB_wrtn
sdc	6813.00	0.00	1498640.00	0	1498640

Device	tps	kB_read/s	kB_wrtn/s	kB_read	kB_wrtn
sdc	6711.00	0.00	1476420.00	0	1476420

The `iostat` output will repeat itself for every second until a `Ctrl-C` is issued to cancel the operation. The second column in the output is `tps`, which stands for transactions per second and is the same as IOPS. A nicer way to visualize the output, which avoids the clutter that a repeating command produces, is to clear the terminal on each run:

```
$ while true; do clear && iostat -d /dev/sdc && sleep 1; done
```

Accurate tests with fio

If `dd` and `iostat` aren't sufficient, the most commonly used tool for performance testing is `fio`. It can help clarify the performance behavior of a device in a read-heavy or write-heavy environment (and even adjust the percentages of reads versus writes).

The output from `fio` is quite verbose. The example below trims it to emphasize the IOPS found on both read and write operations:

```
$ fio --name=sdc-performance --filename=/dev/sdc --ioengine=libaio \
    --iodepth=1 --rw=randrw --bs=32k --direct=0 --size=64m
sdc-performance: (g=0): rw=randwrite, bs=(R) 32.0KiB-32.0KiB,
(W) 32.0KiB-32.0KiB, (T) 32.0KiB-32.0KiB, ioengine=libaio, iodepth=1
fio-3.1
Starting 1 process

sdc-performance: (groupid=0, jobs=1): err= 0: pid=2879:
    read: IOPS=1753, BW=54.8MiB/s (57.4MB/s)(31.1MiB/567msec)
...
    iops        : min= 1718, max= 1718, avg=1718.00, stdev= 0.00, samples=1
  write: IOPS=1858, BW=58.1MiB/s (60.9MB/s)(32.9MiB/567msec)
...
    iops        : min= 1824, max= 1824, avg=1824.00, stdev= 0.00, samples=1
```

The flags used in the example name the *job* `sdc-performance`, point to the */dev/sdc* device directly (will require superuser permissions), use the native Linux asynchronous I/O library, set the `iodepth` to 1 (number of sequential I/O requests to be sent at a time), and define random read and write operations of 32 kilobytes for the buffer size using buffered I/O (can be set to 1 to use unbuffered I/O) on a 64-megabyte file. Quite the lengthy command here!

The `fio` tool has a tremendous number of additional options that can help with most any case where accurate IOPS measurements are needed. For example, it can span the test across many devices at once, do some *I/O warm up*, and even set I/O thresholds for the test if a defined limit shouldn't be surpassed. Finally, the many options in the command line can be configured with INI-style files so that the execution of jobs can be scripted nicely.

Partitions

We tend to default to `fdisk` with its interactive session to create partitions, but in some cases, `fdisk` doesn't work well, such as with large partitions (two terabytes or larger). In those cases, your fallback should be to use `parted`.

A quick interactive session shows how to create a primary partition with `fdisk`, with the default start value and four gibibytes of size. At the end the w key is sent to *write* the changes:

```
$ sudo fdisk /dev/sds

Command (m for help): n
Partition type:
   p   primary (0 primary, 0 extended, 4 free)
   e   extended
Select (default p): p
```

```
Partition number (1-4, default 1):
First sector (2048-22527999, default 2048):
Using default value 2048
Last sector, +sectors or +size{K,M,G} (2048-22527999, default 22527999): +4G
Partition 1 of type Linux and of size 4 GiB is set

Command (m for help): w
The partition table has been altered!

Calling ioctl() to re-read partition table.
Syncing disks.
```

parted accomplishes the same, but with a different interface:

```
$ sudo parted /dev/sdaa
GNU Parted 3.1
Using /dev/sdaa
Welcome to GNU Parted! Type 'help' to view a list of commands.
(parted) mklabel
New disk label type? gpt
(parted) mkpart
Partition name?  []?
File system type?  [ext2]?
Start? 0
End? 40%
```

In the end, you quit with the q key. For programmatic creation of partitions on the command line without any interactive prompts, you accomplish the same result with a couple of commands:

```
$ parted --script /dev/sdaa mklabel gpt
$ parted --script /dev/sdaa mkpart primary 1 40%
$ parted --script /dev/sdaa print
Disk /dev/sdaa: 11.5GB
Sector size (logical/physical): 512B/512B
Partition Table: gpt
Disk Flags:

Number  Start   End     Size    File system  Name    Flags
 1      1049kB  4614MB  4613MB
```

Retrieving Specific Device Information

Sometimes when specific information for a device is needed, either lsblk or blkid are well suited. fdisk doesn't like to work without superuser permissions. Here fdisk lists the information about the */dev/sda* device:

```
$ fdisk -l /dev/sda
fdisk: cannot open /dev/sda: Permission denied

$ sudo fdisk -l /dev/sda
```

```
Disk /dev/sda: 42.9 GB, 42949672960 bytes, 83886080 sectors
Units = sectors of 1 * 512 = 512 bytes
Sector size (logical/physical): 512 bytes / 512 bytes
I/O size (minimum/optimal): 512 bytes / 512 bytes
Disk label type: dos
Disk identifier: 0x0009d9ce

   Device Boot      Start         End      Blocks   Id  System
/dev/sda1   *        2048    83886079    41942016   83  Linux
```

blkid is a bit similar in that it wants superuser permissions as well:

```
$ blkid /dev/sda

$ sudo blkid /dev/sda
/dev/sda: PTTYPE="dos"
```

lsblk allows to get information without higher permissions, and provides the same informational output regardless:

```
$ lsblk /dev/sda
NAME   MAJ:MIN RM SIZE RO TYPE MOUNTPOINT
sda      8:0    0  40G  0 disk
└─sda1   8:1    0  40G  0 part /
$ sudo lsblk /dev/sda
NAME   MAJ:MIN RM SIZE RO TYPE MOUNTPOINT
sda      8:0    0  40G  0 disk
└─sda1   8:1    0  40G  0 part /
```

This command, which uses the -p flag for low-level device probing, is *very thorough* and should give you good enough information for a device:

```
$ blkid -p /dev/sda1
UUID="8e4622c4-1066-4ea8-ab6c-9a19f626755c" TYPE="xfs" USAGE="filesystem"
PART_ENTRY_SCHEME="dos" PART_ENTRY_TYPE="0x83" PART_ENTRY_FLAGS="0x80"
PART_ENTRY_NUMBER="1" PART_ENTRY_OFFSET="2048" PART_ENTRY_SIZE="83884032"
```

lsblk has some default properties to look for:

```
$ lsblk -P /dev/nvme0n1p1
NAME="nvme0n1p1" MAJ:MIN="259:1" RM="0" SIZE="512M" RO="0" TYPE="part"
```

But it also allows you to set specific flags to request a particular property:

```
lsblk -P -o SIZE /dev/nvme0n1p1
SIZE="512M"
```

To access a property in this way makes it easy to script and even consume from the Python side of things.

Network Utilities

Network tooling keeps improving as more and more servers need to be interconnected. A lot of the utilities in this section cover useful one-liners like Secure Shell (SSH) tunneling, but some others go into the details of testing network performance, such as using the Apache Bench tool.

SSH Tunneling

Have you ever tried to reach an HTTP service that runs on a remote server that is not accessible except via SSH? This situation occurs when the HTTP service is enabled but not needed publicly. The last time we saw this happen was when a production instance of RabbitMQ (*https://www.rabbitmq.com*) had the management plug-in enabled, which starts an HTTP service on port 15672. The service isn't exposed and with good reason; there is no need to have it publicly available since it is rarely used, and besides, one can use SSH's tunneling capabilities.

This works by creating an SSH connection with the remote server and then forwarding the remote port (15672, in my case) to a local port on the originating machine. The remote machine has a custom SSH port, which complicates the command slightly. This is is how it looks:

```
$ ssh -L 9998:localhost:15672 -p 2223 adeza@prod1.rabbitmq.ceph.internal -N
```

There are three flags, three numbers, and two addresses. Let's dissect the command to make what is going on here much clearer. The -L flag is the one that signals that we want forwarding enabled and a local port (9998) to bind to a remote port (RabbitMQ's default of 15672). Next, the -p flag indicates that the custom SSH port of the remote server is 2223, and then the username and address are specified. Lastly, the -N means that it shouldn't get us to a remote shell and do the forwarding.

When executed correctly, the command will appear to hang, but it allows you to go into *http://localhost:9998/* and see the login page for the remote RabbitMQ instance. A useful flag to know when tunneling is -f: it will send the process into the background, which is helpful if this connection isn't temporary, leaving the terminal ready and clean to do more work.

Benchmarking HTTP with Apache Benchmark (ab)

We *really* love to hammer servers we work with to ensure they handle load correctly, especially before they get promoted to production. Sometimes we even try to trigger some odd race condition that may happen under heavy load. The Apache Benchmark tool (ab in the command line) is one of those tiny tools that can get you going quickly with just a few flags.

This command will create 100 requests at a time, for a total of 10,000 requests, to a local instance where Nginx is running:

```
$ ab -c 100 -n 10000 http://localhost/
```

That is pretty brutal to handle in a system, but this is a local server, and the requests are just an HTTP GET. The detailed output from ab is very comprehensive and looks like this (trimmed for brevity):

```
Benchmarking localhost (be patient)
...
Completed 10000 requests
Finished 10000 requests

Server Software:        nginx/1.15.9
Server Hostname:        localhost
Server Port:            80

Document Path:          /
Document Length:        612 bytes

Concurrency Level:      100
Time taken for tests:   0.624 seconds
Complete requests:      10000
Failed requests:        0
Total transferred:      8540000 bytes
HTML transferred:       6120000 bytes
Requests per second:    16015.37 [#/sec] (mean)
Time per request:       6.244 [ms] (mean)
Time per request:       0.062 [ms] (mean, across all concurrent requests)
Transfer rate:          13356.57 [Kbytes/sec] received

Connection Times (ms)
              min  mean[+/-sd] median   max
Connect:        0    3   0.6      3       5
Processing:     0    4   0.8      3       8
Waiting:        0    3   0.8      3       6
Total:          0    6   1.0      6       9
```

This type of information and how it is presented is tremendous. At a glance, you can quickly tell if a production server drops connections (in the Failed requests field) and what the averages are. A GET request is used, but ab allows you to use other HTTP verbs, such as POST, and even do a HEAD request. You need to exercise caution with this type of tool because it can easily overload a server. Below are more realistic numbers from an HTTP service in production (trimmed for brevity):

```
...
Benchmarking prod1.ceph.internal (be patient)

Server Software:        nginx
Server Hostname:        prod1.ceph.internal
Server Port:            443
```

```
SSL/TLS Protocol:      TLSv1.2,ECDHE-RSA-AES256-GCM-SHA384,2048,256
Server Temp Key:       ECDH P-256 256 bits
TLS Server Name:       prod1.ceph.internal

Complete requests:     200
Failed requests:       0
Total transferred:     212600 bytes
HTML transferred:      175000 bytes
Requests per second:   83.94 [#/sec] (mean)
Time per request:      1191.324 [ms] (mean)
Time per request:      11.913 [ms] (mean, across all concurrent requests)
Transfer rate:         87.14 [Kbytes/sec] received
....
```

Now the numbers look different, it hits a service with SSL enabled, and ab lists what the protocols are. At 83 requests per second, we think it could do better, but this is an API server that produces JSON, and it typically doesn't get much load at once, as was just generated.

Load Testing with molotov

The Molotov (*https://molotov.readthedocs.io*) project is an interesting project geared towards load testing. Some of its features are similar to those of Apache Benchmark, but being a Python project, it provides a way to write scenarios with Python and the asyncio module.

This is how the simplest example for molotov looks:

```
import molotov

@molotov.scenario(100)
async def scenario_one(session):
    async with session.get("http://localhost:5000") as resp:
        assert resp.status == 200
```

Save the file as *load_test.py*, create a small Flask application that handles both POST and GET requests at its main URL, and save it as *small.py*:

```
from flask import Flask, redirect, request

app = Flask('basic app')

@app.route('/', methods=['GET', 'POST'])
def index():
    if request.method == 'POST':
        redirect('https://www.google.com/search?q=%s' % request.args['q'])
    else:
        return '<h1>GET request from Flask!</h1>'
```

Start the Flask application with FLASK_APP=small.py flask run, and then run molotov with the *load_test.py* file created previously:

```
$ molotov -v -r 100 load_test.py
**** Molotov v1.6. Happy breaking! ****
Preparing 1 worker...
OK
SUCCESSES: 100 | FAILURES: 0 WORKERS: 0
*** Bye ***
```

One hundred requests on a single worker ran against the local Flask instance. The tool really shines when the load testing is extended to do more per request. It has concepts similar to unit testing, such as setup, teardown, and even code, that can react to certain events. Since the small Flask application can handle a POST that redirects to a Google search, add another scenario to the *load_test*.py_ file. This time change the weight so that 100% of the requests do a POST:

```
@molotov.scenario(100)
async def scenario_post(session):
    resp = await session.post("http://localhost:5000", params={'q': 'devops'})
    redirect_status = resp.history[0].status
    error = "unexpected redirect status: %s" % redirect_status
    assert redirect_status == 301, error
```

Run this new scenario for a single request to show the following:

```
$ molotov -v -r 1 --processes 1 load_test.py
**** Molotov v1.6. Happy breaking! ****
Preparing 1 worker...
OK
AssertionError('unexpected redirect status: 302',)
  File ".venv/lib/python3.6/site-packages/molotov/worker.py", line 206, in step
    **scenario['kw'])
  File "load_test.py", line 12, in scenario_two
    assert redirect_status == 301, error
SUCCESSES: 0 | FAILURES: 1
*** Bye ***
```

A single request (with -r 1) was enough to make this fail. The assertion needs to be updated to check for a 302 instead of a 301. Once that status is updated, change the weight of the POST scenario to 80 so that other requests (with a GET) are sent to the Flask application. This is how the file looks in the end:

```
import molotov


@molotov.scenario()
async def scenario_one(session):
    async with session.get("http://localhost:5000/") as resp:
        assert resp.status == 200


@molotov.scenario(80)
async def scenario_two(session):
    resp = await session.post("http://localhost:5000", params={'q': 'devops'})
    redirect_status = resp.history[0].status
```

```
    error = "unexpected redirect status: %s" % redirect_status
    assert redirect_status == 301, error
```

Run *load_test.py* for 10 requests to distribute the requests, two for a GET and the rest with a POST:

```
127.0.0.1 - - [04/Sep/2019 12:10:54] "POST /?q=devops HTTP/1.1" 302 -
127.0.0.1 - - [04/Sep/2019 12:10:56] "POST /?q=devops HTTP/1.1" 302 -
127.0.0.1 - - [04/Sep/2019 12:10:57] "POST /?q=devops HTTP/1.1" 302 -
127.0.0.1 - - [04/Sep/2019 12:10:58] "GET / HTTP/1.1" 200 -
127.0.0.1 - - [04/Sep/2019 12:10:58] "POST /?q=devops HTTP/1.1" 302 -
127.0.0.1 - - [04/Sep/2019 12:10:59] "POST /?q=devops HTTP/1.1" 302 -
127.0.0.1 - - [04/Sep/2019 12:11:00] "POST /?q=devops HTTP/1.1" 302 -
127.0.0.1 - - [04/Sep/2019 12:11:01] "GET / HTTP/1.1" 200 -
127.0.0.1 - - [04/Sep/2019 12:11:01] "POST /?q=devops HTTP/1.1" 302 -
127.0.0.1 - - [04/Sep/2019 12:11:02] "POST /?q=devops HTTP/1.1" 302 -
```

As you can see, molotov is easily extensible with pure Python and can be modified to suit other, more complex, needs. These examples scratch the surface of what the tool can do.

CPU Utilities

There are two important CPU utilities: top and htop. You can find top preinstalled in most Linux distributions today, but if you are able to install packages, htop is fantastic to work with and we prefer its customizable interface over top. There are a few other tools out there that provide CPU visualization and perhaps even monitoring, but none are as complete and as widely available as both top and htop. For example, it is entirely possible to get CPU utilization from the ps command:

```
$ ps -eo pcpu,pid,user,args | sort -r | head -10
%CPU   PID USER     COMMAND
 0.3   719 vagrant  -bash
 0.1   718 vagrant  sshd: vagrant@pts/0
 0.1   668 vagrant  /lib/systemd/systemd --user
 0.0     9 root     [rcu_bh]
 0.0    95 root     [ipv6_addrconf]
 0.0    91 root     [kworker/u4:3]
 0.0     8 root     [rcu_sched]
 0.0    89 root     [scsi_tmf_1]
```

The ps command takes some custom fields. The first one is pcpu, which gives the CPU usage, followed by the process ID, the user, and finally, the command. That *pipes* into a sorted reverse because by default it goes from less CPU usage to more, and you need to have the most CPU usage at the top. Finally, since the command displays this information for every single process, it filters the top 10 results with the head command.

But the command is quite a mouthful, is a challenge to remember, and is not updated on the fly. Even if aliased, you are better off with top or htop. As you will see, both have extensive features.

Viewing Processes with htop

The htop tool is just like top (an interactive process viewer) but is fully cross-platform (works on OS X, FreeBSD, OpenBSD, and Linux), offers support for better visualizations (see Figure 4-1), and is a pleasure to use. Visit *https://hisham.hm/htop* for a screenshot of htop running on a server. One of the main caveats of htop is that all the shortcuts you may know about top are not compatible, so you will have to rewire your brain to understand and use them for htop.

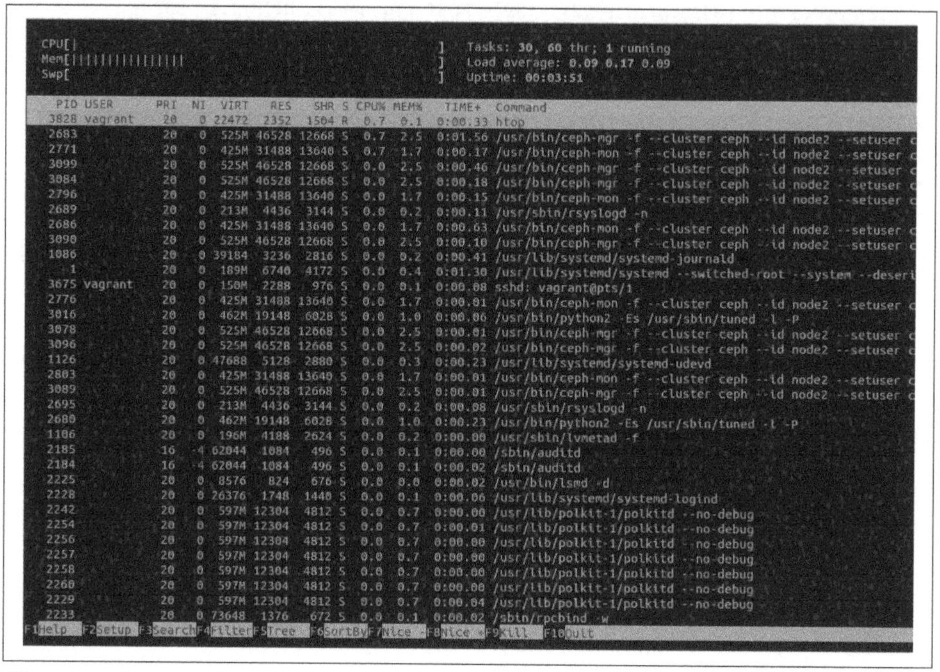

Figure 4-1. htop running on a server

Right away, the look and feel of the information displayed in Figure 4-1 is different. The CPU, Memory, and Swap are nicely shown at the top left, and they move as the system changes. The arrow keys scroll up or down and even left to right, providing a view of the whole command of the process.

Want to kill a process? Move to it with the arrow keys, or hit / to incrementally search (and filter) the process, and then press k. A new menu will show all the signals that can be sent to the process—for example, SIGTERM instead of SIGKILL. It is possible to "*tag*" more than one process to kill. Press the space bar to tag the selected process, highlighting it with a different color. Made a mistake and want to un-tag? Press the space bar again. This all feels very intuitive.

One problem with htop is that it has lots of actions mapped to F keys, and you may not have any. For example, F1 is for help. The alternative is to use the equivalent mappings when possible. To access the help menu, use the h key; to access the setup, use Shift s instead of F2.

The t (again, how intuitive!) enables (toggles) the process list as a tree. Probably the most used functionality is sorting. Press > and a menu appears to select what type of sorting you want: PID, user, memory, priority, and CPU percentage are just a few. There are also shortcuts to sort directly (skips the menu selection) by memory (Shift i), CPU (Shift p), and Time (Shift t).

Finally, two incredible features: you can run strace or lsof directly in the selected process as long as these are installed and available to the user. If the processes require superuser permissions, htop will report that, and it will require sudo to run as a privileged user. To run strace on a selected process, use the s key; for lsof, use the l key.

If either strace or lsof is used, the search and filter options are available with the / character. What an incredibly useful tool! Hopefully, one day other non-F key mappings will be possible, even though most work can be done with the alternative mappings.

 If htop is customized via its interactive session, the changes get persisted in a configuration file that is usually located at ~/.config/htop/htoprc. If you define configurations there and later change them in the session, then the session will overwrite whatever was defined previously in the htoprc file.

Working with Bash and ZSH

It all starts with customization. Both Bash and ZSH will usually come with a *"dotfile,"* a file prefixed with a dot that holds configuration but by default is hidden when directory contents are listed, and lives in the home directory of the user. For Bash this is *.bashrc*, and for ZSH it is *.zshrc*. Both shells support several layers of places that will get loaded in a predefined order, which ends in the configuration file for the user.

When ZSH is installed, a .zshrc is usually not created. This is how a minimal version of it looks in a CentOS distro (all comments removed for brevity):

```
$ cat /etc/skel/.zshrc
autoload -U compinit
compinit

setopt COMPLETE_IN_WORD
```

Bash has a couple of additional items in it but nothing surprising. You will no doubt get to the point of being extremely annoyed at some behavior or thing you saw in some other server that you want to replicate. We can't live without colors in the terminal, so whatever the shell, it has to have color enabled. Before you know it, you are deep into configurations and want to add a bunch of useful aliases and functions.

Soon after, the text editor configurations come in, and it all feels unmanageable on different machines or when new ones are added and all those useful aliases are not set up, and it is *unbelievable*, but no one has enabled color support anywhere. Everyone has a way to solve this problem in an entirely nontransferable, ad hoc way: Alfredo uses a *Makefile* at some point, and his coworkers use either nothing at all or a Bash script. A new project called Dotdrop (*https://deadc0de.re/dotdrop*) has lots of features to get all those dotfiles in working order, with features such as copying, symlinking, and keeping separate *profiles* for development and other machines—pretty useful when you move from one machine to another.

You can use Dotdrop for a Python project, and although you can install it via the regular virtualenv and pip tooling, it is recommended to include it as a submodule to your repository of dotfiles. If you haven't done so already, it is very convenient to keep all your dotfiles in version control to keep track of changes. Alfredo's dotfiles (*https://oreil.ly/LV1AH*) are publicly available, and he tries to keep them as up-to-date as possible.

Independent of what is used, keeping track of changes via version control, and making sure everything is always updated, is a good strategy.

Customizing the Python Shell

You can customize the Python shell with helpers and import useful modules in a Python file that then has to be exported as an environment variable. I keep my configuration files in a repository called *dotfiles*, so in my shell configuration file (*$HOME/.zshrc* for me) I define the following export:

```
export PYTHONSTARTUP=$HOME/dotfiles/pythonstartup.py
```

To try this out, create a new Python file called *pythonstartup.py* (although it can be named anything) that looks like this:

```
import types
import uuid

helpers = types.ModuleType('helpers')
helpers.uuid4 = uuid.uuid4()
```

Now open up a new Python shell and specify the newly created *pythonstartup.py*:

```
$ PYTHONSTARTUP=pythonstartup.py python
Python 3.7.3 (default, Apr  3 2019, 06:39:12)
[GCC 8.3.0] on linux
```

```
Type "help", "copyright", "credits" or "license" for more information.
>>> helpers
<module 'helpers'>
>>> helpers.uuid4()
UUID('966d7dbe-7835-4ac7-bbbf-06bf33db5302')
```

The helpers object is immediately available. Since we added the uuid4 property, we can access it as helpers.uuid4(). As you may be able to tell, all the imports and definitions are going to be available in the Python shell. This is a convenient way to extend behavior that can be useful with the default shell.

Recursive Globbing

Recursive globbing is enabled in ZSH by default, but Bash (versions 4 and higher) requires shopt to set it. Recursive globbing is a cool setting that allows you to traverse a path with the following syntax:

```
$ ls **/*.py
```

That snippet would go through each file and directory recursively and list every single file that ends in .py. This is how to enable it in Bash 4:

```
$ shopt -s globstar
```

Searching and Replacing with Confirmation Prompts

Vim has a nice feature in its search and replace engine that prompts for confirmation to perform the replacement or skip it. This is particularly useful when you can't nail the exact regular expression that matches what you need but want to ignore some other close matches. We know regular expressions, but we've tried to avoid being an expert at them because it would be very tempting to use them for everything. Most of the time, you will want to perform a simple search and replace and not bang your head against the wall to come up with the perfect regex.

The c flag needs to be appended at the end of the command to enable the confirmation prompt in Vim:

```
:%s/original term/replacement term/gc
```

The above translates to: search for *original term* in the whole file and replace it with *replacement term*, but at each instance, prompt so that one can decide to change it or skip it. If a match is found, Vim will display a message like this one:

```
replace with replacement term (y/n/a/q/l/^E/^Y)?
```

The whole confirmation workflow might seem silly but allows you to relax the constraints on the regular expression, or even not use one at all for a simpler match and replace. A quick example of this is a recent API change in a production tool that changed an object's attribute for a callable. The code returned True or False to inform if superuser permissions were required or not. The actual replacement in a single file would look like this:

```
:%s/needs_root/needs_root()/gc
```

The added difficulty here is that `needs_root` was also splattered in comments and doc strings, so it wasn't easy to come up with a regular expression that would allow skipping the replacement when inside a comment block or in part of a doc string. With the c flag, you can just hit Y or N and move on. No regular expression needed at all!

With recursive globbing enabled (`shopt -s globstar` in Bash 4), this powerful one-liner will go through all the matching files, perform the search, and replace the item according to the prompts if the pattern is found inside the files:

```
vim -c "bufdo! set eventignore-=Syntax | %s/needs_root/needs_root()/gce" **/*.py
```

There is a lot to unpack here, but the above example will traverse recursively to find all the files ending in .py, load them into Vim, and perform the search and replace with confirmation only if there is a match. If there isn't a match, it skips the file. The `set eventignore-=Syntax` is used because otherwise Vim will not load the syntax files when executing it this way; we like syntax highlighting and expect it to work when this type of replacement is used. The next part after the | character is the replacement with the confirmation flag and the e flag, which helps ignore any errors that would prevent a smooth workflow from being interrupted with errors.

 There are numerous other flags and variations that you can use to enhance the replacement command. To learn more about the special flags with a search and replace in Vim, take a look at `:help sub stitute`, specifically at the `s_flags` section.

Make the complicated one-liner easier to remember with a function that takes two parameters (search and replace terms) and the path:

```
vsed() {
  search=$1
  replace=$2
  shift
  shift
  vim -c "bufdo! set eventignore-=Syntax| %s/$search/$replace/gce" $*
}
```

Name it `vsed`, as a mix of Vim and the `sed` tool, so that it is easier to remember. In the terminal, it looks straightforward and allows you to make changes to multiple files easily and with confidence, since you can accept or deny each replacement:

```
$ vsed needs_root needs_root() **/*.py
```

Removing Temporary Python Files

Python's pyc, and more recently its *pycache* directories, can sometimes get in the way. This simple one-liner aliased to pyclean uses the find command to remove pyc, then goes on to find *pycache* directories and recursively deletes them with the tool's built-in delete flag:

```
alias pyclean='find . \
    \( -type f -name "*.py[co]" -o -type d -name "__pycache__" \) -delete &&
    echo "Removed pycs and __pycache__"'
```

Listing and Filtering Processes

Process listing to view what runs in a machine and then filtering to check on a specific application is one of the things that you'll do several times a day at the very least. It is not at all surprising that everyone has a variation on either the flags or the order of the flags for the ps tool (we usually use aux). It is something you end up doing so many times a day that the order and the flags get ingrained in your brain and it is hard to do it any other way.

As a good starting point to list the processes and some information, such as process IDs, try this:

```
$ ps auxw
```

This command lists all processes with the *BSD-style* flags (flags that aren't prefixed with a dash -) regardless or whether they have a terminal (tty) or not, and includes the user that owns the process. Finally, it gives more space to the output (w flag).

Most of the times, you are filtering with grep to get information about a specific process. For example, if you want to check if Nginx is running, you pipe the output into grep and pass nginx as an argument:

```
$ ps auxw | grep nginx
root      29640  1536 ?        Ss   10:11   0:00 nginx: master process
www-data 29648  5440 ?        S    10:11   0:00 nginx: worker process
alfredo  30024   924 pts/14   S+   10:12   0:00 grep nginx
```

That is great, but it is annoying to have the grep command included. This is particularly maddening when there are no results except for the grep:

```
$ ps auxw | grep apache
alfredo  31351  0.0  0.0   8856   912 pts/13  S+   10:15   0:00 grep apache
```

No apache process is found, but the visuals may mislead you to think it is, and double-checking that this is indeed just grep being included because of the argument can get tiring pretty quickly. A way to solve this is to add another pipe to grep to filter itself from the output:

```
$ ps auxw | grep apache | grep -v grep
```

To have to always remember to add that extra `grep` can be equally annoying, so an alias comes to the rescue:

```
alias pg='ps aux | grep -v grep | grep $1'
```

The new alias will filter the first `grep` line out and leave only the interesting output (if any):

```
$ pg vim
alfredo  31585  77836 20624 pts/3    S+   18:39   0:00 vim /home/alfredo/.zshrc
```

Unix Timestamp

To get the widely used Unix timestamp in Python is very easy:

```
In [1]: import time

In [2]: int(time.time())
Out[2]: 1566168361
```

But in the shell, it can be a bit more involved. This alias works in OS X, which has the BSD-flavored version of the `date` tool:

```
alias timestamp='date -j -f "%a %b %d %T %Z %Y" "`date`" "+%s"'
```

OS X can be awkward with its tooling, and it may be confusing to never remember why a given utility (like `date` in this case) behaves completely differently. In the Linux version of `date`, a far simpler approach works the same way:

```
alias timestamp='date "+%s"'
```

Mixing Python with Bash and ZSH

It never occurred to us to try and mix Python with a shell, like ZSH or Bash. It feels like going against common sense, but there are a few good cases here that you can use almost daily. In general, our rule of thumb is that 10 lines of shell script is the limit; anything beyond that is a bug waiting to make you waste time because the error reporting isn't there to help you out.

Random Password Generator

The amount of accounts and passwords that you need on a week-to-week basis is only going to keep increasing, even for throwaway accounts that you can use Python for to generate robust passwords. Create a useful, randomized password generator that sends the contents to the clipboard to easily paste it:

```
In [1]: import os

In [2]: import base64
```

```
In [3]: print(base64.b64encode(os.urandom(64)).decode('utf-8'))
gHHlGXnqnbsALbAZrGaw+LmvipTeFi3tA/9uBltNf9g2S9qTQ8hTpBYrXStp+i/o5TseeVo6wcX2A==
```

Porting that to a shell function that can take an arbitrary length (useful when a site restricts length to a certain number) looks like this:

```
mpass() {
    if [ $1 ]; then
        length=$1
    else
        length=12
    fi
    _hash=`python3 -c "
import os,base64
exec('print(base64.b64encode(os.urandom(64))[:${length}].decode(\'utf-8\'))')
"`
    echo $_hash | xclip -selection clipboard
    echo "new password copied to the system clipboard"
}
```

Now the mpass function defaults to generate 12-character passwords by slicing the output, and then sends the contents of the generated string to xclip so that it gets copied to the clipboard for easy pasting.

 xclip is not installed by default in many distros, so you need to ensure that it is installed for the function to work properly. If xclip is not available, any other utility that can help manage the system clipboard will work fine.

Does My Module Exist?

Find out if a module exists, and if it does, get the path to that module. This is useful when reused for other functions that can take that output for processing:

```
try() {
    python -c "
exec('''
try:
    import ${1} as _
    print(_.__file__)
except Exception as e:
    print(e)
''')"
}
```

Changing Directories to a Module's Path

"Where does this module live?" is often asked when debugging libraries and dependencies, or even when poking around at the source of modules. Python's way to install and distribute modules isn't straightforward, and in different Linux distributions the paths are entirely different and have separate conventions. You can find out the path of a module if you import it and then use `print`:

```
In [1]: import os

In [2]: print(os)
<module 'os' from '.virtualenvs/python-devops/lib/python3.6/os.py'>
```

It isn't convenient if all you want is the path so that you can change directories to it and look at the module. This function will try to import the module as an argument, print it out (this is shell, so `return` doesn't do anything for us), and then change directory to it:

```
cdp() {
    MODULE_DIRECTORY=`python -c "
exec('''
try:
    import os.path as _, ${module}
    print(_.dirname(_.realpath(${module}.__file__)))
except Exception as e:
    print(e)
''')"`
    if [[ -d $MODULE_DIRECTORY ]]; then
        cd $MODULE_DIRECTORY
    else
        echo "Module ${1} not found or is not importable: $MODULE_DIRECTORY"
    fi
}
```

Let's make it more robust, in case the package name has a dash and the module uses an underscore, by adding:

```
module=$(sed 's/-/_/g' <<< $1)
```

If the input has a dash, the little function can solve this on the fly and get us to where we need to be:

```
$ cdp pkg-resources
$ pwd
/usr/lib/python2.7/dist-packages/pkg_resources
```

Converting a CSV File to JSON

Python comes with a few built-ins that are surprising if you've never dealt with them. It can handle JSON natively, as well as CSV files. It only takes a couple of lines to load a CSV file and then *"dump"* its contents as JSON. Use the following CSV file (*addresses.csv*) to see the contents when JSON is dumped in the Python shell:

```
John,Doe,120 Main St.,Riverside, NJ, 08075
Jack,Jhonson,220 St. Vernardeen Av.,Phila, PA,09119
John,Howards,120 Monroe St.,Riverside, NJ,08075
Alfred, Reynolds, 271 Terrell Trace Dr., Marietta, GA, 30068
Jim, Harrison, 100 Sandy Plains Plc., Houston, TX, 77005

>>> import csv
>>> import json
>>> contents = open("addresses.csv").readlines()
>>> json.dumps(list(csv.reader(contents)))
'[["John", "Doe", "120 Main St.", "Riverside", " NJ", " 08075"],
["Jack", "Jhonson", "220 St. Vernardeen Av.", "Phila", " PA", "09119"],
["John", "Howards", "120 Monroe St.", "Riverside", " NJ", "08075"],
["Alfred", " Reynolds", " 271 Terrell Trace Dr.", " Marietta", " GA", " 30068"],
["Jim", " Harrison", " 100 Sandy Plains Plc.", " Houston", " TX", " 77005"]]'
```

Port the interactive session to a function that can do this on the command line:

```
csv2json () {
        python3 -c "
exec('''
import csv,json
print(json.dumps(list(csv.reader(open(\'${1}\')))))
''')
"
}
```

Use it in the shell, which is much simpler than remembering all the calls and modules:

```
$ csv2json addresses.csv
[["John", "Doe", "120 Main St.", "Riverside", " NJ", " 08075"],
["Jack", "Jhonson", "220 St. Vernardeen Av.", "Phila", " PA", "09119"],
["John", "Howards", "120 Monroe St.", "Riverside", " NJ", "08075"],
["Alfred", " Reynolds", " 271 Terrell Trace Dr.", " Marietta", " GA", " 30068"],
["Jim", " Harrison", " 100 Sandy Plains Plc.", " Houston", " TX", " 77005"]]
```

Python One-Liners

In general, writing a long, single line of Python is not considered good practice. The PEP 8 (*https://oreil.ly/3P_qQ*) guide even frowns on compounding statements with a semicolon (it is possible to use semicolons in Python!). But quick debug statements and calls to a debugger are fine. They are, after all, temporary.

Debuggers

A few programmers out there swear by the `print()` statement as the best strategy to debug running code. In some cases, that might work fine, but most of the time we use the Python debugger (with the `pdb` module) or `ipdb`, which uses IPython as a backend. By creating a break point, you can poke around at variables and go up and down the stack. These single-line statements are important enough that you should memorize them:

Set a break point and drop to the Python debugger (`pdb`):

```
import pdb;pdb.set_trace()
```

Set a break point and drop to a Python debugger based on IPython (`ipdb`):

```
import ipdb;ipdb.set_trace()
```

Although not technically a debugger (you can't move forward or backward in the stack), this one-liner allows you to start an IPython session when the execution gets to it:

```
import IPython; IPython.embed()
```

 Everyone seems to have a favorite debugger tool. We find `pdb` to be too rough (no auto-completion, no syntax highlighting), so we tend to like `ipdb` better. Don't be surprised if someone comes along with a different debugger! In the end, it's useful to know how `pdb` works, as it's the base needed to be proficient regardless of the debugger. In systems you can't control, use `pdb` directly because you can't install dependencies; you may not like it, but you can still manage your way around.

How Fast Is this Snippet?

Python has a module to run a piece of code several times over and get some performance metrics from it. Lots of users like to ask if there are efficient ways to handle a loop or update a dictionary, and there are lots of knowledgeable people that love the `timeit` module to prove performance.

As you have probably seen, we are fans of IPython (*https://ipython.org*), and its interactive shell comes with a *"magic"* special function for the `timeit` module. "Magic" functions are prefixed with the % character and perform a distinct operation within the shell. An all-time favorite regarding performance is whether list comprehension is faster than just appending to a list. The two examples below use the `timeit` module to find out:

```
In [1]: def f(x):
   ...:     return x*x
```

```
    ...:

In [2]: %timeit for x in range(100): f(x)
100000 loops, best of 3: 20.3 us per loop
```

In the standard Python shell (or interpreter), you import the module and access it directly. The invocation looks a bit different in this case:

```
>>> array = []
>>> def appending():
...     for i in range(100):
...         array.append(i)
...
>>> timeit.repeat("appending()", "from __main__ import appending")
[5.298534262983594, 5.32031941099558, 5.359099322988186]
>>> timeit.repeat("[i for i in range(100)]")
[2.2052824340062216, 2.1648171059787273, 2.1733458579983562]
```

The output is a bit odd, but that's because it's meant to be processed by another module or library, and is not meant for human readability. The averages favor the list comprehension. This is how it looks in IPython:

```
In [1]: def appending():
    ...:     array = []
    ...:     for i in range(100):
    ...:         array.append(i)
    ...:

In [2]: %timeit appending()
5.39 µs ± 95.1 ns per loop (mean ± std. dev. of 7 runs, 100000 loops each)

In [3]: %timeit [i for i in range(100)]
2.1 µs ± 15.2 ns per loop (mean ± std. dev. of 7 runs, 100000 loops each)
```

Because IPython exposes timeit as a special command (notice the prefix with %), the output is human readable and more helpful to view, and it doesn't require the weird import, as in the standard Python shell.

strace

The ability to tell how a program is interacting with the operating system becomes crucial when applications aren't logging the interesting parts or not logging at all. Output from strace can be rough, but with some understanding of the basics, it becomes easier to understand what is going on with a problematic application. One time, Alfredo was trying to understand why permission to access a file was being denied. This file was inside of a symlink that seemed to have all the right permissions. What was going on? It was difficult to tell by just looking at logs, since those weren't particularly useful in displaying permissions as they tried to access files.

strace included these two lines in the output:

```
stat("/var/lib/ceph/osd/block.db", 0x7fd) = -1 EACCES (Permission denied)
lstat("/var/lib/ceph/osd/block.db", {st_mode=S_IFLNK|0777, st_size=22}) = 0
```

The program was setting ownership on the parent directory, which happened to be a link, and *block.db*, which in this case was also a link to a block device. The block device itself had the right permissions, so what was the problem? It turns out that the link in the directory had a *sticky bit* that prevented other links from changing the path —including the block device. The chown tool has a special flag (-h or --no-dereference) to indicate that the change in ownership should also affect the links.

This type of debugging would be difficult (if not impossible) without something like strace. To try it out, create a file called *follow.py* with the following contents:

```
import subprocess

subprocess.call(['ls', '-alh'])
```

It imports the subprocess module to do a system call. It will output the contents of the system call to ls. Instead of a direct call with Python, prefix the command with strace to see what happens:

```
$ strace python follow.py
```

A lot of output should've filled the terminal, and probably most of it will look very foreign. Force yourself to go through each line, regardless of whether you understand what is going on. Some lines will be easier to tell apart than others. There are a lot of read and fstat calls; you'll see actual system calls and what the process is doing at each step. There are also open and close operations on some files, and there is a particular section that should show up with a few stat calls:

```
stat("/home/alfredo/go/bin/python", 0x7ff) = -1 ENOENT (No such file)
stat("/usr/local/go/bin/python", 0x7ff) = -1 ENOENT (No such file)
stat("/usr/local/bin/python", 0x7ff) = -1 ENOENT (No such file)
stat("/home/alfredo/bin/python", 0x7ff) = -1 ENOENT (No such file)
stat("/usr/local/sbin/python", 0x7ff) = -1 ENOENT (No such file)
stat("/usr/local/bin/python", 0x7ff) = -1 ENOENT (No such file)
stat("/usr/sbin/python", 0x7ff) = -1 ENOENT (No such file)
stat("/usr/bin/python", {st_mode=S_IFREG|0755, st_size=3691008, ...}) = 0
readlink("/usr/bin/python", "python2", 4096) = 7
readlink("/usr/bin/python2", "python2.7", 4096) = 9
readlink("/usr/bin/python2.7", 0x7ff, 4096) = -1 EINVAL (Invalid argument)
stat("/usr/bin/Modules/Setup", 0x7ff) = -1 ENOENT (No such file)
stat("/usr/bin/lib/python2.7/os.py", 0x7ffd) = -1 ENOENT (No such file)
stat("/usr/bin/lib/python2.7/os.pyc", 0x7ff) = -1 ENOENT (No such file)
stat("/usr/lib/python2.7/os.py", {st_mode=S_IFREG|0644, ...}) = 0
stat("/usr/bin/pybuilddir.txt", 0x7ff) = -1 ENOENT (No such file)
stat("/usr/bin/lib/python2.7/lib-dynload", 0x7ff) = -1 ENOENT (No such file)
stat("/usr/lib/python2.7/lib-dynload", {st_mode=S_IFDIR|0755, ...}) = 0
```

This system is pretty old, and python in the output means python2.7, so it pokes around the filesystem to try and find the right executable. It goes through a few until it reaches */usr/bin/python*, which is a link that points to */usr/bin/python2*, which in turn is another link that sends the process to */usr/bin/python2.7*. It then calls stat on */usr/bin/Modules/Setup*, which we've never heard of as Python developers, only to continue to the os module.

It continues to *pybuilddir.txt* and *lib-dynload*. What a trip. Without strace we would've probably tried to read the code that executes this to try and figure out where it goes next. But strace makes this tremendously easier, including all the interesting steps along the way, with useful information for each call.

The tool has many flags that are worth looking into; for example, it can *attach itself to a PID*. If you know the PID of a process, you can tell strace to produce output on what exactly is going on with it.

One of those useful flags is -f; it will follow child processes as they are created by the initial program. In the example Python file, a call to subprocess is made, and it calls out to ls; if the command to strace is modified to use -f, the output becomes richer, with details about that call.

When *follow.py* runs in the home directory, there are a quite a few differences with the -f flag. You can see calls to lstat and readlink for the dotfiles (some of which are symlinked):

```
[pid 30127] lstat(".vimrc", {st_mode=S_IFLNK|0777, st_size=29, ...}) = 0
[pid 30127] lgetxattr(".vimrc", "security.selinux", 0x55c5a36f4720, 255)
[pid 30127] readlink(".vimrc", "/home/alfredo/dotfiles/.vimrc", 30) = 29
[pid 30127] lstat(".config", {st_mode=S_IFDIR|0700, st_size=4096, ...}) = 0
```

Not only do the calls to these files show, but the PID is prefixed in the output, which helps identify which (child) process is doing what. A call to strace without the -f flag would not show a PID, for example.

Finally, to analyze the output in detail, it can be helpful to save it to a file. This is possible with the -o flag:

```
$ strace -o output.txt python follow.py
```

Exercises

- Define what IOPS is.
- Explain what the difference is between throughput and IOPS.
- Name a limitation with `fdisk` for creating partitions that `parted` doesn't have.
- Name three tools that can provide disk information.
- What can an SSH tunnel do? When is it useful?

Case Study Question

- Create a load test using the `molotov` tool that tests a `JSON` response from a server with an HTTP status of `200`.

## CHAPTER 5

Package Management

Often, small scripts grow in usefulness and importance, which creates a need to share and distribute their contents. Python libraries, as well as other code projects, require packaging. Without packaging, distributing code becomes problematic and brittle.

Once past the proof of concept stage, it is helpful to keep track of changes, advertise the type of change (for example, when introducing a backward-incompatible update), and provide a way for users to depend on a specific version. Even in the most straightforward use cases, it is beneficial to follow a few (packaging) guidelines. This, at the very least, should mean keeping track of a changelog and determining a version.

There are several strategies to follow for package management, and knowing a few of the ones most commonly used allows you to adopt the best option to solve a problem. For example, it might be easier to distribute a Python library through the Python Package Index (PyPI) instead of making it a system package like Debian and RPM. If a Python script needs to run at specific intervals or if it is a long-running process, then system packaging working together with systemd might work better.

Although systemd is not a packaging tool, it does play well on systems that depend on it to manage processes and the server startup sequence. Learning how to handle processes with a few systemd configuration settings and some packaging is a great way to increase the capabilities of a Python project further.

The native Python packaging tools have a public hosting instance for packages (PyPI). However, for Debian and RPM packages, it requires some effort to provide a local repository. This chapter covers a few tools that make it easier to create and manage a package repository, including a local alternative to PyPI.

Having a good understanding of the different packaging strategies, and healthy practices like proper versioning and keeping a changelog, provide a stable, consistent experience when distributing software.

Why Is Packaging Important?

Several factors make packaging software an essential feature of a project (regardless of size!). Keeping track of versions and changes (via a changelog) is an excellent way to provide some insight into new features and bug fixes. Versioning allows others to determine better what might work within a project.

When trying to identify issues and bugs, a changelog with an accurate description of changes is an invaluable tool to help identify potential causes of system breakage.

It takes discipline and hard work to version a project, describe changes in a changelog, and provide a way for others to install and use a project. However, the benefits when distributing, debugging, upgrading, or even uninstalling are significant.

When Packaging Might Not Be Needed

Sometimes you don't need to distribute a project to other systems at all. Ansible playbooks are usually run from one server to manage other systems in the network. In cases like Ansible, it might be enough to follow versioning and keep a changelog.

Version control systems like Git make this easy with the use of tags. Tagging in Git would still be useful if a project does need to get packaged, since most tooling can consume the tag (as long as a tag represents a version) to produce a package.

Recently, there was a long debug session to determine why an installer for a large software project had stopped working. Suddenly, all the functional tests for a small Python tool that depended on the installer completing its deployment were failing. The installer did have versions and kept those versions synchronized with version control, but there was no changelog whatsoever that would have explained that recent changes were going to break an existing API. To find the issue, we had to go through all the recent commits to determine what could be the problem.

Going through a few commits shouldn't be difficult, but try doing so on a project with more than four thousand commits! After finding the cause, two tickets were opened: one that explained the bug and another one to ask for a changelog.

Packaging Guidelines

Before packaging, a few things are worth considering so that the process is as smooth as possible. Even when you don't plan to package a product, these guidelines help to improve a project overall.

Projects in version control are always ready to be packaged.

Descriptive Versioning

There are many ways to version software, but it is a good idea to follow a well-known schema. The Python developer's guide has a clear definition (*https://oreil.ly/C3YKO*) for acceptable forms of versioning.

The versioning schema is meant to be extremely flexible, while keeping an eye on consistency so that installer tooling can make sense and prioritize accordingly (for example, a stable version over a beta one). In its purest form, and most commonly in Python packages, the following two variants are used: `major.minor` or `major.minor.micro`.

Valid versions would then look like:

- `0.0.1`
- `1.0`
- `2.1.1`

 Although there are many variations described by the excellent Python developer's guide, concentrate on the simpler forms (listed above). They are good enough to produce packages, while adhering to most guidelines for both system and native Python packages.

A commonly accepted format for releases is `major.minor.micro` (and also used by the Semantic Versioning scheme (*https://semver.org*)):

- `major` for backward-incompatible changes
- `minor` adds features that are also backward compatible
- `micro` adds backward-compatible bug fixes

Following the listed versions above, you can deduce that a dependency on an application with version `1.0.0` might break with version `2.0.0`.

Once the decision for a release occurs, then it is easy to determine the version number. Assuming the current released version of the project under development is `1.0.0`, it means the following outcomes are possible:

- If the release has backward-incompatible changes, the version is: `2.0.0`
- If the release has added features that do not break compatibility, the version is `1.1.0`
- If the release is to fix issues that also do not break compatibility, the version is `1.0.1`

Once a schema is being followed, then a release process is immediately descriptive. Although it would be nice for all software to follow a similar pattern, some projects have a completely different schema of their own. For example, the Ceph (*https:// ceph.com*) project uses the following: `major.[0|1|2].minor`

- `major` indicates a major release, while not necessarily breaking backward-compatibility.
- `0`, `1`, or `2` mean (in order) development release, release candidate, or stable version.
- `minor` is used only for bug fixes and never for features.

That schema would mean that `14.0.0` is a development release, while `14.2.1` is a bug fix release for the stable version of the major release (`14` in this case).

The changelog

As we have mentioned already, it is important to keep track of releases and what they mean in the context of a version number. Keeping a changelog is not that difficult, once a versioning schema is chosen. Although it can be a single file, large projects tend to break it down into smaller files in a directory. Best practice is using a simple format that is descriptive and easy to maintain.

The following example is an actual portion of a *changelog* file in a production Python tool:

```
1.1.3
^^^^^
22-Mar-2019

* No code changes - adding packaging files for Debian

1.1.2
^^^^^
13-Mar-2019

* Try a few different executables (not only ``python``) to check for a working
  one, in order of preference, starting with ``python3`` and ultimately falling
  back to the connection interpreter
```

The example provides four essential pieces of information:

1. The latest version number released
2. Whether the latest release is backward compatible
3. The release date of the last version
4. Changes included in the release

The file doesn't need to be of a specific format, as long as it is consistent and informative. A proper changelog can provide several pieces of information with little effort. It is tempting to try and automate the task of writing a changelog with every release, but we would advise against a fully automated process: nothing beats a well-written, thoughtful entry about a bug fix or a feature added.

A poorly automated changelog is one that uses all the version control commits included in the release. This is not a good practice, since you can get the same information by listing the commits.

Choosing a Strategy

Understanding the type of distribution needed and what infrastructure services are available helps determine what type of packaging to use. Pure Python libraries that extend functionality for other Python projects are suitable as a native Python package, hosted on the Python Package Index (PyPI) or a local index.

Standalone scripts and long-running processes are good candidates for system packages like RPM or Debian, but ultimately, it depends on what type of systems are available and if it is at all possible to host (and manage) a repository. In the case of long-running processes, the packaging can have rules to configure a systemd unit that makes it available as a controllable process. systemd allows for the graceful handling of start, stop, or restart operations. These are things that aren't possible with native Python packaging.

In general, the more a script or process needs to interact with a system, the better it is suited to a system package or a container. When writing a Python-only script, conventional Python packaging is the right choice.

 There aren't hard requirements on what strategy to choose. It depends! Pick the best environment available for distribution (RPM if the servers are CentOS, for example). Different types of packaging are not mutually exclusive; one project can offer multiple packaging formats at the same time.

Packaging Solutions

In this section, the details on how to create a package and host it are covered.

To simplify the code examples, assume a small Python project called `hello-world` with the following structure:

```
hello-world
└── hello_world
    ├── __init__.py
    └── main.py

1 directory, 2 files
```

The project has a top-level directory called `hello-world` and a subdirectory (`hello_world`) with two files in it. Depending on the packaging choice, different files are needed to create a package.

Native Python Packaging

By far the simplest solution is using the native Python packaging tooling and hosting (via PyPI). Like the rest of the other packaging strategies, the project requires some files used by `setuptools`.

 One easy way to source a virtual environment is to create a bash or zsh alias that both cd's into the directory and sources the environment, like this: `alias sugar="source ~/.sugar/bin/activate && cd ~/src/sugar"`

To continue, create a new virtual environment and then activate:

```
$ python3 -m venv /tmp/packaging
$ source /tmp/packaging/bin/activate
```

 `setuptools` is a requirement to produce a native Python package. It is a collection of tools and helpers to create and distribute Python packages.

Once the virtual environment is active, the following dependencies exist:

setuptools
    A set of utilities for packaging

twine
    A tool for registering and uploading packages

Install them by running the following command:

```
$ pip install setuptools twine
```

 A very easy way to figure out what is installed is to use IPython and this snippet to list all of the Python packages as a JSON data structure:

```
In [1]: !pip list --format=json
```

```
[{"name": "appnope", "version": "0.1.0"},
 {"name": "astroid", "version": "2.2.5"},
 {"name": "atomicwrites", "version": "1.3.0"},
 {"name": "attrs", "version": "19.1.0"}]
```

Package files

To produce the native Python package, we have to add a few files. To keep things simple, focus on the minimum amount of files needed to produce the package. The file that describes the package to setuptools is named *setup.py*. It exists at the top-level directory. For the example project, this is how that file looks:

```
from setuptools import setup, find_packages

setup(
    name="hello-world",
    version="0.0.1",
    author="Example Author",
    author_email="author@example.com",
    url="example.com",
    description="A hello-world example package",
    packages=find_packages(),
    classifiers=[
        "Programming Language :: Python :: 3",
        "License :: OSI Approved :: MIT License",
        "Operating System :: OS Independent",
    ],
)
```

The *setup.py* file will import two helpers from the setuptools module: setup and find_packages. The setup function is what requires the rich description about the package. The find_packages function is a utility to automatically detect where the Python files are. Additionally, the file imports classifiers that describe certain aspects of the package, such as the license, operating systems supported, and Python versions. These *classifiers* are called *trove classifiers*, and the Python Package Index (*https://pypi.org/classifiers*) has a detailed description of other classifiers available. Detailed descriptions make a package get discovered when uploaded to PyPI.

With just the addition of this one file, we can already produce a package, in this case, a *source distribution* package. Without a *README* file, a warning appears when running the commands. To prevent this, add an empty one in the top-level directory with the command: touch README.

The contents of the project directory should look like this:

```
hello-world
├── hello_world
│   ├── __init__.py
│   └── main.py
└── README
└── setup.py


1 directory, 4 files
```

To produce the *source distribution* from it, run the following command:

```
python3 setup sdist
```

The output should look similar to the following:

```
$ python3 setup.py sdist
running sdist
running egg_info
writing hello_world.egg-info/PKG-INFO
writing top-level names to hello_world.egg-info/top_level.txt
writing dependency_links to hello_world.egg-info/dependency_links.txt
reading manifest file 'hello_world.egg-info/SOURCES.txt'
writing manifest file 'hello_world.egg-info/SOURCES.txt'
running check
creating hello-world-0.0.1
creating hello-world-0.0.1/hello_world
creating hello-world-0.0.1/hello_world.egg-info
copying files to hello-world-0.0.1...
copying README -> hello-world-0.0.1
copying setup.py -> hello-world-0.0.1
copying hello_world/__init__.py -> hello-world-0.0.1/hello_world
copying hello_world/main.py -> hello-world-0.0.1/hello_world
Writing hello-world-0.0.1/setup.cfg
Creating tar archive
removing 'hello-world-0.0.1' (and everything under it)
```

At the top-level directory of the project, a new directory called *dist* is there; it contains the *source distribution*: a file *hello-world-0.0.1.tar.gz*. If we check the contents of the directory, it has changed once again:

```
hello-world
├── dist
│   └── hello-world-0.0.1.tar.gz
├── hello_world
│   ├── __init__.py
│   └── main.py
```

```
├── hello_world.egg-info
│   ├── dependency_links.txt
│   ├── PKG-INFO
│   ├── SOURCES.txt
│   └── top_level.txt
├── README
└── setup.py

3 directories, 9 files
```

The newly created *tar.gz* file is an installable package! This package can now be uploaded to PyPI for others to install directly from it. By following the version schema, it allows installers to ask for a specific version (0.0.1 in this case), and the extra metadata passed into the setup() function enables other tools to discover it and show information about it, such as the author, description, and version.

The Python installer tool pip can be used to install the *tar.gz* file directly. To try it out, use the path to the file as an argument:

```
$ pip install dist/hello-world-0.0.1.tar.gz
Processing ./dist/hello-world-0.0.1.tar.gz
Building wheels for collected packages: hello-world
  Building wheel for hello-world (setup.py) ... done
Successfully built hello-world
Installing collected packages: hello-world
Successfully installed hello-world-0.0.1
```

The Python Package Index

The Python Package Index (PyPI) is a repository of Python software that allows users to host Python packages and also install from it. It is maintained by and for the community with the help of sponsors and donations as part of the Python Software Foundation (*https://www.python.org/psf*).

> This section requires registration for the *test instance* of PyPI. Make sure you have an account already or register online (*https://oreil.ly/lyVVx*). You need your username and password for the account to upload packages.

In the sample *setup.py* file, an example email address contains a placeholder. If the package is going to get published to the index, this needs to be updated to reflect the same email address that owns the project at PyPI. Update any other fields, like the author, url, and description, to more accurately reflect the project being built.

To make sure things work correctly, and to avoid *pushing to production*, the package is tested by uploading it to the test instance of PyPI. This test instance behaves the same as production and verifies that a package works correctly.

The setuptools and the *setup.py* file is the traditional method of uploading a package to PyPI. A new approach, called twine, can simplify things.

At the beginning of this section, twine got installed in the virtual environment. Next, it can be used to upload the package to the test instance of PyPI. The following command uploads the *tar.gz* file and prompts for the username and password:

```
$ twine upload --repository-url https://test.pypi.org/legacy/ \
  dist/hello-world-0.0.1.tar.gz
Uploading distributions to https://test.pypi.org/legacy/
Enter your username:
Enter your password:
```

To test out whether the package made it, we can try and install it with pip:

```
$ python3 -m pip install --index-url https://test.pypi.org/simple/ hello-world
```

The command looks like it has a space in the PyPI URL, but the index URL ends in /simple/, and hello-world is another argument that indicates the name of the Python package to be installed.

For an actual production release, an account would need to exist or be created (*https://pypi.org/account/register*). The same steps that are taken to upload to the test instance, including the validation, would also work for the *real* PyPI.

Older Python packaging guides may reference commands such as:

```
$ python setup.py register
$ python setup.py upload
```

These may still work and are part of the setuptools set of utilities to package and upload projects to a package index. However, twine offers secure authentication over HTTPS, and allows signing with gpg. Twine works regardless if python setup.py upload doesn't, and finally, it provides a way to test a package before uploading to the index.

A final item to point out is that it may be helpful to create a Makefile and put a make command in it that automatically deploys your project and builds the documentation for you. Here is an example of how that could work:

```
deploy-pypi:
    pandoc --from=markdown --to=rst README.md -o README.rst
    python setup.py check --restructuredtext --strict --metadata
    rm -rf dist
    python setup.py sdist
    twine upload dist/*
    rm -f README.rst
```

Hosting an internal package index

In some situations, it might be preferable to host an internal PyPI.

A company where Alfredo used to work had private libraries that were not supposed to be public at all, so it was a requirement to host an instance of PyPI. Hosting has its caveats, though. All dependencies and versions of those dependencies have to exist in the instance; otherwise, installs can fail. An installer can't fetch dependencies from different sources at the same time! On more than one occasion, a new version had a missing component, so that package had to be uploaded for the install to complete correctly.

If package *A* is hosted internally and has requirements on packages *B* and *C*, all three need to exist (along with their required versions) in the same instance.

An internal PyPI makes installations go faster, can keep packages private, and at its core, isn't challenging to accomplish.

 A highly recommended full-featured tool for hosting an internal PyPI is devpi. It has features like mirroring, staging, replication, and Jenkins integration. The project documentation (*http:// doc.devpi.net*) has great examples and detailed information.

First, create a new directory called pypi so that you can create a proper structure for hosting packages, and then create a subdirectory with the name of our example package (hello-world). The names of subdirectories are the names of the packages themselves:

```
$ mkdir -p pypi/hello-world
$ tree pypi
pypi
└── hello-world

1 directory, 0 files
```

Now copy the *tar.gz* file into the *hello-world* directory. The final version of this directory structure should look like this:

```
$ tree pypi
pypi
└── hello-world
    └── hello-world-0.0.1.tar.gz

1 directory, 1 file
```

The next step is to create a web server with auto indexing enabled. Python comes with a built-in web server that is good enough to try this out, and it even has the auto indexing enabled by default! Change directories to the *pypi* directory containing the hello-world package and start the built-in web server:

```
$ python3 -m http.server
Serving HTTP on 0.0.0.0 port 8000 (http://0.0.0.0:8000/) ...
```

In a new terminal session, create a temporary virtual environment to try out installing the hello-world package from the local PyPI instance. Activate it, and finally, try installing it by pointing pip to the custom local URL:

```
$ python3 -m venv /tmp/local-pypi
$ source /tmp/local-pypi/bin/activate
(local-pypi) $ pip install -i http://localhost:8000/ hello-world
Looking in indexes: http://localhost:8000/
Collecting hello-world
  Downloading http://localhost:8000/hello-world/hello-world-0.0.1.tar.gz
Building wheels for collected packages: hello-world
  Building wheel for hello-world (setup.py) ... done
Successfully built hello-world
Installing collected packages: hello-world
Successfully installed hello-world-0.0.1
```

In the session where the http.server module is running, there should be some logs demonstrating all the requests the installer made to retrieve the hello-world package:

```
Serving HTTP on 0.0.0.0 port 8000 (http://0.0.0.0:8000/) ...
127.0.0.1 [09:58:37] "GET / HTTP/1.1" 200 -
127.0.0.1 [09:59:39] "GET /hello-world/ HTTP/1.1" 200 -
127.0.0.1 [09:59:39] "GET /hello-world/hello-world-0.0.1.tar.gz HTTP/1.1" 200
```

A production environment needs a better-performing web server. The http.server module is used in this example for simplicity, but it isn't meant to handle simultaneous multiple requests or scaling out.

When building a local index without a tool like devpi, there is a defined specification that includes descriptions of normalized names for the directory structure. This specification can be found in PEP 503 (*https://oreil.ly/sRcAe*).

Debian Packaging

If targeting Debian (or a Debian-based distribution such as Ubuntu) for distributing a project, additional files are required. Understanding what these files are and how the Debian packaging tools use them improves the process of producing an installable .deb package and troubleshooting issues.

Some of these plain-text files require a *very* strict formatting, and if the format is even slightly incorrect, the packaging cannot install.

This section assumes the packaging is in a Debian or Debian-based distro, so that it is easier to install and use the required packaging tools.

Package files

Debian packaging needs a *debian* directory with a few files in it. To narrow the scope of what is needed to produce a package, most of the available options are skipped, such as running a test suite before completing a build or declaring multiple Python versions.

Create the *debian* directory where all required files exist. In the end, the `hello-world` project structure should look like this:

```
$ tree
.
├── debian
├── hello_world
│   ├── __init__.py
│   └── main.py
├── README
└── setup.py

2 directories, 4 files
```

Note that the directory includes the *setup.py* and *README* file from the native Python packaging section. It is required because Debian tooling uses these to produce the `.deb` package.

The changelog file. This file can be complicated to get right if done by hand. The errors produced when this file is not formatted correctly are not easy to debug. Most Debian packaging workflows rely on the `dch` tool to enhance debuggability.

I've ignored my advice before and have tried to manually create this file. In the end I wasted time because error reporting is not very good, and spotting issues is very difficult. Below is an example of an entry in the *changelog* file that caused a problem:

```
--Alfredo Deza <alfredo@example.com> Sat, 11 May 2013 2:12:00 -0800
```

That entry produced the following error:

```
parsechangelog/debian: warning: debian/changelog(l7): found start of entry where
    expected more change data or trailer
```

Can you spot the fix?

```
-- Alfredo Deza <alfredo@example.com> Sat, 11 May 2013 2:12:00 -0800
```

A *space* between the dashes and my name was the cause. Save yourself the heartache and use dch. The tool is part of the `devscripts` package:

```
$ sudo apt-get install devscripts
```

The dch command-line tool has many options, and it is useful to go through its documentation (the main page is comprehensive). We are going to run it to create the changelog for the first time (this requires the one-time use of the `--create` flag). Before running it, export your full name and email so that they get into the generated file:

```
$ export DEBEMAIL="alfredo@example.com"
$ export DEBFULLNAME="Alfredo Deza"
```

Now run dch to produce the changelog:

```
$ dch --package "hello-world" --create -v "0.0.1" \
    -D stable "New upstream release"
```

The newly created file should look similar to this:

```
hello-world (0.0.1) stable; urgency=medium

  * New upstream release

 -- Alfredo Deza <alfredo@example.com>  Thu, 11 Apr 2019 20:28:08 -0400
```

 The Debian changelog is specific to Debian packaging. It is fine to have a separate changelog for the project when the format doesn't fit or if other information needs updating. Lots of projects keep the Debian *changelog* file as a separate Debian-only file.

The control file. This is the file that defines the package name, its description, and any dependencies needed for building and running the project. It also has a strict format, but it doesn't need to change much (unlike the *changelog*). The file ensures that Python 3 is required and that it follows Debian's Python naming guidelines.

 In the transition from Python 2 to Python 3, most distributions settled on using the following schema for Python 3 packages: `python3-{package name}`.

After adding the dependencies, naming conventions, and a short description, this is how the file should look:

```
Source: hello-world
Maintainer: Alfredo Deza <alfredo@example.com>
Section: python
```

```
Priority: optional
Build-Depends:
 debhelper (>= 11~),
 dh-python,
 python3-all
 python3-setuptools
Standards-Version: 4.3.0

Package: python3-hello-world
Architecture: all
Depends: ${misc:Depends}, ${python3:Depends}
Description: An example hello-world package built with Python 3
```

Other required files. There are a few other files needed to produce a Debian package. Most of them are just a couple of lines long and change infrequently.

The *rules* file is an executable file that tells Debian what to run to produce the package; in this case it should look like the following:

```
#!/usr/bin/make -f

export DH_VERBOSE=1

export PYBUILD_NAME=remoto

%:
        dh $@ --with python3 --buildsystem=pybuild
```

The *compat* file sets the corresponding debhelper (another packaging tool) compatibility, recommended to be set to 10 here. You might check to see whether a higher value is required if an error message complains about it:

```
$ cat compat
10
```

Without a license, the build process might not work, and it is a good idea to state the license explicitly. This particular example uses the MIT license, and this is how it should look in *debian/copyright*:

```
Format: http://www.debian.org/doc/packaging-manuals/copyright-format/1.0
Upstream-Name: hello-world
Source: https://example.com/hello-world

Files: *
Copyright: 2019 Alfredo Deza
License: Expat

License: Expat
  Permission is hereby granted, free of charge, to any person obtaining a
  copy of this software and associated documentation files (the "Software"),
  to deal in the Software without restriction, including without limitation
  the rights to use, copy, modify, merge, publish, distribute, sublicense,
```

Finally, after adding all these new files to the debian directory, the hello-world
project looks like this:

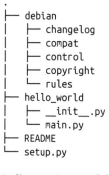

```
.
├── debian
│   ├── changelog
│   ├── compat
│   ├── control
│   ├── copyright
│   └── rules
├── hello_world
│   ├── __init__.py
│   └── main.py
├── README
└── setup.py

2 directories, 9 files
```

Producing the binary

To produce the binary, use the debuild command-line tool. For this example project,
the package remains unsigned (the signing process requires a GPG key), and the
debuild documentation uses an example that allows skipping the signing. The script
is run from inside the source tree to build only the binary package. This command
works for the hello-world project (truncated version shown here):

```
$ debuild -i -us -uc -b
...
dpkg-deb: building package 'python3-hello-world'
in '../python3-hello-world_0.0.1_all.deb'.
...
 dpkg-genbuildinfo --build=binary
 dpkg-genchanges --build=binary >../hello-world_0.0.1_amd64.changes
dpkg-genchanges: info: binary-only upload (no source code included)
 dpkg-source -i --after-build hello-world-debian
dpkg-buildpackage: info: binary-only upload (no source included)
Now running lintian hello-world_0.0.1_amd64.changes ...
```

```
E: hello-world changes: bad-distribution-in-changes-file stable
Finished running lintian.
```

A *python3-hello-world_0.0.1_all.deb* should now exist in the upper directory. The lintian call (a Debian packaging linter) complains at the very end that the *changelog* file has an invalid distribution, which is fine because we aren't targeting a single distribution in particular (for example, Debian Buster). Rather, we are building a package that will most likely install in any Debian-base distro that complies with the dependencies (only Python 3, in this case).

Debian repositories

There are many tools to automate Debian repositories, but it is useful to understand how to go about creating one (Alfredo even helped develop one (*https://oreil.ly/ hJMgY*) for both RPM and Debian!). To continue, ensure that the binary package created previously is available at a known location:

```
$ mkdir /opt/binaries
$ cp python3-hello-world_0.0.1_all.deb /opt/binaries/
```

For this section, the `reprepro` tool needs to be installed:

```
$ sudo apt-get install reprepro
```

Create a new directory somewhere in the system to hold packages. This example uses */opt/repo*. The basic configuration for a repository needs a file, called `distribu tions`, that describes the contents and looks like this:

```
Codename: sid
Origin: example.com
Label: example.com
Architectures: amd64 source
DscIndices: Sources Release .gz .bz2
DebIndices: Packages Release . .gz .bz2
Components: main
Suite: stable
Description: example repo for hello-world package
Contents: .gz .bz2
```

Save this file at */opt/repo/conf/distributions*. Create another directory to hold the actual repo:

```
$ mkdir /opt/repo/debian/sid
```

To create the repository, instruct `reprepro` to use the *distributions* file created, and that the base directory is */opt/repo/debian/sid*. Finally, add the binary previously created as a target for the Debian sid distribution:

```
$ reprepro --confdir /opt/repo/conf/distributions -b /opt/repo/debian/sid \
  -C main includedeb sid /opt/binaries/python3-hello-world_0.0.1_all.deb
Exporting indices...
```

This command creates the repo for the Debian sid distribution! This command can be adapted for a different Debian-based distribution such as Ubuntu Bionic, for example. To do so would only require replacing sid with bionic.

Now that the repo exists, the next step is to ensure that it works as expected. For a production environment, a robust web server like Apache or Nginx would be a good choice, but to test this, use Python's http.server module. Change directories to the directory containing the repository, and start the server:

```
$ cd /opt/repo/debian/sid
$ python3 -m http.server
Serving HTTP on 0.0.0.0 port 8000 (http://0.0.0.0:8000/) ...
```

Aptitude (or apt, the Debian package manager) needs some configuration to be aware of this new location for packages. This configuration is a simple file with a single line in it pointing to the URL and components of our repo. Create a file at */etc/apt/sources.lists.d/hello-world.list*. It should look like this:

```
$ cat /etc/apt/sources.list.d/hello-world.list
deb [trusted=yes] http://localhost:8000/ sid main
```

The [trusted=yes] configuration tells apt not to enforce signed packages. On repositories that are properly signed, this step is not necessary.

After adding the file, update apt so that it recognizes the new location, and look for (and install) the hello-world package:

```
$ sudo apt-get update
Ign:1 http://localhost:8000 sid InRelease
Get:2 http://localhost:8000 sid Release [2,699 B]
Ign:3 http://localhost:8000 sid Release.gpg
Get:4 http://localhost:8000 sid/main amd64 Packages [381 B]
Get:5 http://localhost:8000 sid/main amd64 Contents (deb) [265 B]
Fetched 3,345 B in 1s (6,382 B/s)
Reading package lists... Done
```

Searching for the python3-hello-world package provides the description added in the *distributions* file when configuring reprepro:

```
$ apt-cache search python3-hello-world
python3-hello-world - An example hello-world package built with Python 3
```

Installing and removing the package should work without a problem:

```
$ sudo apt-get install python3-hello-world
Reading package lists... Done
Building dependency tree
Reading state information... Done
The following NEW packages will be installed:
  python3-hello-world
0 upgraded, 1 newly installed, 0 to remove and 48 not upgraded.
Need to get 2,796 B of archives.
```

```
Fetched 2,796 B in 0s (129 kB/s)
Selecting previously unselected package python3-hello-world.
(Reading database ... 242590 files and directories currently installed.)
Preparing to unpack .../python3-hello-world_0.0.1_all.deb ...
Unpacking python3-hello-world (0.0.1) ...
Setting up python3-hello-world (0.0.1) ...
$ sudo apt-get remove --purge python3-hello-world
Reading package lists... Done
Building dependency tree
Reading state information... Done
The following packages will be REMOVED:
  python3-hello-world*
0 upgraded, 0 newly installed, 1 to remove and 48 not upgraded.
After this operation, 19.5 kB disk space will be freed.
Do you want to continue? [Y/n] Y
(Reading database ... 242599 files and directories currently installed.)
Removing python3-hello-world (0.0.1) ...
```

RPM Packaging

Just as with Debian packaging, when working in RPM, it is necessary to have the native Python packaging done already. It should be possible to produce a Python package with a *setup.py* file. However, very unlike Debian, in which many files are needed, RPM packaging can work with just one: the *spec* file. If targeting a distribution like CentOS or Fedora, the RPM Package Manager (formerly known as Red Hat Package Manager) is the way to go.

The spec file

In its simplest form, the *spec* file (named *hello-world.spec* for this example) is not difficult to understand, and most sections are self-explanatory. It can even be generated by using `setuptools`:

```
$ python3 setup.py bdist_rpm --spec-only
running bdist_rpm
running egg_info
writing hello_world.egg-info/PKG-INFO
writing dependency_links to hello_world.egg-info/dependency_links.txt
writing top-level names to hello_world.egg-info/top_level.txt
reading manifest file 'hello_world.egg-info/SOURCES.txt'
writing manifest file 'hello_world.egg-info/SOURCES.txt'
writing 'dist/hello-world.spec'
```

The output file in *dist/hello-world.spec* should look similar to this:

```
%define name hello-world
%define version 0.0.1
%define unmangled_version 0.0.1
%define release 1

Summary: A hello-world example pacakge
```

```
Name: %{name}
Version: %{version}
Release: %{release}
Source0: %{name}-%{unmangled_version}.tar.gz
License: MIT
Group: Development/Libraries
BuildRoot: %{_tmppath}/%{name}-%{version}-%{release}-buildroot
Prefix: %{_prefix}
BuildArch: noarch
Vendor: Example Author <author@example.com>
Url: example.com

%description
A Python3 hello-world package

%prep
%setup -n %{name}-%{unmangled_version} -n %{name}-%{unmangled_version}

%build
python3 setup.py build

%install
python3 setup.py install --single-version-externally-managed -O1 \
--root=$RPM_BUILD_ROOT --record=INSTALLED_FILES

%clean
rm -rf $RPM_BUILD_ROOT

%files -f INSTALLED_FILES
%defattr(-,root,root)
```

Although it looks simple, it is already creating a potential issue: the version is input and requires updating every time. This process is similar to Debian's *changelog* file, which needs to have the version *bumped* on each release.

The `setuptools` integration is advantageous, allows further modification to this file if needed, and copies to the root directory of the project for a permanent location. Some projects use a base template that gets populated to generate the spec file as part of the build process. This process is useful if following a rigorous release workflow. In the case of the Ceph project (*https://ceph.com*), the release is tagged via version control (Git), and the release scripts use that tag to apply it to the template via a `Make file`. It is worth noting that additional methods exist to automate this process further.

Generating a *spec* file is not always useful, because certain sections might need to be hardcoded to follow some distribution rule or a specific dependency that is not part of the generated file. In such cases, it is best to generate it once and configure it further to finally save it and make the *spec* file a formal part of the project.

Producing the binary

There are a few different tools to produce RPM binaries; one in particular is the rpmbuild command-line tool:

```
$ sudo yum install rpm-build
```

 The command-line tool is rpmbuild but the package is called rpm-build, so make sure that rpmbuild (the command-line tool) is available in the terminal.

A directory structure is required by rpmbuild to create the binary. After the directories are created, the *source* file (the *tar.gz* file generated by setuptools) needs to be present in the *SOURCES* directory. This is how the structure should be created and how it will look once it is done:

```
$ mkdir -p /opt/repo/centos/{SOURCES,SRPMS,SPECS,RPMS,BUILD}
$ cp dist/hello-world-0.0.1.tar.gz /opt/repo/centos/SOURCES/
$ tree /opt/repo/centos
/opt/repo/centos
├── BUILD
├── BUILDROOT
├── RPMS
├── SOURCES
│   └── hello-world-0.0.1.tar.gz
├── SPECS
└── SRPMS

6 directories, 1 file
```

The directory structure is always needed, and by default, rpmbuild requires it in the home directory. To keep things isolated, a different location (in */opt/repo/centos*) is used. This process means configure rpmbuild uses this directory instead. This process produces both a binary and a *source* package with the -ba flag (output is abbreviated):

```
$ rpmbuild -ba --define "_topdir /opt/repo/centos"  dist/hello-world.spec
...
Executing(%build): /bin/sh -e /var/tmp/rpm-tmp.CmGOdp
running build
running build_py
creating build
creating build/lib
creating build/lib/hello_world
copying hello_world/main.py -> build/lib/hello_world
copying hello_world/__init__.py -> build/lib/hello_world
Executing(%install): /bin/sh -e /var/tmp/rpm-tmp.CQgOKD
+ python3 setup.py install --single-version-externally-managed \
-01 --root=/opt/repo/centos/BUILDROOT/hello-world-0.0.1-1.x86_64
```

```
running install
writing hello_world.egg-info/PKG-INFO
writing dependency_links to hello_world.egg-info/dependency_links.txt
writing top-level names to hello_world.egg-info/top_level.txt
reading manifest file 'hello_world.egg-info/SOURCES.txt'
writing manifest file 'hello_world.egg-info/SOURCES.txt'
running install_scripts
writing list of installed files to 'INSTALLED_FILES'
Processing files: hello-world-0.0.1-1.noarch
Provides: hello-world = 0.0.1-1
Wrote: /opt/repo/centos/SRPMS/hello-world-0.0.1-1.src.rpm
Wrote: /opt/repo/centos/RPMS/noarch/hello-world-0.0.1-1.noarch.rpm
Executing(%clean): /bin/sh -e /var/tmp/rpm-tmp.gcIJgT
+ umask 022
+ cd /opt/repo/centos//BUILD
+ cd hello-world-0.0.1
+ rm -rf /opt/repo/centos/BUILDROOT/hello-world-0.0.1-1.x86_64
+ exit 0
```

The directory structure at */opt/repo/centos* will have lots of new files, but we are only interested in the one that has the noarch RPM:

```
$ tree /opt/repo/centos/RPMS
/opt/repo/centos/RPMS
└── noarch
    └── hello-world-0.0.1-1.noarch.rpm

1 directory, 1 file
```

The noarch RPM is an installable RPM package! The tool produced other useful packages that can be published as well (look at */opt/repo/centos/SRPMS*, for example).

RPM repositories

To create an RPM repository, use the createrepo command-line tool. It handles the creation of the repository metadata (XML-based RPM metadata) from the binaries it finds in a given directory. In this section, create (and host) the noarch binary:

```
$ sudo yum install createrepo
```

You can create the repository in the same location used to produce the noarch package, or use a new (clean) directory. Create new binaries if needed. Once that is completed, the package copies:

```
$ mkdir -p /var/www/repos/centos
$ cp -r /opt/repo/centos/RPMS/noarch /var/www/repos/centos
```

To create the metadata, run the createrepo tool:

```
$ createrepo -v /var/www/repos/centos/noarch
Spawning worker 0 with 1 pkgs
Worker 0: reading hello-world-0.0.1-1.noarch.rpm
Workers Finished
```

```
Saving Primary metadata
Saving file lists metadata
Saving other metadata
Generating sqlite DBs
Starting other db creation: Thu Apr 18 09:13:35 2019
Ending other db creation: Thu Apr 18 09:13:35 2019
Starting filelists db creation: Thu Apr 18 09:13:35 2019
Ending filelists db creation: Thu Apr 18 09:13:35 2019
Starting primary db creation: Thu Apr 18 09:13:35 2019
Ending primary db creation: Thu Apr 18 09:13:35 2019
Sqlite DBs complete
```

Although an x86_64 package does not exist, repeat the `createrepo` call for this new directory so that yum doesn't complain about it later:

```
$ mkdir /var/www/repos/centos/x86_64
$ createrepo -v /var/www/repos/centos/x86_64
```

We are going to use the `http.server` module to serve this directory over HTTP:

```
$ python3 -m http.server
Serving HTTP on 0.0.0.0 port 8000 (http://0.0.0.0:8000/) ...
```

To access this repository, yum needs to be configured with a *repo file*. Create one at */etc/yum.repos.d/hello-world.repo*. It should look like this:

```
[hello-world]
name=hello-world example repo for noarch packages
baseurl=http://0.0.0.0:8000/$basearch
enabled=1
gpgcheck=0
type=rpm-md
priority=1

[hello-world-noarch]
name=hello-world example repo for noarch packages
baseurl=http://0.0.0.0:8000/noarch
enabled=1
gpgcheck=0
type=rpm-md
priority=1
```

Note how the `gpgcheck` value is 0. This means we haven't signed any packages and yum should not try to verify a signature, preventing a failure in this example. Searching for the package should now be possible, giving us the description as part of the output:

```
$ yum --enablerepo=hello-world search hello-world
Loaded plugins: fastestmirror, priorities
Loading mirror speeds from cached hostfile
 * base: reflector.westga.edu
 * epel: mirror.vcu.edu
 * extras: mirror.steadfastnet.com
```

```
      * updates: mirror.mobap.edu
     base                                                      | 3.6 kB
     extras                                                    | 3.4 kB
     hello- world                                              | 2.9 kB
     hello-world-noarch                                        | 2.9 kB
     updates                                                   | 3.4 kB
     8 packages excluded due to repository priority protections
     ==========================================================================
     matched: hello-world
     ==========================================================================
     hello-world.noarch : A hello-world example pacakge
```

The search function works correctly; installing the package should work as well:

```
$ yum --enablerepo=hello-world install hello-world
Loaded plugins: fastestmirror, priorities
Loading mirror speeds from cached hostfile
 * base: reflector.westga.edu
 * epel: mirror.vcu.edu
 * extras: mirror.steadfastnet.com
 * updates: mirror.mobap.edu
8 packages excluded due to repository priority protections
Resolving Dependencies
--> Running transaction check
---> Package hello-world.noarch 0:0.0.1-1 will be installed
--> Finished Dependency Resolution

Dependencies Resolved
Installing:
 hello-world           noarch        0.0.1-1           hello-world-noarch

Transaction Summary
Install  1 Package

Total download size: 8.1 k
Installed size: 1.3 k
Downloading packages:
hello-world-0.0.1-1.noarch.rpm                               | 8.1 kB
Running transaction check
Running transaction test
Transaction test succeeded
Running transaction
  Installing : hello-world-0.0.1-1.noarch
  Verifying  : hello-world-0.0.1-1.noarch

Installed:
  hello-world.noarch 0:0.0.1-1

Complete!
```

Removing has to work as well:

```
$ yum remove hello-world
Loaded plugins: fastestmirror, priorities
```

```
Resolving Dependencies
--> Running transaction check
---> Package hello-world.noarch 0:0.0.1-1 will be erased
--> Finished Dependency Resolution

Dependencies Resolved
Removing:
 hello-world            noarch          0.0.1-1           @hello-world-noarch

Transaction Summary
Remove  1 Package

Installed size: 1.3 k
Is this ok [y/N]: y
Downloading packages:
Running transaction check
Running transaction test
Transaction test succeeded
Running transaction
  Erasing    : hello-world-0.0.1-1.noarch
  Verifying  : hello-world-0.0.1-1.noarch
Removed:
  hello-world.noarch 0:0.0.1-1
Complete!
```

The `http.server` module should display some activity, demonstrating that `yum` was reaching out to get the `hello-world` package:

```
[18/Apr/2019 03:37:24] "GET /x86_64/repodata/repomd.xml HTTP/1.1"
[18/Apr/2019 03:37:24] "GET /noarch/repodata/repomd.xml HTTP/1.1"
[18/Apr/2019 03:37:25] "GET /x86_64/repodata/primary.sqlite.bz2 HTTP/1.1"
[18/Apr/2019 03:37:25] "GET /noarch/repodata/primary.sqlite.bz2 HTTP/1.1"
[18/Apr/2019 03:56:49] "GET /noarch/hello-world-0.0.1-1.noarch.rpm HTTP/1.1"
```

Management with systemd

`systemd` is a *system and service manager* for Linux (also known as *init system*). It is the default init system for many distributions, such as Debian and Red Hat. Here are some of the many features `systemd` provides:

- Easy parallelization
- Hooks and triggers for on-demand behavior
- Logging integration
- Ability to depend on other units for orchestrating complicated startups

There are plenty of other exciting aspects of `systemd`, such as network, DNS, and even mounting for devices. The idea of handling processes with ease in Python has always been challenging; at one point there were a few *init-like* projects in Python to choose from, all with their configuration and handling APIs. Using systemd allows portability and makes it easy to collaborate with others since it is widely available.

Two well-known process handlers in Python are supervisord (*http://supervisord.org*) and circus (*https://oreil.ly/adGEj*).

Not long ago, Alfredo wrote a small Python HTTP API that needed to go into production. The project had transitioned from supervisord to circus, and things were working fine. Unfortunately, production constraints meant the integration of systemd with the OS. The transition was rough because systemd was reasonably new, but once things were in place, we benefited from having the same production-like handling for development and catching integration issues earlier in the development cycle. When the API went into the release, we already felt comfortable with systemd to troubleshoot problems and even fine-tune the configuration to cope with external issues. (Have you ever seen an init script fail because the network was not operational?)

In this section we build a small HTTP service that needs to be available when the system boots and can restart at any moment. The unit configuration handles logging and ensures that specific system resources are available before attempting to start.

Long-Running Processes

Processes that are meant to be running all the time are excellent candidates to be handled with systemd. Consider how a DNS or mail server works; these are *always on* programs, and they need some handling to capture logging or restart when configuration changes.

We are going to use a small HTTP API server, based on the Pecan web framework (*https://www.pecanpy.org*).

There is nothing specific in this section as to how Pecan works, so that the examples can be used for other frameworks or long-running services.

Setting It Up

Pick a permanent location for the project to create a directory at */opt/http*, and then create a new virtual environment and install the Pecan framework:

```
$ mkdir -p /opt/http
$ cd /opt/http
```

```
$ python3 -m venv .
$ source bin/activate
(http) $ pip install "pecan==1.3.3"
```

Pecan has some built-in helpers that can create the necessary files and directories for an example project. Pecan can be used to create a basic "vanilla" HTTP API project that hooks up to systemd. Version 1.3.3 has two options: the base and the rest-api flavors:

```
$ pecan create api rest-api
Creating /opt/http/api
Recursing into +package+
  Creating /opt/http/api/api
...
Copying scaffolds/rest-api/config.py_tmpl to /opt/http/api/config.py
Copying scaffolds/rest-api/setup.cfg_tmpl to /opt/http/api/setup.cfg
Copying scaffolds/rest-api/setup.py_tmpl to /opt/http/api/setup.py
```

 It is important to use a consistent path, because it is used later when configuring the service with systemd.

By including the project scaffolding, we now have a fully functional project with no effort. It even has a *setup.py* file with everything in it, ready to become a native Python package! Let's install the project so that we can run it:

```
(http) $ python setup.py install
running install
running bdist_egg
running egg_info
creating api.egg-info
...
creating dist
creating 'dist/api-0.1-py3.6.egg' and adding 'build/bdist.linux-x86_64/egg'
removing 'build/bdist.linux-x86_64/egg' (and everything under it)
Processing api-0.1-py3.6.egg
creating /opt/http/lib/python3.6/site-packages/api-0.1-py3.6.egg
Extracting api-0.1-py3.6.egg to /opt/http/lib/python3.6/site-packages
...
Installed /opt/http/lib/python3.6/site-packages/api-0.1-py3.6.egg
Processing dependencies for api==0.1
Finished processing dependencies for api==0.1
```

The pecan command-line tool requires a configuration file. The configuration file has already been created for you by the scaffolding, and it lives in the top directory. Start the server with the *config.py* file:

```
(http) $ pecan serve config.py
Starting server in PID 17517
serving on 0.0.0.0:8080, view at http://127.0.0.1:8080
```

Testing it out on the browser should produce a plain-text message. This is how it shows with the `curl` command:

```
(http) $ curl localhost:8080
Hello, World!
```

A long-running process starts with `pecan serve config.py`. The only way to stop this process is to send a `KeyboardInterrupt` with `Control-C`. Starting it again requires the virtual environment to be activated, and the same `pecan serve` command runs again.

The systemd Unit File

Unlike older init systems that work with executable scripts, `systemd` works with plain text files. The final version of the unit file looks like this:

```
[Unit]
Description=hello world pecan service
After=network.target

[Service]
Type=simple
ExecStart=/opt/http/bin/pecan serve /opt/http/api/config.py
WorkingDirectory=/opt/http/api
StandardOutput=journal
StandardError=journal

[Install]
WantedBy=multi-user.target
```

Save this file as `hello-world.service`. It will be copied into its final destination later in this section.

It is essential to get all the section names and the configuration directives correct, as all are case-sensitive. If names don't match exactly, things won't work. Let's go into detail for each section of the HTTP service:

Unit

Provides a description and includes an `After` directive that tells `systemd` that this service unit needs to have an operational network environment before being started. Other units may have more complex requirements, not only to start the service but even *after* it starts! `Condition` and `Wants` are other directives that are very useful.

Service

This section is only needed when configuring a *service* unit. It defaults to `Type=simple`. Services of this type should not fork—they have to stay in the foreground so that `systemd` can handle their operation. The `ExecStart` line explains what the command should run to start the service. It is *crucial* to use absolute paths to avoid problems finding the right files.

Although not required, I've included the `WorkingDirectory` directive to ensure that the process is in the same directory where the application lives. If anything updates later, it might benefit from already being in a position relative to the application.

Both the `StandardOutput` and `StandardError` directives are great to work with, and show how much `systemd` has to offer here. It will handle all the logging emitted via `stdout` and `stderr` through `systemd` machinery. We will demonstrate this further when explaining how to interact with the service.

Install

The `WantedBy` directive explains how this unit handles once it is enabled. The `multi-user.target` is equivalent to `runlevel 3` (the normal run level for a server that boots into a terminal). This type of configuration allows the system to determine how it behaves once enabled. Once enabled, a symlink is created in the *multi-user.target.wants* directory.

Installing the Unit

The configuration file itself has to go to a specific location so that `systemd` can pick it up and *load it*. Various locations are supported, but */etc/systemd/system* is for units that are created or managed by an administrator.

It is useful to make sure that the `ExecStart` directive works with those paths. Using absolute paths increases the chance of introducing a typo. To verify, run the whole line in the terminal and look for output similar to this:

```
$ /opt/http/bin/pecan serve /opt/http/api/config.py
Starting server in PID 20621
serving on 0.0.0.0:8080, view at http://127.0.0.1:8080
```

After verifying that the command works, copy the unit file into this directory using `hello-world.service` as the name:

```
$ cp hello-world.service /etc/systemd/system/
```

Once in place, `systemd` needs to be reloaded to make it aware of this new unit:

```
$ systemctl daemon-reload
```

The service is now fully functional and can be started and stopped. This process is verified by using the `status` subcommand. Let's go through the different commands you can use to interact with the service. First, let's see if `systemd` recognizes it. This is how it should behave and what the output looks like:

```
$ systemctl status hello-world
● hello-world.service - hello world pecan service
   Loaded: loaded (/etc/systemd/system/hello-world.service; disabled; )
   Active: inactive (dead)
```

Since the service is not running, it is not surprising to see it reported as dead. Start the service next and check the status once again (`curl` should report nothing is running on port 8080):

```
$ curl localhost:8080
curl: (7) Failed to connect to localhost port 8080: Connection refused
$ systemctl start hello-world
$ systemctl status hello-world
● hello-world.service - hello world pecan service
   Loaded: loaded (/etc/systemd/system/hello-world.service; disabled; )
   Active: active (running) since Tue 2019-04-23 13:44:20 EDT; 5s ago
 Main PID: 23980 (pecan)
    Tasks: 1 (limit: 4915)
   Memory: 20.1M
   CGroup: /system.slice/hello-world.service
           └─23980 /opt/http/bin/python /opt/http/bin/pecan serve config.py

Apr 23 13:44:20 huando systemd[1]: Started hello world pecan service.
```

The service is running and fully operational. Verify it once again on port 8080 to make sure that the framework is up and running and responding to requests:

```
$ curl localhost:8080
Hello, World!
```

If you stop the service with `systemctl stop hello-world`, the `curl` command will report a connection failure once again.

So far, we have created and installed the unit, verified it works by starting and stopping the service, and checked if the Pecan framework is responding to requests on its default port. You want this service up and running if the server reboots at any time, and this is where the `Install` section helps. Let's enable the service:

```
$ systemctl enable hello-world
Created symlink hello-world.service → /etc/systemd/system/hello-world.service.
```

When the server restarts, the small HTTP API service is up and running.

Log Handling

Since this is a configured service with logging configuration (all `stdout` and `stderr` is going directly into `systemd`), the handling works *for free*. No need to configure file-based logging, rotation, or even expiration. There are a few interesting and very nice features provided by `systemd` that allow you to interact with logs, such as limiting the time range and filtering by unit or process ID.

The command to interact with logs from a unit is done through the `journalctl` command-line tool. This process might be a surprise if expecting another subcommand from `systemd` to provide the logging helpers.

Since we started the service and sent some requests to it via `curl` in the previous section, let's see what the logs say:

```
$ journalctl -u hello-world
-- Logs begin at Mon 2019-04-15 09:05:11 EDT, end at Tue 2019-04-23
Apr 23 13:44:20 srv1 systemd[1]: Started hello world pecan service.
Apr 23 13:44:44 srv1 pecan[23980] [INFO    ] [pecan.commands.serve] GET / 200
Apr 23 13:44:55 srv1 systemd[1]: Stopping hello world pecan service...
Apr 23 13:44:55 srv1 systemd[1]: hello-world.service: Main process exited
Apr 23 13:44:55 srv1 systemd[1]: hello-world.service: Succeeded.
Apr 23 13:44:55 srv1 systemd[1]: Stopped hello world pecan service.
```

The `-u` flag specifies the *unit*, which in this case is `hello-world`, but you can also use a pattern or even specify multiple units.

A common way to *follow* a log as it produces entries is to use the `tail` command. Specifically, this looks like:

```
$ tail -f pecan-access.log
```

The command to accomplish the same thing with `journalctl` looks slightly different, but it *works in the same way*:

```
$ journalctl -fu hello-world
Apr 23 13:44:44 srv1 pecan[23980][INFO][pecan.commands.serve] GET / 200
Apr 23 13:44:44 srv1 pecan[23980][INFO][pecan.commands.serve] GET / 200
Apr 23 13:44:44 srv1 pecan[23980][INFO][pecan.commands.serve] GET / 200
```

If the `systemd` package is available with the `pcre2` engine, it allows you to use `--grep`. This further filters out log entries based on a pattern.

The -f flag means to *follow* the log, and it starts from the most recent entries and continues to show the entries as they happen, just like `tail -f` would. In production, the number of logs may be too many, and errors might have been showing up *today*. In those cases, you can use a combination of `--since` and `--until`. Both these flags accept a few different types of parameters:

- today
- yesterday
- "3 hours ago"
- -1h
- -15min
- -1h35min

In our small example, `journalctl` is unable to find anything for the last 15 minutes. At the beginning of the output, it informs us of the range and produces the entries, if any:

```
$ journalctl -u hello-world --since "-15min"
-- Logs begin at Mon 2019-04-15 09:05:11 EDT, end at Tue 2019-04-23
-- No entries --
```

Exercises

- Use three different commands to get log output from `systemd` using `journalctl`.
- Explain what the `WorkinDirectory` configuration option is for `systemd` units.
- Why is a changelog important?
- What is a *setup.py* file for?
- Name three differences between Debian and RPM packages.

Case Study Question

- Create a local instance of PyPI using `devpi`, upload a Python package, and then try to install that Python package from the local `devpi` instance.

## CHAPTER 6

Continuous Integration and Continuous Deployment

Author: Noah

The practices of continuous integration (CI) and continuous deployment (CD) are essential to a modern software development life cycle process. A CI system clones the codebase for the software under consideration from a source control system such as GitHub, builds the software into an artifact that can be a binary, a tar archive, or a Docker image, and, very importantly, also runs unit and/or integration tests for the software. A CD system deploys the artifacts built by the CI system to a target environment. This deployment can be automated for nonproduction environments, but usually includes a manual approval step for production. A more advanced type of such systems is a continuous delivery platform, which automates the deployment step to production and is capable of rolling back the deployment based on metrics obtained from monitoring and logging platforms.

Real-World Case Study: Converting a Poorly Maintained WordPress Site to Hugo

A while back, a friend asked for a favor fixing their company website. The company sold very expensive, used scientific equipment and its inventory was served via a WordPress site that was frequently hacked, performed horribly, or was down for days. Typically I try to avoid getting sucked into projects like this, but since it was a friend, I decided to help. You can reference the code for the conversion project at this Git repository (*https://oreil.ly/myos1*).

Each step of the conversion process is covered in the GitHub repo. The steps include:

1. Backup
2. Convert
3. Upgrade
4. Deploy

 The story had a funny ending. After creating a bulletproof, "tank" of a website that had incredible performance, security, auto-deployment, and incredible SEO, it ran for years with zero vulnerabilities or downtime. Long after I had forgotten about the project, I got a text from my friend. It had been a couple years since I had last talked with him. He said the website was down and he needed my help.

I texted back to him to ask how this was possible. It is running off Amazon S3 which has 99.999999999% uptime. He texted back that he had recently converted it back to WordPress because it was "easier" to make changes. I laughed and told him I wasn't a good fit for his project. As they say, no good deed is left unpunished.

Some of the requirements I considered were:

- It needed to be continuously deployed.
- It needed to be fast to run and develop against!
- It should be a static site hosted from a cloud provider.
- There should be a reasonable workflow for converting from WordPress.
- It should be possible to create a reasonable search interface using Python.

In the end I decided to use Hugo (*https://gohugo.io*), AWS (*https://aws.amazon.com*), and Algolia (*https://www.algolia.com*). The general architecture looked like Figure 6-1.

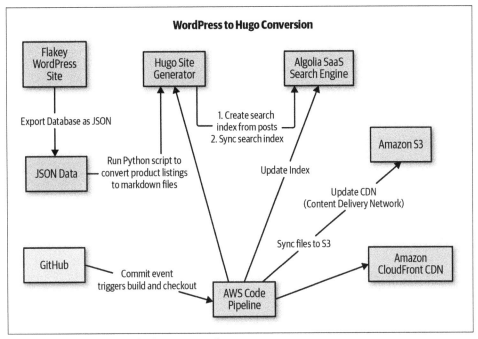

Figure 6-1. Continuous deployment with Hugo

Setting Up Hugo

Getting started with Hugo is very straightforward (see the getting started Hugo guide (*https://oreil.ly/r_Rcg*)). First, install the software. On my OS X machine I did it this way:

```
brew install hugo
```

If you already installed Hugo, you may need to upgrade:

```
Error: hugo 0.40.3 is already installed
To upgrade to 0.57.2, run brew upgrade hugo.
```

If you are on another platform, you can follow instructions here (*https://oreil.ly/ FfWdo*). To verify things are working, run `hugo version`:

```
(.python-devops) ➜ ~ hugo version
Hugo Static Site Generator v0.57.2/extended darwin/amd64 BuildDate: unknown
```

The only thing left to do is to initialize a skeleton Hugo app and install a theme:

```
hugo new site quickstart
```

This creates a new site called `quickstart`. You can build this site again, VERY QUICKLY, by running `hugo`. This compiles the markdown files to HTML and CSS.

Converting WordPress to Hugo Posts

Next, I converted the WordPress database to JSON via a raw dump. Then I wrote a Python script to convert this data into Hugo posts in markdown format. Here is that code:

```python
"""Conversion code of old database fields into markdown example.

If you did a database dump of WordPress and then converted it to JSON, you could
tweak this."""

import os
import shutil
from category import CAT
from new_picture_products import PICTURES

def check_all_category():
  ares = {}
  REC = []
  for pic in PICTURES:
    res  = check_category(pic)
    if not res:
      pic["categories"] = "Other"
      REC.append(pic)
      continue

    title,key = res
    if key:
      print("FOUND MATCH: TITLE--[%s], CATEGORY--[%s]" %\
        (title, key))
      ares[title]= key
      pic["categories"] = key
      REC.append(pic)
  return ares, REC

def check_category(rec):

  title = str(rec['title'])
  for key, values in CAT.items():
    print("KEY: %s, VALUE: %s" % (key, values))
    if title in key:
      return title,key
    for val in values:
      if title in val:
        return title,key

def move_image(val):
  """Creates a new copy of the uploaded images to img dir"""

  source_picture = "static/uploads/%s" % val["picture"]
  destination_dir = "static/img/"
  shutil.copy(source_picture, destination_dir)
```

```python
def new_image_metadata(vals):
    new_paths = []
    for val in vals:
        pic = val['picture'].split("/")[-1:].pop()
        destination_dir = "static/img/%s" % pic
        val['picture'] = destination_dir
        new_paths.append(val)
    return new_paths

CAT_LOOKUP = {'2100': 'Foo',
 'a': 'Biz',
 'b': 'Bam',
 'c': 'Bar',
 '1': 'Foobar',
 '2': 'bizbar',
 '3': 'bam'}

def write_post(val):

    tags = val["tags"]
    date = val["date"]
    title = val["title"]
    picture = val["picture"]
    categories = val["categories"]
    out = """
+++
tags = ["%s"]
categories = ["%s"]
date = "%s"
title = "%s"
banner = "%s"
+++
[![%s](%s)](%s)
 **Product Name**: %s""" % \
 (tags, categories, date, title, picture.lstrip("/"),
   title, picture, picture, title)

    filename = "../content/blog/%s.md" % title
    if os.path.exists(filename):
        print("Removing: %s" % filename)
        os.unlink(filename)

    with open(filename, 'a') as the_file:
        the_file.write(out)

if __name__ == '__main__':
    from new_pic_category import PRODUCT
    for product in PRODUCT:
        write_post(product)
```

Creating an Algolia Index and Updating It

With the database products converted to markdown posts, the next step is to write some Python code that creates an Algolia index and syncs it. Algolia (*https://www.algolia.com*) is a great tool to use because it quickly solves the search engine problem and has nice Python support as well.

This script crawls through all of the markdown files and generates a search index that can be uploaded to Algolia:

```python
"""
Creates a very simple JSON index for Hugo to import into Algolia. Easy to extend.

#might be useful to run this on content directory to remove spaces
for f in *\ *; do mv "$f" "${f// /_}"; done

"""
import os
import json

CONTENT_ROOT = "../content/products"
CONFIG = "../config.toml"
INDEX_PATH = "../index.json"

def get_base_url():
    for line in open(CONFIG):
        if line.startswith("baseurl"):
            url = line.split("=")[-1].strip().strip('"')
            return url

def build_url(base_url, title):

    url = "<a href='%sproducts/%s'>%s</a>" %\
        (base_url.strip(), title.lower(), title)
    return url

def clean_title(title):
    title_one = title.replace("_", " ")
    title_two = title_one.replace("-", " ")
    title_three = title_two.capitalize()
    return title_three

def build_index():
    baseurl = get_base_url()
    index =[]
    posts = os.listdir(CONTENT_ROOT)
    for line in posts:
        print("FILE NAME: %s" % line)
        record = {}
        title = line.strip(".md")
        record['url'] = build_url(baseurl, title)
        record['title'] = clean_title(title)
```

```
        print("INDEX RECORD: %s" % record)
        index.append(record)
    return index

def write_index():
    index = build_index()
    with open(INDEX_PATH, 'w') as outfile:
        json.dump(index,outfile)

if __name__ == '__main__':
    write_index()
```

Finally, the index can be sent to Algolia with this snippet:

```
import json
from algoliasearch import algoliasearch

def update_index():
    """Deletes index, then updates it"""
    print("Starting Updating Index")
    client = algoliasearch.Client("YOUR_KEY", "YOUR_VALUE")
    index = client.init_index("your_INDEX")
    print("Clearing index")
    index.clear_index()
    print("Loading index")
    batch = json.load(open('../index.json'))
    index.add_objects(batch)

if __name__ == '__main__':
    update_index()
```

Orchestrating with a Makefile

Using a `Makefile` allows you to replicate the steps your deployment process will use later. I typically set up a `Makefile` to orchestrate this locally. Here is what the entire build and deploy process looks like:

```
build:
  rm -rf public
  hugo

watch: clean
  hugo server -w

create-index:
  cd algolia;python make_algolia_index.py;cd ..

update-index:
  cd algolia;python sync_algolia_index.py;cd ..

make-index: create-index update-index
```

```
clean:
  -rm -rf public

sync:
  aws s3 --profile <yourawsprofile> sync --acl \
    "public-read" public/ s3://example.com

build-deploy-local: build sync

all: build-deploy-local
```

Deploying with AWS CodePipeline

Amazon Web Services (AWS) is a common deployment target for hosting a static website via Amazon S3, Amazon Route 53, and Amazon CloudFront. AWS CodePipeline, their build server service, works very well as the deployment mechanism for these sites. You can log into AWS CodePipeline, set up a new build project, and tell it to use a *buildspec.yml* file. The code can be customized and the portions that are templated out can be replaced with actual values.

As soon as GitHub gets a change event, CodePipeline runs the install in a container. First it grabs the specific version of Hugo specified. Next it builds the Hugo pages. Thousands of Hugo pages can be rendered subsecond because of the speed of Go.

Finally, the HTML pages are synced to Amazon S3. Because this is running inside of AWS and is synced, it is also extremely fast. The final step is that CloudFront is invalidated:

```
version: 0.1

environment_variables:
  plaintext:
    HUGO_VERSION: "0.42"

phases:
  install:
    commands:
      - cd /tmp
      - wget https://github.com/gohugoio/hugo/releases/\
      download/v${HUGO_VERSION}/hugo_${HUGO_VERSION}_Linux-64bit.tar.gz
      - tar -xzf hugo_${HUGO_VERSION}_Linux-64bit.tar.gz
      - mv hugo /usr/bin/hugo
      - cd -
      - rm -rf /tmp/*
  build:
    commands:
      - rm -rf public
      - hugo
  post_build:
    commands:
      - aws s3 sync public/ s3://<yourwebsite>.com/ --region us-west-2 --delete
```

```
  - aws s3 cp s3://<yourwebsite>.com/\
  s3://<yourwebsite>.com/ --metadata-directive REPLACE \
    --cache-control 'max-age=604800' --recursive
  - aws cloudfront create-invalidation --distribution-id=<YOURID> --paths '/*'
  - echo Build completed on `date`
```

Real-World Case Study: Deploying a Python App Engine Application with Google Cloud Build

Back in 2008 I wrote the very first article on using Google App Engine. You have to use the Wayback Machine to get it from the O'Reilly blog (*https://oreil.ly/8LoIf*).

Here is a reboot for the modern era. This is another version of Google App Engine, but this time it uses Google Cloud Build (*https://oreil.ly/MllhM*). The Google Cloud Platform (GCP) Cloud Build works a lot like AWS CodePipeline. Here is a config file that is checked into a GitHub repo. The config file is named *cloudbuild.yaml*. You can see all of the source code for this project in this Git repository (*https://oreil.ly/vxsnc*):

```
steps:
- name: python:3.7
  id: INSTALL
  entrypoint: python3
  args:
  - '-m'
  - 'pip'
  - 'install'
  - '-t'
  - '.'
  - '-r'
  - 'requirements.txt'
- name: python:3.7
  entrypoint: ./pylint_runner
  id: LINT
  waitFor:
  - INSTALL
- name: "gcr.io/cloud-builders/gcloud"
  args: ["app", "deploy"]
timeout: "1600s"
images: ['gcr.io/$PROJECT_ID/pylint']
```

Note that the *cloudbuild.yaml* file installs the packages seen here in the *require-ments.txt* file and also runs `gcloud app deploy`, which deploys the App Engine application on check-in to GitHub:

```
Flask==1.0.2
gunicorn==19.9.0
pylint==2.3.1
```

Here is a walk-through of how to set up this entire project:

1. Create the project.
2. Activate the cloud shell.
3. Refer to the hello world docs for the Python 3 App Engine (*https://oreil.ly/zgf5J*).
4. Run describe:

```bash
verify project is working
```
```bash
gcloud projects describe $GOOGLE_CLOUD_PROJECT
```

```bash
output of command:
```
```bash
createTime: '2019-05-29T21:21:10.187Z'
lifecycleState: ACTIVE
name: helloml
projectId: helloml-xxxxx
projectNumber: '881692383648'
```

5. You may want to verify that you have the correct project. If not, do this to switch:

```
gcloud config set project $GOOGLE_CLOUD_PROJECT
```

6. Create the App Engine app:

```
gcloud app create
```

   This will ask for the region. Go ahead and pick us-central [12].

```
Creating App Engine application in project [helloml-xxx]
and region [us-central]....done.
Success! The app is now created.
Please use `gcloud app deploy` to deploy your first app.
```

7. Clone the hello world sample app repo:

```
git clone https://github.com/GoogleCloudPlatform/python-docs-samples
```

8. cd into the repo:

```
cd python-docs-samples/appengine/standard_python37/hello_world
```

9. Update the Cloudshell image (note that this is optional):

```
git clone https://github.com/noahgift/gcp-hello-ml.git
# Update .cloudshellcustomimagerepo.json with project and image name
# TIP: enable "Boost Mode" in in Cloudshell
cloudshell env build-local
cloudshell env push
cloudshell env update-default-image
# Restart Cloudshell VM
```

10. Create and source the virtual environment:

```
virtualenv --python $(which python) venv
source venv/bin/activate
```

Double-check that it works:

```
which python
/home/noah_gift/python-docs-samples/appengine/\
    standard_python37/hello_world/venv/bin/python
```

11. Activate the cloud shell editor.

12. Install the packages:

```
pip install -r requirements.txt
```

This should install Flask:

```
Flask==1.0.2
```

13. Run Flask locally. This runs Flask locally in the GCP shell:

```
python main.py
```

14. Use the web preview (see Figure 6-2).

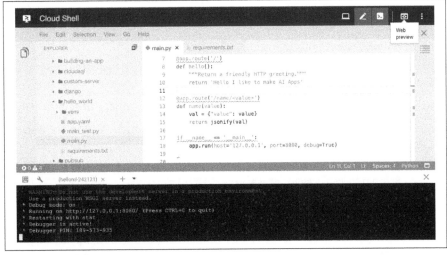

Figure 6-2. Web preview

15. Update *main.py*:

```
from flask import Flask
from flask import jsonify

app = Flask(__name__)

@app.route('/')
def hello():
    """Return a friendly HTTP greeting."""
```

```
    return 'Hello I like to make AI Apps'

@app.route('/name/<value>')
def name(value):
    val = {"value": value}
    return jsonify(val)

if __name__ == '__main__':
    app.run(host='127.0.0.1', port=8080, debug=True)
```

16. Test out passing in parameters to exercise this function:

```
@app.route('/name/<value>')
def name(value):
    val = {"value": value}
    return jsonify(val)
```

For example, calling this route will take the word *lion* and pass it into the name function in Flask:

```
https://8080-dot-3104625-dot-devshell.appspot.com/name/lion
```

Returns a value in the web browser:

```
{
value: "lion"
}
```

17. Now deploy the app:

```
gcloud app deploy
```

Be warned! The first deploy could take about 10 minutes. You might also need to enable the cloud build API.

```
Do you want to continue (Y/n)?  y
Beginning deployment of service [default]...
╔═══════════════════════════════════════════════════════╗
╠═ Uploading 934 files to Google Cloud Storage         ═╣
```

18. Now stream the log files:

```
gcloud app logs tail -s default
```

19. The production app is deployed and should like this:

```
Setting traffic split for service [default]...done.
Deployed service [default] to [https://helloml-xxx.appspot.com]
You can stream logs from the command line by running:
  $ gcloud app logs tail -s default

  $ gcloud app browse
(venv) noah_gift@cloudshell:~/python-docs-samples/appengine/\
  standard_python37/hello_world (helloml-242121)$ gcloud app
 logs tail -s default
Waiting for new log entries...
```

```
2019-05-29 22:45:02 default[2019]    [2019-05-29 22:45:02 +0000] [8]
2019-05-29 22:45:02 default[2019]    [2019-05-29 22:45:02 +0000] [8]
 (8)
2019-05-29 22:45:02 default[2019]    [2019-05-29 22:45:02 +0000] [8]
2019-05-29 22:45:02 default[2019]    [2019-05-29 22:45:02 +0000] [25]
2019-05-29 22:45:02 default[2019]    [2019-05-29 22:45:02 +0000] [27]
2019-05-29 22:45:04 default[2019]    "GET /favicon.ico HTTP/1.1" 404
2019-05-29 22:46:25 default[2019]    "GET /name/usf HTTP/1.1" 200
```

20. Add a new route and test it out:

```
@app.route('/html')
def html():
    """"Returns some custom HTML"""
    return """
    <title>This is a Hello World World Page</title>
    <p>Hello</p>
    <p><b>World</b></p>
    """
```

21. Install Pandas and return JSON results. At this point, you may want to consider creating a Makefile and doing this:

```
touch Makefile
#this goes inside that file
install:
    pip install -r requirements.txt
```

You also may want to set up lint:

```
pylint --disable=R,C main.py
-----------------------------------
Your code has been rated at 10.00/10
```

The web route syntax looks like the following block. Add Pandas import at the top:

```
import pandas as pd

@app.route('/pandas')
def pandas_sugar():
    df = pd.read_csv(
      "https://raw.githubusercontent.com/noahgift/sugar/\
      master/data/education_sugar_cdc_2003.csv")
    return jsonify(df.to_dict())
```

When you call the route https://<yourapp>.appspot.com/pandas, you should get something like Figure 6-3.

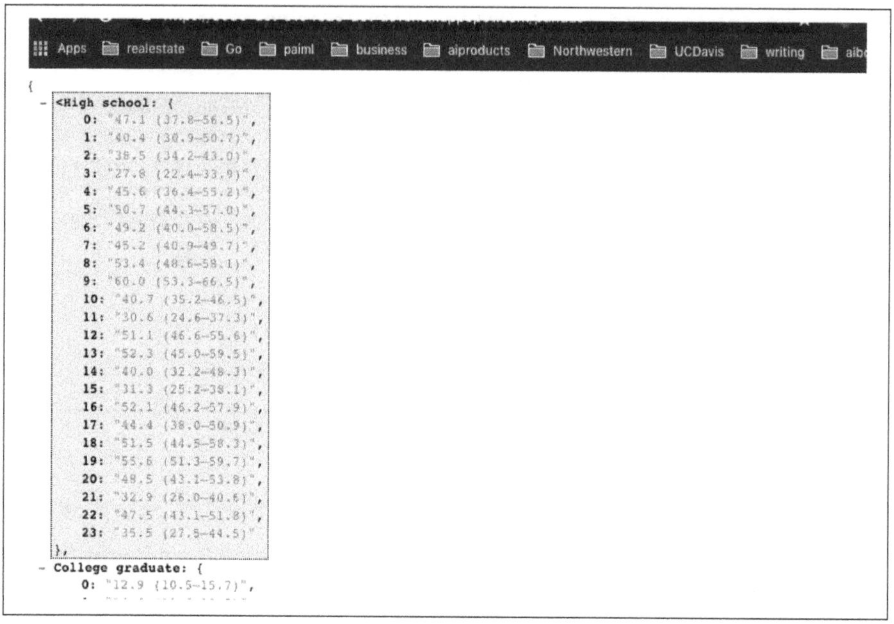

Figure 6-3. Example of JSON out

22. Add this Wikipedia route:

```
import wikipedia
@app.route('/wikipedia/<company>')
def wikipedia_route(company):
    result = wikipedia.summary(company, sentences=10)
    return result
```

23. Add NLP to the app:

   a. Run IPython Notebook (*https://oreil.ly/c564z*).

   b. Enable the Cloud Natural Language API.

   c. Run `pip install google-cloud-language`:

```
In [1]: from google.cloud import language
   ...: from google.cloud.language import enums
   ...:
   ...: from google.cloud.language import types
In [2]:
In [2]: text = "LeBron James plays for the Cleveland Cavaliers."
   ...: client = language.LanguageServiceClient()
   ...: document = types.Document(
   ...:         content=text,
   ...:         type=enums.Document.Type.PLAIN_TEXT)
   ...: entities = client.analyze_entities(document).entities
In [3]: entities
```

24. Here is an end-to-end AI API example:

```python
from flask import Flask
from flask import jsonify
import pandas as pd
import wikipedia


app = Flask(__name__)

@app.route('/')
def hello():
    """Return a friendly HTTP greeting."""
    return 'Hello I like to make AI Apps'

@app.route('/name/<value>')
def name(value):
    val = {"value": value}
    return jsonify(val)

@app.route('/html')
def html():
    """Returns some custom HTML"""
    return """
    <title>This is a Hello World World Page</title>
    <p>Hello</p>
    <p><b>World</b></p>
    """
@app.route('/pandas')
def pandas_sugar():
    df = pd.read_csv(
        "https://raw.githubusercontent.com/noahgift/sugar/\
        master/data/education_sugar_cdc_2003.csv")
    return jsonify(df.to_dict())

@app.route('/wikipedia/<company>')
def wikipedia_route(company):

    # Imports the Google Cloud client library
    from google.cloud import language
    from google.cloud.language import enums
    from google.cloud.language import types
    result = wikipedia.summary(company, sentences=10)

    client = language.LanguageServiceClient()
    document = types.Document(
        content=result,
        type=enums.Document.Type.PLAIN_TEXT)
    entities = client.analyze_entities(document).entities
    return str(entities)
```

```
if __name__ == '__main__':
    app.run(host='127.0.0.1', port=8080, debug=True)
```

This section has shown how to both set up an App Engine application from scratch in the Google Cloud Shell, as well as how to do continuous delivery using GCP Cloud Build.

Real-World Case Study: NFSOPS

NFOPS is an operational technique that uses NFS (Network File System) mount points to manage clusters of computers. It sounds like it is a new thing, but it has been around since Unix has been around. Noah used NFS mount points on Caltech's Unix systems back in 2000 to manage and maintain software. What is old is new again.

As a part-time consultant at a virtual reality startup in San Francisco, one problem I faced was how to build a jobs framework, quickly, that would dispatch work to thousands of AWS Spot Instances.

The solution that ultimately worked was to use NFSOPS (Figure 6-4) to deploy Python code to thousands of Computer Vision Spot Instances subsecond.

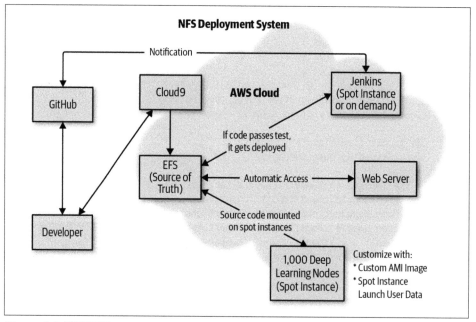

Figure 6-4. NFSOPS

NFSOPS works by using a build server, in this case Jenkins, to mount several Amazon Elastic File System (EFS) mount points (DEV, STAGE, PROD). When a continuous integration build is performed, the final step is an rsync to the respective mount point:

```
#Jenkins deploy build step
rsync -az --delete * /dev-efs/code/
```

The "deploy" is then subsecond to the mount point. When spot instances are launched by the thousands, they are preconfigured to mount EFS (the NFS mount points) and use the source code. This is a handy deployment pattern that optimizes for simplicity and speed. It can also work quite well in tandom with IAC, Amazon Machine Image (AMI), or Ansible.

## CHAPTER 7

Monitoring and Logging

When Noah worked in startups in San Francisco, he used his lunch break to exercise. He would play basketball, run up to Coit Tower, or practice Brazilian Jiu-Jitsu. Most of the startups Noah worked at would have a catered lunch.

He discovered a very unusual pattern coming back from lunch. There was never anything unhealthy left to eat. The leftovers were often full salads, fruit, vegetables, or healthy lean meats. The hordes of startup workers ate all of the unhealthy options while he was exercising, leaving zero temptation to eat bad food. There is something to be said for not following the crowd.

Likewise, the easy path is to ignore operations when developing machine learning models, mobile apps, and web apps. Ignoring operations is so typical it is like eating the chips, soda, and ice cream at the catered lunch. Being normal isn't necessarily preferred, though. In this chapter, the "salad and lean meats" approach to software development is described.

Key Concepts in Building Reliable Systems

Having built companies for a while, it's fun to look at what worked on the software engineering portion versus what didn't. One of the best antipatterns out there is "trust me." Any sane DevOps professional will not trust humans. They are flawed, make emotional mistakes, and can destroy entire companies on a whim. Especially if they are the company's founder.

Instead of a hierarchy based on complete nonsense, a better approach to building reliable systems is to build them piece by piece. In additional, when creating the platform, failure should be expected regularly. The only thing that will affect this truism is if a powerful person is involved in building the architecture. In that case, this truism will be exponentially increased.

You may have heard of the chaos monkey from Netflix, but why bother with that? Instead, let the founders of your company, the CTO, or the VP of Engineering do drive-by coding and second-guess your architecture and codebase. The human chaos monkey will run circles around Netflix. Better yet, let them compile jar files in the middle of production outages and put them on nodes one by one, via SSH, all the while yelling, "This will do the trick!" In this way, the harmonic mean of chaos and ego is achieved.

What is the action item for a sane DevOps professional? Automation is greater than hierarchy. The only solution to the chaos of startups is automation, skepticism, humility, and immutable DevOps principles.

Immutable DevOps Principles

It is hard to imagine a better place to start to build a reliable system than this immutable principle. If the CTO is building Java `.jar` files from a laptop to fix production fires, you should just quit your job. There is nothing that will save your company. We should know—we've been there!

No matter how smart/powerful/charismatic/creative/rich a person is, if they are manually applying critical changes in a crisis to your software platform, you are already dead. You just don't know it yet. The alternative to this monstrous existence is automation.

Humans cannot be involved in deploying software in the long term. This is the #1 antipattern that exists in the software industry. It is essentially a back door for hooligans to wreak havoc on your platform. Instead, deploying software, testing software, and building software needs to be 100% automated.

The most significant initial impact you can have in a company is to set up continuous integration and continuous delivery. Everything else pales in comparison.

Centralized Logging

Logging follows close behind automation in importance. In large-scale, distributed systems, logging isn't optional. Special attention must be paid to logging at both the application level and the environment level.

For example, exceptions should always be sent to the centralized logging system. On the other hand, while developing software, it is often a good idea to create debug logging instead of print statements. Why do this? Many hours are spent developing heuristics to debug the source code. Why not capture that so it can be turned on if a problem surfaces in production again?

The trick here is logging levels. By creating debug log levels that only appear in the nonproduction environment, it allows the logic of debugging to be kept in the source code. Likewise, instead of having overly verbose logs appear in production and add confusion, they can be toggled on and off.

An example of logging in large-scale distributed systems is what Ceph (*https://ceph.com*) uses: daemons can have up to 20 debug levels! All of these levels are handled in code, allowing the system to fine-tune the amount of logging. Ceph furthers this strategy by being able to restrict the amount of logging per daemon. The system has a few daemons, and the logging can be increased for one or all of them.

Case Study: Production Database Kills Hard Drives

Another vital strategy for logging is solving scalability. Once the application is large enough, it might not be feasible to store all logs in a file anymore. Alfredo was once tasked to debug a problem with the primary database of an extensive web application that hosted about one hundred newspaper, radio station, and television station sites. These sites generated lots of traffic and produced massive amounts of logs. So much log output was created that the logging for PostgreSQL was set to a minimum, and he couldn't debug the problem because it required raising the log level. If the log level was raised, the application would stop working from the intense I/O generated. Every day at around five o'clock in the morning, the database load spiked. It had gotten progressively worse.

The database administrators were opposed to raising the log levels to see the most expensive queries (PostgreSQL can include query information in the logs) for a whole day, so we compromised: fifteen minutes at around five o'clock in the morning. As soon as he was able to get those logs, Alfredo immediately got to rate the slowest queries and how often they were run. There was a clear winner: a SELECT * query that was taking so long to complete that the fifteen-minute window was not enough to capture its runtime. The application didn't do any queries that selected everything from any table; what could it be?

After much persuasion, we got access to the database server. If the spike in load happens at around five o'clock in the morning *every single day*, is it possible that there is some recurrent script? We looked into crontab (the program that keeps track of what runs at given intervals), which showed a suspicious script: *backup.sh*. The contents of the script had a few SQL statements that included several SELECT *. The database administrators were using this to back up the primary database, and as the size of the database grew, so did the load until it was no longer tolerable. The solution? Stop using the script, and back up one of the four secondary (replica) databases.

That saved the backup problem, but it didn't help the inability to have access to logs. Thinking ahead on distributing logging output is the right approach. Tools like rsyslog (*https://www.rsyslog.com*) are meant to solve this, and if added from the start, it can save you from being unable to solve a production outage.

Did You Build It or Buy It?

It is incredible how much *vendor lock-in* gets press. Vendor lock-in, though, is in the eye of the beholder. You can pretty much throw a rock in any direction in downtown San Francisco and hit someone preaching the evils of vendor lock-in. When you dig a little deeper though, you wonder what their alternative is.

In Economics, there is a principle called comparative advantage. In a nutshell, it means there is an economic benefit to focusing on what you are best at and outsourcing other tasks to other people. With the cloud, in particular, there is continuous improvement, and end-users benefit from that improvement without an aggregated cost—and most of the time with less complexity than before.

Unless your company is operating at the scale of one of the giants in technology, there is almost no way to implement, maintain, and improve a private cloud and be able to save money and improve the business at the same time. For example, in 2017, Amazon released the ability to deploy multimaster databases with automatic failover across multiple *Availability Zones*. As someone who has attempted this, I can say that it is borderline impossible and tremendously hard to add the ability of automatic failover in such a scenario. One of the golden questions to consider regarding outsourcing is: *"Is this a core competency of the business?"* A company that runs its own mail server but its core competency is selling car parts is playing with fire and probably already losing money.

Fault Tolerance

Fault tolerance is a fascinating topic but it can be very confusing. What is meant by fault tolerance, and how can you achieve it? A great place to learn more about fault tolerance is to read as many white papers from AWS (*https://oreil.ly/zYuls*) as you can.

When designing fault-tolerant systems, it's useful to start by trying to answer the following question: when this service goes down, what can I implement to eliminate (or reduce) manual interaction? Nobody likes getting notifications that a critical system is down, especially when this means numerous steps to recover, even less when it takes communication with other services to ensure everything is back to normal. Note that the question is not being framed as an improbable event, it explicitly acknowledges that the service will go down and that some work will needed done to get it up and running.

A while ago, a full redesign of a complex build system was planned. The build system did several things, most of them related to packaging and releasing the software: dependencies had to be in check, make and other tooling built binaries, RPM and Debian packages were produced, and repositories for different Linux distributions (like CentOS, Debian, and Ubuntu) were created and hosted. The main requirement for this build system was that it had to be fast.

Although speed was one of the primary objectives, when designing a system that involves several steps and different components, it is useful to address the known pain points and try hard to prevent new ones. There are always going to be unknowns in large systems, but using the right strategies for logging (and logging aggregation), monitoring, and recovery are crucial.

Turning our attention back to the build system, one of the problems was that the machines that created the repositories were somewhat complex: an HTTP API received packages for a particular project at a specific version, and repositories were generated automatically. This process involved a database, a RabbitMQ service for asynchronous task handling, and massive amounts of storage to keep repositories around, served by Nginx. Finally, some status reporting would be sent to a central dashboard, so developers could check where in the build process their branch was. It was *crucial* to design everything around the possibility of this service going down.

A big note was added to the whiteboard that read: "ERROR: the repo service is down because the disk is full." The task was not necessarily to prevent a disk being full, but to create a system that can continue working with a full disk, and when the problem is solved, almost no effort is required to put it back into the system. The "full disk" error was a fictional one that could've been anything, like RabbitMQ not running, or a DNS problem, but exemplified the task at hand perfectly.

It is difficult to understand the importance of monitoring, logging, and sound design patterns until a piece of the puzzle doesn't work, and it is impossible to determine the *why* and the *how*. You need to know why it went down so that prevention steps can be instrumented (alerts, monitoring, and self-recovery) to avoid this problem from repeating itself in the future.

To allow this system to continue to work, we split the load into five machines, all of them equal and doing the same work: creating and hosting repositories. The nodes creating the binaries would query an API for a healthy repo machine, which in turn would send an HTTP request to query the /health/ endpoint of the next build server on its list. If the server reported healthy, the binaries would go there; otherwise, the API would pick the next one on the list. If a node failed a health check three times in a row, it was put out of rotation. All a sysadmin had to do to get it back into rotation after a fix was to restart the repository service. (The repository service had a self-health assessment that if successful would notify the API that it was ready to do work.)

Although the implementation was not bulletproof (work was still needed to get a server up, and notifications weren't always accurate), it had a tremendous impact on the maintenance of the service when restoration was required, and kept everything still functioning in a degraded state. This is what fault tolerance is all about!

Monitoring

Monitoring is one of those things where one can do almost nothing and still claim that a monitoring system is in place (as an intern, Alfredo once used a `curl` cronjob to check a production website), but can grow to be so complicated that the production environment seems nimble in comparison. When done right, monitoring and reporting, in general, can help answer the most difficult questions of a production life cycle. It's crucial to have and difficult to get right. This is why there are many companies that specialize in monitoring, alerting, and metric visualization.

At its core, there are two paradigms most services fall into: pull and push. This chapter will cover Prometheus (pull) and Graphite with StatsD (push). Understanding when one is a better choice than the other, and the caveats, is useful when adding monitoring to environments. Most importantly, it's practical to know both and have the ability to deploy whichever services that will work best in a given scenario.

Reliable time-series software has to withstand incredibly high rates of incoming transactional information, be able to store that information, correlate it with time, support querying, and offer a graphical interface that can be customized with filters and queries. In essence, it must almost be like a high-performing database, but specific to time, data manipulation, and visualization.

Graphite

Graphite is a data store for numerical time-based data: it keeps numeric information that correlates to the time it was captured and saves it according to customizable rules. It offers a *very powerful* API that can be queried for information about its data, with time ranges, and also apply *functions* that can transform or perform computations in data.

An important aspect of Graphite (*https://oreil.ly/-0YEs*) is that it *does not collect data*; instead, it concentrates on its API and ability to handle immense amounts of data for periods of time. This forces users to think about what collecting software to deploy along with Graphite. There are quite a few options to choose from for shipping metrics over to Graphite; in this chapter we will cover one of those options, StatsD.

Another interesting aspect of Graphite is that although it comes with a web application that can render graphs on demand, it is common to deploy a different service that can use Graphite directly as a backend for graphs. An excellent example of this is the fantastic Grafana project (*https://grafana.com*), which provides a fully-featured web application for rendering metrics.

StatsD

Graphite allows you to push metrics to it via TCP or UDP, but using something like StatsD is especially nice because there are instrumentation options in Python that allow workflows such as aggregating metrics over UDP and then shipping them over to Graphite. This type of setup makes sense for Python applications that shouldn't block to send data over (TCP connections will block until a response is received; UDP will not). If a very time-expensive Python loop is being captured for metrics, it wouldn't make sense to add the time it takes to communicate to a service that is capturing metrics.

In short, sending metrics to a StatsD service feels like no cost at all (as it should be!). With the Python instrumentation available, measuring everything is very straightforward. Once a StatsD service has enough metrics to ship to Graphite, it will start the process to send the metrics over. All of this occurs in a completely asynchronous fashion, helping the application to continue. Metrics, monitoring, and logging should never impact a production application in any way!

When using StatsD, the data pushed to it is aggregated and flushed to a configurable backend (such as Graphite) at given intervals (which default to 10 seconds). Having deployed a combination of Graphite and StatsD in several production environments, it has been easier to use one StatsD instance on every application server instead of a single instance for all applications. That type of deployment allows more straightforward configuration and tighter security: configuration on all app servers will point to the `localhost` StatsD service and no external ports will need to be opened. At the end, StatsD will ship the metrics over to Graphite in an outbound UDP connection. This also helps by spreading the load by pushing the scalability further down the pipeline into Graphite.

StatsD is a `Node.js` daemon, so installing it means pulling in the `Node.js` dependency. It is certainly *not* a Python project!

Prometheus

In a lot of ways, Prometheus (*https://prometheus.io*) is very similar to Graphite (powerful queries and visualization). The main difference is that it *pulls* information from sources, and it does this over HTTP. This requires services to expose HTTP endpoints to allow Prometheus to gather metric data. Another significant difference from Graphite is that it has baked-in alerting, where rules can be configured to trigger alerts or make use of the `Alertmanager`: a component in charge of dealing with alerts, silencing them, aggregating them, and relaying them to different systems such as email, chat, and on-call platforms.

Some projects like Ceph (*https://ceph.com*) already have configurable options to enable Prometheus to scrape information at specific intervals. It's great when this type of integration is offered out of the box; otherwise, it requires running an HTTP instance somewhere that can expose metric data for a service. For example, in the case of the PostgreSQL database (*https://www.postgresql.org*), the Prometheus exporter is a container that runs an HTTP service exposing data. This might be *fine* in a lot of cases, but if there are already integrations to gather data with something, such as collectd (*https://collectd.org*), then running HTTP services might not work that well.

Prometheus is a great choice for short-lived data or time data that frequently changes, whereas Graphite is better suited for long-term historical information. Both offer a very advanced query language, but Prometheus is more powerful.

For Python, the `prometheus_client` (*https://oreil.ly/t9NtW*) is an excellent utility to start shipping metrics over to Prometheus; if the application is already web-based, the client has integrations for lots of different Python webservers, such as Twisted, WSGI, Flask, and even Gunicorn. Aside from that, it can also export all its data to expose it directly at a defined endpoint (versus doing it on a separate HTTP instance). If you want your web application exposing in `/metrics/`, then adding a handler that calls `prometheus_client.generate_latest()` will return the contents in the format that the Prometheus parser understands.

Create a small Flask application (save it to `web.py`) to get an idea how simple `gener ate_latest()` is to use, and make sure to install the `prometheus_client` package:

```
from flask import Response, Flask
import prometheus_client

app = Flask('prometheus-app')

@app.route('/metrics/')
def metrics():
    return Response(
        prometheus_client.generate_latest(),
        mimetype='text/plain; version=0.0.4; charset=utf-8'
    )
```

Run the app with the development server:

```
$ FLASK_APP=web.py flask run
 * Serving Flask app "web.py"
 * Environment: production
   WARNING: This is a development server.
   Use a production WSGI server instead.
 * Running on http://127.0.0.1:5000/ (Press CTRL+C to quit)
127.0.0.1 - - [07/Jul/2019 10:16:20] "GET /metrics HTTP/1.1" 308 -
127.0.0.1 - - [07/Jul/2019 10:16:20] "GET /metrics/ HTTP/1.1" 200 -
```

While the application is running, open a web browser and type in the URL *http://localhost:5000/metrics*. It starts generating output that Prometheus can collect, even if there is nothing really significant:

```
...
# HELP process_cpu_seconds_total Total user and system CPU time in seconds.
# TYPE process_cpu_seconds_total counter
process_cpu_seconds_total 0.27
# HELP process_open_fds Number of open file descriptors.
# TYPE process_open_fds gauge
process_open_fds 6.0
# HELP process_max_fds Maximum number of open file descriptors.
# TYPE process_max_fds gauge
process_max_fds 1024.0
```

Most production-grade web servers like Nginx and Apache can produce extensive metrics on response times and latency. For example, if adding that type of metric data to a Flask application, the middleware, where all requests can get recorded, would be a good fit. Apps will usually do other interesting things in a request, so let's add two more endpoints—one with a counter, and the other with a timer. These two new endpoints will generate metrics that will get processed by the prometheus_client library and reported when the /metrics/ endpoint gets requested over HTTP.

Adding a counter to our small app involves a couple of small changes. Create a new index endpoint:

```
@app.route('/')
def index():
    return '<h1>Development Prometheus-backed Flask App</h1>'
```

Now define the Counter object. Add the name of the counter (requests), a short description (Application Request Count), and at least one useful label (such as end point). This label will help identify where this counter is coming from:

```
from prometheus_client import Counter

REQUESTS = Counter(
    'requests', 'Application Request Count',
    ['endpoint']
)

@app.route('/')
def index():
    REQUESTS.labels(endpoint='/').inc()
    return '<h1>Development Prometheus-backed Flask App</h1>'
```

With the REQUESTS counter defined, include it in the index() function, restart the application, and make a couple of requests. If /metrics/ is then requested, the output should show some new activity we've created:

```
...
# HELP requests_total Application Request Count
# TYPE requests_total counter
requests_total{endpoint="/"} 3.0
# TYPE requests_created gauge
requests_created{endpoint="/"} 1.562512871203272e+09
```

Now add a `Histogram` object to capture details on an endpoint that sometimes takes a bit longer to reply. The code simulated this by sleeping for a randomized amount of time. Just like the index function, a new endpoint is needed as well, where the `Histogram` object is used:

```
from prometheus_client import Histogram

TIMER = Histogram(
    'slow', 'Slow Requests',
    ['endpoint']
)
```

The simulated expensive operation will use a function that tracks the start time and end time and then passes that information to the histogram object:

```
import time
import random

@app.route('/database/')
def database():
    with TIMER.labels('/database').time():
        # simulated database response time
        sleep(random.uniform(1, 3))
    return '<h1>Completed expensive database operation</h1>'
```

Two new modules are needed: `time` and `random`. Those will help calculate the time passed onto the histogram and simulate the expensive operation being performed in the database. Running the application once again and requesting the /database/ endpoint will start producing content when /metrics/ is polled. Several items that are measuring our simulation times should now appear:

```
# HELP slow Slow Requests
# TYPE slow histogram
slow_bucket{endpoint="/database",le="0.005"} 0.0
slow_bucket{endpoint="/database",le="0.01"} 0.0
slow_bucket{endpoint="/database",le="0.025"} 0.0
slow_bucket{endpoint="/database",le="0.05"} 0.0
slow_bucket{endpoint="/database",le="0.075"} 0.0
slow_bucket{endpoint="/database",le="0.1"} 0.0
slow_bucket{endpoint="/database",le="0.25"} 0.0
slow_bucket{endpoint="/database",le="0.5"} 0.0
slow_bucket{endpoint="/database",le="0.75"} 0.0
slow_bucket{endpoint="/database",le="1.0"} 0.0
slow_bucket{endpoint="/database",le="2.5"} 2.0
slow_bucket{endpoint="/database",le="5.0"} 2.0
```

```
slow_bucket{endpoint="/database",le="7.5"} 2.0
slow_bucket{endpoint="/database",le="10.0"} 2.0
slow_bucket{endpoint="/database",le="+Inf"} 2.0
slow_count{endpoint="/database"} 2.0
slow_sum{endpoint="/database"} 2.0021886825561523
```

The Histogram object is flexible enough that it can operate as a context manager, a decorator, or take in values directly. Having this flexibility is incredibly powerful and helps produce instrumentation that can work in most environments with little effort.

Instrumentation

At a company we are familiar with, there was this massive application that was used by several different newspapers—a giant monolithic web application that had no runtime monitoring. The ops team was doing a great job keeping an eye on system resources such as memory and CPU usage, but there was nothing checking how many API calls per second were going to the third-party video vendor, and how expensive these calls were. One could argue that that type of measurement is achievable with logging, and that wouldn't be wrong, but again, this is a massive monolithic application with absurd amounts of logging already.

The question here was how to introduce robust metrics with easy visualization and querying that wouldn't take three days of implementation training for developers and make it as easy as adding a logging statement in the code. Instrumentation of any technology at runtime has to be as close to the previous statement as possible. Any solution that drifts from that premise will have trouble being successful. If it is hard to query and visualize, then few people will care or pay attention. If it is hard to implement (and maintain!), then it might get dropped. If it is cumbersome for developers to add at runtime, then it doesn't matter if all the infrastructure and services are ready to receive metrics; nothing will get shipped over (or at least, nothing meaningful).

The python-statsd is an excellent (and tiny) library that pushes metrics over to StatsD (which later can be relayed to Graphite) and can help you understand how metrics can be instrumented easily. Having a dedicated module in an application that wraps the library is useful, because you will need to add customization that would become tedious if repeated everywhere.

 The Python client for StatsD has a few packages available on PyPI. For the purposes of these examples, use the python-statsd package. Install it in a virtual environment with pip install python-statsd. Failing to use the right client might cause import errors!

One of the simplest use cases is a counter, and the examples for `python-statsd` show something similar to this:

```
>>> import statsd
>>>
>>> counter = statsd.Counter('app')
>>> counter += 1
```

This example assumes a StatsD is running locally. Therefore there is no need to create a connection; the defaults work great here. But the call to the `Counter` class is passing a name (*app*) that will not work in a production environment. As described in "Naming Conventions" on page 176, it is crucial to have a good scheme that helps identify environments and locations of the stats, but it would be very repetitive if you had to do this everywhere. In some Graphite environments, a *secret* has to prefix the namespace on all metrics being sent as a means of authentication. This adds another layer that needs to be abstracted away so that it isn't needed when instrumenting metrics.

Some parts of the namespace, such as the secret, have to be configurable, and others can be programmatically assigned. Assuming there is a way to optionally prefix the namespace with a function called `get_prefix()`, this is how the `Counter` would get wrapped to provide a smooth interaction in a separate module. For the examples to work, create the new module, name it *metrics.py*, and add the following:

```
import statsd
import get_prefix


def Counter(name):
    return statsd.Counter("%s.%s" % (get_prefix(), name))
```

By following the same example used in "Naming Conventions" on page 176 for a small Python application that calls to the Amazon S3 API in a path such as *web/api/ aws.py*, the `Counter` can get instantiated like this:

```
from metrics import Counter

counter = Counter(__name__)

counter += 1
```

By using `__name__`, the `Counter` object is created with the full Python namespace of the module that will appear on the receiving side as `web.api.aws.Counter`. This works nicely, but it isn't flexible enough if we need more than one counter in loops that happen in different places. We must modify the wrapper so that a suffix is allowed:

```
import statsd
import get_prefix

def Counter(name, suffix=None):
```

```
    if suffix:
        name_parts = name.split('.')
        name_parts.append(suffix)
        name = '.'.join(name_parts)
    return statsd.Counter("%s.%s" % (get_prefix(), name))
```

If the *aws.py* file contains two places that require a counter, say a read and a write function for S3, then we can easily suffix them:

```
from metrics import Counter
import boto

def s3_write(bucket, filename):
    counter = Counter(__name__, 's3.write')
    conn = boto.connect_s3()
    bucket = conn.get_bucket(bucket)
    key = boto.s3.key.Key(bucket, filename)
    with open(filename) as f:
        key.send_file(f)
    counter += 1

def s3_read(bucket, filename):
    counter = Counter(__name__, 's3.read')
    conn = boto.connect_s3()
    bucket = conn.get_bucket(bucket)
    k = Key(bucket)
    k.key = filename
    counter += 1
    return k
```

These two helpers now have unique counters from the same wrapper, and if configured in a production environment, the metrics appear in a namespace similar to `secret.app1.web.api.aws.s3.write.Counter`. This level of granularity is helpful when trying to identify metrics per operation. Even if there are cases where granularity isn't needed, it is always better to have it and ignore it than to need it and not have it. Most metric dashboards allow customization for grouping metrics.

The suffix is useful when added to function names (or class methods) that hardly represent what they are or what they do, so improving the naming by using something meaningful is another benefit to this added flexibility:

```
def helper_for_expensive_operations_on_large_files():
    counter = Counter(__name__, suffix='large_file_operations')
    while slow_operation:
        ...
        counter +=1
```

Counters and other metric types such as gauges can be so easy to add that it might be tempting to include them in a loop, but for performance-critical code blocks that run thousands of times per second, it might be impactful to add these types of instrumentation. Limiting the metrics that are being sent or sending them later are good options to consider.

This section showed how to instrument metrics for a local StatsD service. This instance will end up relaying its metric data to a configured backend like Graphite, but these simplistic examples aren't meant to be a StatsD-only solution. To the contrary, they demonstrate that adding helpers and utilities to wrap common usage is a must, and when easy instrumentation exists, developers will want to add it everywhere. The problem of having too much metric data is preferable to having no metrics at all.

Naming Conventions

In most monitoring and metric services such as Graphite, Grafana, Prometheus, and even StatsD, there is a notion of namespaces. Namespaces are very important, and it is worth thinking carefully on a convention that will allow easy identification of system components, while at the same time allow enough flexibility to accommodate for growth or even change. These namespaces are similar to how Python uses them: a dot separates each name, and each separated part represents a step in a hierarchy from left to right. The first item from the left is the parent, and every subsequent part is a child.

For example, let's assume we have some API calls to AWS in a nimble Python application that serves images on a website. The Python module where we have the spot we want metrics is in a path like this: *web/api/aws.py*. The natural namespace choice for this path could be: `web.api.aws`, but what if we have more than one production app server? Once the metrics ship with one namespace, it's hard (almost impossible!) to change to a different scheme. Let's improve the namespace to help identify production servers: `{server_name}.web.api.aws`

Much better! But can you see another issue? When shipping metrics, a trailing name is sent over. In the case of counters example, the name would be something like: `{server_name}.web.api.aws.counter`. That is a problem because our little application does several calls to AWS like S3 and we may want to talk to other AWS services in the future. It is easier to fix child naming than parent naming, so in this case, it just requires developers to match metrics as granularly as possible to what is measured. For example, if we had an S3 module inside the *aws.py* file, it would make sense to include it to distinguish it from other pieces. The child portion of that metric would look like `aws.s3`, and a counter metric would end up looking like `aws.s3.counter`.

Having so many variables for namespaces can feel cumbersome, but most established metric services allow easy combinations, such as "show me count average for all S3 calls last week but only from production servers in the East Coast." Pretty powerful, huh?

There is another potential issue here. What do we do with production and staging environments? What if I'm developing and testing in a virtual machine somewhere? The {server_name} part might not help much here if everyone calls their development machine srv1. If deploying to different regions, or even if there is a plan to scale beyond a single region or country, an extra addition to the namespace can make sense as well. There are numerous ways to expand on namespaces to better fit an environment, but something like this is a suitable prefix: {region}.{prod|staging| dev}.{server_name}

Logging

It can be daunting to configure logging in Python correctly. The logging module is very performant and has several different outlets that can receive its output. Once you grasp its initial configuration, it isn't that complicated to add to it. We've been guilty of rewriting an alternative way of logging because of the dislike for configuring the logging module properly. This was a mistake, because it almost never accounted for all the things that the standard library module does well: multithreaded environments, unicode, and supporting multiple destinations other than STDOUT, just to name a few.

Python's logging module is so big and can be made to accommodate so many different uses (just like almost all software in this very distilled chapter), that not even a whole chapter would be sufficient to cover it all. This section will offer short examples for the simplest use cases, and then move progressively toward more complex uses. Once a few scenarios are well understood, it isn't hard to keep expanding logging into other configurations.

Even though it is complex and can take some time to fully comprehend, it is one of the *crucial pillars* of DevOps. You cannot be a successful DevOps person without it.

Why Is It Hard?

Python applications, like command-line tools and one-shot types of tools, usually have a top-to-bottom design and are very procedural. When you start learning development with something like Python (or perhaps Bash), it is reasonable to get used to that flow. Even when moving to more object-oriented programming and using more classes and modules, there is still this sense of declaring what you need, instantiating objects to use them, and so on. Modules and objects aren't usually preconfigured at import time, and it is not common to see some imported module be configured globally for the whole project even before being instantiated.

There is this sense of *"somehow this is configured and how is it possible if I haven't even called it yet."* Logging is like that; once configured at runtime, the module somehow persists this configuration regardless of where it is imported and used, and before creating loggers. This is all very convenient, but it is hard to get used to when almost nothing else works this way in the Python standard library!

The basicconfig

The easiest way out of logging configuration misery is to simply use `basicconfig`. It is a straightforward way to get logging working, with lots of defaults and about three lines worth of work:

```
>>> import logging
>>> logging.basicConfig()
>>> logger = logging.getLogger()
>>> logger.critical("this can't be that easy")
CRITICAL:root:this can't be that easy
```

With almost no need to understand anything about logging, messages appear and the module appears to be configured correctly. It is also good that it can support more customization and a few options that are well-suited for small applications that don't need highly customized logging interfaces. The format of the log messages and setting the verbosity are achieved with ease:

```
>>> import logging
>>> FORMAT = '%(asctime)s %(name)s %(levelname)s %(message)s'
>>> logging.basicConfig(format=FORMAT, level=logging.INFO)
>>> logger = logging.getLogger()
>>> logger.debug('this will probably not show up')
>>> logger.warning('warning is above info, should appear')
2019-07-08 08:31:08,493 root WARNING warning is above info, should appear
```

This example was configured to set the minimum level at INFO, which is why the debug message didn't emit anything. Formatting was passed into the `basicConfig` call to set the time, the name of the logging (more on that later in this section), the level name, and finally, the message. That is plenty for most applications, and it is good to know that a simple entry into logging can do so much already.

The problem with this type of configuration is that it will not be sufficient to take advantage of more complex scenarios. This configuration has a lot of defaults that might not be acceptable and will be cumbersome to change. If there is any possibility that the application will need something a bit more complicated, it is recommended to fully configure logging and go through the pain of understanding how to do that.

Deeper Configuration

The logging module has several different *loggers*; these loggers can be configured independently, and they can also inherit configuration from a *parent* logger. The top-most logger is the root logger, and all other loggers are child loggers (root is the parent). When configuring the root logger, you are essentially setting the configuration for *everything* globally. This way of organizing logging makes sense when different applications or different parts of a single application require different types of logging interfaces and settings.

If a web application wants to send WSGI server errors over email but log everything else to a file, this would be impossible to do if a single root-level logger was being configured. This is similar to "Naming Conventions" on page 176 in that the names are separated by dots, and every dot indicates a new child level. It means that app.wsgi could be configured to send error logs over email, while app.requests can be set separately with file-based logging.

 A nice way of dealing with this namespace is by using the same namespace as Python instead of using something custom. Do this by using *name* to create loggers in modules. Using the same namespace for both the project and logging prevents confusion.

Configuration of logging should be set as *early as possible*. If the application is a command-line tool, then the right place for it is at the main entry point, probably even before parsing arguments. For web applications, the logging configuration is usually through the framework's helpers. Most popular web frameworks today have a facility for logging configuration: Django, Flask, Pecan, and Pyramid all offer an interface for early logging configuration. Take advantage of it!

This example shows how to configure a command-line tool; you can see that there are a few similarities to basicConfig:

```
import logging
import os

BASE_FORMAT = "[%(name)s][%(levelname)-6s] %(message)s"
FILE_FORMAT = "[%(asctime)s]" + BASE_FORMAT

root_logger = logging.getLogger()
root_logger.setLevel(logging.DEBUG)

try:
    file_logger = logging.FileHandler('application.log')
except (OSError, IOError):
    file_logger = logging.FileHandler('/tmp/application.log')
```

```
file_logger.setLevel(logging.INFO)
file_logger.setFormatter(logging.Formatter(BASE_FORMAT))
root_logger.addHandler(file_logger)
```

A lot is happening here. The root logger is requested by calling getLogger() without any arguments, and the level is set at DEBUG. This is a good default to have, since other child loggers can modify the level. Next, the file logger gets configured. In this case, it tries to create the file logger that will fall back to a temporary location if it can't write to it. It then gets set at the INFO level, and its message format is changed to include a timestamp (useful for file-based log files).

Note how at the end, the file logger gets added to the root_logger. It feels counter-intuitive, but in this case, the root configuration is being set to handle everything. Adding a *stream handler* to the root logger will make the application send logs to both the file and standard error at the same time:

```
console_logger = logging.StreamHandler()
console_logger.setFormatter(BASE_FORMAT)
console_logger.setLevel(logging.WARNING)
root_logger.addHandler(console_logger)
```

In this case, the BASE_FORMAT was used, because it's going to the terminal, where time-stamps can cause excessive noise. As you can see, it takes quite a bit of configuration and settings, and it gets very complicated once we start dealing with different loggers. To minimize this, a separate module with a helper that sets all these options is preferable. As an alternative to this type of configuration, the logging module offers a dictionary-based configuration, where the settings are set in a key-value interface. The example below shows how the configuration would look for the same example.

To see it in action, add a couple of log calls at the end of the file, execute directly with Python, and save it in a file called *log_test.py*:

```
# root logger
logger = logging.getLogger()
logger.warning('this is an info message from the root logger')

app_logger = logging.getLogger('my-app')
app_logger.warning('an info message from my-app')
```

The root logger is the parent, and a new logger called my-app is introduced. Executing the file directly gives output in the terminal as well as in a file called *application.log*:

```
$ python log_test.py
[root][WARNING] this is an info message from the root logger
[my-app][WARNING] an info message from my-app
$ cat application.log
[2019-09-08 12:28:25,190][root][WARNING] this is an info message from the root
logger
[2019-09-08 12:28:25,190][my-app][WARNING] an info message from my-app
```

The output is repeated because we configured both, but that doesn't mean they need to be. The formatting changed for the file-based logger, allowing a cleaner view in the console:

```
from logging.config import dictConfig

dictConfig({
    'version': 1,
    'formatters': {
        'BASE_FORMAT': {
            'format': '[%(name)s][%(levelname)-6s] %(message)s',
        },
        'FILE_FORMAT': {
            'format': '[%(asctime)s] [%(name)s][%(levelname)-6s] %(message)s',
        },
    },
    'handlers': {
        'console': {
            'class': 'logging.StreamHandler',
            'level': 'INFO',
            'formatter': 'BASE_FORMAT'
        },
        'file': {
            'class': 'logging.FileHandler',
            'level': 'DEBUG',
            'formatter': 'FILE_FORMAT'
        }

    },
    'root': {
        'level': 'INFO',
        'handlers': ['console', 'file']
    }
})
```

Using dictConfig helps better visualize where things go and how they all tie together versus the more manual example earlier. For complicated setups where more than one logger is needed, the dictConfig way is better. Most of the web frameworks use the dictionary-based configuration exclusively.

Sometimes, the logging format is overlooked. It's often seen as something cosmetic that provides visual appeal to a human reading the logs. While that is partly true, it is nice to have some square brackets to designate the logging level (for example, [CRITI CAL]), but it can also be instrumental when other specifics of the environment, such as production, staging, or development, need separation. It might be immediately clear to a developer that the logs are from the development version, but it is extremely important to identify them if they are being forwarded around or collected in a central place. Dynamically applying this is done with environment variables and the use of logging.Filter in the dictConfig:

```python
import os
from logging.config import dictConfig

import logging

class EnvironFilter(logging.Filter):
    def filter(self, record):
        record.app_environment = os.environ.get('APP_ENVIRON', 'DEVEL')
        return True

dictConfig({
    'version': 1,
    'filters' : {
        'environ_filter' : {
            '()': EnvironFilter
        }
    },
    'formatters': {
        'BASE_FORMAT': {
            'format':
                '[%(app_environment)s][%(name)s][%(levelname)-6s] %(message)s',
        }
    },
    'handlers': {
        'console': {
            'class': 'logging.StreamHandler',
            'level': 'INFO',
            'formatter': 'BASE_FORMAT',
            'filters': ['environ_filter'],
        }
    },
    'root': {
        'level': 'INFO',
        'handlers': ['console']
    }
})
```

There is a lot going on in this example. It might be easy to miss a few things that got updated. First, a new class called EnvironFilter, which uses the logging.Filter as a base class, was added, and it defined a method called filter that accepts a record argument. This is how the base class wants this method to be defined. The record argument gets extended to include the APP_ENVIRON environment variable that defaults to *DEVEL*.

Then, in the dictConfig, a new key is added (filters) that names this filter the envi ron_filter, pointing to the EnvironFilter class. Finally, in the handlers key, we added the filters key that accepts a list, and in this case it will only have a single filter added: environ_filter.

The defining and naming of the filter feels cumbersome, but this is because our example is trivial. In more complex environments, it allows you to extend and configure without *boilerplate* filling the dictionary, making it easier to update or extend further.

A quick test in the command line indicates how the new filter shows the environment. In this example, a basic Pecan (*https://www.pecanpy.org*) application is used:

```
$ pecan serve config.py
Starting server in PID 25585
serving on 0.0.0.0:8080, view at http://127.0.0.1:8080
2019-08-12 07:57:28,157 [DEVEL][INFO    ] [pecan.commands.serve] GET / 200
```

The default environment of DEVEL works, and changing it to production is one environment variable away:

```
$ APP_ENVIRON='PRODUCTION' pecan serve config.py
Starting server in PID 2832
serving on 0.0.0.0:8080, view at http://127.0.0.1:8080
2019-08-12 08:15:46,552 [PRODUCTION][INFO    ] [pecan.commands.serve] GET / 200
```

Common Patterns

The logging module offers a few good patterns that aren't immediately obvious but are quite good to use as much as possible. One of these patterns is using the log ging.exception helper. A common workflow looks like this:

```
try:
    return expensive_operation()
except TypeError as error:
    logging.error("Running expensive_operation caused error: %s" % str(error))
```

This type of workflow is problematic on several fronts: it primarily *eats* the exception and just reports the string representation of it. If the exception isn't obvious or if it happens in a location that is not immediately evident, then reporting TypeError is useless. When string replacement fails, you can get a ValueError, but if the code is obscuring the traceback, then the error doesn't help:

```
[ERROR] Running expensive_operation caused an error:
    TypeError: not all arguments converted during string formatting
```

Where did that happen? We know it happens when expensive_operation() is called, but where? In what function, class, or file? This type of logging is not only unhelpful, it is infuriating! The logging module can help us log the full exception traceback:

```
try:
    return expensive_operation()
except TypeError:
    logging.exception("Running expensive_operation caused error")
```

The `logging.exception` helper will push the full traceback to the log output magically. The implementation doesn't need to worry about capturing `error` as it was doing before, or even try to retrieve useful information from the exception. The logging module is taking care of everything.

Another useful pattern is to use the built-in capabilities of the logging module for string interpolation. Take this piece of code as an example:

```
>>> logging.error(
"An error was produced when calling: expensive_operation, \
with arguments: %s, %s" % (arguments))
```

The statement is requiring two string replacements, and it is assuming that `argu ments` is going to have two items. If `arguments` fails to have two arguments, the above statement will break the production code. You *never* want to break production code because of logging. The module has a helper to catch this, report it as a problem, and allow the program to continue:

```
>>> logging.error("An error was produced when calling: expensive_operation, \
with arguments: %s, %s", arguments)
```

This is safe, and it is the recommended way to pass items to the statement.

The ELK Stack

Just like Linux, Apache, MySQL, and PHP were known as *LAMP*, you will often hear about the *ELK* stack: Elasticsearch, Logstash, and Kibana. This stack allows you to extract information from logs, capture useful metadata, and send it to a document store (Elasticsearch) which then uses a powerful dashboard (Kibana) to display the information. Understanding each piece is crucial for an effective strategy when consuming logs. Each component of the stack is equally essential, and although you may find similar applications for each, this section concentrates on their actual roles in an example application.

Most production systems have been around for a while, and you will rarely get the chance to redo infrastructure from scratch. Even if you are lucky enough to get to design infrastructure from the ground up, it is possible to overlook the importance of log structure. A proper log structure is as important as capturing useful information, but when the structure is lacking, Logstash can help. When installing Nginx, the default logging output is similar to this:

```
192.168.111.1 - - [03/Aug/2019:07:28:41 +0000] "GET / HTTP/1.1" 200 3700 "-" \
"Mozilla/5.0 (X11; Ubuntu; Linux x86_64; rv:68.0) Gecko/20100101 Firefox/68.0"
```

Some parts of the log statement are straightforward, such as the HTTP method (a GET) and the timestamp. If you can control the information, drop what is not meaningful, or include needed data, that is fine as long as you have a clear understanding of what all of these components are. The configuration for the HTTP server has these details in */etc/nginx/nginx.conf*:

```
http {
    log_format  main  '$remote_addr - $remote_user [$time_local] "$request" '
                      '$status $body_bytes_sent "$http_referer" '
                      '"$http_user_agent" "$http_x_forwarded_for"';
    ...
```

When you first look at the output, you might think that the dashes were for missing information, but this is not entirely correct. In the log output example, *two* dashes follow the IP; one is just cosmetic, and the second one is for missing information. The configuration tells us that a single dash follows the IP and then by $remote_user, which is useful when authentication is involved so that the authenticated user is captured. If this is an HTTP server that doesn't have authentication enabled, the $remote_user can be dropped from the configuration (if you have access and permission to change the *nginx.conf* file), or it can be ignored with rules that extract the metadata from the logs. Let's see in the next section how Logstash can help with its vast number of input plug-ins.

 Elasticsearch, Logstash, and Kibana are usually *not* available in Linux distributions. Depending on the flavor of the distribution, the proper signing keys need to get imported, and the package manager needs to be configured to pull from the right repositories. Refer to the install sections on the official documentation (*https:// oreil.ly/A-EwN*). Make sure that the Filebeat package is also installed. This is a lightweight (yet powerful) utility for log forwarding. It will be used to send logs to Logstash later.

Logstash

The first step after deciding to go with the ELK stack is to hack some Logstash rules to extract information from a given source, filter it, and then ship it to a service (like Elasticsearch in this case). After Logstash gets installed, the path */etc/logstash/* becomes available with a useful *conf.d* directory where we can add multiple configurations for different services. Our use case is capturing Nginx information, filtering it, and then shipping it over to a local Elasticsearch service that should already be installed and running.

To consume logs, the `filebeat` utility needs to be installed. This is available from the same repositories that you enabled to install Elasticsearch, Kibana, and Logstash. Before configuring Logstash, we need to ensure that Filebeat is configured for the Nginx log files and the location of Logstash.

After installing Filebeat, add the log paths for Nginx and the default Logstash port for localhost (5044). The configuration in */etc/filebeat/filebeat.yml* should have these lines defined (or uncommented):

```
filebeat.inputs:

- type: log
  enabled: true

  paths:
    - /var/log/nginx/*.log

output.logstash:
  hosts: ["localhost:5044"]
```

This allows Filebeat to look at every single path in */var/log/nginx/* and then forward it to the localhost instance of Logstash. If a separate log file for another Nginx application is required, it gets added here. Other defaults in the configuration file might be present, and those should be fine to leave as is. Now start the service:

```
$ systemctl start filebeat
```

Now create a new file in the Logstash configuration directory (in */etc/logstash/conf.d/*), and name it *nginx.conf*. The first section that you should add handles the input:

```
input {
  beats {
    port => "5044"
  }
}
```

The input section indicates that the source of the information will come from the Filebeat service using port 5044. Since all the file path configuration is done in the Filbeat configuration, not much else is necessary here.

Next, we need to extract the information and map it to keys (or fields). Some parsing rules need to be put in place to make sense of the unstructured data we are dealing with. For this type of parsing, use the grok plug-in; append the following configuration to the same file:

```
filter {
  grok {
    match => { "message" => "%{COMBINEDAPACHELOG}"}
  }
}
```

The filter section now defines the usage of the grok plug-in that takes the incoming line and applies the powerful COMBINEDAPACHELOG, a collection of regular expressions that can accurately find and map all the components of the web server logs coming from Nginx.

Finally, the output section needs to set where the newly structured data should go:

```
output {
  elasticsearch {
    hosts => ["localhost:9200"]
  }
}
```

This means that all structured data gets sent over to the local instance of Elasticsearch. As you can see, the configuration for Logstash (and the Filebeat service) was very minimal. There are several plug-ins and configuration options that can be added to further fine-tune the log collection and parsing. This *batteries included* approach is excellent for getting started without having to figure out extensions or plug-ins. If you are curious, browse through the Logstash source code and search for the *grok-patterns* file that contains COMBINEDAPACHELOG; the collection of regular expressions is quite the sight.

Elasticsearch and Kibana

After installing the elasticsearch package, there is little that you need to do to have a local setup running and ready to receive structured data from Logstash. Make sure the service is started and running without problems:

```
$ systemctl start elasticsearch
```

Similarly, install the kibana package and start the service up:

```
$ systemctl start kibana
```

Even though Kibana is a dashboard, and the ELK stack is not built with Python, these services are so well integrated that it demonstrates what great platform design and architecture truly are. After starting Kibana for the first time, while browsing through the log output it immediately starts looking for an instance of Elasticsearch running on the host. This is the default behavior of its own Elasticsearch plug-in with no extra configuration. The behavior is transparent, and the messaging tells you that is was able to initialize the plug-in and reach Elasticsearch:

```
{"type":"log","@timestamp":"2019-08-09T12:34:43Z",
"tags":["status","plugin:elasticsearch@7.3.0","info"],"pid":7885,
"state":"yellow",
"message":"Status changed from uninitialized to yellow",
"prevState":"uninitialized","prevMsg":"uninitialized"}

{"type":"log","@timestamp":"2019-08-09T12:34:45Z",
"tags":["status","plugin:elasticsearch@7.3.0","info"],"pid":7885,
"state":"green","message":"Status changed from yellow to green - Ready",
"prevState":"yellow","prevMsg":"Waiting for Elasticsearch"}
```

After changing the configuration to an incorrect port, the logs are very clear that the automatic behavior is not quite working:

```
{"type":"log","@timestamp":"2019-08-09T12:59:27Z",
"tags":["error","elasticsearch","data"],"pid":8022,
"message":"Request error, retrying
  GET http://localhost:9199/_xpack => connect ECONNREFUSED 127.0.0.1:9199"}

{"type":"log","@timestamp":"2019-08-09T12:59:27Z",
"tags":["warning","elasticsearch","data"],"pid":8022,
"message":"Unable to revive connection: http://localhost:9199/"}
```

Once Kibana is up and running, along with Elasticsearch (on the correct port!), Filebeat, and Logstash, you will be greeted with a full-featured dashboard and plenty of options to get started, as in Figure 7-1.

Figure 7-1. Kibana's landing dashboard page

Hit the local instance of Nginx to get some activity in the logs and start the data processing. For this example, the Apache Benchmarking Tool (ab) is used, but you can try it with your browser or directly with curl:

```
$ ab -c 8 -n 50 http://localhost/
This is ApacheBench, Version 2.3 <$Revision: 1430300 $>
Copyright 1996 Adam Twiss, Zeus Technology Ltd, http://www.zeustech.net/
Licensed to The Apache Software Foundation, http://www.apache.org/

Benchmarking localhost (be patient).....done
```

Without doing anything specific to configure Kibana further, open the default URL and port where it is running: *http://localhost:5601*. The default view offers lots of options to add. In the *discover* section, you will see all the structured information from the requests. This is an example JSON fragment that Logstash processed and is available in Kibana (which is sourcing the data from Elasticsearch):

```
...
    "input": {
      "type": "log"
    },
    "auth": "-",
    "ident": "-",
    "request": "/",
    "response": "200",
    "@timestamp": "2019-08-08T21:03:46.513Z",
    "verb": "GET",
    "@version": "1",
    "referrer": "\"-\"",
    "httpversion": "1.1",
    "message": "::1 - - [08/Aug/2019:21:03:45 +0000] \"GET / HTTP/1.1\" 200",
    "clientip": "::1",
    "geoip": {},
    "ecs": {
      "version": "1.0.1"
    },
    "host": {
      "os": {
        "codename": "Core",
        "name": "CentOS Linux",
        "version": "7 (Core)",
        "platform": "centos",
        "kernel": "3.10.0-957.1.3.el7.x86_64",
        "family": "redhat"
      },
      "id": "0a75ccb95b4644df88f159c41fdc7cfa",
      "hostname": "node2",
      "name": "node2",
      "architecture": "x86_64",
      "containerized": false
    },
    "bytes": "3700"
  },
  "fields": {
    "@timestamp": [
      "2019-08-08T21:03:46.513Z"
    ]
  }
...
```

Critical keys like `verb`, `timestamp`, `request`, and `response` have been parsed and captured by Logstash. There is lots of work to do with this initial setup to convert it into something more useful and practical. The captured metadata can help render traffic (including geolocation), and Kibana can even set threshold alerts for data, for when specific metrics go above or below a determined value.

In the dashboard, this structured data is available to be picked apart and used to create meaningful graphs and representations, as shown in Figure 7-2.

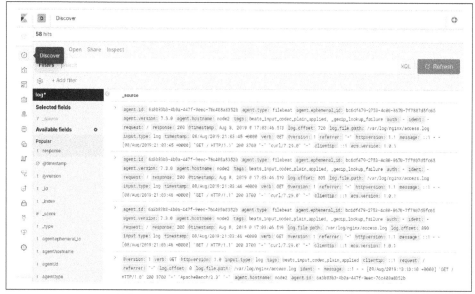

Figure 7-2. Structured data in Kibana

As we've seen, the ELK stack can get you started capturing and parsing through logs with minimal configuration and almost no effort. The examples are trivial, but should already demonstrate the immense capabilities of its components. More often than we would like to admit, we've been faced with infrastructure with a `cron` entry that is *tailing* logs and *grepping* for some pattern to send an email or submit an alert to Nagios. Using capable software components and understanding how much they can do for you, even in their simplest forms, is essential to better infrastructure, and in this case, better visibility of what that infrastructure is doing.

Exercises

- What is fault tolerance and how can it help infrastructure systems?
- What can be done for systems that produce huge amounts of logging?
- Explain why UDP might be preferred when pushing metrics to other systems. Why would TCP be problematic?

- Describe the differences between *pull* and *push* systems. When would one be better than the other?
- Produce a naming convention for storing metrics that accommodates production environments, web and database servers, and different application names.

Case Study Question

- Create a Flask application that fully implements logging at different levels (info, debug, warning, and error) and sends a metric (like a Counter) to a remote Graphite instance via a StatsD service when an exception is produced.

## CHAPTER 8

Pytest for DevOps

Continuous integration, continuous delivery, deployments, and any pipeline work-flow in general with some thought put into it will be filled with validation. This *vali-dation* can happen at every step of the way and when achieving important objectives.

For example, if in the middle of a long list of steps to produce a deployment, a `curl` command is called to get an all-important file, do you think the build should con-tinue if it fails? Probably not! `curl` has a flag that can be used to produce a nonzero exit status (`--fail`) if an HTTP error happens. That simple flag usage is a form of validation: ensure that the request succeeded, otherwise fail the build step. The *key word* is to *ensure* that something succeeded, and that is at the core of this chapter: validation and testing strategies that can help you build better infrastructure.

Thinking about validation becomes all the more satisfying when Python gets in the mix, harnessing testing frameworks like `pytest` to handle the verification of systems.

This chapter reviews some of the basics associated with testing in Python using the phenomenal `pytest` framework, then dives into some advanced features of the framework, and finally goes into detail about the *TestInfra* project, a plug-in to `pyt est` that can do system verification.

Testing Superpowers with pytest

We can't say enough good things about the `pytest` framework. Created by Holger Krekel, it is now maintained by quite a few people that do an incredible job at pro-ducing a high-quality piece of software that is usually part of our everyday work. As a full-featured framework, it is tough to narrow down the scope enough to provide a useful introduction without repeating the project's complete documentation.

The pytest project has lots of information, examples, and feature details in its documentation (*https://oreil.ly/PSAu2*) that are worth reviewing. There are always new things to learn as the project continues to provide new releases and different ways to improve testing.

When Alfredo was first introduced to the framework, he was struggling to write tests, and found it cumbersome to adhere to Python's built-in way of testing with unittest (this chapter goes through the differences later). It took him a couple of minutes to get hooked into pytest's magical reporting. It wasn't forcing him to move away from how he had written his tests, and it worked right out of the box with no modifications! This flexibility shows throughout the project, and even when things might not be possible today, you can extend its functionality via plug-ins or its configuration files.

By understanding how to write more straightforward test cases, and by taking advantage of the command-line tool, reporting engine, plug-in extensibility, and framework utilities, you will want to write more tests that will undoubtedly be better all around.

Getting Started with pytest

In its simplest form, pytest is a command-line tool that discovers Python tests and executes them. It doesn't force a user to understand its internals, which makes it easy to get started with. This section demonstrates some of the most basic features, from writing tests to laying out files (so that they get automatically discovered), and finally, looking at the main differences between it and Python's built-in testing framework, unittest.

Most *Integrated Development Environments* (IDEs), such as PyCharm and Visual Studio Code, have built-in support for running pytest. If using a text editor like Vim, there is support via the pytest.vim (*https://oreil.ly/HowKu*) plug-in. Using pytest from the editor saves time and makes debugging failures easier, but be aware that not every option or plug-in is supported.

Testing with pytest

Make sure that you have pytest installed and available in the command line:

```
$ python3 -m venv testing
$ source testing/bin/activate
```

Create a file called *test_basic.py*; it should look like this:

```
def test_simple():
    assert True

def test_fails():
    assert False
```

If `pytest` runs without any arguments, it should show a pass and a failure:

```
$ (testing) pytest
============================ test session starts ============================
platform linux -- Python 3.6.8, pytest-4.4.1, py-1.8.0, pluggy-0.9.0
rootdir: /home/alfredo/python/testing
collected 2 items

test_basic.py .F                                                    [100%]

================================== FAILURES ==================================
_____ test_fails _____

    def test_fails():
>       assert False
E       assert False

test_basic.py:6: AssertionError
===================== 1 failed, 1 passed in 0.02 seconds =====================
```

The output is beneficial from the start; it displays how many tests were collected, how many passed, and which one failed—including its line number.

 The default output from `pytest` is handy, but it might be too verbose. You can control the amount of output with configuration, reducing it with the `-q` flag.

There was no need to create a class to include the tests; functions were discovered and ran correctly. A test suite can have a mix of both, and the framework works fine in such an environment.

Layouts and conventions

When testing in Python, there are a few conventions that `pytest` follows implicitly. Most of these conventions are about naming and structure. For example, try renaming the *test_basic.py* file to *basic.py* and run `pytest` to see what happens:

```
$ (testing) pytest -q

no tests ran in 0.00 seconds
```

No tests ran because of the convention of prefixing test files with *test_*. If you rename the file back to *test_basic.py*, it should be automatically discovered and tests should run.

 Layouts and conventions are helpful for automatic test discovery. It is possible to configure the framework to use other naming conventions or to directly test a file that has a unique name. However, it is useful to follow through with basic expectations to avoid confusion when tests don't run.

These are conventions that will allow the tool to discover tests:

- The testing directory needs to be named *tests*.
- Test files need to be prefixed with *test*; for example, *test_basic.py*, or suffixed with *test.py*.
- Test functions need to be prefixed with `test_`; for example, `def testsimple():`.
- Test classes need to be prefixed with `Test`; for example, `class TestSimple`.
- Test methods follow the same conventions as functions, prefixed with `test_`; for example, `def test_method(self):`.

Because prefixing with `test_` is a requirement for automatic discovery and execution of tests, it allows introducing helper functions and other nontest code with different names, so that they get excluded automatically.

Differences with unittest

Python already comes with a set of utilities and helpers for testing, and they are part of the `unittest` module. It is useful to understand how `pytest` is different and why it is highly recommended.

The `unittest` module forces the use of classes and class inheritance. For an experienced developer who understands object-oriented programming and class inheritance, this shouldn't be a problem, but for beginners, *it is an obstacle*. Using classes and inheritance shouldn't be a requisite for writing basic tests!

Part of forcing users to inherit from `unittest.TestCase` is that you are required to understand (and remember) most of the assertion methods that are used to verify results. With `pytest`, there is a single assertion helper that can do it all: `assert`.

These are a few of the assert methods that can be used when writing tests with `unittest`. Some of them are easy to grasp, while others are very confusing:

- `self.assertEqual(a, b)`
- `self.assertNotEqual(a, b)`
- `self.assertTrue(x)`
- `self.assertFalse(x)`
- `self.assertIs(a, b)`
- `self.assertIsNot(a, b)`
- `self.assertIsNone(x)`
- `self.assertIsNotNone(x)`
- `self.assertIn(a, b)`
- `self.assertNotIn(a, b)`
- `self.assertIsInstance(a, b)`
- `self.assertNotIsInstance(a, b)`
- `self.assertRaises(exc, fun, *args, **kwds)`
- `self.assertRaisesRegex(exc, r, fun, *args, **kwds)`
- `self.assertWarns(warn, fun, *args, **kwds)`
- `self.assertWarnsRegex(warn, r, fun, *args, **kwds)`
- `self.assertLogs(logger, level)`
- `self.assertMultiLineEqual(a, b)`
- `self.assertSequenceEqual(a, b)`
- `self.assertListEqual(a, b)`
- `self.assertTupleEqual(a, b)`
- `self.assertSetEqual(a, b)`
- `self.assertDictEqual(a, b)`
- `self.assertAlmostEqual(a, b)`
- `self.assertNotAlmostEqual(a, b)`
- `self.assertGreater(a, b)`
- `self.assertGreaterEqual(a, b)`
- `self.assertLess(a, b)`
- `self.assertLessEqual(a, b)`
- `self.assertRegex(s, r)`
- `self.assertNotRegex(s, r)`

- `self.assertCountEqual(a, b)`

`pytest` allows you to use `assert` exclusively and does not force you to use any of the above. Moreover, it *does allow* you to write tests using `unittest`, and it even executes them. We strongly advise against doing that and suggest you concentrate on just using plain asserts.

Not only is it easier to use plain asserts, but `pytest` also provides a rich comparison engine on failures (more on this in the next section).

pytest Features

Aside from making it easier to write tests and execute them, the framework provides lots of extensible options, such as hooks. Hooks allow you to interact with the framework internals at different points in the runtime. If you want to alter the collection of tests, for example, a hook for the collection engine can be added. Another useful example is if you want to implement a nicer report when a test fails.

While developing an HTTP API, we found that sometimes the failures in the tests that used HTTP requests against the application weren't beneficial: an assertion failure would be reported because the expected response (an HTTP 200) was an HTTP 500 error. We wanted to know more about the request: to what URL endpoint? If it was a POST request, did it have data? What did it look like? These are things that were already available in the HTTP response object, so we wrote a hook to poke inside this object and include all these items as part of the failure report.

Hooks are an advanced feature of `pytest` that you might not need at all, but it is useful to understand that the framework can be flexible enough to accommodate different requirements. The next sections cover how to extend the framework, why using `assert` is so valuable, how to parametrize tests to reduce repetition, how to make helpers with `fixtures`, and how to use the built-in ones.

conftest.py

Most software lets you extend functionality via plug-ins (web browsers call them *extensions*, for example); similarly, `pytest` has a rich API for developing plug-ins. The complete API is not covered here, but its simpler approach is: the *conftest.py* file. In this file, the tool can be extended *just like a plug-in can*. There is no need to fully understand how to create a separate plug-in, package it, and install it. If a *conftest.py* file is present, the framework will load it and consume any specific directives in it. It all happens automatically!

Usually, you will find that a *conftest.py* file is used to hold hooks, fixtures, and helpers for those fixtures. Those *fixtures* can then be used within tests if declared as arguments (that process is described later in the fixture section).

It makes sense to add fixtures and helpers to this file when more than one test module will use it. If there is only a single test file, or if only one file is going to make use of a fixture or hook, there is no need to create or use a *conftest.py* file. Fixtures and helpers can be defined within the same file as the test and behave the same.

The only condition for loading a *conftest.py* file is to be present in the *tests* directory and match the name correctly. Also, although this name is configurable, we advise against changing it and encourage you to follow the default naming conventions to avoid potential issues.

The Amazing assert

When we have to describe how great the `pytest` tooling is, we start by describing the important uses of the `assert` statement. Behind the scenes, the framework is inspecting objects and providing a rich comparison engine to better describe errors. This is usually met with resistance because a bare `assert` in Python is terrible at describing errors. Compare two long strings as an example:

```
>>> assert "using assert for errors" == "using asert for errors"
Traceback (most recent call last):
  File "<stdin>", line 1, in <module>
AssertionError
```

Where is the difference? It is hard to tell without spending some time looking at those two long lines closely. This will cause people to recommend against it. A small test shows how `pytest` augments when reporting the failure:

```
$ (testing) pytest test_long_lines.py
============================= test session starts ==============================
platform linux -- Python 3.6.8, pytest-4.4.1, py-1.8.0, pluggy-0.9.0
collected 1 item

test_long_lines.py F                                                     [100%]

=================================== FAILURES ===================================
_____ test_long_lines _____

    def test_long_lines():
>       assert "using assert for errors" == "using asert for errors"
E       AssertionError: assert '...rt for errors' == '...rt for errors'
E         - using assert for errors
E         ?            -
E         + using asert for errors

test_long_lines.py:2: AssertionError
========================== 1 failed in 0.04 seconds ===========================
```

Can you tell where the error is? This is *tremendously easier*. Not only does it tell you it fails, but it points to exactly *where* the failure is. The example is a simple assert with a long string, but the framework handles other data structures like lists and dictionaries without a problem. Have you ever compared very long lists in tests? It is impossible to easily tell what items are different. Here is a small snippet with long lists:

```
assert ['a', 'very', 'long', 'list', 'of', 'items'] == [
        'a', 'very', 'long', 'list', 'items']
E   AssertionError: assert [...'of', 'items'] == [...ist', 'items']
E     At index 4 diff: 'of' != 'items'
E     Left contains more items, first extra item: 'items'
E     Use -v to get the full diff
```

After informing the user that the test failed, it points exactly to the index number (index four or fifth item), and finally, it says that one list has one extra item. Without this level of introspection, debugging failures would take a very long time. The bonus in reporting is that, by default, it omits very long items when making comparisons, so that only the relevant portion shows in the output. After all, what you want is to know not only that the lists (or any other data structure) are different but *exactly where they* are different.

Parametrization

Parametrization is one of the features that can take a while to understand because it doesn't exist in the unittest module and is a feature unique to the pytest framework. It can be clear once you find yourself writing very similar tests that had minor changes in the inputs but are testing the same thing. Take, for example, this class that is testing a function that returns True if a string is implying a truthful value. The string_to_bool is the function under test:

```
from my_module import string_to_bool

class TestStringToBool(object):

    def test_it_detects_lowercase_yes(self):
        assert string_to_bool('yes')

    def test_it_detects_odd_case_yes(self):
        assert string_to_bool('YeS')

    def test_it_detects_uppercase_yes(self):
        assert string_to_bool('YES')

    def test_it_detects_positive_str_integers(self):
        assert string_to_bool('1')

    def test_it_detects_true(self):
        assert string_to_bool('true')
```

```
        def test_it_detects_true_with_trailing_spaces(self):
            assert string_to_bool('true ')

        def test_it_detects_true_with_leading_spaces(self):
            assert string_to_bool(' true')
```

See how all these tests are evaluating the same result from similar inputs? This is where parametrization shines because it can group all these values and pass them to the test; it can effectively reduce them to a single test:

```
import pytest
from my_module import string_to_bool

true_values = ['yes', '1', 'Yes', 'TRUE', 'TruE', 'True', 'true']

class TestStrToBool(object):

    @pytest.mark.parametrize('value', true_values)
    def test_it_detects_truish_strings(self, value)
        assert string_to_bool(value)
```

There are a couple of things happening here. First `pytest` is imported (the framework) to use the `pytest.mark.parametrize` module, then `true_values` is defined as a (list) variable of all the values to use that should evaluate the same, and finally, it replaces all the test methods to a single one. The test method uses the `parametrize` decorator, which defines two arguments. The first is a string, *value*, and the second is the name of the list defined previously. This can look a bit odd, but it is telling the framework that *value* is the name to use for the argument in the test method. That is where the `value` argument comes from!

If the verbosity is increased when running, the output will show exactly what value was passed in. It almost looks like the single test got cloned into every single iteration passed in:

```
test_long_lines.py::TestLongLines::test_detects_truish_strings[yes] PASSED
test_long_lines.py::TestLongLines::test_detects_truish_strings[1] PASSED
test_long_lines.py::TestLongLines::test_detects_truish_strings[Yes] PASSED
test_long_lines.py::TestLongLines::test_detects_truish_strings[TRUE] PASSED
test_long_lines.py::TestLongLines::test_detects_truish_strings[TruE] PASSED
test_long_lines.py::TestLongLines::test_detects_truish_strings[True] PASSED
test_long_lines.py::TestLongLines::test_detects_truish_strings[true] PASSED
```

The output includes the values used in each iteration of the *single test* in brackets. It is reducing the very verbose test class into a single test method, thanks to `parametrize`. The next time you find yourself writing tests that seem very similar and that assert the same outcome with different inputs, you will know that you can make it simpler with the `parametrize` decorator.

Fixtures

We think of `pytest` fixtures (*https://oreil.ly/gPoM5*) like little helpers that can get injected into a test. Regardless of whether you are writing a single test function or a bunch of test methods, fixtures can be used in the same way. If they aren't going to be shared among other test files, it is fine to define them in the same test file; otherwise they can go into the *conftest.py* file. Fixtures, just like helper functions, can be almost anything you need for a test, from simple data structures that get pre-created to more complex ones like setting a database for a web application.

These helpers can also have a defined *scope*. They can have specific code that cleans up for every test method, class, and module, or even allows setting them up once for the whole test session. By defining them in a test method (or test function), you are effectively getting the fixture injected at runtime. If this sounds a bit confusing, it will become clear through examples in the next few sections.

Getting Started

Fixtures are so easy to define and use that they are often abused. We know we've created a few that could have been simple helper methods! As we've mentioned already, there are many different use cases for fixtures—from simple data structures to more complex ones, such as setting up whole databases for a single test.

Recently, Alfredo had to test a small application that parses the contents of a particular file called a *keyring file*. It has some structure similar to an INI file, with some values that have to be unique and follow a specific format. The file structure can be very tedious to recreate on every test, so a fixture was created to help. This is how the keyring file looks:

```
[mon.]
    key = AQBvaBFZAAAAABAA9VHgwCg3rWn8fMaX8KL01A==
    caps mon = "allow *"
```

The fixture is a function that returns the contents of the keyring file. Let's create a new file called test_keyring.py with the contents of the fixture, and a small test function that verifies the default key:

```
import pytest
import random


@pytest.fixture
def mon_keyring():
    def make_keyring(default=False):
        if default:
            key = "AQBvaBFZAAAAABAA9VHgwCg3rWn8fMaX8KL01A=="
        else:
            key = "%032x==" % random.getrandbits(128)
```

```
        return """
    [mon.]
        key = %s
            caps mon = "allow *"
        """ % key
    return make_keyring

def test_default_key(mon_keyring):
    contents = mon_keyring(default=True)
    assert "AQBvaBFZAAAAABAA9VHgwCg3rWn8fMaX8KL01A==" in contents
```

The fixture is using a nested function that does the heavy lifting, allows using a *default* key value, and returns the nested function in case the caller wants to have a randomized key. Inside the test, it receives the fixture by declaring it part of the argument of the test function (mon_keyring in this case), and is calling the fixture with default=True so that the default key is used, and then verifying it is generated as expected.

In a real-world scenario, the generated contents would be passed to the parser, ensuring expected behavior after parsing and that no errors happen.

The production code that used this fixture eventually grew to do other kinds of testing, and at some point, the test wanted to verify that the parser could handle files in different conditions. The fixture was returning a string, so it needed extending. Existing tests already made use of the mon_keyring fixture, so to extend the functionality without altering the current fixture, a new one was created that used a feature from the framework. Fixtures can *request* other fixtures! You define the required fixture as an argument (like a test function or test method would), so the framework injects it when it gets executed.

This is how the new fixture that creates (and returns) the file looks:

```
@pytest.fixture
def keyring_file(mon_keyring, tmpdir):
    def generate_file(default=False):
        keyring = tmpdir.join('keyring')
        keyring.write_text(mon_keyring(default=default))
        return keyring.strpath
    return generate_file
```

Going line by line, the pytest.fixture decorator tells the framework that this function is a fixture, then the fixture is defined, asking for *two fixtures* as arguments: mon_keyring and tmpdir. The first is the one created previously in the *test_keyring.py* file earlier, and the second one is a built-in fixture from the framework (more on built-in fixtures in the next section). The tmpdir fixture allows you to use a temporary directory that gets removed after the test completes, then the *keyring* file is created, and the text generated by the mon_keyring fixture is written, passing the default argument. Finally, it returns the absolute path of the new file created so that the test can use it.

This is how the test function would use it:

```
def test_keyring_file_contents(keyring_file):
    keyring_path = keyring_file(default=True)
    with open(keyring_path) as fp:
        contents = fp.read()
    assert "AQBvaBFZAAAAABAA9VHgwCg3rWn8fMaX8KL01A==" in contents
```

You should now have a good idea of what fixtures are, where can you define them, and how to consume them in tests. The next section goes through a few of the most useful built-in fixtures that are part of the framework.

Built-in Fixtures

The previous section briefly touched on one of the many built-in fixtures that pytest has to offer: the tmpdir fixture. The framework provides a few more fixtures. To verify the full list of available fixtures, run the following command:

```
$ (testing) pytest  -q --fixtures
```

There are two fixtures that we use a lot: monkeypatch and capsys, and they are in the list produced when the above command is run. This is the brief description you will see in the terminal:

```
capsys
    enables capturing of writes to sys.stdout/sys.stderr and makes
    captured output available via ``capsys.readouterr()`` method calls
    which return a ``(out, err)`` tuple.
monkeypatch
    The returned ``monkeypatch`` funcarg provides these
    helper methods to modify objects, dictionaries or os.environ::

    monkeypatch.setattr(obj, name, value, raising=True)
    monkeypatch.delattr(obj, name, raising=True)
    monkeypatch.setitem(mapping, name, value)
    monkeypatch.delitem(obj, name, raising=True)
    monkeypatch.setenv(name, value, prepend=False)
    monkeypatch.delenv(name, value, raising=True)
    monkeypatch.syspath_prepend(path)
    monkeypatch.chdir(path)

    All modifications will be undone after the requesting
    test function has finished. The ``raising``
    parameter determines if a KeyError or AttributeError
    will be raised if the set/deletion operation has no target.
```

capsys captures any stdout or stderr produced in a test. Have you ever tried to verify some command output or logging in a unit test? It is challenging to get right and is something that requires a separate plug-in or library to *patch* Python's internals and then inspect its contents.

These are two test functions that verify the output produced on stderr and stdout, respectively:

```python
import sys

def stderr_logging():
    sys.stderr.write('stderr output being produced')

def stdout_logging():
    sys.stdout.write('stdout output being produced')

def test_verify_stderr(capsys):
    stderr_logging()
    out, err = capsys.readouterr()
    assert out == ''
    assert err == 'stderr output being produced'

def test_verify_stdout(capsys):
    stdout_logging()
    out, err = capsys.readouterr()
    assert out == 'stdout output being produced'
    assert err == ''
```

The capsys fixture handles all the patching, setup, and helpers to retrieve the stderr and stdout produced in the test. The content is reset for every test, which ensures that the variables populate with the correct output.

monkeypatch is probably the fixture that we use the most. When testing, there are situations where the code under test is out of our control, and *patching* needs to happen to override a module or function to have a specific behavior. There are quite a few *patching* and *mocking* libraries (*mocks* are helpers to set behavior on patched objects) available for Python, but monkeypatch is good enough that you might not need to install a separate library to help out.

The following function runs a system command to capture details from a device, then parses the output, and returns a property (the ID_PART_ENTRY_TYPE as reported by blkid):

```python
import subprocess

def get_part_entry_type(device):
    """
    Parses the ``ID_PART_ENTRY_TYPE`` from the "low level" (bypasses the cache)
    output that uses the ``udev`` type of output.
    """
```

```
stdout = subprocess.check_output(['blkid', '-p', '-o', 'udev', device])
for line in stdout.split('\n'):
    if 'ID_PART_ENTRY_TYPE=' in line:
        return line.split('=')[-1].strip()
return ''
```

To test it, set the desired behavior on the check_output attribute of the subprocess
module. This is how the test function looks using the monkeypatch fixture:

```
def test_parses_id_entry_type(monkeypatch):
    monkeypatch.setattr(
        'subprocess.check_output',
        lambda cmd: '\nID_PART_ENTRY_TYPE=aaaaa')
    assert get_part_entry_type('/dev/sda') == 'aaaa'
```

The setattr call *sets the attribute* on the patched callable (check_output in this case).
It *patches* it with a lambda function that returns the one interesting line. Since the
subprocess.check_output function is not under our direct control, and the
get_part_entry_type function doesn't allow any other way to inject the values,
patching is the only way.

We tend to favor using other techniques like injecting values (known as *dependency
injection*) before attempting to patch, but sometimes there is no other way. Providing
a library that can patch and handle all the cleanup on testing is one more reason pyt
est is a joy to work with.

Infrastructure Testing

This section explains how to do infrastructure testing and validation with the Testinfra project (*https://oreil.ly/e7Afx*). It is a pytest plug-in for infrastructure that relies
heavily on fixtures and allows you to write Python tests as if testing code.

The previous sections went into some detail on pytest usage and examples, and this
chapter started with the idea of verification at a system level. The way we explain
infrastructure testing is by asking a question: *How can you tell that the deployment
was successful?* Most of the time, this means some manual checks, such as loading a
website or looking at processes, which is insufficient; it is error-prone and can get
tedious if the system is significant.

Although you can initially get introduced to pytest as a tool to write and run Python
unit tests, it can be advantageous to repurpose it for infrastructure testing. A few
years ago Alfredo was tasked to produce an installer that exposed its features over an
HTTP API. This installer was to create a Ceph cluster (*https://ceph.com*), involving
many machines. During the QA portion of launching the API, it was common to get
reports where the cluster wouldn't work as expected, so he would get the credentials
to log in to these machines and inspect them. There is a multiplier effect once you
have to debug a distributed system comprising several machines: multiple

configuration files, different hard drives, network setups, anything and everything can be different even if they appear to be similar.

Every time Alfredo had to debug these systems, he had an ever-growing list of things to check. Is the configuration the same on all servers? Are the permissions as expected? Does a specific user exist? He would eventually forget something and spend time trying to figure out what he was missing. It was an unsustainable process. *What if I could write simple test cases against the cluster?* Alfredo wrote a few simple tests to verify the items on the list to execute them against the machines making up the cluster. Before he knew it, he had a good set of tests that took a few seconds to run that would identify all kinds of issues.

That was an incredible eye-opener for improving the delivery process. He could even execute these (functional) tests while developing the installer and catch things that weren't quite right. If the QA team caught any issues, he could run the same tests against their setup. Sometimes tests caught environmental issues: a drive was *dirty* and caused the deployment to fail; a configuration file from a different cluster was left behind and caused issues. Automation, granular tests, and the ability to run them often made the work better and alleviated the amount of work the QA team had to put up with.

The TestInfra project has all kinds of fixtures to test a system efficiently, and it includes a complete set of backends to connect to servers; regardless of their deployment type: Ansible, Docker, SSH, and Kubernetes are some of the supported connections. By supporting many different connection backends, you can execute the same set of tests regardless of infrastructure changes.

The next sections go through different backends and get into examples of a production project.

What Is System Validation?

System validation can happen at different levels (with monitoring and alert systems) and at different stages in the life cycle of an application, such as during pre-deployment, at runtime, or during deployment. An application that Alfredo recently put into production needed to handle client connections gracefully without any disruption, even when restarted. To sustain traffic, the application is load balanced: when the system is under heavy loads, new connections get sent to other servers with a lighter load.

When a new release gets deployed, the application *has to be restarted*. Restarting means that clients experience an odd behavior at best, or a very broken experience at the worst. To avoid this, the restart process waits for all client connections to terminate, the system refuses new connections, allowing it to finish work from existing clients, and the rest of the system picks up the work. When no connections are active, the deployment continues and stops services to get the newer code in.

There is validation at every step of the way: before the deployment to tell the balancer to stop sending new clients and later, verifying that no new clients are active. If that workflow converts to a test, the title could be something like: `make sure that no clients are currently running`. Once the new code is in, another validation step checks whether the balancer has acknowledged that the server is ready to produce work once again. Another test here could be: `balancer has server as active`. Finally, it makes sure that the server is receiving new client connections—yet another test to write!

Throughout these steps, verification is in place, and tests can be written to verify this type of workflow.

System validation can also be tied to monitoring the overall health of a server (or servers in a clustered environment) or be part of the continuous integration while developing the application and testing functionally. The basics of validation apply to these situations and anything else that might benefit from status verification. It shouldn't be used exclusively for testing, although that is a good start!

Introduction to Testinfra

Writing unit tests against infrastructure is a powerful concept, and having used Testinfra for over a year, we can say that it has improved the quality of production applications we've had to deliver. The following sections go into specifics, such as connecting to different nodes and executing validation tests, and explore what type of fixtures are available.

To create a new virtual environment, install `pytest`:

```
$ python3 -m venv validation
$ source testing/bin/activate
(validation) $ pip install pytest
```

Install `testinfra`, ensuring that version 2.1.0 is used:

```
(validation) $ pip install "testinfra==2.1.0"
```

 `pytest` fixtures provide all the test functionality offered by the Testinfra project. To take advantage of this section, you will need to know how they work.

Connecting to Remote Nodes

Because different backend connection types exist, when the connection is not specified directly, Testinfra defaults to certain ones. It is better to be explicit about the connection type and define it in the command line.

These are all the connection types that Testinfra supports:

- local
- Paramiko (an SSH implementation in Python)
- Docker
- SSH
- Salt
- Ansible
- Kubernetes (via kubectl)
- WinRM
- LXC

A `testinfra` section appears in the help menu with some context on the flags that are
provided. This is a neat feature from `pytest` and its integration with Testinfra. The
help for both projects comes from the same command:

```
(validation) $ pytest --help
...

testinfra:
  --connection=CONNECTION
                        Remote connection backend (paramiko, ssh, safe-ssh,
                        salt, docker, ansible)
  --hosts=HOSTS         Hosts list (comma separated)
  --ssh-config=SSH_CONFIG
                        SSH config file
  --ssh-identity-file=SSH_IDENTITY_FILE
                        SSH identify file
  --sudo                Use sudo
  --sudo-user=SUDO_USER
                        sudo user
  --ansible-inventory=ANSIBLE_INVENTORY
                        Ansible inventory file
  --nagios              Nagios plugin
```

There are two servers up and running. To demonstrate the connection options, let's
check if they are running CentOS 7 by poking inside the */etc/os-release* file. This is
how the test function looks (saved as `test_remote.py`):

```
def test_release_file(host):
    release_file = host.file("/etc/os-release")
    assert release_file.contains('CentOS')
    assert release_file.contains('VERSION="7 (Core)"')
```

It is a single test function that accepts the host fixture, which runs against all the nodes specified.

The --hosts flag accepts a list of hosts with a connection scheme (SSH would use *ssh://hostname* for example), and some other variations using globbing are allowed. If testing against more than a couple of remote servers at a time, passing them on the command line becomes cumbersome. This is how it would look to test against two servers using SSH:

```
(validation) $ pytest -v --hosts='ssh://node1,ssh://node2' test_remote.py
============================== test session starts ==============================
platform linux -- Python 3.6.8, pytest-4.4.1, py-1.8.0, pluggy-0.9.0
cachedir: .pytest_cache
rootdir: /home/alfredo/python/python-devops/samples/chapter16
plugins: testinfra-3.0.0, xdist-1.28.0, forked-1.0.2
collected 2 items

test_remote.py::test_release_file[ssh://node1] PASSED                    [ 50%]
test_remote.py::test_release_file[ssh://node2] PASSED                    [100%]

========================== 2 passed in 3.82 seconds ==========================
```

The increased verbosity (with the -v flag) shows that Testinfra is executing the one test function in the two remote servers specified in the invocation.

> When setting up the hosts, it is important to have a passwordless connection. There shouldn't be any password prompts, and if using SSH, a key-based configuration should be used.

When automating these types of tests (as part of a job in a CI system, for example), you can benefit from generating the hosts, determining how they connect, and any other special directives. Testinfra can consume an SSH configuration file to determine what hosts to connect to. For the previous test run, Vagrant (*https://www.vagrantup.com*) was used, which created these servers with special keys and connection settings. Vagrant can generate an ad-hoc SSH config file for the servers it has created:

```
(validation) $ vagrant ssh-config

Host node1
  HostName 127.0.0.1
  User vagrant
  Port 2200
```

```
  UserKnownHostsFile /dev/null
  StrictHostKeyChecking no
  PasswordAuthentication no
  IdentityFile /home/alfredo/.vagrant.d/insecure_private_key
  IdentitiesOnly yes
  LogLevel FATAL

Host node2
  HostName 127.0.0.1
  User vagrant
  Port 2222
  UserKnownHostsFile /dev/null
  StrictHostKeyChecking no
  PasswordAuthentication no
  IdentityFile /home/alfredo/.vagrant.d/insecure_private_key
  IdentitiesOnly yes
  LogLevel FATAL
```

Exporting the contents of the output to a file and then passing that to Testinfra offers greater flexibility if using more than one host:

```
(validation) $ vagrant ssh-config > ssh-config
(validation) $ pytest --hosts=default --ssh-config=ssh-config test_remote.py
```

Using `--hosts=default` avoids having to specify them directly in the command line, and the engine feeds from the SSH configuration. Even without Vagrant, the SSH configuration tip is still useful if connecting to many hosts with specific directives.

Ansible (*https://www.ansible.com*) is another option if the nodes are local, SSH, or Docker containers. The test setup can benefit from using an inventory of hosts (much like the SSH config), which can group the hosts into different sections. The host groups can also be specified so that you can single out hosts to test against, instead of executing against all.

For `node1` and `node2` used in the previous example, this is how the inventory file is defined (and saved as `hosts`):

```
[all]
node1
node2
```

If executing against all of them, the command changes to:

```
$ pytest --connection=ansible --ansible-inventory=hosts test_remote.py
```

If defining other hosts in the inventory that need an exclusion, a group can be specified as well. Assuming that both nodes are web servers and are in the `nginx` group, this command would run the tests on only that one group:

```
$ pytest --hosts='ansible://nginx' --connection=ansible \
  --ansible-inventory=hosts test_remote.py
```

A lot of system commands require superuser privileges. To allow escalation of privileges, Testinfra allows specifying --sudo or --sudo-user. The --sudo flag makes the engine use sudo when executing the commands, while the --sudo-user command allows running with higher privileges as a different user.The fixture can be used directly as well.

Features and Special Fixtures

So far, the host fixture is the only one used in examples to check for a file and its contents. However, this is deceptive. The host fixture is an *all-included* fixture; it contains all the other powerful fixtures that Testinfra provides. This means that the example has already used the host.file, which has lots of extras packed in it. It is also possible to use the fixture directly:

```
In [1]: import testinfra

In [2]: host = testinfra.get_host('local://')

In [3]: node_file = host.file('/tmp')

In [4]: node_file.is_directory
Out[4]: True

In [5]: node_file.user
Out[5]: 'root'
```

The all-in-one host fixture makes use of the extensive API from Testinfra, which loads everything for each host it connects to. The idea is to write a single test that gets executed against different nodes, all accessible from the same host fixture.

These are a couple dozen (*https://oreil.ly/2_J-o*) attributes available. These are some of the most used ones:

host.ansible
:   Provides full access to any of the Ansible properties at runtime, such as hosts, inventory, and vars

host.addr
:   Network utilities, like checks for IPV4 and IPV6, is host reachable, is host resolvable

host.docker
:   Proxy to the Docker API, allows interacting with containers, and checks if they are running

host.interface
:   Helpers for inspecting addresses from a given interface

`host.iptables`

Helpers for verifying firewall rules as seen by `host.iptables`

`host.mount_point`

Check mounts, filesystem types as they exist in paths, and mount options

`host.package`

Very useful to query if a package is installed and at what version

`host.process`

Check for running processes

`host.sudo`

Allows you to execute commands with `host.sudo` or as a different user

`host.system_info`

All kinds of system metadata, such as distribution version, release, and codename

`host.check_output`

Runs a system command, checks its output if runs successfully, and can be used in combination with `host.sudo`

`host.run`

Runs a command, allows you to check the return code, `host.stderr`, and `host.stdout`

`host.run_expect`

Verifies that the return code is as expected

Examples

A frictionless way to start developing system validation tests is to do so while creating the actual deployment. Somewhat similar to *Test Driven Development* (TDD), any progress warrants a new test. In this section, a web server needs to be installed and configured to run on port 80 to serve a static landing page. While making progress, tests will be added. Part of writing tests is understanding failures, so a few problems will be introduced to help us figure out what to fix.

With a *vanilla* Ubuntu server, start by installing the Nginx package:

```
$ apt install nginx
```

Create a new test file called *test_webserver.py* for adding new tests after making progress. After Nginx installs, let's create another test:

```
def test_nginx_is_installed(host):
    assert host.package('nginx').is_installed
```

Reduce the verbosity in pytest output with the -q flag to concentrate on failures. The remote server is called node4 and SSH is used to connect to it. This is the command to run the first test:

```
(validate) $ pytest -q --hosts='ssh://node4' test_webserver.py
.
1 passed in 1.44 seconds
```

Progress! The web server needs to be up and running, so a new test is added to verify that behavior:

```
def test_nginx_is_running(host):
    assert host.service('nginx').is_running
```

Running again *should* work once again:

```
(validate) $ pytest -q --hosts='ssh://node4' test_webserver.py
.F
================================ FAILURES ====================================
_____ test_nginx_is_running[ssh://node4] _____

host = <testinfra.host.Host object at 0x7f629bf1d668>

    def test_nginx_is_running(host):
>       assert host.service('nginx').is_running
E       AssertionError: assert False
E        +  where False = <service nginx>.is_running
E        +    where <service nginx> = <class 'SystemdService'>('nginx')

test_webserver.py:7: AssertionError
1 failed, 1 passed in 2.45 seconds
```

Some Linux distributions do not allow packages to start the services when they get installed. Moreover, the test has caught the Nginx service not running, as reported by systemd (the default unit service). Starting Nginx manually and running the test should make everything pass once again:

```
(validate) $ systemctl start nginx
(validate) $ pytest -q --hosts='ssh://node4' test_webserver.py
..
2 passed in 2.38 seconds
```

As mentioned at the beginning of this section, the web server should be serving a static landing page on port 80. Adding another test (in *test_webserver.py*) to verify the port is the next step:

```
def test_nginx_listens_on_port_80(host):
    assert host.socket("tcp://0.0.0.0:80").is_listening
```

This test is more involved and needs attention to some details. It opts to check for TCP connections on port 80 on *any IP in the server*. While this is fine for this test, if the server has multiple interfaces and is configured to bind to a specific address, then a new test would have to be added. Adding another test that checks if port 80 is listening on a given address might seem like overkill, but if you think about the reporting, it helps explain what is going on:

1. Test nginx listens on port 80 : PASS

2. Test nginx listens on address 192.168.0.2 and port 80: FAIL

The above tells us that Nginx is binding to port 80, *just not to the right interface*. An extra test is an excellent way to provide granularity (at the expense of extra verbosity).

Run the newly added test again:

```
(validate) $ pytest -q --hosts='ssh://node4' test_webserver.py
..F
================================== FAILURES ==================================
_____ test_nginx_listens_on_port_80[ssh://node4] _____

host = <testinfra.host.Host object at 0x7fbaa64f26a0>

    def test_nginx_listens_on_port_80(host):
>       assert host.socket("tcp://0.0.0.0:80").is_listening
E       AssertionError: assert False
E       + where False = <socket tcp://0.0.0.0:80>.is_listening
E       +   where <socket tcp://0.0.0.0:80> = <class 'LinuxSocketSS'>

test_webserver.py:11: AssertionError
1 failed, 2 passed in 2.98 seconds
```

No address has anything listening on port 80. Looking at the configuration for Nginx reveals that it is set to listen on port 8080 using a directive in the default site that configures the port:

```
(validate) $ grep "listen 8080" /etc/nginx/sites-available/default
    listen 8080 default_server;
```

After changing it back to port 80 and restarting the nginx service, the tests pass again:

```
(validate) $ grep "listen 80" /etc/nginx/sites-available/default
    listen 80 default_server;
(validate) $ systemctl restart nginx
(validate) $ pytest -q --hosts='ssh://node4' test_webserver.py
...
3 passed in 2.92 seconds
```

Since there isn't a built-in fixture to handle HTTP requests to an address, the final test uses the wget utility to retrieve the contents of the running website and make assertions on the output to ensure that the static site renders:

```
def test_get_content_from_site(host):
    output = host.check_output('wget -qO- 0.0.0.0:80')
    assert 'Welcome to nginx' in output
```

Running *test_webserver.py* once more verifies that all our assumptions are correct:

```
(validate) $ pytest -q --hosts='ssh://node4' test_webserver.py
....
4 passed in 3.29 seconds
```

Understanding the concepts of testing in Python, and repurposing those for system validation, is incredibly powerful. Automating test runs while developing applications or even writing and running tests on existing infrastructure are both excellent ways to simplify day-to-day operations that can become error-prone. pytest and Testinfra are great projects that can help you get started, and make it easy when extending is needed. Testing is a *level up* on skills.

Testing Jupyter Notebooks with pytest

One easy way to introduce big problems into your company is to forget about applying software engineering best practices when it comes to data science and machine learning. One way to fix this is to use the nbval plug-in for pytest that allows you to test your notebooks. Take a look at this Makefile:

```
setup:
	python3 -m venv ~/.myrepo

install:
	pip install -r requirements.txt

test:
	python -m pytest -vv --cov=myrepolib tests/*.py
	python -m pytest --nbval notebook.ipynb

lint:
	pylint --disable=R,C myrepolib cli web

all: install lint test
```

The key item is the --nbval flag that also allows the notebook in the repo to be tested by the build server.

Exercises

- Name at least three conventions needed so that pytest can discover a test.
- What is the *conftest.py* file for?
- Explain parametrization of tests.
- What is a fixture and how can it be used in tests? Is it convenient? Why?
- Explain how to use the monkeypatch fixture.

Case Study Question

- Create a test module to use `testinfra` to connect to a remote server. Test that Nginx is installed, is running with `systemd`, and the server is binding to port 80. When all tests pass, try to make them fail by configuring Nginx to listen on a different port.

CHAPTER 9
Cloud Computing

Cloud computing is a term that creates the same confusion as other popular modern buzzwords, such as Big Data, AI, and Agile. When a term gets popular enough, it eventually means many things to many people. Here is a precise definition. The cloud is the delivery of on-demand computing services where you pay for what you use, just like any other utility: natural gas, electricity, or water.

The top benefits of cloud computing include cost, speed, global scale, productivity, performance, reliability, and security. Let's break down each one of these.

Cost
> There is no up-front cost and resources can be precisely metered to meet demand.

Speed
> The cloud offers self-service, so an expert user can leverage the resources to build solutions quickly.

Global scale
> All major cloud providers have a global scale, which means services can be provisioned all over the world to meet demand in a geographic region.

Productivity
> Many tasks, such as racking servers, configuring network hardware, and physically securing a data center, no longer exist. Companies can focus on building core intellectual property versus reinventing the wheel.

Performance
> Unlike hardware you own, cloud hardware is continually upgraded, meaning that the fastest and latest hardware is always available on demand. All of the hardware

is also joined together on low-latency and high-bandwidth infrastructure, creating an ideal high-performance environment.

Reliability

The core architecture of the cloud offers redundancy at every step. There are multiple regions and multiple data centers in each region. Cloud native architecture can design around these capabilities, leading to highly available architectures. Additionally, many core cloud services are themselves highly available, like Amazon S3, which has nine nines, or 99.999999999% reliability.

Security

You are only as good as your weakest link with security. By consolidating to centralized security, a higher level of security occurs. Problems such as physical access to a data center or encryption at rest become industry standard on day one.

Cloud Computing Foundations

In some ways, it is hard to think about DevOps without also thinking about the cloud. Amazon describes the following as DevOps best practices: Continous Integration, Continous Delivery, Microservices, Infrastructure as Code, Monitoring and Logging, and Communication and Collaboration. Of these best practices, you could argue that all of them depend on the cloud's existence. Even the harder to define practice of "Communication and Collaboration" is made possible by a modern suite of SaaS communication tools: Jira, Trello, Slack, GitHub, and others. Where do all of these SaaS communication tools run? In the cloud.

What is unique about the modern cloud era? There are at least three defining characteristics: theoretical infinite computing resources, on-demand access computing resources, and no up-front commitment of capital. Hidden inside these characteristics is DevOps skills Pareto distribution.

In practice, the cloud becomes incredibly cost effective when used in a manner that supports the real efficiencies of the cloud. On the other hand, for unsophisticated organizations using the cloud, it can be incredibly expensive because they are not taking advantage of the core features of the cloud. It is probably fair to say that 80% of the gross profits of the cloud in the early days were derived from unsophisticated users who left instances idle, chose the wrong instances (too big), didn't architect for auto-scaling, or used software architectures that were noncloud native, such as shoving everything into a relational database. Likewise, the remaining 20% of gross profits were derived from incredibly thrifty organizations with exceptional DevOps skills.

Before the cloud existed, there was a fixed cost that never went away. This cost was fixed both in terms of money and in developer time. A data center had to be maintained by a team of people, and that was a full-time job and very expensive. As the cloud has grown in maturity, only the best of the best now work in data centers, and they are working for incredibly sophisticated organizations like Google, Microsoft, and Amazon. It isn't statistically possible for a small company to have the hardware talent of a data center engineer at that level, at least over the long term.

A fundamental law of economics is the principle of comparative advantage. Instead of looking at what the cloud costs and thinking that you can save money by doing it yourself, look at the *opportunity cost* of not doing something else. Most organizations have concluded that:

1. They cannot compete at the level of Google, Amazon, and Microsoft in data center expertise.

2. Paying for cloud services allows the company to focus on other areas where they can use their unique skills.

Netflix has decided to focus on delivering streaming services and creating original content than running its own data centers. If you look at the Netflix 11-year stock price from 2008 to 2019 (Figure 9-1), it's hard to argue with this strategy.

Figure 9-1. Netflix 11-year stock price

What is unique about Netflix, though, is its dedication to operational excellence in the cloud. Current or former Netflix employees have given numerous talks at conferences, developed and released tools on GitHub, and written articles and books on DevOps and cloud computing topics. This further supports the point that it isn't enough to realize that the cloud is the correct choice, but this decision must be backed up by operational excellence. Otherwise, an organization risks being the equivalent of the gym member who signs up for a year membership, yet only goes for three weeks. The members that don't go to the gym subsidize the cost of the gym for the other members who attend regularly.

Types of Cloud Computing

There are several main types of cloud computing: public cloud, private cloud, hybrid cloud, and multicloud. The majority of the time when you hear about the cloud, it is about a public cloud. It is isn't the only type of cloud, however. A private cloud is used exclusively by an organization, and is either physically located in that organization's data center, or it can be hosted for an organization by another company. Some examples of private cloud providers are HPE, VMware, Dell, and Oracle. A popular open source private cloud option is OpenStack. An excellent example of how that could look in practice is that Rackspace, a more niche alternative in the hosting space, is one of the largest providers of OpenStack private clouds as a service.

A more flexible option is the hybrid cloud. The hybrid cloud combines both a private and public cloud. An example of this type of architecture involves using the public cloud for situations that require scalability and extra capacity, and using a private cloud for day-to-day operations. Another example could involve a specialized hardware architecture, say, a farm of GPUs that perform deep learning in a private cloud, and the connected public cloud serves at the core infrastructure. Even major cloud vendors are entering this space. A good example is the Anthos platform (*https://cloud.google.com/anthos*) from Google. This platform does the hard work of linking an on-premises data center with GCP to allow workflows, such as running Kubernetes clusters in both locations in a seamless manner.

Finally, multicloud is a choice that is enabled partially by modern DevOps technologies such as Docker containers, and IaC solutions such as Terraform. A multicloud strategy is one that involves using multiple clouds at the same time. An excellent example of this is running jobs in containers on multiple clouds simultaneously. Why would you do this? For one reason, you could decide to run jobs on AWS Spot Instances when the price was suitable to make a profit, but on GCP when AWS was too expensive. Tools like Terraform allow you to abstract away cloud concepts into a familiar configuration language, while containers allow code and an execution environment to travel to any destination that can run a container.

Types of Cloud Services

There are five main types of cloud services: Infrastructure as a Service (IaaS), Metal as a Service (MaaS), Platform as a Service (PaaS), serverless, and Software as a Service (SaaS). Each of these cloud services works at a different layer of abstraction and has pros and cons. Let's break down each service.

Infrastructure as a Service

IaaS is a lower-level category that includes the ability to rent virtual machines by the minute, access object storage, provision software-defined network (SDN) and software-defined storage (SDS), and bid for an available virtual machine. This level of service is most closely associated with AWS, especially in the early years (2006) when Amazon launched S3 cloud storage, SQS (Simple Queue Service), and EC2 (virtual machines).

The advantage of this service for an organization with strong expertise in DevOps is that it can be incredibly cost-effective and reliable with a small team of people. The disadvantage is that IaaS has a steep learning curve, and when administered inefficiently, it can be expensive in terms of cost and human labor. In the Bay Area during 2009–2019, this scenario played out in real-time on AWS at many companies.

One story that brings this home occurred when Noah ran engineering at a SaaS company that provided monitoring and search tools. During his first month on the job, there were two mission-critical problems involving the cloud. The first problem, which occurred during week one, was that the SaaS billing system misconfigured the storage system. The company was deleting data from paying customers! The gist of the problem was that they didn't have the necessary DevOps infrastructure needed to succeed in the cloud: no build server, no testing, no real isolated development environments, no code review, and limited ability to deploy software automatically. The fix Noah implemented were these DevOps practices, while a figurative raging fire burned.

 A developer did set fire to the office by cooking bacon in a toaster oven. Noah thought he smelled smoke, so he walked into the kitchen and flames were crawling up the walls and the ceiling. He was so stunned at the sheer irony of the situation that he sat there for a few seconds, soaking it in. Fortunately, a quick-thinking co-worker (his product manager) grabbed the fire extinguisher and put out the fire.

A second, more serious, problem with our cloud architecture occurred shortly afterward. All of the developers in the company had to be on call so that there would be 24/7 coverage (except the CTO/founder who often wrote code that was directly or indirectly responsible for outages. . .more on that later). One night when Noah was on call, he was awoken at 2 A.M. by a call from the CEO/founder on his cell phone. He told Noah they had been hacked and that the entire SaaS system did not exist anymore. There were no web servers, search endpoints, or any other virtual machine running the platform in existence. Noah asked why he hadn't received a page, and the CEO said the monitoring system was also deleted. Noah decided to drive into work at 2 A.M. and work on the problem from there.

As more information surfaced, the issue became apparent. The CEO and founder had set up the AWS account initially, and all emails about service interruptions went to his email. For several months, Amazon had been sending him emails about how virtual machines in our region, Northern Virginia, needed to be retired, and that in the coming months they would be deleted. Well, that day eventually came, and in the middle of the night, that entire company's servers ceased to exist.

Noah found this out as he drove into work, so he then focused on building an entire SaaS company again from scratch, using the source code in GitHub. It was at this point that Noah began to understand both the power and the complexity of AWS. It took him from 2 A.M. until about 8 P.M. to get the SaaS system operational and able to accept data, process payments, and serve out dashboards. It took another 48 hours to completely restore all of the data from backups.

One of the reasons it took so long to get things running again is that the deployment process was centralized around a forked version of Puppet that a previous employee created but never checked into version control. Fortunately, Noah was able to find a copy of that version of Puppet at around 6 A.M. on one lone machine that survived the carnage. If this machine hadn't existed, it might have been the end of the company. It would have taken perhaps a week to completely rebuild a company of that complexity without some Infrastructure as Code (IAC) scaffolding.

An experience this stressful that had a reasonably happy ending taught him a lot. Noah realized this was the trade-off of the cloud; it was incredibly powerful, but the learning curve was crushing even for VC-funded startups in the Bay Area. Now back to the CTO/founder who wasn't on call, but checked code into production (without using a build server or continuous integration system). This person wasn't the villain of the story. It is possible that if Noah himself was the CTO/founder of a company at a certain point in his career, he might have made the same mistakes.

The real issue is the power dynamic. Hierarchy does not equal being correct. It is easy to get drunk on your power and believe that because you are in charge, what you do always makes sense. When Noah ran a company, he made similar mistakes. The key takeaway is that the process has to be right, not the individual. If it isn't automated, it is broken. If it isn't going through some type of automated quality control test, then it is also broken. If the deployment isn't repeatable, it is also broken.

One final story to share about this company involves monitoring. After those two initial crises, the symptoms resolved, but the underlying diseases were still malignant. There was an ineffective engineering process in the company. Another story highlights the underlying problem. There was a homegrown monitoring system (again, initially created by the founders) that on average generated alerts every 3-4 hours, 24 hours a day.

Because everyone in engineering except the CTO was on call, most of the engineering staff was always sleep deprived because they received alerts about the system not working every night. The "fix" to the alerts was to restart services. Noah volunteered to be on call for one month straight to allow engineering the time to fix the problem. This sustained period of suffering and lack of sleep led him to realize several things. One, the monitoring system was no better than random. He could potentially replace the entire system with this Python script:

```
from  random import choices

hours = list(range(1,25))
status = ["Alert", "No Alert"]
for hour in hours:
    print(f"Hour: {hour} -- {choices(status)}"
```

```
✗ python random_alert.py
Hour: 1 -- ['No Alert']
Hour: 2 -- ['No Alert']
Hour: 3 -- ['Alert']
Hour: 4 -- ['No Alert']
Hour: 5 -- ['Alert']
Hour: 6 -- ['Alert']
Hour: 7 -- ['Alert']
Hour: 8 -- ['No Alert']
Hour: 9 -- ['Alert']
Hour: 10 -- ['Alert']
Hour: 11 -- ['No Alert']
Hour: 12 -- ['Alert']
Hour: 13 -- ['No Alert']
Hour: 14 -- ['No Alert']
Hour: 15 -- ['No Alert']
Hour: 16 -- ['Alert']
Hour: 17 -- ['Alert']
Hour: 18 -- ['Alert']
Hour: 19 -- ['Alert']
Hour: 20 -- ['No Alert']
Hour: 21 -- ['Alert']
Hour: 22 -- ['Alert']
Hour: 23 -- ['No Alert']
Hour: 24 -- ['Alert']
```

Once he realized this, he dug into the data and created a historical picture of every single alert for the last year by day (note that these alerts were meant to be actionable and to "wake you up"). From Figure 9-2, you can see that not only did the alerts not make sense, but they were increasing to a frequency that was ridiculous in hindsight. They were "cargo culting" engineering best practices and figuratively waving palm tree branches at a dirt runway filled with airplanes built out of straw.

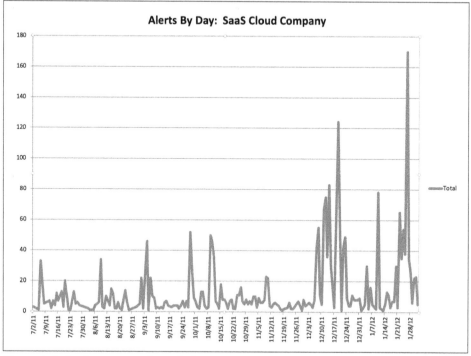

Figure 9-2. SaaS company alerts daily

In looking at the data, it was even more distressing to learn that engineers had spent YEARS of their lives responding to pages and getting woken up at night, and it was utterly useless. The suffering and sacrifice accomplished nothing and reinforced the sad truth that life is not fair. The unfairness of the situation was quite depressing, and it took quite a bit of convincing to get people to agree to turn off the alerts. There is a built-in bias in human behavior to continue to do what you have always done. Additionally, because the suffering was so severe and sustained, there was a tendency to attribute a deeper meaning to it. Ultimately, it was a false god.

The retrospective on using AWS cloud IaaS for that particular company is, in fact, the selling points of DevOps:

1. You must have a delivery pipeline and feedback loop: build, test, release, monitor, and then plan.

2. Development and operations are not silos. If the CTO is writing code, they should also be on call (the pain and suffering from years of being woken up would serve as the correct feedback loop).

3. Status in a hierarchy is not more important than the process. There should be a collaboration between team members that emphasizes ownership and accountability, regardless of title, pay, or experience level.

4. Speed is a fundamental requirement of DevOps. As a result, microservices and continuous delivery are requirements because they let teams take ownership of their services and release software more quickly.

5. Rapid delivery is a fundamental requirement of DevOps, but it also requires continuous integration, continuous delivery, and effective and actionable monitoring and logging.

6. It provides the ability to manage infrastructure and development processes at scale. Automation and consistency are hard requirements. Using IaC to manage development, testing, and production environments in a repeatable and automated manner are the solution.

Metal as a Service

MaaS allows you to treat physical servers like virtual machines. The same ease of use in managing clusters of virtual machines works for physical hardware. MaaS is the name of a service offering by Canonical, which the owner of Canonical, Mark Shuttleworth, describes as "cloud semantics" to the bare metal world. MaaS could also refer to the concept of using physical hardware from a vendor that treats hardware much like virtualized hardware. An excellent example of a company like this is SoftLayer, a bare metal provider acquired by IBM.

In the pro category, having full control over hardware does have a certain appeal for niche applications. An excellent example of this could be using a GPU-based database. In practice, a regular public cloud could offer similar services, so a full cost-benefit analysis helps when justifying when to use MaaS.

Platform as a Service

PaaS is a complete development and deployment environment that has all of the resources necessary to create cloud services. Examples of this include Heroku and Google App Engine. PaaS differs from IaaS in that it has development tools, database management tools, and high-level services that offer "point and click" integration. Examples of the types of services that can be bundled are an authentication service, a database service, or a web application service.

A justifiable criticism of PaaS is that it can be much more expensive in the long term than IaaS, as discussed previously; however this depends on the environment. If the organization is unable to enact DevOps behaviors, then the cost is a moot point. In that case, it would be better to pay for a more expensive service that provides more of those capabilities. The opportunity cost of an organization that needs to learn the advanced capabilities of managing an IaaS deployment may be too high for the short life span of a startup. It may be smarter for an organization to offload those capabilities to a PaaS provider.

Serverless Computing

Serverless is one of the newer categories of cloud computing, and it is still actively in development. The real promise of serverless is the ability to spend more time building applications and services and less or no time thinking about how they run. Every major cloud platform has a serverless solution.

The building block for serverless solutions is a compute node or Function as a Service (FaaS). AWS has Lambda, GCP has Cloud Functions, and Microsoft has Azure Functions. Traditionally, the underlying execution of these cloud functions has been abstracted away for a runtime, i.e., Python 2.7, Python 3.6, or Python 3.7. All of these vendors support Python runtimes, and in some cases, they also support customizing the underlying runtime via a customized Docker container. Here is an example of a straightforward AWS Lambda function that grabs the first page of Wikipedia.

There are a few things to point out about this Lambda function. The logic itself is in the `lambda_handler` and it takes two arguments. The first argument, `event`, is from whatever has triggered it. The Lambda could be anything from an Amazon Cloud Watch event timer to running it with a payload crafted from the AWS Lambda Console. The second argument, `context`, has methods and properties that provide information about the invocation, function, and execution environment.

```
import json
import wikipedia

print('Loading function')

def lambda_handler(event, context):
    """Wikipedia Summarizer"""

    entity = event["entity"]
    res = wikipedia.summary(entity, sentences=1)
    print(f"Response from wikipedia API: {res}")
    response = {
    "statusCode": "200",
    "headers": { "Content-type": "application/json" },
    "body": json.dumps({"message": res})
```

```
    }
    return response
```

To use the Lambda function a `JSON` payload is sent in:

```
{"entity":"google"}
```

The output of the Lambda is also a `JSON` payload:

```
Response
{
    "statusCode": "200",
    "headers": {
        "Content-type": "application/json"
    },
    "body": "{\"message\": \"Google LLC is an American multinational technology"}
}
```

One of the most potent aspects of FaaS is the ability to write code that responds to events versus code that is continuously running: i.e., a Ruby on Rails application. FaaS is a cloud-native capability that truly exploits what a cloud is best at—elasticity. Additionally, the development environment for writing lambda functions has evolved considerably.

Cloud9 on AWS is a browser-based development environment with deep integrations into AWS (Figure 9-3).

Figure 9-3. Using AWS Cloud9

Cloud9 is now my preferred environment for writing AWS Lambda functions and for running code that needs the AWS API keys. Cloud9 has built-in tools for writing AWS Lambda functions that make it straightforward to build and test them locally, as well as deploy them into AWS.

Figure 9-4 shows how you can pass in JSON payload and test a lambda locally in Cloud9. Testing this way is a significant advantage of the evolving platform.

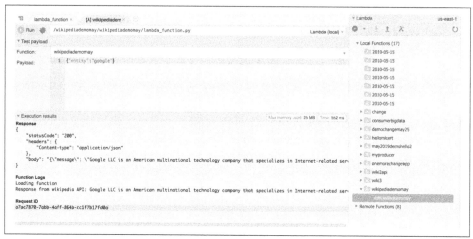

Figure 9-4. Running Lambda Function in Cloud9

Likewise, Google Cloud starts you off with the GCP Cloud Shell environment (see Figure 9-5). Cloud Shell also allows you to bootstrap development quickly, with access to critical command-line tools and a full development environment.

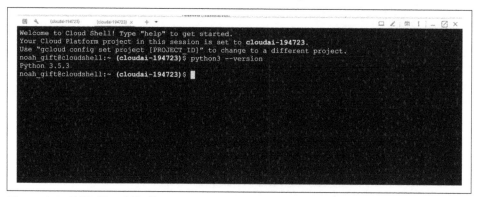

Figure 9-5. GCP Cloud Shell

The GCP Cloud Shell editor (see Figure 9-6) is a full-fledged IDE with syntax highlighting, a file explorer, and many other tools generally found in a traditional IDE.

Figure 9-6. GCP Cloud Shell editor

The key takeaway is that with the cloud, it is also best to use native development tools when possible. It reduces security holes, limits slowdowns from transferring data from your laptop to the cloud, and increases productivity due to the deep integration with its native environment.

Software as a Service

SaaS and the cloud have been joined together from day one. As the cloud gets features, SaaS products continue to distribute innovation on top of the innovations of the cloud. There are many advantages of SaaS products, especially in the DevOps space. For example, why build a monitoring solution yourself if you can *rent it*, especially when first starting. Additionally, many core DevOps principles, such as continuous integration and continuous delivery, are also made available by SaaS applications offered by cloud vendors, such as AWS CodePipeline, or third-party SaaS solutions like CircleCI.

In many cases, the ability to mix IaaS, PaaS, and SaaS allows modern companies to develop products in a much more reliable and efficient manner than they could 10 years prior. Every year it gets easier to build software, thanks to the rapid evolution not just of the cloud, but of the SaaS companies building solutions on top of the cloud.

Infrastructure as Code

IaC is covered in much greater detail in Chapter 10; refer to that chapter for a more detailed breakdown of IaC. Regarding the cloud and DevOps, though, IaC is a fundamental aspect of real-world cloud computing. IaC is a must-have capability to implement DevOps practices on the cloud.

Continuous Delivery

Continuous delivery is a newer term that can be easily confused between continuous integration and continuous deployment. The critical difference is that software is *delivered* to some environment, say a staging environment, where it can undergo both automated and manual testing. Although it doesn't require deployment immediately, it is in a deployable state. More detailed explanations of build systems can be found in Chapter 15, but it is also worth pointing out that this is a fundamental requirement to using the cloud correctly.

Virtualization and Containers

There is no more fundamental component of the cloud then virtualization. When AWS officially launched in 2006, Amazon Elastic Compute Cloud (EC2) was one of the core services released. There are a few key areas of virtualization to discuss.

Hardware Virtualization

The first virtualization abstraction released by AWS was hardware virtualization. Hardware virtualization comes in two flavors: paravirtual (PV) or hardware virtual machine (HVM). The best performance comes from HVM. The critical difference in performance is that HVM can take advantage of hardware extensions that tap into the host's hardware, essentially making the virtual machine a first-class member of the host's hardware, rather than merely a guest that is unaware of what the host is doing.

Hardware virtualization provides the ability to run multiple operating systems on one host and the ability to partition CPU, I/O (both network and disk), and memory to the guest operating system. There are many advantages to this approach, and it is the foundation of the modern cloud, but there are also some unique challenges to Python itself. One issue is that often the layer of granularity is too large for Python to fully exploit the environment. Because of the limitations of Python and threads (they don't work on multiple cores), a virtual machine that has two cores could be wasting one core. With hardware virtualization and the Python language, there can be a tremendous waste of resources due to a lack of true multithreading. A virtual machine configuration for a Python application can often leave one or more cores idle, wasting both money and energy. Fortunately, the cloud has presented new solutions that help eliminate these defects in the Python language. In particular, containers and serverless eliminate this problem because they treat the cloud as an operating system, and instead of threads, there are lambdas or containers. Instead of threads that listen on queues, lambdas respond to events from a cloud queue, such as SQS.

Software Defined Networks

Software Defined Networks (SDNs) are an essential component of cloud computing. The killer feature of SDNs is the ability to dynamically and programmatically change network behavior. Before this capability, this often rested in the hands of a networking guru who managed this F5 load balancer with an iron fist. Noah once worked at a large telecommunications company where there was a daily meeting called "Change Management" with a single individual—let's call him Bob—who controlled every piece of software that was released.

It takes a unique personality to be a Bob. There were often yelling matches between Bob and people in the company. It was the classic IT Operations versus Development battle, and Bob delighted in saying no. The cloud and DevOps completely eliminate this role, the hardware, and the weekly shouting matches. Continuous delivery processes are building and deploying software consistently with the exact configuration, software, and data needed for a production environment. Bob's role melted into ones and zeros deep inside the Matrix, replaced by some Terraform code.

Software Defined Storage

Software Defined Storage (SDS) is an abstraction that allows storage to provision on demand. This storage can be configured with granular Disk I/O and Network I/O. A good example is Amazon EBS volumes where you can configure provisioned Disk I/O. Typically, cloud SDS grows Disk I/O automatically with the volume size. An excellent example of how that works in practice is Amazon Elastic File System (EFS). EFS increases Disk I/O as the storage size grows (this occurs automatically) and is designed to support requests from thousands of EC2 instances concurrently. It also has deep integration with Amazon EC2 instances that allow pending writes to buffer and occur asynchronously.

Noah has good experience using EFS in precisely this situation. Before AWS Batch was available, he architected and wrote a system that employed thousands of spot instances that mounted EFS volumes, where they performed distributed computer vision jobs they collected from Amazon SQS. The ability to use a distributed filesystem that is always on is a massive advantage for distributed computing, and it simplifies everything from deployment to cluster computing.

Containers

Containers have been around for decades, and they refer to OS-level virtualization. The kernel allows the existence of isolated user-space instances. In the early 2000s, there was an explosion of hosting companies that used virtual hosting of Apache websites as a form of OS-level virtualization. Mainframes and classic Unix operating systems such as AIX, HP-UX, and Solaris have also had sophisticated forms of containers for years. As a developer, Noah worked with Solaris LDOM technology when it came out in 2007 and was in awe at how he could install full operating systems that allowed granular control of CPU, memory, and I/O all from telneting into a machine with a lights-out management card.

The modern version of containers is under rapid development, borrows the best things from the mainframe era, and combines them with newer ideas like source control. In particular, one of the significant revolutions with containers is to treat them as projects that check out of version control. Docker containers are now the standard format for containers, and all major cloud vendors support Dockerfile containers, along with Kubernetes container management software. There is more information on containers in Chapter 12, but the essential items that relate to the cloud are listed here:

Container registry
 All cloud providers have a container registry where they keep your containers.

Kubernetes management service
 All cloud providers have a Kubernetes offering, and this is now the standard for managing container-based deployments.

Dockerfile format
 This is the standard for building containers, and it is a simple file format. It is a best practice to use lint tools like hadolint (*https://oreil.ly/XboVE*) in your build process to ensure simple bugs don't leak through.

Continuous integration with containers
 All cloud providers have cloud-based build systems that allow integration with containers. Google has Cloud Build (*https://oreil.ly/xy6Ag*), Amazon has AWS CodePipeline (*https://oreil.ly/I5bdH*), and Azure has Azure Pipelines (*https://oreil.ly/aEOx4*). They all can build containers and register them into a container registry, as well as build projects using containers.

Deep container integration into all cloud services
 When you get into managed services in platforms on clouds, you can rest assured they all have one thing in common—containers! Amazon SageMaker, a managed machine learning platform, uses containers. The cloud development

environment Google Cloud Shell uses containers to allow you to customize your development environment.

Challenges and Opportunities in Distributed Computing

One of the most challenging areas of computer science is distributed computing. In the modern era of cloud computing, there a few fundamental shifts that have changed everything. One of the most significant shifts is the rise of multicore machines and the end of Moore's Law. See Figure 9-7.

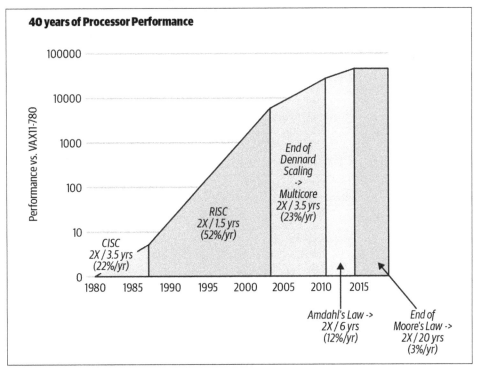

Figure 9-7. End of Moore's Law (Source: John Hennessy and David Patterson, Computer Architecture: A Quantitative Approach, 6/e. 2018)

Moore's Law exposed two fundamental problems that manifest themselves in the cloud era. The first problem is that CPUs are designed to be multipurpose processors. They are not specialized to run parallel workloads. If you couple that with the ultimate physical limits of increasing CPU speed, the CPU has become less critical in the cloud era. In 2015, Moore's Law was effectively over, and gains are at 3% a year.

The second problem is that making multiple core machines to counteract the limitations of single processor speed has led to a ripple effect on software languages. Many languages previously had substantial problems taking advantage of multiple cores because they were designed in an era before multiple processors existed, let alone the internet. Python is a good case in point here. What makes things even more challenging, Figure 9-8 shows that there is "no free lunch" by adding more cores to a problem that is not mostly parallel.

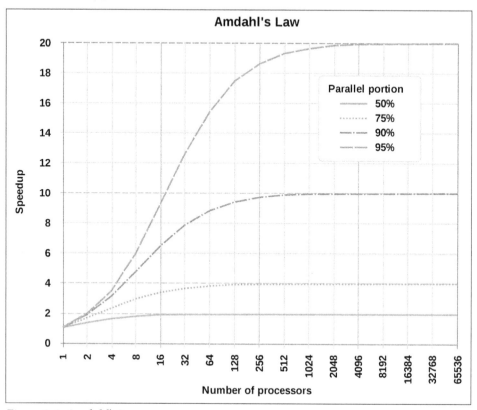

Figure 9-8. Amdahl's Law

The opportunity is in the cloud and different architectures like application-specific integrated circuits (ASICs). These include graphic processing units (GPUs), field-programmable gate arrays (FPGAs), and tensor processing units (TPUs). These specialized chips are increasingly being used in machine learning workloads and are paving the way for cloud architectures that use a combination of different hardware to tackle complex problems in distributed computing.

Python Concurrency, Performance, and Process Management in the Cloud Era

Imagine walking down a dark street in San Francisco late at night in a dangerous part of the city. In this scenario, you are a black belt in Brazilian Jiu-Jitsu. You are alone and notice that a stranger seems to be following you. Your heart starts to race as they approach and you think about your years of martial arts training. Will you have to fight a stranger in the street? You actively spar with opponents at your gym several times per week. You feel prepared to defend yourself if you need to. You also know that Brazilian Jiu-Jitsu is an efficient martial art, and it works in real-world situations.

On the other hand, fighting someone is still something to avoid. It is dangerous. Weapons could be involved. You could win the fight, yet seriously injure your opponent. You could lose the fight and become seriously injured yourself. Even an expert in Brazilian Jiu-Jitsu knows that a street fight is not a preferred scenario, despite the high probability of winning.

Concurrency in Python is very similar. There are some handy patterns like multiprocessing and asyncio. It is better to use concurrency sparingly. Often the other option is to use the platform's concurrency options (serverless, batch processing, spot instances) versus the concurrency you create yourself via a programming language.

Process Management

Process management in Python is a standout capability of the language. When Python acts as a glue to other platforms, languages, and processes, this is when it is at its best. Also, the actual implementation of process management has dramatically changed over the years and continues to improve.

Manage Processes with Subprocess

The simplest and most effective way to launch processes with the standard library is to use the run() function. As long as you have python 3.7 or higher installed, start here and simplify your code. A hello world example is just a line of code:

```
out = subprocess.run(["ls", "-l"], capture_output=True)
```

This line does almost everything you might want. It invokes a shell command in a Python subprocess and captures the output. The return value is an object of type CompletedProcess. This has the args used to launch the process: the returncode, stdout, stderr, and check_returncode.

This one-liner replaces and streamlines overly verbose and complicated methods of invoking shell commands. This is great for a developer who frequently writes Python

---

code mixed with shell commands. Here are a few more tips that might be helpful to follow.

Avoid shell=True

It is a security best practice to invoke a command as items in a list:

```
subprocess.run["ls", "-la"]
```

It is best to avoid using a string:

```
#AVOID THIS
subprocess.run("ls -la", shell=True)
```

The reason for this is straightforward. It is easy to introduce a security hole accidentally if you accept any string and execute it. Let's suppose you wrote a simple program that allowed a user to list a directory. A user can backdoor any command they want and hitchhike on your program. Writing an accidental backdoor is very scary and hopefully illustrates what a bad idea it is to use shell=True!

```
#This is input by a malicious user and causes permanent data loss
user_input = 'some_dir && rm -rf /some/important/directory'
my_command = "ls -l " + user_input
subprocess.run(my_command, shell=True)
```

Instead, you can completely prevent that by not allowing strings:

```
#This is input by a malicious user and does nothing
user_input = 'some_dir && rm -rf /some/important/directory'
subprocess.run(["ls", "-l", user_input])
```

Set timeouts and handle them when appropriate

If you are writing code that invokes a process that may take some time to run, you should create a sensible default timeout. An easy way to experiment with how this works is to use the Unix sleep command. Here is an example of a sleep command that finishes before the timeout triggers in the IPython shell. It returns a Completed Process object:

```
In [1]: subprocess.run(["sleep", "3"], timeout=4)
Out[1]: CompletedProcess(args=['sleep', '3'], returncode=0)
```

Here is a second version that throws an exception. In most cases, it would be wise to do something useful with this exception:

```
----> 1 subprocess.run(["sleep", "3"], timeout=1)

/Library/Frameworks/Python.framework/Versions/3.7/lib/python3.7/subprocess.py
  in run(input, capture_output, timeout, check, *popenargs, **kwargs)
    477             stdout, stderr = process.communicate()
    478             raise TimeoutExpired(process.args, timeout, output=stdout,
--> 479                                  stderr=stderr)
```

```
480        except:  # Including KeyboardInterrupt, communicate handled that.
481            process.kill()
```

```
TimeoutExpired: Command '['sleep', '3']' timed out after 1 seconds
```

A reasonable approach is to catch this exception `TimeoutExpired` and then to log the exception and implement some cleanup code:

```
import logging
import subprocess

try:
    subprocess.run(["sleep", "3"], timeout=4)
except subprocess.TimeoutExpired:
    logging.exception("Sleep command timed out")
```

Logging exceptions are critically important when building systems at the professional level. If this code is later deployed on many machines, it could become impossible to track down an error without a centralized logging system that is searchable. For DevOps professionals, it is critically essential to follow this pattern and evangelize its usefulness.

The problem with Python threads

You may have had a friend your parents told you not to hang out with when you were growing up. If so, it was most likely because your parents were trying to help you avoid bad choices. Python threads are a lot like that lousy friend you had growing up. Things are not going to end well if you keep associating yourself with them.

Threads in other languages are a reasonable trade-off. In a language like C#, you can execute thread pools that connect to queues and expect that each thread that spawned can take advantage of all of the cores on the device. This well-proven pattern of using threads with queues decreases the downsides of manually setting and removing locks in code.

Python doesn't work this way. If you spawn threads, it won't use all of the cores on your machine, and it can often behave in a nondeterministic fashion, bouncing from core to core and even "slowing down your code." Why use something like this when there are alternatives?

If you are interested in learning more about DevOps, then chances are you're focused on pragmatism. You only want to learn and apply the knowledge that is practical and makes sense. Pragmatism is yet another reason to avoid threads in Python. In theory, you could use threads in some situations and get a performance increase if the problem was I/O bound. However, again, why use an unreliable tool when reliable tools exist? Using Python threads is like driving a car that requires you to push it and jump-start it by popping the clutch because the battery is flaky. What happens the day you don't have room to jump-start it, or can't park the car on a hill? Using this strategy is pure madness!

There are no examples of using threads in this chapter. Why show something that is incorrect? Instead of using threads, focus on other alternatives outlined in this chapter.

Using Multiprocessing to Solve Problems

The multiprocessing library is the only unified way to use all of the cores on a machine using the standard library in Python. In looking at Figure 9-9, there are a couple of options at the operating system level: multiprocessing and containers.

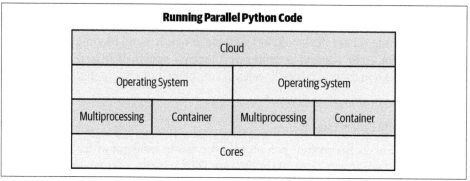

Figure 9-9. Running parallel Python code

Using containers as an alternative is a crucial distinction. If the purpose of using the multiprocessing library is to invoke a process many times without interprocess communication, a strong argument could be made to use a container, virtual machine, or cloud-native construct such as Function as a Service. A popular and effective cloud-native option is AWS Lambda.

Likewise, a container has many advantages over forking processes yourself. There are many advantages to containers. Container definitions are code. Containers can be sized precisely at the level needed: i.e., memory, CPU, or disk I/O. They are a direct competitor and often a better replacement for forking processes yourself. In practice, they can also be much easier to fit into a DevOps mindset.

From a DevOps perspective, if you buy into the idea that you should avoid concurrency in Python that you implement yourself unless it is the only option, then even the scenario when you use the multiprocessing module is limited. It may be that multiprocessing is best used as a tool in development and experimentation only, since much better options exist at both the container and cloud level.

Another way to put this is to ask who you trust to fork processes: the multiprocessing code you wrote in Python, the developers from Google who wrote Kubernetes, or the developers at Amazon who wrote AWS Lambda? Experience tells me that I make the best decisions when I stand on the shoulders of giants. With that philosophical consideration out of the way, here are some ways to use multiprocessing effectively.

Forking Processes with Pool()

A straightforward way to test out the ability to fork multiple processes and run a function against them is to calculate KMeans clustering with the sklearn machine learning library. A KMeans calculation is computed intensively and has a time complexity of $O(n^{**}2)$, which means it grows exponentially slower with more data. This example is a perfect type of operation to parallelize, either at the macro or the micro level. In the following example, the make_blobs method creates a dataset with 100k records and 10 features. This process has timing for each KMeans algorithm as well as the total time it takes:

```
from sklearn.datasets.samples_generator import make_blobs
from sklearn.cluster import KMeans
import time

def do_kmeans():
    """KMeans clustering on generated data"""

    X,_ = make_blobs(n_samples=100000, centers=3, n_features=10,
                random_state=0)
    kmeans = KMeans(n_clusters=3)
    t0 = time.time()
    kmeans.fit(X)
    print(f"KMeans cluster fit in {time.time()-t0}")

def main():
    """Run Everything"""

    count = 10
    t0 = time.time()
    for _ in range(count):
        do_kmeans()
    print(f"Performed {count} KMeans in total time: {time.time()-t0}")


if __name__ == "__main__":
    main()
```

The runtime of the KMeans algorithm shows that it is an expensive operation and to run 10 iterations takes 3.5 seconds:

```
(.python-devops) → python kmeans_sequential.py
KMeans cluster fit in 0.29854321479797363
KMeans cluster fit in 0.2869119644165039
KMeans cluster fit in 0.2811620235443115
KMeans cluster fit in 0.28687286376953125
```

```
KMeans cluster fit in 0.2845759391784668
KMeans cluster fit in 0.2866239547729492
KMeans cluster fit in 0.2843656539916992
KMeans cluster fit in 0.2885470390319824
KMeans cluster fit in 0.2878849506378174
KMeans cluster fit in 0.28443288803100586
Performed 10 KMeans in total time: 3.510640859603882
```

In the following example, the `multiprocessing.Pool.map`, the method is used to distribute 10 KMeans cluster operations to a pool of 10 processes. This example occurs by mapping the argument of 100000 to the function do_kmeans:

```python
from multiprocessing import Pool
from sklearn.datasets.samples_generator import make_blobs
from sklearn.cluster import KMeans
import time

def do_kmeans(n_samples):
    """KMeans clustering on generated data"""

    X,_ = make_blobs(n_samples, centers=3, n_features=10,
                random_state=0)
    kmeans = KMeans(n_clusters=3)
    t0 = time.time()
    kmeans.fit(X)
    print(f"KMeans cluster fit in {time.time()-t0}")

def main():
    """Run Everything"""

    count = 10
    t0 = time.time()
    with Pool(count) as p:
        p.map(do_kmeans, [100000,100000,100000,100000,100000,
                    100000,100000,100000,100000,100000])

    print(f"Performed {count} KMeans in total time: {time.time()-t0}")


if __name__ == "__main__":
    main()
```

The run time of each KMeans operation is slower, but the overall speedup is double. This is a common issue with concurrency frameworks; there is overhead to distribute parallel work. There isn't a "free lunch" to run the parallel code. The cost is that each task has a ramp-up time of about one second:

```
(.python-devops) → python kmeans_multiprocessing.py
KMeans cluster fit in 1.3836050033569336
KMeans cluster fit in 1.3868029117584229
KMeans cluster fit in 1.3955950736999512
KMeans cluster fit in 1.3925609588623047
```

```
KMeans cluster fit in 1.3877739906311035
KMeans cluster fit in 1.4068050384521484
KMeans cluster fit in 1.41087007522583
KMeans cluster fit in 1.3935530185699463
KMeans cluster fit in 1.4161033630371094
KMeans cluster fit in 1.4132652282714844
Performed 10 KMeans in total time: 1.6691410541534424
```

This example shows why it is essential to profile code and also be careful about immediately jumping to concurrency. If the problem is small scale, then the overhead of the parallelization approach could slow the code down in addition to making it more complex to debug.

From a DevOps perspective, the most straightforward and most maintainable approach should always be the top priority. In practice, this could mean that this style of multiprocessing parallelization is a reasonable approach, but not before a macro-ready level parallelization approach has first been tried. Some alternative Macro approaches could be using containers, using FaaS (AWS Lambda or some other serverless technology), or using a high-performance server that Python runs workers against (RabbitMQ or Redis).

Function as a Service and Serverless

The modern AI era has created pressures that have enabled new paradigms. CPU clock speed increases have ground to a halt, and this has effectively ended Moore's Law. At the same time, the explosion of data, the rise of cloud computing, and the availability of application specific integrated circuits (ASICs) have picked up that slack. Now a function as a unit of work has become an essential concept.

Serverless and FaaS can be used somewhat interchangeably, and they describe the ability to run a function as a unit of work on a cloud platform.

High Performance Python with Numba

Numba is a very cool library to experiment with for distributed problem-solving. Using it is a lot like modifying your car with high-performance aftermarket parts. It also leverages the trend of using ASICs to solve specific problems.

Using Numba Just in Time Compiler

Let's take a look at the officially documented example (*https://oreil.ly/KlW5s*) of Numba Just in Time Compiler (JIT), tweak it a bit, and then break down what is happening.

This example is a Python function that is decorated by the JIT. The argument nopython=True enforces that the code passes through the JIT and is optimized using the

LLVM compiler. If this option isn't selected, it means that if something doesn't translate to LLVM, it stays as regular Python code:

```
import numpy as np
from numba import jit

@jit(nopython=True)
def go_fast(a):
    """Expects Numpy Array"""

    count = 0
    for i in range(a.shape[0]):
        count += np.tanh(a[i, i])
    return count + trace
```

Next, a numpy array is created, and the IPython magic function is used to time it:

```
x = np.arange(100).reshape(10, 10)
%timeit go_fast(x)
```

The output shows that it took 855 nanoseconds to run the code:

```
The slowest run took 33.43 times longer than the fastest. This example could mean
that an intermediate result is cached. 1000000 loops, best of 3: 855 ns per loop
```

The regular version can be run using this trick to avoid the decorator:

```
%timeit go_fast.py_func(x)
```

The output shows that without the JIT, regular Python code is 20 times slower:

```
The slowest run took 4.15 times longer than the fastest. This result could mean
that an intermediate run is cached. 10000 loops, best of 3: 20.5 µs per loop
```

With the Numba JIT, for loops are an optimization that it can speed up. It also optimizes numpy functions and numpy data structure. The main takeaway here is that it might be worth looking at existing code that has been running for years and seeing if critical parts of a Python infrastructure could benefit from being compiled with the Numba JIT.

Using High-Performance Servers

Self-actualization is an essential concept in human development. The simplest definition of self-actualization is an individual reaching their real potential. To do this, they must also accept their human nature with all of its flaws. One theory is that less than 1% of people have fully self-actualized.

The same concept can be applied to Python, the language. Fully accepting the strengths and weaknesses of the language allows a developer to utilize it fully. Python is not a high-performance language. Python is not a language optimized for writing servers like other languages are: Go, Java, C, C++, C#, or Erlang. Instead, Python is a language for applying high-level logic on top of high-performance code written in a high-performance language or platform.

Python is widely popular because it fits into the natural thought process of the human mind. With sufficient experience using the language, you can think in Python, just like you can think in your native language. Logic can be expressed in many ways: language, symbolic notation, code, pictures, sound, and art. Computer science constructs such as memory management, type declaration, concurrency primitives, and object-oriented design can be abstracted away from pure logic. They are optional to the expression of an idea.

The power of a language like Python is that it allows the user to work at the logic level, not the computer science level. What is the takeaway? Use the right tool for the job, and often this is the cloud or service in another language.

Conclusion

Both DevOps and data science share a common thread in that they are both job titles and capabilities. Some of the benefits of DevOps methodologies are speed, automation, reliability, scale, and security accomplished through pragmatism. Using macro-level solutions for concurrency and management of processes increases operation efficiency. Using micro-level solutions before looking at available frameworks and solutions is a dangerous DevOps antipattern.

What are the takeaways for Python in the cloud era?

- Learn to master the right concurrency technique for the task at hand.
- Learn to use the high-performance computing library Numba to turbocharge your code with real threads, JIT, and the GPU.
- Learn to use FaaS to solve unique problems elegantly.
- Treat the cloud as an operating system and make it do the hard work of concurrency.
- Embrace cloud-native constructs such as continuous delivery, Docker format containers, and serverless.

Exercises

- What is IaaS?
- What is PaaS?
- What does elasticity mean?
- What does availability mean?

- What is block storage?

- What are the different types of cloud computing services?

- What is serverless?

- What are some key differences between IaaS and PaaS?

- What is the CAP Theorem?

- What is Amdahl's Law?

Case Study Questions

- A company is hesitant to move into cloud computing because it has heard it can be more expensive. What are some ways to mitigate the cost risks of adopting cloud computing?

- What is an example of a cloud-native architecture? Draw an architectural diagram of a cloud-native system and list the key features.

- What do spot or preemptible instances do? How can they save money? What problems are they suitable for? What problems are they not suitable for?

## CHAPTER 10

Infrastructure as Code

Before we had fancy DevOps titles and job descriptions, we were lowly system administrators, or sysadmins for short. Those were the dark, pre-cloud days when we had to load the trunks of our cars with bare-metal servers and drive to a colocation (colo) facility to rack the servers, wire them, attach a wheeled monitor/keyboard/mouse to them, and set them up one by one. Grig still shudders to think about the hours he spent in colos, in blinding light and freezing A/C. We had to be wizards at Bash scripting, then we graduated to Perl, and the more fortunate of us to Python. As the saying went, the internet circa 2004 was held together with duct tape and bubble gum.

Somewhere during the period of 2006 to 2007, we discovered the magical world of Amazon EC2 instances. We were able to provision servers through a simple point-and-click interface, or through command-line tools. No more driving to colocation facilities, no more stacking and wiring bare-metal servers. We could go wild and launch 10 EC2 instances at a time. Or even 20! Or even 100! The sky was the limit. However, we quickly figured out that manually connecting to each EC2 instance using SSH and then setting up our applications on every instance separately was not going to scale. It was fairly easy to provision the instances themselves. What was difficult was to install the required packages for our applications, add the correct users, make sure the file permissions looked right, and finally install and configure our applications. To scratch this itch, the first generation of infrastructure automation software came into being, represented by "configuration management" tools. Puppet was the first well-known configuration management tool, released in 2005 and predated the release of Amazon EC2. Other such tools that were launched on the heels of Puppet were Chef in 2008, followed by SaltStack in 2011, and Ansible in 2012.

By 2009, the world was ready to welcome the arrival of a new term: DevOps. To this day, there are competing definitions of DevOps. What is interesting is that it came into being in the tumultuous early days of infrastructure software automation. While there are important people and culture aspects to DevOps, one thing stands out in this chapter: the ability to automate the provisioning, configuration, and deployment of infrastructure and applications.

By 2011, it was getting hard to keep track of all the services comprising the Amazon Web Services (AWS) suite. The cloud was much more complicated than raw compute power (Amazon EC2) and object storage (Amazon S3). Applications started to rely on multiple services interacting with each other, and tools were needed to help automate the provisioning of these services. Amazon didn't wait long to fill this need, and in 2011 it started offering just such a tool: AWS CloudFormation. This was one of the first moments when we could truly say that we were able to describe our infrastructure through code. CloudFormation opened the doors to a new generation of Infrastructure as Code (IaC) tools, which were operating at the layer of the cloud infrastructure itself, underneath the layer served by the first-generation configuration management tools.

By 2014, AWS had launched dozens of services. That was the year when another important tool in the world of IaC came into being: Terraform, by HashiCorp. To this day, the two most used IaC tools are CloudFormation and Terraform.

Another important development in the world of IaC and DevOps was taking place sometime between late 2013 and early 2014: the release of Docker, which came to be synonymous with container technologies. Although containers had been around for a number of years, the great benefit that Docker brought to the table was that it wrapped technologies such as Linux containers and cgroups into an easy-to-use API and command-line interface (CLI) toolset that significantly lowered the barrier of entry for people who wanted to package their applications into containers that could be deployed and run wherever Docker was running. Container technologies and container orchestration platforms are discussed in detail in Chapters 11 and 12.

The usage and mindshare of Docker exploded and damaged the popularity of the first-generation configuration management tools (Puppet, Chef, Ansible, SaltStack). The companies behind these tools are reeling at the moment and are all trying to stay afloat and current by reinventing themselves as cloud friendly. Before the advent of Docker, you would provision the infrastructure for your application with an IaC tool such as CloudFormation or Terraform, then deploy the application itself (code and configuration) with a configuration management tool such as Puppet, Chef, Ansible, or SaltStack. Docker suddenly made these configuration management tools obsolete, since it provided a means for you to package your application (code + configuration) in a Docker container that would then run inside the infrastructure provisioned by the IaC tools.

A Classification of Infrastructure Automation Tools

Fast-forward to 2020 and it is easy to feel lost as a DevOps practitioner when faced with the multitude of infrastructure automation tools available.

One way to differentiate IaC tools is by looking at the layer at which they operate. Tools such as CloudFormation and Terraform operate at the cloud infrastructure layer. They allow you to provision cloud resources such as compute, storage, and networking, as well as various services such as databases, message queues, data analytics, and many others. Configuration management tools such as Puppet, Chef, Ansible, and SaltStack typically operate at the application layer, making sure that all the required packages are installed for your application, and that the application itself is configured correctly (although many of these tools also have modules that can provision cloud resources). Docker also operates at the application layer.

Another way to compare IaC tools is by dividing them into declarative versus imperative categories. You can tell an automation tool what to do in a declarative manner where you describe the state of the system that you are trying to achieve. Puppet, CloudFormation, and Terraform operate in a declarative manner. Alternatively, you can use an automation tool in a procedural or imperative manner, where you specify the exact steps needed by the tool to achieve the desired system state. Chef and Ansible operate in an imperative manner. SaltStack can operate in both declarative and imperative manners.

Let's look at the desired state of the system as a blueprint for the construction of a building, let's say a stadium. You use procedural tools like Chef and Ansible to build the stadium, section by section and row by row inside each section. You need to keep track of the state of the stadium and the progress of the construction. Using declarative tools such as Puppet, CloudFormation, and Terraform, you first put together the blueprint for the stadium. The tool then makes sure that the construction achieves the state depicted in the blueprint.

Given this chapter's title, we will focus the remaining discussion on IaC tools, which can be further classified along several dimensions.

One dimension is the way you specify the desired state of the system. In CloudFormation, you do it with JSON or YAML syntax, while in Terraform you do it with the proprietary HashiCorp Configuration Language (HCL) syntax. In contrast, Pulumi and the AWS Cloud Development Kit (CDK) allow you to use real programming languages, including Python, for specifying the desired state of the system.

Another dimension is the cloud providers supported by each tool. Since CloudFormation is an Amazon service, it stands to reason that it focuses on AWS (although one can define non-AWS resources with CloudFormation when using the custom resources feature). The same is true for the AWS CDK. In contrast, Terraform supports many cloud providers, as does Pulumi.

Because this is a book about Python, we would like to mention a tool called troposphere (*https://oreil.ly/Zdid-*), which allows you to specify CloudFormation stack templates using Python code, and then exports them to JSON or YAML. Troposphere stops at the generation of the stack templates, which means that you need to provision the stacks using CloudFormation. One other tool that also uses Python and is worth mentioning is stacker (*https://oreil.ly/gBF_N*). It uses troposphere under the covers, but it also provisions the generated CloudFormation stack templates.

The rest of this chapter shows two of these automation tools, Terraform and Pulumi, in action, each working on a common scenario, which is the deployment of a static website in Amazon S3, which is fronted by the Amazon CloudFront CDN and secured by an SSL certificate provisioned via the AWS Certificate Manager (ACM) service.

> Some of the commands used in the following examples produce large amounts of output. Except for cases where it is critical to the understanding of the command, we will omit the majority of the output lines to save trees and enable you to focus better on the text.

Manual Provisioning

We started by working through the scenario manually, using the AWS web-based console. Nothing like experiencing the pain of doing things manually so that you can better enjoy the results of automating tedious work!

We first followed the documentation from AWS website for hosting in S3 (*https://oreil.ly/kdv8T*).

We already had a domain name bought via Namecheap: devops4all.dev. We created a hosted zone in Amazon Route 53 for the domain, and pointed the name servers for this domain in Namecheap to AWS DNS servers handling the hosted domain.

We provisioned two S3 buckets, one for the root URL of the site (devops4all.dev) and one for the www URL (www.devops4all.dev). The idea was to redirect requests to www to the root URL. We also went through the guide and configured the buckets for static site hosting, with the proper permissions. We uploaded an *index.html* file and a JPG image to the root S3 bucket.

The next step was to provision an SSL certificate to handle both the root domain name (devops4all.dev) and any subdomain of that domain (*.devops4all.dev). For verification, we used DNS records that we added to the Route 53 hosted zone.

The ACM certificate needs to be provisioned in the us-east-1 AWS region so that it can be used in CloudFront.

We then created an AWS CloudFront CDN distribution pointing to the root S3 bucket and used the ACM certificate provisioned in the previous step. We specified that HTTP requests should be redirected to HTTPS. Once the distribution was deployed (which took approximately 15 minutes), we added Route 53 records for the root domain and the www domain as A records of type Alias pointing to the Cloud-Front distribution endpoint DNS name.

At the end of this exercise, we were able to go to *http://devops4all.dev*, be redirected automatically to *https://devops4all.dev*, and see the home page of the site showing the image we uploaded. We also tried going to *http://www.devops4all.dev* and were redirected to *https://devops4all.dev*.

The manual creation of all the AWS resources we mentioned took approximately 30 minutes. We also spent 15 minutes waiting for the CloudFront distribution propagation, for a total of 45 minutes. Note that we had done all this before, so we knew exactly what to do, with only minimal reference to the AWS guide.

It is worth taking a moment to appreciate how easy it is these days to provision a free SSL certificate. Gone are the days when you had to wait hours or even days for the SSL certificate provider to approve your request, only after you submitted proof that your company existed. Between AWS ACM, and Let's Encrypt, there is no excuse not to have SSL enabled on all pages of your site in 2020.

Automated Infrastructure Provisioning with Terraform

We decided to use Terraform as the first IaC tool for the automation of these tasks, even though Terraform is not directly related to Python. It has several advantages, such as maturity, strong ecosystem, and multicloud provisioners.

The recommended way of writing Terraform code is to use modules, which are reusable components of Terraform configuration code. There is a common registry (*https://registry.terraform.io*) of Terraform modules hosted by HashiCorp where you can search for ready-made modules that you might use for provisioning the resources you need. In this example, we will write our own modules.

The version of Terraform used here is 0.12.1, which is the latest version at the time of this writing. Install it on a Mac by using brew:

```
$ brew install terraform
```

Provisioning an S3 Bucket

Create a *modules* directory and underneath it an *s3* directory containing three files: *main.tf*, *variables.tf*, and *outputs.tf*. The *main.tf* file in the *s3* directory tells Terraform to create an S3 bucket with a specific policy. It uses a variable called domain_name that is declared in *variables.tf* and whose value is passed to it by the caller of this module. It outputs the DNS endpoint of the S3 bucket, which will be used by other modules as an input variable.

Here are the three files in *modules/s3*:

```
$ cat modules/s3/main.tf
resource "aws_s3_bucket" "www" {
  bucket = "www.${var.domain_name}"
  acl = "public-read"
  policy = <<POLICY
{
  "Version":"2012-10-17",
  "Statement":[
    {
      "Sid":"AddPerm",
      "Effect":"Allow",
      "Principal": "*",
      "Action":["s3:GetObject"],
      "Resource":["arn:aws:s3:::www.${var.domain_name}/*"]
    }
  ]
}
POLICY

  website {
    index_document = "index.html"
  }
}

$ cat modules/s3/variables.tf
variable "domain_name" {}

$ cat modules/s3/outputs.tf
output "s3_www_website_endpoint" {
  value = "${aws_s3_bucket.www.website_endpoint}"
}
```

> The policy attribute of the aws_s3_bucket resource above is an example of an S3 bucket policy that allows public access to the bucket. If you work with S3 buckets in an IaC context, it pays to familiarize yourself with the official AWS documentation on bucket and user policies (*https://oreil.ly/QtTYd*).

The main Terraform script which ties together all the modules is a file called *main.tf*
in the current directory:

```
$ cat main.tf
provider "aws" {
  region = "${var.aws_region}"
}

module "s3" {
  source = "./modules/s3"
  domain_name = "${var.domain_name}"
}
```

It refers to variables that are defined in a separate file called *variables.tf*:

```
$ cat variables.tf
variable "aws_region" {
  default = "us-east-1"
}

variable "domain_name" {
  default = "devops4all.dev"
}
```

Here is the current directory tree at this point:

```
|____main.tf
|____variables.tf
|____modules
| |____s3
| | |____outputs.tf
| | |____main.tf
| | |____variables.tf
```

The first step in running Terraform is to invoke the `terraform init` command,
which will read the contents of any module referenced by the main file.

The next step is to run the `terraform plan` command, which creates the blueprint
mentioned in the earlier discussion.

To create the resources specified in the plan, run `terraform apply`:

```
$ terraform apply

An execution plan has been generated and is shown below.
Resource actions are indicated with the following symbols:
  + create

Terraform will perform the following actions:

  # module.s3.aws_s3_bucket.www will be created
  + resource "aws_s3_bucket" "www" {
      + acceleration_status = (known after apply)
      + acl  = "public-read"
```

```
    + arn  = (known after apply)
    + bucket  = "www.devops4all.dev"
    + bucket_domain_name  = (known after apply)
    + bucket_regional_domain_name = (known after apply)
    + force_destroy = false
    + hosted_zone_id= (known after apply)
    + id= (known after apply)
    + policy  = jsonencode(
        {
          + Statement = [
              + {
                  + Action = [
                      + "s3:GetObject",
                    ]
                  + Effect = "Allow"
                  + Principal = "*"
                  + Resource  = [
                      + "arn:aws:s3:::www.devops4all.dev/*",
                    ]
                  + Sid = "AddPerm"
                },
            ]
          + Version= "2012-10-17"
        }
      )
    + region  = (known after apply)
    + request_payer = (known after apply)
    + website_domain= (known after apply)
    + website_endpoint = (known after apply)

    + versioning {
        + enabled = (known after apply)
        + mfa_delete = (known after apply)
      }

    + website {
        + index_document = "index.html"
      }
  }

Plan: 1 to add, 0 to change, 0 to destroy.

Do you want to perform these actions?
  Terraform will perform the actions described above.
  Only 'yes' will be accepted to approve.

  Enter a value: yes

module.s3.aws_s3_bucket.www: Creating...
module.s3.aws_s3_bucket.www: Creation complete after 7s [www.devops4all.dev]

Apply complete! Resources: 1 added, 0 changed, 0 destroyed.
```

At this point, check that the S3 bucket was created using the AWS web console UI.

Provisioning an SSL Certificate with AWS ACM

The next module is created for the provisioning of an SSL certificate using the AWS Certificate Manager service. Create a directory called *modules/acm* with three files: *main.tf*, *variables.tf*, and *outputs.tf*. The *main.tf* file in the *acm* directory tells Terraform to create an ACM SSL certificate using DNS as the validation method. It uses a variable called domain_name which is declared in *variables.tf* and whose value is passed to it by the caller of this module. It outputs the ARN identifier of the certificate, which will be used by other modules as an input variable.

```
$ cat modules/acm/main.tf
resource "aws_acm_certificate" "certificate" {
  domain_name = "*.${var.domain_name}"
  validation_method = "DNS"
  subject_alternative_names = ["*.${var.domain_name}"]
}

$ cat modules/acm/variables.tf
variable "domain_name" {
}

$ cat modules/acm/outputs.tf
output "certificate_arn" {
  value = "${aws_acm_certificate.certificate.arn}"
}
```

Add a reference to the new acm module in the main Terraform file:

```
$ cat main.tf
provider "aws" {
  region = "${var.aws_region}"
}

module "s3" {
  source = "./modules/s3"
  domain_name = "${var.domain_name}"
}

module "acm" {
  source = "./modules/acm"
  domain_name = "${var.domain_name}"
}
```

The next three steps are the same as in the S3 bucket creation sequence: terraform init, terraform plan, and terraform apply.

Use the AWS console to add the necessary Route 53 records for the validation process. The certificate is normally validated and issued in a few minutes.

Provisioning an Amazon CloudFront Distribution

The next module is created for the provisioning of an Amazon CloudFront distribution. Create a directory called *modules/cloudfront* with three files: *main.tf*, *variables.tf*, and *outputs.tf*. The *main.tf* file in the *cloudfront* directory tells Terraform to create a CloudFront distribution resource. It uses several variables that are declared in *variables.tf* and whose values are passed to it by the caller of this module. It outputs the DNS domain name for the CloudFront endpoint and the hosted Route 53 zone ID for the CloudFront distribution, which will be used by other modules as input variables:

```
$ cat modules/cloudfront/main.tf
resource "aws_cloudfront_distribution" "www_distribution" {
  origin {
    custom_origin_config {
      // These are all the defaults.
      http_port= "80"
      https_port  = "443"
      origin_protocol_policy = "http-only"
      origin_ssl_protocols= ["TLSv1", "TLSv1.1", "TLSv1.2"]
    }

    domain_name = "${var.s3_www_website_endpoint}"
    origin_id= "www.${var.domain_name}"
  }

  enabled  = true
  default_root_object = "index.html"

  default_cache_behavior {
    viewer_protocol_policy = "redirect-to-https"
    compress = true
    allowed_methods= ["GET", "HEAD"]
    cached_methods = ["GET", "HEAD"]
    target_origin_id = "www.${var.domain_name}"
    min_ttl  = 0
    default_ttl = 86400
    max_ttl  = 31536000

    forwarded_values {
      query_string = false
      cookies {
        forward = "none"
      }
    }
  }

  aliases = ["www.${var.domain_name}"]

  restrictions {
    geo_restriction {
      restriction_type = "none"
```

```
    }
  }

  viewer_certificate {
    acm_certificate_arn = "${var.acm_certificate_arn}"
    ssl_support_method  = "sni-only"
  }
}

$ cat modules/cloudfront/variables.tf
variable "domain_name" {}
variable "acm_certificate_arn" {}
variable "s3_www_website_endpoint" {}

$ cat modules/cloudfront/outputs.tf
output "domain_name" {
  value = "${aws_cloudfront_distribution.www_distribution.domain_name}"
}

output "hosted_zone_id" {
  value = "${aws_cloudfront_distribution.www_distribution.hosted_zone_id}"
}
```

Add a reference to the cloudfront module in the main Terraform file. Pass s3_www_website_endpoint and acm_certificate_arn as input variables to the cloud front module. Their values are retrieved from the outputs of the other modules, s3 and acm, respectively.

 ARN stands for Amazon Resource Name. It is a string that uniquely identifies a given AWS resource. You will see many ARN values generated and passed around as variables when you use IaC tools that operate within AWS.

```
$ cat main.tf
provider "aws" {
  region = "${var.aws_region}"
}

module "s3" {
  source = "./modules/s3"
  domain_name = "${var.domain_name}"
}

module "acm" {
  source = "./modules/acm"
  domain_name = "${var.domain_name}"
}

module "cloudfront" {
  source = "./modules/cloudfront"
```

```
  domain_name = "${var.domain_name}"
  s3_www_website_endpoint = "${module.s3.s3_www_website_endpoint}"
  acm_certificate_arn = "${module.acm.certificate_arn}"
}
```

The next three steps are the usual ones for the provisioning of resources with Terraform: `terraform init`, `terraform plan`, and `terraform apply`.

The `terraform apply` step took almost 23 minutes in this case. Provisioning an Amazon CloudFront distribution is one of the lengthiest operations in AWS, because the distribution is being deployed globally by Amazon behind the scenes.

Provisioning a Route 53 DNS Record

The next module was for the creation of a Route 53 DNS record for the main domain of the site www.devops4all.dev. Create a directory called *modules/route53* with two files: *main.tf* and *variables.tf*. The *main.tf* file in the *route53* directory tells Terraform to create a Route 53 DNS record of type `A` as an alias to the DNS name of the Cloud-Front endpoint. It uses several variables that are declared in *variables.tf* and whose values are passed to it by the caller of this module:

```
$ cat modules/route53/main.tf
resource "aws_route53_record" "www" {
  zone_id = "${var.zone_id}"
  name = "www.${var.domain_name}"
  type = "A"

  alias {
    name  = "${var.cloudfront_domain_name}"
    zone_id  = "${var.cloudfront_zone_id}"
    evaluate_target_health = false
  }
}

$ cat modules/route53/variables.tf
variable "domain_name" {}
variable "zone_id" {}
variable "cloudfront_domain_name" {}
variable "cloudfront_zone_id" {}
```

Add a reference to the `route53` module in the *main.tf* Terraform file. Pass `zone_id`, `cloudfront_domain_name`, and `cloudfront_zone_id` as input variables to the `route53` module. The value of `zone_id` is declared in *variables.tf* in the current directory, while the other values are retrieved from the outputs of the `cloudfront` module:

```
$ cat main.tf
provider "aws" {
  region = "${var.aws_region}"
}
```

```
module "s3" {
  source = "./modules/s3"
  domain_name = "${var.domain_name}"
}

module "acm" {
  source = "./modules/acm"
  domain_name = "${var.domain_name}"
}

module "cloudfront" {
  source = "./modules/cloudfront"
  domain_name = "${var.domain_name}"
  s3_www_website_endpoint = "${module.s3.s3_www_website_endpoint}"
  acm_certificate_arn = "${module.acm.certificate_arn}"
}

module "route53" {
  source = "./modules/route53"
  domain_name = "${var.domain_name}"
  zone_id = "${var.zone_id}"
  cloudfront_domain_name = "${module.cloudfront.domain_name}"
  cloudfront_zone_id = "${module.cloudfront.hosted_zone_id}"
}

$ cat variables.tf
variable "aws_region" {
  default = "us-east-1"
}

variable "domain_name" {
  default = "devops4all.dev"
}

variable "zone_id" {
  default = "ZWX18ZIVHAA5O"
}
```

The next three steps, which should be very familiar to you by now, are for the provisioning of resources with Terraform: `terraform init`, `terraform plan`, and `terraform apply`.

Copying Static Files to S3

To test the provisioning of the static website from end to end, create a simple file called *index.html* that includes a JPEG image, and copy both files to the S3 bucket previously provisioned with Terraform. Make sure that the `AWS_PROFILE` environment variable is set to a correct value already present in the *~/.aws/credentials* file:

```
$ echo $AWS_PROFILE
gheorghiu-net
```

```
$ aws s3 cp static_files/index.html s3://www.devops4all.dev/index.html
upload: static_files/index.html to s3://www.devops4all.dev/index.html
$ aws s3 cp static_files/devops4all.jpg s3://www.devops4all.dev/devops4all.jpg
upload: static_files/devops4all.jpg to s3://www.devops4all.dev/devops4all.jpg
```

Visit *https://www.devops4all.dev/* and verify that you can see the JPG image that was uploaded.

Deleting All AWS Resources Provisioned with Terraform

Whenever you provision cloud resources, you need to be mindful of the cost associated with them. It is very easy to forget about them, and you may be surprised by the AWS bill you receive at the end of the month. Make sure to delete all the resources provisioned above. Remove these resources by running the `terraform destroy` command. One more thing to note is that the contents of the S3 bucket need to be removed before running `terraform destroy` because Terraform will not delete a nonempty bucket.

Before running the `terraform destroy` command, make sure you will not delete resources that might still be used in production!

Automated Infrastructure Provisioning with Pulumi

Pulumi is one of the new kids on the block when it comes to IaC tools. The keyword here is *new*, which means it is still somewhat rough around the edges, especially in regards to Python support.

Pulumi allows you to specify the desired state of your infrastructure by telling it which resources to provision using real programming languages. TypeScript was the first language supported by Pulumi, but nowadays Go and Python are also supported.

It is important to understand the difference between writing infrastructure automation code in Python using Pulumi and an AWS automation library such as Boto.

With Pulumi, your Python code describes the resources that you want to be provisioned. You are, in effect, creating the blueprint or the state discussed at the beginning of the chapter. This makes Pulumi similar to Terraform, but the big difference is that Pulumi gives you the full power of a programming language such as Python in terms of writing functions, loops, using variables, etc. You are not hampered by the use of a markup language such as Terraform's HCL. Pulumi combines the power of a declarative approach, where you describe the desired end state, with the power of a real programming language.

With an AWS automation library such as Boto, you both describe and provision individual AWS resources through the code you write. There is no overall blueprint or state. You need to keep track of the provisioned resources yourself, and to orchestrate their creation and removal. This is the imperative or procedural approach for automation tools. You still get the advantage of writing Python code.

To start using Pulumi, create a free account on their website pulumi.io. Then you can install the `pulumi` command-line tool on your local machine. On a Macintosh, use Homebrew to install `pulumi`.

The first command to run locally is `pulumi login`:

```
$ pulumi login
Logged into pulumi.com as griggheo (https://app.pulumi.com/griggheo)
```

Creating a New Pulumi Python Project for AWS

Create a directory called *proj1*, run `pulumi new` in that directory, and chose the aws-python template. As part of the project creation, `pulumi` asks for the name of a stack. Call it `staging`:

```
$ mkdir proj1
$ cd proj1
$ pulumi new
Please choose a template: aws-python        A minimal AWS Python Pulumi program
This command will walk you through creating a new Pulumi project.

Enter a value or leave blank to accept the (default), and press <ENTER>.
Press ^C at any time to quit.

project name: (proj1)
project description: (A minimal AWS Python Pulumi program)
Created project 'proj1'

stack name: (dev) staging
Created stack 'staging'

aws:region: The AWS region to deploy into: (us-east-1)
Saved config

Your new project is ready to go!
To perform an initial deployment, run the following commands:

   1. virtualenv -p python3 venv
   2. source venv/bin/activate
   3. pip3 install -r requirements.txt

Then, run 'pulumi up'
```

It is important to understand the difference between a Pulumi project and a Pulumi stack. A project is the code you write for specifying the desired state of the system, the resources you want Pulumi to provision. A stack is a specific deployment of the project. For example, a stack can correspond to an environment such as development, staging, or production. In the examples that follow, we will create two Pulumi stacks, one called staging that corresponds to a staging environment, and further down the line, another stack called prod that corresponds to a production environment.

Here are the files automatically generated by the pulumi new command as part of the aws-python template:

```
$ ls -la
total 40
drwxr-xr-x    7 ggheo  staff   224 Jun 13 21:43 .
drwxr-xr-x   11 ggheo  staff   352 Jun 13 21:42 ..
-rw-------    1 ggheo  staff    12 Jun 13 21:43 .gitignore
-rw-r--r--    1 ggheo  staff    32 Jun 13 21:43 Pulumi.staging.yaml
-rw-------    1 ggheo  staff    77 Jun 13 21:43 Pulumi.yaml
-rw-------    1 ggheo  staff   184 Jun 13 21:43 __main__.py
-rw-------    1 ggheo  staff    34 Jun 13 21:43 requirements.txt
```

Follow the instructions in the output of pulumi new and install virtualenv, then create a new virtualenv environment and install the libraries specified in *requirements.txt*:

```
$ pip3 install virtualenv
$ virtualenv -p python3 venv
$ source venv/bin/activate
(venv) pip3 install -r requirements.txt
```

 Before provisioning any AWS resources with pulumi up, make sure you are using the AWS account that you are expecting to target. One way to specify the desired AWS account is to set the AWS_PRO FILE environment variable in your current shell. In our case, an AWS profile called gheorghiu-net was already set up in the local *~/.aws/credentials* file.

```
(venv) export AWS_PROFILE=gheorghiu-net
```

The *__main__.py* file generated by Pulumi as part of the aws-python template is as follows:

```
$ cat __main__.py
import pulumi
from pulumi_aws import s3

# Create an AWS resource (S3 Bucket)
bucket = s3.Bucket('my-bucket')

# Export the name of the bucket
pulumi.export('bucket_name', bucket.id)
```

Clone the Pulumi examples GitHub repository (*https://oreil.ly/SIT-v*) locally, then copy *__main__.py* and the *www* directory from *pulumi-examples/aws-py-s3-folder* into the current directory.

Here is the new *__main__.py* file in the current directory:

```
$ cat __main__.py
import json
import mimetypes
import os

from pulumi import export, FileAsset
from pulumi_aws import s3

web_bucket = s3.Bucket('s3-website-bucket', website={
    "index_document": "index.html"
})

content_dir = "www"
for file in os.listdir(content_dir):
    filepath = os.path.join(content_dir, file)
    mime_type, _ = mimetypes.guess_type(filepath)
    obj = s3.BucketObject(file,
        bucket=web_bucket.id,
        source=FileAsset(filepath),
        content_type=mime_type)

def public_read_policy_for_bucket(bucket_name):
    return json.dumps({
        "Version": "2012-10-17",
        "Statement": [{
            "Effect": "Allow",
            "Principal": "*",
            "Action": [
                "s3:GetObject"
            ],
            "Resource": [
                f"arn:aws:s3:::{bucket_name}/*",
            ]
        }]
    })

bucket_name = web_bucket.id
bucket_policy = s3.BucketPolicy("bucket-policy",
    bucket=bucket_name,
    policy=bucket_name.apply(public_read_policy_for_bucket))

# Export the name of the bucket
export('bucket_name',  web_bucket.id)
export('website_url', web_bucket.website_endpoint)
```

Note the use of Python variables for content_dir and bucket_name, the use of a for loop, and also the use of a regular Python function public_read_pol icy_for_bucket. It is refreshing to be able to use regular Python constructs in IaC programs!

Now it's time to run pulumi up to provision the resources specified in __main__.py. This command will show all the resources that will be created. Moving the current choice to yes will kick off the provisioning process:

```
(venv) pulumi up
Previewing update (staging):

        Type                      Name                Plan
    +   pulumi:pulumi:Stack       proj1-staging       create
    +   ├─ aws:s3:Bucket          s3-website-bucket   create
    +   ├─ aws:s3:BucketObject    favicon.png         create
    +   ├─ aws:s3:BucketPolicy    bucket-policy       create
    +   ├─ aws:s3:BucketObject    python.png          create
    +   └─ aws:s3:BucketObject    index.html          create

Resources:
    + 6 to create

Do you want to perform this update? yes
Updating (staging):

        Type                      Name                Status
    +   pulumi:pulumi:Stack       proj1-staging       created
    +   ├─ aws:s3:Bucket          s3-website-bucket   created
    +   ├─ aws:s3:BucketObject    index.html          created
    +   ├─ aws:s3:BucketObject    python.png          created
    +   ├─ aws:s3:BucketObject    favicon.png         created
    +   └─ aws:s3:BucketPolicy    bucket-policy       created

Outputs:
    bucket_name: "s3-website-bucket-8e08f8f"
    website_url: "s3-website-bucket-8e08f8f.s3-website-us-east-1.amazonaws.com"

Resources:
    + 6 created

Duration: 14s
```

Inspect the existing Pulumi stacks:

```
(venv) pulumi stack ls
NAME        LAST UPDATE     RESOURCE COUNT   URL
staging*    2 minutes ago   7                https://app.pulumi.com/griggheo/proj1/staging

(venv) pulumi stack
Current stack is staging:
    Owner: griggheo
```

```
       Last updated: 3 minutes ago (2019-06-13 22:05:38.088773 -0700 PDT)
       Pulumi version: v0.17.16
   Current stack resources (7):
       TYPE                                NAME
       pulumi:pulumi:Stack                 proj1-staging
       pulumi:providers:aws                default
       aws:s3/bucket:Bucket                s3-website-bucket
       aws:s3/bucketPolicy:BucketPolicy    bucket-policy
       aws:s3/bucketObject:BucketObject    index.html
       aws:s3/bucketObject:BucketObject    favicon.png
       aws:s3/bucketObject:BucketObject    python.png
```

Inspect the outputs of the current stack:

```
(venv) pulumi stack output
Current stack outputs (2):
    OUTPUT          VALUE
    bucket_name     s3-website-bucket-8e08f8f
    website_url     s3-website-bucket-8e08f8f.s3-website-us-east-1.amazonaws.com
```

Visit the URL specified in the website_url output (*http://s3-website-bucket-8e08f8f.s3-website-us-east-1.amazonaws.com*) and make sure you can see the static site.

In the sections that follow, the Pulumi project will be enhanced by specifying more AWS resources to be provisioned. The goal is to have parity with the resources that were provisioned with Terraform: an ACM SSL certificate, a CloudFront distribution, and a Route 53 DNS record for the site URL.

Creating Configuration Values for the Staging Stack

The current stack is staging. Rename the existing *www* directory to *www-staging*, then use the pulumi config set command to specify two configuration values for the current staging stack: domain_name and local_webdir.

> For more details on how Pulumi manages configuration values and secrets, see the Pulumi reference documentation (*https://oreil.ly/D_Cy5*).

```
(venv) mv www www-staging
(venv) pulumi config set local_webdir www-staging
(venv) pulumi config set domain_name staging.devops4all.dev
```

To inspect the existing configuration values for the current stack, run:

```
(venv) pulumi config
KEY             VALUE
aws:region      us-east-1
```

```
domain_name    staging.devops4all.dev
local_webdir   www-staging
```

Once the configuration values are set, use them in the Pulumi code:

```
import pulumi

config = pulumi.Config('proj1')  # proj1 is project name defined in Pulumi.yaml

content_dir = config.require('local_webdir')
domain_name = config.require('domain_name')
```

Now that the configuration values are in place; next we will provision an SSL certificate with the AWS Certificate Manager service.

Provisioning an ACM SSL Certificate

Around this point, Pulumi starts to show its rough edges when it comes to its Python SDK. Just reading the Pulumi Python SDK reference for the acm (*https://oreil.ly/ Niwaj*) module is not sufficient to make sense of what you need to do in your Pulumi program.

Fortunately, there are many Pulumi examples in TypeScript that you can take inspiration from. One such example that illustrated our use case is aws-ts-static-website (*https://oreil.ly/7F39c*).

Here is the TypeScript code for creating a new ACM certificate (from index.ts (*https://oreil.ly/mlSr1*)):

```
const certificate = new aws.acm.Certificate("certificate", {
    domainName: config.targetDomain,
    validationMethod: "DNS",
}, { provider: eastRegion });
```

Here is the equivalent Python code that we wrote:

```
from pulumi_aws import acm

cert = acm.Certificate('certificate', domain_name=domain_name,
    validation_method='DNS')
```

> A rule of thumb in porting Pulumi code from TypeScript to Python is that parameter names that are camelCased in TypeScript become snake_cased in Python. As you can see in the earlier example, domainName becomes domain_name and validationMethod becomes validation_method.

Our next step was to provision a Route 53 zone and in that zone a DNS validation record for the ACM SSL certificate.

Provisioning a Route 53 Zone and DNS Records

Provisioning a new Route 53 zone with Pulumi is easy if you follow the Pulumi SDK reference for route53 (*https://oreil.ly/cU9Yj*).

```
from pulumi_aws import route53

domain_name = config.require('domain_name')

# Split a domain name into its subdomain and parent domain names.
# e.g. "www.example.com" => "www", "example.com".
def get_domain_and_subdomain(domain):
  names = domain.split(".")
  if len(names) < 3:
    return('', domain)
  subdomain = names[0]
  parent_domain = ".".join(names[1:])
  return (subdomain, parent_domain)

(subdomain, parent_domain) = get_domain_and_subdomain(domain_name)
zone = route53.Zone("route53_zone", name=parent_domain)
```

The preceding snippet shows how to use a regular Python function to split the configuration value read into the domain_name variable into two parts. If domain_name is staging.devops4all.dev, the function will split it into subdomain (staging) and parent_domain (devops4all.dev).

The parent_domain variable is then used as a parameter to the constructor of the zone object, which tells Pulumi to provision a route53.Zone resource.

> Once the Route 53 zone was created, we had to point the Namecheap name servers at the name servers specified in the DNS record for the new zone so that the zone can be publicly accessible.

All was well and good so far. The next step was to create both the ACM certificate and a DNS record to validate the certificate.

We first tried to port the example TypeScript code by applying the rule of thumb of turning camelCase parameter names into snake_case.

TypeScript:

```
const certificateValidationDomain = new aws.route53.Record(
    `${config.targetDomain}-validation`, {
    name: certificate.domainValidationOptions[0].resourceRecordName,
    zoneId: hostedZoneId,
    type: certificate.domainValidationOptions[0].resourceRecordType,
    records: [certificate.domainValidationOptions[0].resourceRecordValue],
```

```
        ttl: tenMinutes,
    });
```

The first attempt at porting to Python by switching camelCase to snake_case:

```
cert = acm.Certificate('certificate',
    domain_name=domain_name, validation_method='DNS')

domain_validation_options = cert.domain_validation_options[0]

cert_validation_record = route53.Record(
  'cert-validation-record',
  name=domain_validation_options.resource_record_name,
  zone_id=zone.id,
  type=domain_validation_options.resource_record_type,
  records=[domain_validation_options.resource_record_value],
  ttl=600)
```

No luck. `pulumi up` shows this error:

```
AttributeError: 'dict' object has no attribute 'resource_record_name'
```

At this point, we were stumped, because the Python SDK documentation doesn't include this level of detail. We did not know what attributes we needed to specify for the `domain_validation_options` object.

We were only able to get past this by adding the `domain_validation_options` object to the list of Pulumi exports, which are printed out by Pulumi at the end of the `pulumi up` operation:

```
export('domain_validation_options', domain_validation_options)
```

The output from `pulumi up` was:

```
+ domain_validation_options: {
  + domain_name        : "staging.devops4all.dev"
  + resourceRecordName : "_c5f82e0f032d0f4f6c7de17fc2c.staging.devops4all.dev."
  + resourceRecordType : "CNAME"
  + resourceRecordValue: "_08e3d475bf3aeda0c98.ltfvzjuylp.acm-validations.aws."
    }
```

Bingo! It turns out that the attributes of the `domain_validation_options` object are still camelCased.

Here is the second attempt at porting to Python, which was successful:

```
cert_validation_record = route53.Record(
  'cert-validation-record',
  name=domain_validation_options['resourceRecordName'],
  zone_id=zone.id,
  type=domain_validation_options['resourceRecordType'],
  records=[domain_validation_options['resourceRecordValue']],
  ttl=600)
```

Next, specify a new type of resource to be provisioned: a certificate validation completion resource. This causes the `pulumi up` operation to wait until ACM validates the certificate by checking the Route 53 validation record created earlier.

```
cert_validation_completion = acm.CertificateValidation(
        'cert-validation-completion',
        certificate_arn=cert.arn,
        validation_record_fqdns=[cert_validation_dns_record.fqdn])

cert_arn = cert_validation_completion.certificate_arn
```

At this point, you have a fully automated way of provisioning an ACM SSL certificate and of validating it via DNS.

The next step is to provision the CloudFront distribution in front of the S3 bucket hosting the static files for the site.

Provisioning a CloudFront Distribution

Use the SDK reference for the Pulumi `cloudfront` module (*https://oreil.ly/4n98-*) to figure out which constructor parameters to pass to `cloudfront.Distribution`. Inspect the TypeScript code to know what the proper values are for those parameters.

Here is the final result:

```
log_bucket = s3.Bucket('cdn-log-bucket', acl='private')

cloudfront_distro = cloudfront.Distribution ( 'cloudfront-distro',
    enabled=True,
    aliases=[ domain_name ],
    origins=[
        {
          'originId': web_bucket.arn,
          'domainName': web_bucket.website_endpoint,
          'customOriginConfig': {
              'originProtocolPolicy': "http-only",
              'httpPort': 80,
              'httpsPort': 443,
              'originSslProtocols': ["TLSv1.2"],
            },
        },
    ],

    default_root_object="index.html",
    default_cache_behavior={
        'targetOriginId': web_bucket.arn,

        'viewerProtocolPolicy': "redirect-to-https",
        'allowedMethods': ["GET", "HEAD", "OPTIONS"],
        'cachedMethods': ["GET", "HEAD", "OPTIONS"],
```

```
    'forwardedValues': {
        'cookies': { 'forward': "none" },
        'queryString': False,
    },

    'minTtl': 0,
    'defaultTtl': 600,
    'maxTtl': 600,
},
price_class="PriceClass_100",
custom_error_responses=[
    { 'errorCode': 404, 'responseCode': 404,
      'responsePagePath': "/404.html" },
],

restrictions={
    'geoRestriction': {
        'restrictionType': "none",
    },
},
viewer_certificate={
    'acmCertificateArn': cert_arn,
    'sslSupportMethod': "sni-only",
},
logging_config={
    'bucket': log_bucket.bucket_domain_name,
    'includeCookies': False,
    'prefix': domain_name,
})
```

Run pulumi up to provision the CloudFront distribution.

Provisioning a Route 53 DNS Record for the Site URL

The last step in the end-to-end provisioning of the resources for the staging stack was the relatively simple task of specifying a DNS record of type A as an alias to the domain of the CloudFront endpoint:

```
site_dns_record = route53.Record(
        'site-dns-record',
        name=subdomain,
        zone_id=zone.id,
        type="A",
        aliases=[
        {
            'name': cloudfront_distro.domain_name,
            'zoneId': cloudfront_distro.hosted_zone_id,
            'evaluateTargetHealth': True
        }
    ])
```

Run pulumi up as usual.

Visit *https://staging.devops4all.dev* and see the files uploaded to S3. Go to the logging bucket in the AWS console and make sure the CloudFront logs are there.

Let's see how to deploy the same Pulumi project to a new environment, represented by a new Pulumi stack.

Creating and Deploying a New Stack

We decided to modify the Pulumi program so that it does not provision a new Route 53 zone, but instead uses the value of the zone ID for an existing zone as a configuration value.

To create the prod stack, use the command `pulumi stack init` and specify prod for its name:

```
(venv) pulumi stack init
Please enter your desired stack name: prod
Created stack 'prod'
```

Listing the stacks now shows the two stacks, staging and prod, with an asterisk next to prod signifying that prod is the current stack:

```
(venv) pulumi stack ls
NAME      LAST UPDATE     RESOURCE COUNT   URL
prod*     n/a             n/a              https://app.pulumi.com/griggheo/proj1/prod
staging   14 minutes ago  14               https://app.pulumi.com/griggheo/proj1/staging
```

Now it's time to set the proper configuration values for the prod stack. Use a new dns_zone_id configuration value, set to the ID of the zone that was already created by Pulumi when it provisioned the staging stack:

```
(venv) pulumi config set aws:region us-east-1
(venv) pulumi config set local_webdir www-prod
(venv) pulumi config set domain_name www.devops4all.dev
(venv) pulumi config set dns_zone_id Z2FTL2X8M0EBTW
```

Change the code to read zone_id from the configuration and to not create the Route 53 zone object.

Run `pulumi up` to provision the AWS resources:

```
(venv) pulumi up
Previewing update (prod):

       Type                              Name               Plan
       pulumi:pulumi:Stack               proj1-prod
   +   ├─ aws:cloudfront:Distribution    cloudfront-distro  create
   +   └─ aws:route53:Record             site-dns-record    create

Resources:
    + 2 to create
    10 unchanged
```

```
Do you want to perform this update? yes
Updating (prod):

        Type                              Name              Status
        pulumi:pulumi:Stack               proj1-prod
    +   ├─ aws:cloudfront:Distribution    cloudfront-distro created
    +   └─ aws:route53:Record             site-dns-record   created

Outputs:
  + cloudfront_domain: "d3uhgbdw67nmlc.cloudfront.net"
  + log_bucket_id    : "cdn-log-bucket-53d8ea3"
  + web_bucket_id    : "s3-website-bucket-cde"
  + website_url      : "s3-website-bucket-cde.s3-website-us-east-1.amazonaws.com"

Resources:
    + 2 created
    10 unchanged

Duration: 18m54s
```

Success! The `prod` stack was fully deployed.

However, the contents of the *www-prod* directory containing the static files for the site are identical at this point to the contents of the *www-staging* directory.

Modify *www-prod/index.html* to change "Hello, S3!" to "Hello, S3 production!", then run `pulumi up` again to detect the changes and upload the modified file to S3:

```
(venv) pulumi up
Previewing update (prod):

        Type                   Name          Plan      Info
        pulumi:pulumi:Stack    proj1-prod
    ~   └─ aws:s3:BucketObject index.html    update    [diff: ~source]

Resources:
    ~ 1 to update
    11 unchanged

Do you want to perform this update? yes
Updating (prod):

        Type                   Name          Status    Info
        pulumi:pulumi:Stack    proj1-prod
    ~   └─ aws:s3:BucketObject index.html    updated   [diff: ~source]

Outputs:
cloudfront_domain: "d3uhgbdw67nmlc.cloudfront.net"
log_bucket_id    : "cdn-log-bucket-53d8ea3"
web_bucket_id    : "s3-website-bucket-cde"
website_url      : "s3-website-bucket-cde.s3-website-us-east-1.amazonaws.com"
```

```
Resources:
    ~ 1 updated
     11 unchanged

Duration: 4s
```

Invalidate the cache of the CloudFront distribution to see the change.

Visit *https://www.devops4all.dev* and see the message: `Hello, S3 production!`

One caveat about IaC tools that keep track of the state of the system: there are situations when the state as seen by the tool will be different from the actual state. In that case, it is important to synchronize the two states; otherwise, they will drift apart more and more and you will be in the situation where you don't dare make any more changes for fear that you will break production. It's not for nothing that the word *Code* is prominent in *Infrastructure as Code*. Once you commit to using an IaC tool, best practices say that you should provision all resources via code, and no longer spin up any resource manually. It is hard to maintain this discipline, but it pays dividends in the long run.

Exercises

- Provision the same set of AWS resources by using the AWS Cloud Development Kit (*https://aws.amazon.com/cdk*).
- Use Terraform or Pulumi to provision cloud resources from other cloud providers, such as Google Cloud Platform or Microsoft Azure.

## CHAPTER 11

Container Technologies: Docker and Docker Compose

Virtualization technologies have been around since the days of the IBM mainframes. Most people have not had a chance to work on a mainframe, but we are sure some readers of this book remember the days when they had to set up or use a bare-metal server from a manufacturer such as HP or Dell. These manufacturers are still around today, and you can still use bare-metal servers hosted in a colocation facility, like in the good old days of the dot-com era.

When most people think of virtualization, however, they do not automatically have a mainframe in mind. Instead, they most likely imagine a virtual machine (VM) running a guest operating system (OS) such as Fedora or Ubuntu on top of a hypervisor such as VMware ESX or Citrix/Xen. The big advantage of VMs over regular bare-metal servers is that by using VMs, you can optimize the server's resources (CPU, memory, disk) by splitting them across several virtual machines. You can also run several operating systems, each in its own VM, on top of one shared bare-metal server, instead of buying a dedicated server per targeted OS. Cloud computing services such as Amazon EC2 would not have been possible without hypervisors and virtual machines. This type of virtualization can be called kernel-level because each virtual machine runs its own OS kernel.

In the never-ending quest for more bang for their buck, people realized that virtual machines were still wasteful in terms of resources. The next logical step was to isolate an individual application into its own virtual environment. This was achieved by running containers within the same OS kernel. In this case, they were isolated at the file-system level. Linux containers (LXC) and Sun Solaris zones were early examples of such technologies. Their disadvantage was that they were hard to use and were tightly coupled to the OS they were running on. The big breakthrough in container usage came when Docker started to offer an easy way to manage and run filesystem-level containers.

What Is a Docker Container?

A Docker container encapsulates an application together with other software packages and libraries it requires to run. People sometimes use the terms Docker container and Docker image interchangeably, but there is a difference. The filesystem-level object that encapsulates the application is called a Docker image. When you run the image, it becomes a Docker container.

You can run many Docker containers, all using the same OS kernel. The only requirement is that you must install a server-side component called the Docker engine or the Docker daemon on the host where you want to run the containers. In this way, the host resources can be split and utilized in a more granular way across the containers, giving you more bang for your buck.

Docker containers provide more isolation and resource control than regular Linux processes, but provide less than full-fledged virtual machines would. To achieve these properties of isolation and resource control, the Docker engine makes use of Linux kernel features such as namespaces, control groups (or cgroups), and Union File Systems (UnionFS).

The main advantage of Docker containers is portability. Once you create a Docker image, you can run it as a Docker container on any host OS where the Docker server-side daemon is available. These days, all the major operating systems run the Docker daemon: Linux, Windows, and macOS.

All this can sound too theoretical, so it is time for some concrete examples.

Creating, Building, Running, and Removing Docker Images and Containers

Since this is a book on Python and DevOps, we will take the canonical Flask "Hello World" as the first example of an application that runs in a Docker container. The examples shown in this section use the Docker for Mac package. Subsequent sections will show how to install Docker on Linux.

Here is the main file of the Flask application:

```
$ cat app.py
from flask import Flask
app = Flask(__name__)

@app.route('/')
def hello_world():
```

```
    return 'Hello, World! (from a Docker container)'

if __name__ == '__main__':
    app.run(debug=True, host='0.0.0.0')
```

We also need a requirements file that specifies the version of the Flask package to be installed with `pip`:

```
$ cat requirements.txt
Flask==1.0.2
```

Trying to run the *app.py* file directly with Python on a macOS laptop without first installing the requirements results in an error:

```
$ python app.py
Traceback (most recent call last):
  File "app.py", line 1, in <module>
    from flask import Flask
ImportError: No module named flask
```

One obvious way to get past this issue is to install the requirements with `pip` on your local machine. This would make everything specific to the operating system you are running locally. What if the application needs to be deployed on a server running a different OS? The well-known issue of "works on my machine" could arise, where everything works beautifully on a macOS laptop, but for some mysterious reason, usually related to OS-specific versions of Python libraries, everything breaks on the staging or production servers running other operating systems, such as Ubuntu or Red Hat Linux.

Docker offers an elegant solution to this conundrum. We can still do our development locally, using our beloved editors and toolchains, but we package our application's dependencies inside a portable Docker container.

Here is the Dockerfile describing the Docker image that is going to be built:

```
$ cat Dockerfile
FROM python:3.7.3-alpine

ENV APP_HOME /app
WORKDIR $APP_HOME

COPY requirements.txt .

RUN pip install -r requirements.txt

ENTRYPOINT [ "python" ]
CMD [ "app.py" ]
```

A few notes about this Dockerfile:

- Use a prebuilt Docker image for Python 3.7.3 based on the Alpine distribution that produces slimmer Docker images; this Docker image already contains executables such as `python` and `pip`.

- Install the required packages with `pip`.

- Specify an ENTRYPOINT and a CMD. The difference between the two is that when the Docker container runs the image built from this Dockerfile, the program it runs is the ENTRYPOINT, followed by any arguments specified in CMD; in this case, it will run `python app.py`.

 If you do not specify an ENTRYPOINT in your Dockerfile, the following default will be used: `/bin/sh -c`.

To create the Docker image for this application, run `docker build`:

```
$ docker build -t hello-world-docker .
```

To verify that the Docker image was saved locally, run `docker images` followed by the name of the image:

```
$ docker images hello-world-docker
REPOSITORY              TAG      IMAGE ID        CREATED          SIZE
hello-world-docker      latest   dbd84c229002    2 minutes ago    97.7MB
```

To run the Docker image as a Docker container, use the `docker run` command:

```
$ docker run --rm -d -v `pwd`:/app -p 5000:5000 hello-world-docker
c879295baa26d9dff1473460bab810cbf6071c53183890232971d1b473910602
```

A few notes about the `docker run` command arguments:

- The `--rm` argument tells the Docker server to remove this container once it stops running. This is useful to prevent old containers from clogging the local filesystem.

- The `-d` argument tells the Docker server to run this container in the background.

- The `-v` argument specifies that the current directory (*pwd*) is mapped to the */app* directory inside the Docker container. This is essential for the local development workflow we want to achieve because it enables us to edit the application files locally and have them be auto-reloaded by the Flask development server running inside the container.

- The `-p 5000:5000` argument maps the first port (5000) locally to the second port (5000) inside the container.

To list running containers, run `docker ps` and note the container ID because it will be used in other `docker` commands:

```
$ docker ps
CONTAINER ID   IMAGE                        COMMAND          CREATED
c879295baa26   hello-world-docker:latest    "python app.py"  4 seconds ago
STATUS           PORTS                       NAMES
Up 2 seconds     0.0.0.0:5000->5000/tcp      flamboyant_germain
```

To inspect the logs for a given container, run `docker logs` and specify the container name or ID:

```
$ docker logs c879295baa26
 * Serving Flask app "app" (lazy loading)
 * Running on http://0.0.0.0:5000/ (Press CTRL+C to quit)
 * Restarting with stat
 * Debugger is active!
 * Debugger PIN: 647-161-014
```

Hit the endpoint URL with `curl` to verify that the application works. Because port 5000 of the application running inside the Docker container was mapped to port 5000 on the local machine with the `-p` command-line flag, you can use the local IP address 127.0.0.1 with port 5000 as the endpoint for the application.

```
$ curl http://127.0.0.1:5000
Hello, World! (from a Docker container)%
```

Now modify the code in *app.py* with your favorite editor. Change the greeting text to *Hello, World! (from a Docker container with modified code)*. Save *app.py* and notice lines similar to these in the Docker container logs:

```
 * Detected change in '/app/app.py', reloading
 * Restarting with stat
 * Debugger is active!
 * Debugger PIN: 647-161-014
```

This shows that the Flask development server running inside the container has detected the change in *app.py* and has reloaded the application.

Hitting the application endpoint with `curl` will show the modified greeting:

```
$ curl http://127.0.0.1:5000
Hello, World! (from a Docker container with modified code)%
```

To stop a running container, run `docker stop` or `docker kill` and specify the container ID as the argument:

```
$ docker stop c879295baa26
c879295baa26
```

To delete a Docker image from local disk, run docker rmi:

```
$ docker rmi hello-world-docker
Untagged: hello-world-docker:latest
Deleted:sha256:dbd84c229002950550334224b4b42aba948ce450320a4d8388fa253348126402
Deleted:sha256:6a8f3db7658520a1654cc6abee8eafb463a72ddc3aa25f35ac0c5b1eccdf75cd
Deleted:sha256:aee7c3304ef6ff620956850e0b6e6b1a5a5828b58334c1b82b1a1c21afa8651f
Deleted:sha256:dca8a433d31fa06ab72af63ae23952ff27b702186de8cbea51cdea579f9221e8
Deleted:sha256:cb9d58c66b63059f39d2e70f05916fe466e5c99af919b425aa602091c943d424
Deleted:sha256:f0534bdca48bfded3c772c67489f139d1cab72d44a19c5972ed2cd09151564c1
```

This output shows the different filesystem layers comprising a Docker image. When the image is removed, the layers are deleted as well. Consult the Docker storage drivers (*https://oreil.ly/wqNve*) documentation for more details on how Docker uses filesystem layers to build its images.

Publishing Docker Images to a Docker Registry

Once you have a Docker image built locally, you can publish it to what is called a Docker registry. There are several public registries to choose from, and for this example we will use Docker Hub. The purpose of these registries is to allow people and organizations to share pre-built Docker images that can be reused across different machines and operating systems.

First, create a free account on Docker Hub (*https://hub.docker.com*) and then create a repository, either public or private. We created a private repository called flask-hello-world under our griggheo Docker Hub account.

Then, at the command line, run docker login and specify the email and password for your account. At this point, you can interact with Docker Hub via the docker client.

 Before showing you how to publish your locally built Docker image to Docker Hub, we want to point out that best practice is to tag your image with a unique tag. If you don't tag it specifically, the image will be tagged as latest by default. Pushing a new image version with no tag will move the latest tag to the newest image version. When using a Docker image, if you do not specify the exact tag you need, you will get the latest version of the image, which might contain modifications and updates that might break your dependencies. As always, the principle of least surprise should apply: you should use tags both when pushing images to a registry, and when referring to images in a Dockerfile. That being said, you can also tag your desired version of the image as latest so that people who are interested in the latest and greatest can use it without specifying a tag.

When building the Docker image in the previous section, it was automatically tagged as latest, and the repository was set to the name of the image, signifying that the image is local:

```
$ docker images hello-world-docker
REPOSITORY              TAG       IMAGE ID        CREATED         SIZE
hello-world-docker      latest    dbd84c229002    2 minutes ago   97.7MB
```

To tag a Docker image, run docker tag:

```
$ docker tag hello-world-docker hello-world-docker:v1
```

Now you can see both tags for the hello-world-docker image:

```
$ docker images hello-world-docker
REPOSITORY              TAG       IMAGE ID        CREATED           SIZE
hello-world-docker      latest    dbd84c229002    2 minutes ago     97.7MB
hello-world-docker      v1        89bd38cb198f    42 seconds ago    97.7MB
```

Before you can publish the hello-world-docker image to Docker Hub, you also need to tag it with the Docker Hub repository name, which contains your username or your organization name. In our case, this repository is griggheo/hello-world-docker:

```
$ docker tag hello-world-docker:latest griggheo/hello-world-docker:latest
$ docker tag hello-world-docker:v1 griggheo/hello-world-docker:v1
```

Publish both image tags to Docker Hub with docker push:

```
$ docker push griggheo/hello-world-docker:latest
$ docker push griggheo/hello-world-docker:v1
```

If you followed along, you should now be able to see your Docker image published with both tags to the Docker Hub repository you created under your account.

Running a Docker Container with the Same Image on a Different Host

Now that the Docker image is published to Docker Hub, we are ready to show off the portability of Docker by running a container based on the published image on a different host. The scenario considered here is that of collaborating with a colleague who doesn't have macOS but likes to develop on a laptop running Fedora. The scenario includes checking out the application code and modifying it.

Launch an EC2 instance in AWS based on the Linux 2 AMI, which is based on Red-Hat/CentOS/Fedora, and then install the Docker engine. Add the default user on the EC2 Linux AMI, called ec2-user, to the docker group so it can run docker client commands:

```
$ sudo yum update -y
$ sudo amazon-linux-extras install docker
$ sudo service docker start
$ sudo usermod -a -G docker ec2-user
```

Make sure to check out the application code on the remote EC2 instance. In this case, the code consists only of *app.py* file.

Next, run the Docker container based on the image published to Docker Hub. The only difference is that the image used as an argument to the docker run command was griggheo/hello-world-docker:v1 instead of simply hello-world-docker.

Run docker login, then:

```
$ docker run --rm -d -v `pwd`:/app -p 5000:5000 griggheo/hello-world-docker:v1

Unable to find image 'griggheo/hello-world-docker:v1' locally
v1: Pulling from griggheo/hello-world-docker
921b31ab772b: Already exists
1a0c422ed526: Already exists
ec0818a7bbe4: Already exists
b53197ee35ff: Already exists
8b25717b4dbf: Already exists
d997915c3f9c: Pull complete
f1fd8d3cc5a4: Pull complete
10b64b1c3b21: Pull complete
Digest: sha256:af8b74f27a0506a0c4a30255f7ff563c9bf858735baa610fda2a2f638ccfe36d
Status: Downloaded newer image for griggheo/hello-world-docker:v1
9d67dc321ffb49e5e73a455bd80c55c5f09febc4f2d57112303d2b27c4c6da6a
```

Note that the Docker engine on the EC2 instance recognizes that it does not have the Docker image locally, so it downloads it from Docker Hub, then runs a container based on the newly downloaded image.

At this point, access to port 5000 was granted by adding a rule to the security group associated with the EC2 instance. Visit http://54.187.189.51:5000[1] (with 54.187.189.51 being the external IP of the EC2 instance) and see the greeting *Hello, World! (from a Docker container with modified code)*.

When modifying the application code on the remote EC2 instance, the Flask server running inside the Docker container will auto-reload the modified code. Change the greeting to *Hello, World! (from a Docker container on an EC2 Linux 2 AMI instance)* and notice that the Flask server reloaded the application by inspecting the logs of the Docker container:

```
[ec2-user@ip-10-0-0-111 hello-world-docker]$ docker ps
CONTAINER ID   IMAGE                              COMMAND          CREATED
9d67dc321ffb   griggheo/hello-world-docker:v1    "python app.py"  3 minutes ago
```

---

1 This is an example URL address—your IP address will be different.

```
STATUS       PORTS                     NAMES
Up 3 minutes 0.0.0.0:5000->5000/tcp    heuristic_roentgen

[ec2-user@ip-10-0-0-111 hello-world-docker]$ docker logs 9d67dc321ffb
 * Serving Flask app "app" (lazy loading)
 * Debug mode: on
 * Running on http://0.0.0.0:5000/ (Press CTRL+C to quit)
 * Restarting with stat
 * Debugger is active!
 * Debugger PIN: 306-476-204
72.203.107.13 - - [19/Aug/2019 04:43:34] "GET / HTTP/1.1" 200 -
72.203.107.13 - - [19/Aug/2019 04:43:35] "GET /favicon.ico HTTP/1.1" 404 -
 * Detected change in '/app/app.py', reloading
 * Restarting with stat
 * Debugger is active!
 * Debugger PIN: 306-476-204
```

Hitting http://54.187.189.51:5000[2] now shows the new greeting *Hello, World! (from a Docker container on an EC2 Linux 2 AMI instance)*.

It is worth noting that we did not have to install anything related to Python or Flask to get our application to run. By simply running our application inside a container, we were able to take advantage of the portability of Docker. It is not for nothing that Docker chose the name "container" to popularize its technology—one inspiration was how the shipping container revolutionized the global transportation industry.

> Read "Production-ready Docker images" (*https://pythonspeed.com/docker*) by Itamar Turner-Trauring for an extensive collection of articles on Docker container packaging for Python applications.

Running Multiple Docker Containers with Docker Compose

In this section we will use the "Flask By Example" (*https://oreil.ly/prNg7*) tutorial that describes how to build a Flask application that calculates word-frequency pairs based on the text from a given URL.

Start by cloning the Flask By Example GitHub repository (*https://oreil.ly/M-pvc*):

```
$ git clone https://github.com/realpython/flask-by-example.git
```

We will use compose to run multiple Docker containers representing the different parts of the example application. With Compose, you use a YAML file to define and

---

2 Again, your IP address will be different.

configure the services comprising an application, then you use the `docker-compose` command-line utility to create, start, and stop these services that will run as Docker containers.

The first dependency to consider for the example application is PostgreSQL, as described in Part 2 of the tutorial (*https://oreil.ly/iobKp*).

Here is how to run PostgreSQL in a Docker container inside a *docker-compose.yaml* file:

```
$ cat docker-compose.yaml
version: "3"
services:
  db:
    image: "postgres:11"
    container_name: "postgres"
    ports:
      - "5432:5432"
    volumes:
      - dbdata:/var/lib/postgresql/data
volumes:
  dbdata:
```

A few things to note about this file:

- Define a service called `db` based on the `postgres:11` image published on Docker Hub.
- Specify a port mapping from local port 5432 to the container port 5432.
- Specify a Docker volume for the directory where PostgreSQL stores its data, which is */var/lib/postgresql/data*. This is so that the data stored in PostgreSQL will persist across restarts of the container.

The `docker-compose` utility is not part of the Docker engine, so it needs to be installed separately. See the official documentation (*https://docs.docker.com/compose/install*) for instructions on installing it on various operating systems.

To bring up the `db` service defined in *docker-compose.yaml*, run the `docker-compose up -d db` command, which will launch the Docker container for the db service in the background (the `-d` flag):

```
$ docker-compose up -d db
Creating postgres ... done
```

Inspect the logs for the db service with the `docker-compose logs db` command:

```
$ docker-compose logs db
Creating volume "flask-by-example_dbdata" with default driver
Pulling db (postgres:11)...
11: Pulling from library/postgres
Creating postgres ... done
```

```
Attaching to postgres
postgres | PostgreSQL init process complete; ready for start up.
postgres |
postgres | 2019-07-11 21:50:20.987 UTC [1]
LOG:  listening on IPv4 address "0.0.0.0", port 5432
postgres | 2019-07-11 21:50:20.987 UTC [1]
LOG:  listening on IPv6 address "::", port 5432
postgres | 2019-07-11 21:50:20.993 UTC [1]
LOG:  listening on Unix socket "/var/run/postgresql/.s.PGSQL.5432"
postgres | 2019-07-11 21:50:21.009 UTC [51]
LOG:  database system was shut down at 2019-07-11 21:50:20 UTC
postgres | 2019-07-11 21:50:21.014 UTC [1]
LOG:  database system is ready to accept connections
```

Running `docker ps` shows the container running the PostgreSQL database:

```
$ docker ps
dCONTAINER ID    IMAGE    COMMAND    CREATED    STATUS    PORTS    NAMES
83b54ab10099 postgres:11 "docker-entrypoint.s…"  3 minutes ago  Up 3 minutes
         0.0.0.0:5432->5432/tcp    postgres
```

Running `docker volume ls` shows the `dbdata` Docker volume mounted for the Post-greSQL */var/lib/postgresql/data* directory:

```
$ docker volume ls | grep dbdata
local              flask-by-example_dbdata
```

To connect to the PostgreSQL database running in the Docker container associated with the db service, run the command `docker-compose exec db` and pass it the command line `psql -U postgres`:

```
$ docker-compose exec db psql -U postgres
psql (11.4 (Debian 11.4-1.pgdg90+1))
Type "help" for help.

postgres=#
```

Following "Flask by Example, Part 2" (*https://oreil.ly/iobKp*), create a database called wordcount:

```
$ docker-compose exec db psql -U postgres
psql (11.4 (Debian 11.4-1.pgdg90+1))
Type "help" for help.

postgres=# create database wordcount;
CREATE DATABASE

postgres=# \l
```

```
                        List of databases
       Name    |  Owner  | Encoding |  Collate   |   Ctype    |   Access privileges
    -----------+---------+----------+------------+------------+---------------------
     postgres  | postgres | UTF8    | en_US.utf8 | en_US.utf8 |
     template0 | postgres | UTF8    | en_US.utf8 | en_US.utf8 | =c/postgres +
               |         |          |            |            | |postgres=CTc/postgres
     template1 | postgres | UTF8    | en_US.utf8 | en_US.utf8 | =c/postgres +
               |         |          |            |            | |postgres=CTc/postgres
     wordcount | postgres | UTF8|  en_US.utf8 | en_US.utf8 |
    (4 rows)
    postgres=# \q
```

Connect to the `wordcount` database and create a role called `wordcount_dbadmin` that will be used by the Flask application:

```
$ docker-compose exec db psql -U postgres wordcount
wordcount=# CREATE ROLE wordcount_dbadmin;
CREATE ROLE
wordcount=# ALTER ROLE wordcount_dbadmin LOGIN;
ALTER ROLE
wordcount=# ALTER USER wordcount_dbadmin PASSWORD 'MYPASS';
ALTER ROLE
postgres=# \q
```

The next step is to create a Dockerfile for installing all the prerequisites for the Flask application.

Make the following modifications to the *requirements.txt* file:

- Modify the version of the `psycopg2` package from `2.6.1` to `2.7` so that it supports PostgreSQL 11

- Modify the version of the `redis` package from `2.10.5` to `3.2.1` for better Python 3.7 support

- Modify the version of the `rq` package from `0.5.6` to `1.0` for better Python 3.7 support

Here is the Dockerfile:

```
$ cat Dockerfile
FROM python:3.7.3-alpine

ENV APP_HOME /app
WORKDIR $APP_HOME

COPY requirements.txt .

RUN \
 apk add --no-cache postgresql-libs && \
 apk add --no-cache --virtual .build-deps gcc musl-dev postgresql-dev && \
 python3 -m pip install -r requirements.txt --no-cache-dir && \
 apk --purge del .build-deps
```

```
COPY . .

ENTRYPOINT [ "python" ]
CMD ["app.py"]
```

 There is an important difference between this Dockerfile and the version used in the first *hello-world-docker* example. Here the contents of the current directory, which includes the application files, are copied into the Docker image. This is done to illustrate a scenario different from the development workflow shown earlier. In this case, we are more interested in running the application in the most portable way, for example, in a staging or production environment, where we do not want to modify application files via mounted volumes as was done in the development scenario. It is possible and even common to use docker-compose with locally mounted volumes for development purposes, but the focus in this section is on the portability of Docker containers across environments, such as development, staging, and production.

Run docker build -t flask-by-example:v1 . to build a local Docker image. The output of this command is not shown because it is quite lengthy.

The next step in the "Flask By Example" tutorial is to run the Flask migrations.

In the *docker-compose.yaml* file, define a new service called migrations and specify its image, its command, its environment variables, and the fact that it depends on the db service being up and running:

```
$ cat docker-compose.yaml
version: "3"
services:
  migrations:
    image: "flask-by-example:v1"
    command: "manage.py db upgrade"
    environment:
      APP_SETTINGS: config.ProductionConfig
      DATABASE_URL: postgresql://wordcount_dbadmin:$DBPASS@db/wordcount
    depends_on:
      - db
  db:
    image: "postgres:11"
    container_name: "postgres"
    ports:
      - "5432:5432"
    volumes:
      - dbdata:/var/lib/postgresql/data
volumes:
  dbdata:
```

The DATABASE_URL variable uses the name db for the PostgreSQL database host. This is because the name db is defined as a service name in the *docker-compose.yaml* file, and docker-compose knows how to link one service to another by creating an overlay network where all services defined in the *docker-compose.yaml* file can interact with each other by their names. See the docker-compose networking reference (*https://oreil.ly/Io80N*) for more details.

The DATABASE_URL variable definition refers to another variable called DBPASS, instead of hardcoding the password for the wordcount_dbadmin user. The *docker-compose.yaml* file is usually checked into source control, and best practices are not to commit secrets such as database credentials to GitHub. Instead, use an encryption tool such as sops (*https://github.com/mozilla/sops*) to manage a secrets file.

Here is an example of how to create an encrypted file using sops with PGP encryption.

First, install gpg on macOS via brew install gpg, then generate a new PGP key with an empty passphrase:

```
$ gpg --generate-key
pub    rsa2048 2019-07-12 [SC] [expires: 2021-07-11]
       E14104A0890994B9AC9C9F6782C1FF5E679EFF32
uid                      pydevops <my.email@gmail.com>
sub    rsa2048 2019-07-12 [E] [expires: 2021-07-11]
```

Next, download sops from its release page (*https://github.com/mozilla/sops/releases*).

To create a new encrypted file called, for example, *environment.secrets*, run sops with the -pgp flag and give it the fingerprint of the key generated above:

```
$ sops --pgp BBDE7E57E00B98B3F4FBEAF21A1EEF4263996BD0 environment.secrets
```

This will open the default editor and allow for the input of the plain-text secrets. In this example, the contents of the *environment.secrets* file are:

```
export DBPASS=MYPASS
```

After saving the *environment.secrets* file, inspect the file to see that it is encrypted, which makes it safe to add to source control:

```
$ cat environment.secrets
{
        "data": "ENC[AES256_GCM,data:qlQ5zc7e8KgGmu5goC9WmE7PP8gueBoSsmM=,
    iv:xG8BHcRfdfLpH9nUlTijBsYrh4TuSdvDqp5F+2Hqw4I=,
    tag:00IVAm9O/UYGljGCzZerTQ==,type:str]",
        "sops": {
                "kms": null,
                "gcp_kms": null,
                "lastmodified": "2019-07-12T05:03:45Z",
                "mac": "ENC[AES256_GCM,data:wo+zPVbPbAJt9Nl23nYuWs55f68/DZJWj3pc0
    l8T2d/SbuRF6YCuOXHSHIKs1ZBpSlsjmIrPyYTqI+M4Wf7it7fnNS8b7FnclwmxJjptBWgL
```

```
T/A1GzIKT1Vrgw9QgJ+prq+Qcrk5dPzhsOTxOoOhGRPsyN8KjkS4sGuXM=,iv:0VvSMgjF6
ypcK+1J54fonRoI7c5whmcu3iNV8xLH02k=,
tag:YaI7DXvvllvpJ3Talzl8lg==,
type:str]",
                "pgp": [
                    {
                        "created_at": "2019-07-12T05:02:24Z",
                        "enc": "-----BEGIN PGP MESSAGE-----\n\nhQEMA+3cyc
        g5b/Hu0OvU5ONr/F0htZM2MZQSXpxoCiO\nWGB5Czc8FTSlRSwu8/cOx0Ch1FwH+IdLwwL+jd
        oXVe55myuu/3OKUy7H1w/W2R\nPI99Biw1m5u3ir3+9tLXmRpLWkz7+nX7FThl9QnOS25
        NRUSSxS7hNaZMcYjpXW+w\nM3XeaGStgbJ9OgIp4A8YGigZQVZZFl3fAG3bm2c+TNJcAbl
        zDpc40fxlR+7LroJI\njuidzyOEe49k0pq3tzqCnph5wPr3HZ1JeQmsIquf//9D5O9S5xH
        Sa9lkz3Y7V4KC\nefzBiS8pivm55T0s+zPBPB/GWUVlqGaxRhv1TAU=\n=WA4+
        \n-----END PGP MESSAGE-----\n",
                        "fp": "E14104A0890994B9AC9C9F6782C1FF5E679EFF32"
                    }
                ],
                "unencrypted_suffix": "_unencrypted",
                "version": "3.0.5"
            }
    }%
```

To decrypt the file, run:

```
$ sops -d environment.secrets
export DBPASS=MYPASS
```

 There is an issue with sops interacting with gpg on a Macintosh. You will need to run the following commands before being able to decrypt the file with sops:

```
$ GPG_TTY=$(tty)
$ export GPG_TTY
```

The goal here is to run the migrations service defined previously in the docker-compose.yaml_ file. To tie the +sops secret management method into docker-compose, decrypt the *environments.secrets* file with sops -d, source its contents into the current shell, then invoke docker-compose up -d migrations using one command line that will not expose the secret to the shell history:

```
$ source <(sops -d environment.secrets); docker-compose up -d migrations
postgres is up-to-date
Recreating flask-by-example_migrations_1 ... done
```

Verify that the migrations were successfully run by inspecting the database and verifying that two tables were created: alembic_version and results:

```
$ docker-compose exec db psql -U postgres wordcount
psql (11.4 (Debian 11.4-1.pgdg90+1))
Type "help" for help.
```

```
wordcount=# \dt
                List of relations
 Schema |       Name        | Type  |       Owner
--------+-------------------+-------+-------------------
 public | alembic_version   | table | wordcount_dbadmin
 public | results           | table | wordcount_dbadmin
(2 rows)

wordcount=# \q
```

Part 4 (*https://oreil.ly/UY2yw*) in the "Flask By Example" tutorial is to deploy a Python worker process based on Python RQ that talks to an instance of Redis.

First, Redis needs to run. Add it as a service called `redis` into the *docker_compose.yaml* file, and make sure that its internal port 6379 is mapped to port 6379 on the local OS:

```
redis:
  image: "redis:alpine"
  ports:
    - "6379:6379"
```

Start the `redis` service on its own by specifying it as an argument to `docker-compose up -d`:

```
$ docker-compose up -d redis
Starting flask-by-example_redis_1 ... done
```

Run `docker ps` to see a new Docker container running based on the `redis:alpine` image:

```
$ docker ps
CONTAINER ID   IMAGE          COMMAND              CREATED       STATUS       PORTS    NAMES
a1555cc372d6   redis:alpine   "docker-entrypoint.s…" 3 seconds ago Up 1 second
0.0.0.0:6379->6379/tcp    flask-by-example_redis_1
83b54ab10099   postgres:11    "docker-entrypoint.s…" 22 hours ago  Up 16 hours
0.0.0.0:5432->5432/tcp    postgres
```

Use the `docker-compose logs` command to inspect the logs of the `redis` service:

```
$ docker-compose logs redis
Attaching to flask-by-example_redis_1
1:C 12 Jul 2019 20:17:12.966 # oOOoOOOoOOOo Redis is starting oOOoOOOoOOOo
1:C 12 Jul 2019 20:17:12.966 # Redis version=5.0.5, bits=64, commit=00000000,
modified=0, pid=1, just started
1:C 12 Jul 2019 20:17:12.966 # Warning: no config file specified, using the
default config. In order to specify a config file use
redis-server /path/to/redis.conf
1:M 12 Jul 2019 20:17:12.967 * Running mode=standalone, port=6379.
1:M 12 Jul 2019 20:17:12.967 # WARNING: The TCP backlog setting of 511 cannot
be enforced because /proc/sys/net/core/somaxconn
is set to the lower value of 128.
```

```
1:M 12 Jul 2019 20:17:12.967 # Server initialized
1:M 12 Jul 2019 20:17:12.967 * Ready to accept connections
```

The next step is to create a service called worker for the Python RQ worker process in
docker-compose.yaml:

```
worker:
  image: "flask-by-example:v1"
  command: "worker.py"
  environment:
    APP_SETTINGS: config.ProductionConfig
    DATABASE_URL: postgresql://wordcount_dbadmin:$DBPASS@db/wordcount
    REDISTOGO_URL: redis://redis:6379
  depends_on:
    - db
    - redis
```

Run the worker service just like the redis service, with docker-compose up -d:

```
$ docker-compose up -d worker
flask-by-example_redis_1 is up-to-date
Starting flask-by-example_worker_1 ... done
```

Running docker ps will show the worker container:

```
$ docker ps
CONTAINER ID   IMAGE          COMMAND           CREATED      STATUS   PORTS    NAMES
72327ab33073   flask-by-example "python worker.py"     8 minutes ago
Up 14 seconds                             flask-by-example_worker_1
b11b03a5bcc3   redis:alpine     "docker-entrypoint.s…" 15 minutes ago
Up About a minute  0.0.0.0:6379->6379/tc  flask-by-example_redis_1
83b54ab10099   postgres:11      "docker-entrypoint.s…"  23 hours ago
Up 17 hours        0.0.0.0:5432->5432/tcp postgres
```

Look at the worker container logs with docker-compose logs:

```
$ docker-compose logs worker
Attaching to flask-by-example_worker_1
20:46:34 RQ worker 'rq:worker:a66ca38275a14cac86c9b353e946a72e' started,
version 1.0
20:46:34 *** Listening on default...
20:46:34 Cleaning registries for queue: default
```

Now launch the main Flask application in its own container. Create a new service
called app in *docker-compose.yaml*:

```
app:
  image: "flask-by-example:v1"
  command: "manage.py runserver --host=0.0.0.0"
  ports:
    - "5000:5000"
  environment:
    APP_SETTINGS: config.ProductionConfig
    DATABASE_URL: postgresql://wordcount_dbadmin:$DBPASS@db/wordcount
    REDISTOGO_URL: redis://redis:6379
```

```
depends_on:
  - db
  - redis
```

Map port 5000 from the application container (the default port for a Flask application) to port 5000 on the local machine. Pass the command manage.py runserver --host=0.0.0.0 to the application container to ensure that port 5000 is exposed correctly by the Flask application inside the container.

Start up the app service with docker compose up -d, while also running sops -d on the encrypted file containing DBPASS, then sourcing the decrypted file before calling docker-compose:

```
source <(sops -d environment.secrets); docker-compose up -d app
postgres is up-to-date
Recreating flask-by-example_app_1 ... done
```

Notice the new Docker container running the application in the list returned by docker ps:

```
$ docker ps
CONTAINER ID    IMAGE    COMMAND    CREATED    STATUS    PORTS    NAMES
d99168a152f1    flask-by-example "python app.py"  3 seconds ago
Up 2 seconds    0.0.0.0:5000->5000/tcp    flask-by-example_app_1
72327ab33073    flask-by-example "python worker.py" 16 minutes ago
Up 7 minutes                              flask-by-example_worker_1
b11b03a5bcc3    redis:alpine    "docker-entrypoint.s…" 23 minutes ago
Up 9 minutes    0.0.0.0:6379->6379/tcp    flask-by-example_redis_1
83b54ab10099    postgres:11     "docker-entrypoint.s…"  23 hours ago
Up 17 hours     0.0.0.0:5432->5432/tcp    postgres
```

Inspect the logs of the application container with docker-compose logs:

```
$ docker-compose logs app
Attaching to flask-by-example_app_1
app_1        |  * Running on http://0.0.0.0:5000/ (Press CTRL+C to quit)
```

Running docker-compose logs with no other arguments allows us to inspect the logs of all the services defined in the *docker-compose.yaml* file:

```
$ docker-compose logs
Attaching to flask-by-example_app_1,
flask-by-example_worker_1,
flask-by-example_migrations_1,
flask-by-example_redis_1,
postgres
1:C 12 Jul 2019 20:17:12.966 # o000o000o000o Redis is starting o000o000o000o
1:C 12 Jul 2019 20:17:12.966 # Redis version=5.0.5, bits=64, commit=00000000,
modified=0, pid=1, just started
1:C 12 Jul 2019 20:17:12.966 # Warning: no config file specified, using the
default config. In order to specify a config file use
redis-server /path/to/redis.conf
1:M 12 Jul 2019 20:17:12.967 * Running mode=standalone, port=6379.
```

```
1:M 12 Jul 2019 20:17:12.967 # WARNING: The TCP backlog setting of 511 cannot
be enforced because /proc/sys/net/core/somaxconn
is set to the lower value of 128.
1:M 12 Jul 2019 20:17:12.967 # Server initialized
1:M 12 Jul 2019 20:17:12.967 * Ready to accept connections
app_1        |   * Running on http://0.0.0.0:5000/ (Press CTRL+C to quit)
postgres     | 2019-07-12 22:15:19.193 UTC [1]
LOG:  listening on IPv4 address "0.0.0.0", port 5432
postgres     | 2019-07-12 22:15:19.194 UTC [1]
LOG:  listening on IPv6 address "::", port 5432
postgres     | 2019-07-12 22:15:19.199 UTC [1]
LOG:  listening on Unix socket "/var/run/postgresql/.s.PGSQL.5432"
postgres     | 2019-07-12 22:15:19.214 UTC [22]
LOG:  database system was shut down at 2019-07-12 22:15:09 UTC
postgres     | 2019-07-12 22:15:19.225 UTC [1]
LOG:  database system is ready to accept connections
migrations_1 | INFO [alembic.runtime.migration] Context impl PostgresqlImpl.
migrations_1 | INFO [alembic.runtime.migration] Will assume transactional DDL.
worker_1     | 22:15:20
RQ worker 'rq:worker:2edb6a54f30a4aae8a8ca2f4a9850303' started, version 1.0
worker_1     | 22:15:20 *** Listening on default...
worker_1     | 22:15:20 Cleaning registries for queue: default
```

The final step is to test the application. Visit http://127.0.0.1:5000 and enter
python.org in the URL field. At that point, the application sends a job to the worker
process, asking it to execute the function count_and_save_words against the home
page of python.org. The application periodically polls the job for the results, and
upon completion, it displays the word frequencies on the home page.

To make the *docker-compose.yaml* file more portable, push the flask-by-example
Docker image to Docker Hub, and reference the Docker Hub image in the container
section for the app and worker services.

Tag the existing local Docker image flask-by-example:v1 with a name prefixed by a
Docker Hub username, then push the newly tagged image to Docker Hub:

```
$ docker tag flask-by-example:v1 griggheo/flask-by-example:v1
$ docker push griggheo/flask-by-example:v1
```

Change *docker-compose.yaml* to reference the new Docker Hub image. Here is the
final version of *docker-compose.yaml*:

```
$ cat docker-compose.yaml
version: "3"
services:
  app:
    image: "griggheo/flask-by-example:v1"
    command: "manage.py runserver --host=0.0.0.0"
    ports:
      - "5000:5000"
    environment:
      APP_SETTINGS: config.ProductionConfig
```

```
          DATABASE_URL: postgresql://wordcount_dbadmin:$DBPASS@db/wordcount
          REDISTOGO_URL: redis://redis:6379
        depends_on:
          - db
          - redis
    worker:
      image: "griggheo/flask-by-example:v1"
      command: "worker.py"
      environment:
        APP_SETTINGS: config.ProductionConfig
        DATABASE_URL: postgresql://wordcount_dbadmin:$DBPASS@db/wordcount
        REDISTOGO_URL: redis://redis:6379
      depends_on:
        - db
        - redis
    migrations:
      image: "griggheo/flask-by-example:v1"
      command: "manage.py db upgrade"
      environment:
        APP_SETTINGS: config.ProductionConfig
        DATABASE_URL: postgresql://wordcount_dbadmin:$DBPASS@db/wordcount
      depends_on:
        - db
    db:
      image: "postgres:11"
      container_name: "postgres"
      ports:
        - "5432:5432"
      volumes:
        - dbdata:/var/lib/postgresql/data
    redis:
      image: "redis:alpine"
      ports:
        - "6379:6379"
volumes:
  dbdata:
```

To restart the local Docker containers, run docker-compose down followed by docker-compose up -d:

```
$ docker-compose down
Stopping flask-by-example_worker_1 ... done
Stopping flask-by-example_app_1    ... done
Stopping flask-by-example_redis_1  ... done
Stopping postgres                  ... done
Removing flask-by-example_worker_1     ... done
Removing flask-by-example_app_1        ... done
Removing flask-by-example_migrations_1 ... done
Removing flask-by-example_redis_1      ... done
Removing postgres                      ... done
Removing network flask-by-example_default

$ source <(sops -d environment.secrets); docker-compose up -d
```

```
Creating network "flask-by-example_default" with the default driver
Creating flask-by-example_redis_1       ... done
Creating postgres                    ... done
Creating flask-by-example_migrations_1 ... done
Creating flask-by-example_worker_1      ... done
Creating flask-by-example_app_1         ... done
```

Note how easy it is to bring up and down a set of Docker containers with docker-compose.

 Even if you want to run a single Docker container, it is still a good idea to include it in a *docker-compose.yaml* file and launch it with the docker-compose up -d command. It will make your life easier when you want to add a second container into the mix, and it will also serve as a mini Infrastructure as Code example, with the *docker-compose.yaml* file reflecting the state of your local Docker setup for your application.

Porting the docker-compose Services to a New Host and Operating System

We will now show how to take the docker-compose setup from the preceding section and port it to a server running Ubuntu 18.04.

Launch an Amazon EC2 instance running Ubuntu 18.04 and install docker-engine and docker-compose:

```
$ sudo apt-get update
$ sudo apt-get remove docker docker-engine docker.io containerd runc
$ sudo apt-get install \
  apt-transport-https \
  ca-certificates \
  curl \
  gnupg-agent \
  software-properties-common
$ curl -fsSL https://download.docker.com/linux/ubuntu/gpg | sudo apt-key add -
$ sudo add-apt-repository \
  "deb [arch=amd64] https://download.docker.com/linux/ubuntu \
  $(lsb_release -cs) \
  stable"
$ sudo apt-get update
$ sudo apt-get install docker-ce docker-ce-cli containerd.io
$ sudo usermod -a -G docker ubuntu

# download docker-compose
$ sudo curl -L \
"https://github.com/docker/compose/releases/download/1.24.1/docker-compose-\
$(uname -s)-$(uname -m)" -o /usr/local/bin/docker-compose
$ sudo chmod +x /usr/local/bin/docker-compose
```

Copy the *docker-compose.yaml* file to the remote EC2 instance and start the db service first, so that the database used by the application can be created:

```
$ docker-compose up -d db
Starting postgres ...
Starting postgres ... done

$ docker ps
CONTAINER ID   IMAGE   COMMAND   CREATED   STATUS   PORTS   NAMES
49fe88efdb45 postgres:11 "docker-entrypoint.s…" 29 seconds ago
    Up 3 seconds       0.0.0.0:5432->5432/tcp   postgres
```

Use docker exec to run the psql -U postgres command inside the running Docker container for the PostgreSQL database. At the PostgreSQL prompt, create the word count database and wordcount_dbadmin role:

```
$ docker-compose exec db psql -U postgres
psql (11.4 (Debian 11.4-1.pgdg90+1))
Type "help" for help.

postgres=# create database wordcount;
CREATE DATABASE
postgres=# \q

$ docker exec -it 49fe88efdb45 psql -U postgres wordcount
psql (11.4 (Debian 11.4-1.pgdg90+1))
Type "help" for help.

wordcount=# CREATE ROLE wordcount_dbadmin;
CREATE ROLE
wordcount=# ALTER ROLE wordcount_dbadmin LOGIN;
ALTER ROLE
wordcount=# ALTER USER wordcount_dbadmin PASSWORD 'MYPASS';
ALTER ROLE
wordcount=# \q
```

Before launching the containers for the services defined in *docker-compose.yaml*, two things are necessary:

1. Run docker login to be able to pull the Docker image pushed previously to Docker Hub:

   ```
   $ docker login
   ```

2. Set the DBPASS environment variable to the correct value in the current shell. The sops method described in the local macOS setup can be used, but for this example, set it directly in the shell:

   ```
   $ export DOCKER_PASS=MYPASS
   ```

Now launch all the services necessary for the application by running docker-compose
up -d:

```
$ docker-compose up -d
Pulling worker (griggheo/flask-by-example:v1)...
v1: Pulling from griggheo/flask-by-example
921b31ab772b: Already exists
1a0c422ed526: Already exists
ec0818a7bbe4: Already exists
b53197ee35ff: Already exists
8b25717b4dbf: Already exists
9be5e85cacbb: Pull complete
bd62f980b08d: Pull complete
9a89f908ad0a: Pull complete
d787e00a01aa: Pull complete
Digest: sha256:4fc554da6157b394b4a012943b649ec66c999b2acccb839562e89e34b7180e3e
Status: Downloaded newer image for griggheo/flask-by-example:v1
Creating fbe_redis_1      ... done
Creating postgres      ... done
Creating fbe_migrations_1 ... done
Creating fbe_app_1       ... done
Creating fbe_worker_1     ... done

$ docker ps
CONTAINER ID    IMAGE    COMMAND    CREATED    STATUS    PORTS    NAMES
f65fe9631d44   griggheo/flask-by-example:v1 "python3 manage.py r…" 5 seconds ago
Up 2 seconds         0.0.0.0:5000->5000/tcp   fbe_app_1
71fc0b24bce3   griggheo/flask-by-example:v1 "python3 worker.py"    5 seconds ago
Up 2 seconds                        fbe_worker_1
a66d75a20a2d   redis:alpine       "docker-entrypoint.s…"   7 seconds ago
Up 5 seconds         0.0.0.0:6379->6379/tcp   fbe_redis_1
56ff97067637   postgres:11        "docker-entrypoint.s…"   7 seconds ago
Up 5 seconds         0.0.0.0:5432->5432/tcp    postgres
```

At this point, after allowing access to port 5000 in the AWS security group associated
with our Ubuntu EC2 instance, you can hit the external IP of the instance on port
5000 and use the application.

It's worth emphasizing one more time how much Docker simplifies the deployment
of applications. The portability of Docker containers and images means that you can
run your application on any operating system where the Docker engine runs. In the
example shown here, none of the prerequisites needed to be installed on the Ubuntu
server: not Flask, not PostgreSQL, and not Redis. It was also not necessary to copy
the application code over from the local development machine to the Ubuntu server.
The only file needed on the Ubuntu server was *docker-compose.yaml*. Then, the whole
set of services comprising the application was launched with just one command:

```
$ docker-compose up -d
```

Beware of downloading and using Docker images from public Docker repositories, because many of them include serious security vulnerabilities, the most serious of which can allow an attacker to break through the isolation of a Docker container and take over the host operating system. A good practice here is to start with a trusted, pre-built image, or build your own image from scratch. Stay abreast of the latest security patches and software updates, and rebuild your image whenever any of these patches or updates are available. Another good practice is to scan all of your Docker images with one of the many Docker scanning tools available, among them Clair (*https://oreil.ly/OBkkx*), Anchore (*https://oreil.ly/uRI_1*), and Falco (*https://oreil.ly/QXRg6*). Such scanning can be performed as part of a continuous integration/continuous deployment pipeline, when the Docker images usually get built.

Although docker-compose makes it easy to run several containerized services as part of the same application, it is only meant to be run on a single machine, which limits its usefulness in production scenarios. You can really only consider an application deployed with docker-compose to be "production ready" if you are not worried about downtime and you are willing to run everything on a single machine (this being said, Grig has seen hosting providers running Dockerized applications in production with docker-compose). For true "production ready" scenarios, you need a container orchestration engine such as Kubernetes, which will be discussed in the next chapter.

Exercises

- Familiarize yourself with the Dockerfile reference (*https://oreil.ly/kA8ZF*).

- Familiarize yourself with the Docker Compose configuration reference (*https://oreil.ly/ENMsQ*).

- Create an AWS KMS key and use it with sops instead of a local PGP key. This allows you to apply AWS IAM permissions to the key, and restrict access to the key to only the developers who need it.

- Write a shell script that uses docker exec or docker-compose exec to run the PostgreSQL commands necessary for creating a database and a role.

- Experiment with other container technologies, such as Podman (*https://podman.io*).

## CHAPTER 12

Container Orchestration: Kubernetes

If you are experimenting with Docker, or if running a set of Docker containers on a single machine is all you need, then Docker and Docker Compose would be sufficient for your needs. However, as soon as you move from the number 1 (single machine) to the number 2 (multiple machines), you need to start worrying about orchestrating the containers across the network. For production scenarios, this is a given. You need at least two machines to achieve fault tolerance/high availability.

In our age of cloud computing, the recommended way of scaling an infrastructure is "out" (also referred to as "horizontal scalability"), by adding more instances to your overall system, as opposed to the older way of scaling "up" (or "vertical scalability"), by adding more CPUs and memory to a single instance. A Docker orchestration platform uses these many instances or nodes as sources of raw resources (CPU, memory, network) that it then allocates to individual containers running within the platform. This ties into what we mentioned in Chapter 11 in regards to the advantages of using containers over classic virtual machines (VMs): the raw resources at your disposal will be better utilized because containers can get these resources allocated to them on a much more granular basis than VMs, and you will get more bang for your infrastructure buck.

There has also been a shift from provisioning servers for specific purposes and running specific software packages on each instance (such as web server software, cache software, database software) to provisioning them as generic units of resource allocation and running Docker containers on them, coordinated by a Docker orchestration platform. You may be familiar with the distinction between looking at servers as "pets" versus looking at them as "cattle." In the early days of infrastructure design, each server had a definite function (such as the mail server), and many times there was only one server for each specific function. There were naming schemes for such servers (Grig remembers using a planetary system naming scheme in the dot-com days), and a lot of time was spent on their care and feeding, hence the pet designation. When configuration management tools such as Puppet, Chef, and Ansible burst onto the scene, it became easier to provision multiple servers of the same type (for example, a web server farm) at the same time, by using an identical installation procedure on each server. This coincided with the rise of cloud computing, with the concept of horizontal scalability mentioned previously, and also with more concern for fault tolerance and high availability as critical properties of well-designed system infrastructure. The servers or cloud instances were considered cattle, disposable units that have value in their aggregate.

The age of containers and serverless computing also brought about another designation, "insects." Indeed, one can look at the coming and going of containers as a potentially short existence, like an ephemeral insect. Functions-as-a-service are even more fleeting than Docker containers, with a short but intense life coinciding with the duration of their call.

In the case of containers, their ephemerality makes their orchestration and interoperability hard to achieve at a large scale. This is exactly the need that has been filled by container orchestration platforms. There used to be multiple Docker orchestration platforms to choose from, such as Mesosphere and Docker Swarm, but these days we can safely say that Kubernetes has won that game. The rest of the chapter is dedicated to a short overview of Kubernetes, followed by an example of running the same application described in Chapter 11 and porting it from docker-compose to Kubernetes. We will also show how to use Helm, a Kubernetes package manager, to install packages called charts for the monitoring and dashboarding tools Prometheus and Grafana, and how to customize these charts.

Short Overview of Kubernetes Concepts

The best starting point for understanding the many parts comprising a Kubernetes cluster is the official Kubernetes documentation (*https://oreil.ly/TYpdE*).

At a high level, a Kubernetes cluster consists of nodes that can be equated to servers, be they bare-metal or virtual machines running in a cloud. Nodes run pods, which are collections of Docker containers. A pod is the unit of deployment in Kubernetes. All containers in a pod share the same network and can refer to each other as if they were running on the same host. There are many situations in which it is advantageous to run more than one container in a pod. Typically, your application container runs as the main container in the pod, and if needed you will run one or more so-called "sidecar" containers for functionality, such as logging or monitoring. One particular case of sidecar containers is an "init container," which is guaranteed to run first and can be used for housekeeping tasks, such as running database migrations. We'll explore this later in this chapter.

An application will typically use more than one pod for fault tolerance and perfor-mance purposes. The Kubernetes object responsible for launching and maintaining the desired number of pods is called a deployment. For pods to communicate with other pods, Kubernetes provides another kind of object called a service. Services are tied to deployments through selectors. Services are also exposed to external clients, either by exposing a NodePort as a static port on each Kubernetes node, or by creat-ing a LoadBalancer object that corresponds to an actual load balancer, if it is sup-ported by the cloud provider running the Kubernetes cluster.

For managing sensitive information such as passwords, API keys, and other creden-tials, Kubernetes offers the Secret object. We will see an example of using a Secret for storing a database password.

Using Kompose to Create Kubernetes Manifests from docker-compose.yaml

Let's take another look at the *docker_compose.yaml* file for the Flask example applica-tion discussed in Chapter 11:

```
$ cat docker-compose.yaml
version: "3"
services:
  app:
    image: "griggheo/flask-by-example:v1"
    command: "manage.py runserver --host=0.0.0.0"
    ports:
      - "5000:5000"
    environment:
      APP_SETTINGS: config.ProductionConfig
      DATABASE_URL: postgresql://wordcount_dbadmin:$DBPASS@db/wordcount
      REDISTOGO_URL: redis://redis:6379
    depends_on:
      - db
      - redis
  worker:
    image: "griggheo/flask-by-example:v1"
    command: "worker.py"
    environment:
      APP_SETTINGS: config.ProductionConfig
      DATABASE_URL: postgresql://wordcount_dbadmin:$DBPASS@db/wordcount
      REDISTOGO_URL: redis://redis:6379
    depends_on:
      - db
      - redis
  migrations:
    image: "griggheo/flask-by-example:v1"
    command: "manage.py db upgrade"
    environment:
      APP_SETTINGS: config.ProductionConfig
```

```
        DATABASE_URL: postgresql://wordcount_dbadmin:$DBPASS@db/wordcount
      depends_on:
        - db
  db:
    image: "postgres:11"
    container_name: "postgres"
    ports:
      - "5432:5432"
    volumes:
      - dbdata:/var/lib/postgresql/data
  redis:
    image: "redis:alpine"
    ports:
      - "6379:6379"
volumes:
  dbdata:
```

We will use a tool called Kompose to translate this YAML file into a set of Kubernetes manifests.

To get a new version of Kompose on a macOS machine, first download it from the Git repository (*https://oreil.ly/GUqaq*), then move it to */usr/local/bin/kompose*, and make it executable. Note that if you rely on your operating system's package management system (for example, apt on Ubuntu systems or yum on Red Hat systems) for installing Kompose, you may get a much older version that may not be compatible to these instructions.

Run the kompose convert command to create the Kubernetes manifest files from the existing *docker-compose.yaml* file:

```
$ kompose convert
INFO Kubernetes file "app-service.yaml" created
INFO Kubernetes file "db-service.yaml" created
INFO Kubernetes file "redis-service.yaml" created
INFO Kubernetes file "app-deployment.yaml" created
INFO Kubernetes file "db-deployment.yaml" created
INFO Kubernetes file "dbdata-persistentvolumeclaim.yaml" created
INFO Kubernetes file "migrations-deployment.yaml" created
INFO Kubernetes file "redis-deployment.yaml" created
INFO Kubernetes file "worker-deployment.yaml" created
```

At this point, remove the *docker-compose.yaml* file:

```
$ rm docker-compose.yaml
```

Deploying Kubernetes Manifests to a Local Kubernetes Cluster Based on minikube

Our next step is to deploy the Kubernetes manifests to a local Kubernetes cluster based on minikube.

A prerequisite to running minikube on macOS is to install *VirtualBox*. Download the VirtualBox package for macOS from its download page (*https://oreil.ly/BewRq*), install it, and then move it to */usr/local/bin/minikube* to make it executable. Note that at the time of this writing, minikube installed a Kubernetes cluster with version 1.15. If you want to follow along with these examples, specify the version of Kubernetes you want to install with minikube:

```
$ minikube start --kubernetes-version v1.15.0
  minikube v1.2.0 on darwin (amd64)
  Creating virtualbox VM (CPUs=2, Memory=2048MB, Disk=20000MB) ...
  Configuring environment for Kubernetes v1.15.0 on Docker 18.09.6
  Downloading kubeadm v1.15.0
  Downloading kubelet v1.15.0
  Pulling images ...
  Launching Kubernetes ...
  Verifying: apiserver proxy etcd scheduler controller dns
  Done! kubectl is now configured to use "minikube"
```

The main command for interacting with a Kubernetes cluster is kubectl.

Install kubectl on a macOS machine by downloading it from the release page (*https://oreil.ly/f9Wv0*), then moving it to */usr/local/bin/kubectl* and making it executable.

One of the main concepts you will use when running kubectl commands is *context*, which signifies a Kubernetes cluster that you want to interact with. The installation process for minikube already created a context for us called *minikube*. One way to point kubectl to a specific context is with the following command:

```
$ kubectl config use-context minikube
Switched to context "minikube".
```

A different, and more handy, way is to install the kubectx utility from the Git repository (*https://oreil.ly/SIf1U*), then run:

```
$ kubectx minikube
Switched to context "minikube".
```

Another handy client utility for your Kubernetes work is kube-ps1 (*https://oreil.ly/AcE32*). For a macOS setup based on Zsh, add this snippet to the file *~/.zshrc*:

```
source "/usr/local/opt/kube-ps1/share/kube-ps1.sh"
PS1='$(kube_ps1)'$PS1
```

These lines change the shell prompt to show the current Kubernetes context and namespace. As you start interacting with multiple Kubernetes clusters, this will be a lifesaver for distinguishing between a production and a staging cluster.

Now run `kubectl` commands against the local `minikube` cluster. For example, the `kubectl get nodes` command shows the nodes that are part of the cluster. In this case, there is only one node with the role of `master`:

```
$ kubectl get nodes
NAME       STATUS   ROLES    AGE     VERSION
minikube   Ready    master   2m14s   v1.15.0
```

Start by creating the Persistent Volume Claim (PVC) object from the file *dbdata-persistentvolumeclaim.yaml* that was created by Kompose, and which corresponds to the local volume allocated for the PostgreSQL database container, when running it with `docker-compose`:

```
$ cat dbdata-persistentvolumeclaim.yaml
apiVersion: v1
kind: PersistentVolumeClaim
metadata:
  creationTimestamp: null
  labels:
    io.kompose.service: dbdata
  name: dbdata
spec:
  accessModes:
  - ReadWriteOnce
  resources:
    requests:
      storage: 100Mi
status: {}
```

To create this object in Kubernetes, use the `kubectl create` command and specify the file name of the manifest with the `-f` flag:

```
$ kubectl create -f dbdata-persistentvolumeclaim.yaml
persistentvolumeclaim/dbdata created
```

List all the PVCs with the `kubectl get pvc` command to verify that our PVC is there:

```
$ kubectl get pvc
NAME       STATUS   VOLUME                                     CAPACITY
ACCESS MODES   STORAGECLASS   AGE
dbdata     Bound    pvc-39914723-4455-439b-a0f5-82a5f7421475   100Mi
RWO            standard       1m
```

The next step is to create the Deployment object for PostgreSQL. Use the manifest file *db-deployment.yaml* created previously by the Kompose utility:

```
$ cat db-deployment.yaml
apiVersion: extensions/v1beta1
kind: Deployment
metadata:
  annotations:
```

```
    kompose.cmd: kompose convert
    kompose.version: 1.16.0 (0c01309)
  creationTimestamp: null
  labels:
    io.kompose.service: db
  name: db
spec:
  replicas: 1
  strategy:
    type: Recreate
  template:
    metadata:
      creationTimestamp: null
      labels:
        io.kompose.service: db
    spec:
      containers:
      - image: postgres:11
        name: postgres
        ports:
        - containerPort: 5432
        resources: {}
        volumeMounts:
        - mountPath: /var/lib/postgresql/data
          name: dbdata
      restartPolicy: Always
      volumes:
      - name: dbdata
        persistentVolumeClaim:
          claimName: dbdata
status: {}
```

To create the deployment, use the `kubectl create -f` command and point it to the manifest file:

```
$ kubectl create -f db-deployment.yaml
deployment.extensions/db created
```

To verify that the deployment was created, list all deployments in the cluster and list the pods that were created as part of the deployment:

```
$ kubectl get deployments
NAME    READY   UP-TO-DATE   AVAILABLE   AGE
db      1/1     1            1           1m

$ kubectl get pods
NAME                  READY   STATUS    RESTARTS   AGE
db-67659d85bf-vrnw7   1/1     Running   0          1m
```

Next, create the database for the example Flask application. Use a similar command to docker `exec` to run the `psql` command inside a running Docker container. The form of the command in the case of a Kubernetes cluster is kubectl `exec`:

```
$ kubectl exec -it db-67659d85bf-vrnw7 -- psql -U postgres
psql (11.4 (Debian 11.4-1.pgdg90+1))
Type "help" for help.

postgres=# create database wordcount;
CREATE DATABASE
postgres=# \q

$ kubectl exec -it db-67659d85bf-vrnw7 -- psql -U postgres wordcount
psql (11.4 (Debian 11.4-1.pgdg90+1))
Type "help" for help.

wordcount=# CREATE ROLE wordcount_dbadmin;
CREATE ROLE
wordcount=# ALTER ROLE wordcount_dbadmin LOGIN;
ALTER ROLE
wordcount=# ALTER USER wordcount_dbadmin PASSWORD 'MYPASS';
ALTER ROLE
wordcount=# \q
```

The next step is to create the Service object corresponding to the db deployment, that will expose the deployment to the other services running inside the cluster, such as the Redis worker service and the main application service. Here is the manifest file for the db service:

```
$ cat db-service.yaml
apiVersion: v1
kind: Service
metadata:
  annotations:
    kompose.cmd: kompose convert
    kompose.version: 1.16.0 (0c01309)
  creationTimestamp: null
  labels:
    io.kompose.service: db
  name: db
spec:
  ports:
  - name: "5432"
    port: 5432
    targetPort: 5432
  selector:
    io.kompose.service: db
status:
  loadBalancer: {}
```

One thing to note is the following section:

```
labels:
  io.kompose.service: db
```

This section appears in both the deployment manifest and the service manifest and is indeed the way to tie the two together. A service will be associated with any deployment that has the same label.

Create the Service object with the `kubectl create -f` command:

```
$ kubectl create -f db-service.yaml
service/db created
```

List all services and notice that the db service was created:

```
$ kubectl get services
NAME         TYPE        CLUSTER-IP      EXTERNAL-IP   PORT(S)    AGE
db           ClusterIP   10.110.108.96   <none>        5432/TCP   6s
kubernetes   ClusterIP   10.96.0.1       <none>        443/TCP    4h45m
```

The next service to deploy is Redis. Create the Deployment and Service objects based on the manifest files generated by Kompose:

```
$ cat redis-deployment.yaml
apiVersion: extensions/v1beta1
kind: Deployment
metadata:
  annotations:
    kompose.cmd: kompose convert
    kompose.version: 1.16.0 (0c01309)
  creationTimestamp: null
  labels:
    io.kompose.service: redis
  name: redis
spec:
  replicas: 1
  strategy: {}
  template:
    metadata:
      creationTimestamp: null
      labels:
        io.kompose.service: redis
    spec:
      containers:
      - image: redis:alpine
        name: redis
        ports:
        - containerPort: 6379
        resources: {}
      restartPolicy: Always
status: {}

$ kubectl create -f redis-deployment.yaml
```

```
deployment.extensions/redis created

$ kubectl get pods
NAME                        READY   STATUS    RESTARTS   AGE
db-67659d85bf-vrnw7         1/1     Running   0          37m
redis-c6476fbff-8kpqz       1/1     Running   0          11s

$ kubectl create -f redis-service.yaml
service/redis created

$ cat redis-service.yaml
apiVersion: v1
kind: Service
metadata:
  annotations:
    kompose.cmd: kompose convert
    kompose.version: 1.16.0 (0c01309)
  creationTimestamp: null
  labels:
    io.kompose.service: redis
  name: redis
spec:
  ports:
  - name: "6379"
    port: 6379
    targetPort: 6379
  selector:
    io.kompose.service: redis
status:
  loadBalancer: {}

$ kubectl get services
NAME         TYPE        CLUSTER-IP      EXTERNAL-IP   PORT(S)    AGE
db           ClusterIP   10.110.108.96   <none>        5432/TCP   84s
kubernetes   ClusterIP   10.96.0.1       <none>        443/TCP    4h46m
redis        ClusterIP   10.106.44.183   <none>        6379/TCP   10s
```

So far, the two services that have been deployed, db and redis, are independent of each other. The next part of the application is the worker process, which needs to talk to both PostgreSQL and Redis. This is where the advantage of using Kubernetes services comes into play. The worker deployment can refer to the endpoints for PostgreSQL and Redis by using the service names. Kubernetes knows how to route the requests from the client (the containers running as part of the pods in the worker deployment) to the servers (the PostgreSQL and Redis containers running as part of the pods in the db and redis deployments, respectively).

One of the environment variables used in the worker deployment is DATABASE_URL. It contains the database password used by the application. The password should not be exposed in clear text in the deployment manifest file, because this file needs to be checked into version control. Instead, create a Kubernetes Secret object.

First, encode the password string in **base64**:

```
$ echo MYPASS | base64
MYPASSBASE64
```

Then, create a manifest file describing the Kubernetes Secret object that you want to create. Since the **base64** encoding of the password is not secure, use **sops** to edit and save an encrypted manifest file *secrets.yaml.enc*:

```
$ sops --pgp E14104A0890994B9AC9C9F6782C1FF5E679EFF32 secrets.yaml.enc
```

Inside the editor, add these lines:

```
apiVersion: v1
kind: Secret
metadata:
  name: fbe-secret
type: Opaque
data:
  dbpass: MYPASSBASE64
```

The *secrets.yaml.enc* file can now be checked in because it contains the encrypted version of the **base64** value of the password.

To decrypt the encrypted file, use the **sops -d** command:

```
$ sops -d secrets.yaml.enc
apiVersion: v1
kind: Secret
metadata:
  name: fbe-secret
type: Opaque
data:
  dbpass: MYPASSBASE64
```

Pipe the output of **sops -d** to **kubectl create -f** to create the Kubernetes Secret object:

```
$ sops -d secrets.yaml.enc | kubectl create -f -
secret/fbe-secret created
```

Inspect the Kubernetes Secrets and describe the Secret that was created:

```
$ kubectl get secrets
NAME                  TYPE                                  DATA   AGE
default-token-k7652   kubernetes.io/service-account-token   3      3h19m
fbe-secret            Opaque                                1      45s

$ kubectl describe secret fbe-secret
Name:         fbe-secret
Namespace:    default
Labels:       <none>
Annotations:  <none>
```

```
Type: Opaque

Data
dbpass:  12 bytes
```

To get the **base64**-encoded Secret back, use:

```
$ kubectl get secrets fbe-secret -ojson | jq -r ".data.dbpass"
MYPASSBASE64
```

To get the plain-text password back, use the following command on a macOS machine:

```
$ kubectl get secrets fbe-secret -ojson | jq -r ".data.dbpass" | base64 -D
MYPASS
```

On a Linux machine, the proper flag for **base64** decoding is -d, so the correct command would be:

```
$ kubectl get secrets fbe-secret -ojson | jq -r ".data.dbpass" | base64 -d
MYPASS
```

The secret can now be used in the deployment manifest of the worker. Modify the *worker-deployment.yaml* file generated by the Kompose utility and add two environment variables:

- DBPASS is the database password that will be retrieved from the fbe-secret Secret object.
- DATABASE_URL is the full database connection string for PostgreSQL, which includes the database password and references it as ${DBPASS}.

This is the modified version of *worker-deployment.yaml*:

```
$ cat worker-deployment.yaml
apiVersion: extensions/v1beta1
kind: Deployment
metadata:
  annotations:
    kompose.cmd: kompose convert
    kompose.version: 1.16.0 (0c01309)
  creationTimestamp: null
  labels:
    io.kompose.service: worker
  name: worker
spec:
  replicas: 1
  strategy: {}
  template:
    metadata:
      creationTimestamp: null
      labels:
        io.kompose.service: worker
```

```
    spec:
      containers:
      - args:
        - worker.py
        env:
        - name: APP_SETTINGS
          value: config.ProductionConfig
        - name: DBPASS
          valueFrom:
            secretKeyRef:
              name: fbe-secret
              key: dbpass
        - name: DATABASE_URL
          value: postgresql://wordcount_dbadmin:${DBPASS}@db/wordcount
        - name: REDISTOGO_URL
          value: redis://redis:6379
        image: griggheo/flask-by-example:v1
        name: worker
        resources: {}
      restartPolicy: Always
  status: {}
```

Create the worker Deployment object in the same way as for the other deployments, by calling kubectl create -f:

```
$ kubectl create -f worker-deployment.yaml
deployment.extensions/worker created
```

List the pods:

```
$ kubectl get pods
NAME                         READY   STATUS             RESTARTS   AGE
db-67659d85bf-vrnw7          1/1     Running            1          21h
redis-c6476fbff-8kpqz        1/1     Running            1          21h
worker-7dbf5ff56c-vgs42      0/1     Init:ErrImagePull  0          7s
```

Note that the worker pod is shown with status Init:ErrImagePull. To see details about this status, run kubectl describe:

```
$ kubectl describe pod worker-7dbf5ff56c-vgs42 | tail -10
                node.kubernetes.io/unreachable:NoExecute for 300s
Events:
  Type     Reason     Age                    From               Message
  ----     ------     ----                   ----               -------
  Normal   Scheduled  2m51s                  default-scheduler
  Successfully assigned default/worker-7dbf5ff56c-vgs42 to minikube

  Normal   Pulling    76s (x4 over 2m50s)    kubelet, minikube
  Pulling image "griggheo/flask-by-example:v1"

  Warning  Failed     75s (x4 over 2m49s)    kubelet, minikube
  Failed to pull image "griggheo/flask-by-example:v1": rpc error:
  code = Unknown desc = Error response from daemon: pull access denied for
```

```
griggheo/flask-by-example, repository does not exist or may require
'docker login'

Warning  Failed    75s (x4 over 2m49s)  kubelet, minikube
Error: ErrImagePull

Warning  Failed    62s (x6 over 2m48s)  kubelet, minikube
Error: ImagePullBackOff

Normal   BackOff    51s (x7 over 2m48s)  kubelet, minikube
Back-off pulling image "griggheo/flask-by-example:v1"
```

The deployment tried to pull the griggheo/flask-by-example:v1 private Docker
image from Docker Hub, and it lacked the appropriate credentials to access the private Docker registry. Kubernetes includes a special type of object for this very scenario, called an *imagePullSecret*.

Create an encrypted file with sops containing the Docker Hub credentials and the
call to kubectl create secret:

```
$ sops --pgp E14104A0890994B9AC9C9F6782C1FF5E679EFF32 \
create_docker_credentials_secret.sh.enc
```

The contents of the file are:

```
DOCKER_REGISTRY_SERVER=docker.io
DOCKER_USER=Type your dockerhub username, same as when you `docker login`
DOCKER_EMAIL=Type your dockerhub email, same as when you `docker login`
DOCKER_PASSWORD=Type your dockerhub pw, same as when you `docker login`

kubectl create secret docker-registry myregistrykey \
--docker-server=$DOCKER_REGISTRY_SERVER \
--docker-username=$DOCKER_USER \
--docker-password=$DOCKER_PASSWORD \
--docker-email=$DOCKER_EMAIL
```

Decode the encrypted file with sops and run it through bash:

```
$ sops -d create_docker_credentials_secret.sh.enc | bash -
secret/myregistrykey created
```

Inspect the Secret:

```
$ kubectl get secrets myregistrykey -oyaml
apiVersion: v1
data:
  .dockerconfigjson: eyJhdXRocyI6eyJkb2NrZXIuaW8iO
kind: Secret
metadata:
  creationTimestamp: "2019-07-17T22:11:56Z"
  name: myregistrykey
  namespace: default
  resourceVersion: "16062"
  selfLink: /api/v1/namespaces/default/secrets/myregistrykey
```

```
        uid: 47d29ffc-69e4-41df-a237-1138cd9e8971
    type: kubernetes.io/dockerconfigjson
```

The only change to the worker deployment manifest is to add these lines:

```
        imagePullSecrets:
        - name: myregistrykey
```

Include it right after this line:

```
        restartPolicy: Always
```

Delete the worker deployment and recreate it:

```
$ kubectl delete -f worker-deployment.yaml
deployment.extensions "worker" deleted

$ kubectl create -f worker-deployment.yaml
deployment.extensions/worker created
```

Now the worker pod is in a Running state, with no errors:

```
$ kubectl get pods
NAME                      READY   STATUS    RESTARTS   AGE
db-67659d85bf-vrnw7       1/1     Running   1          22h
redis-c6476fbff-8kpqz     1/1     Running   1          21h
worker-7dbf5ff56c-hga37   1/1     Running   0          4m53s
```

Inspect the worker pod's logs with the kubectl logs command:

```
$ kubectl logs worker-7dbf5ff56c-hga37
20:43:13 RQ worker 'rq:worker:040640781edd4055a990b798ac2eb52d'
started, version 1.0
20:43:13 *** Listening on default...
20:43:13 Cleaning registries for queue: default
```

The next step is to tackle the application deployment. When the application was deployed in a docker-compose setup in Chapter 11, a separate Docker container was employed to run the migrations necessary to update the Flask database. This type of task is a good candidate for running as a sidecar container in the same pod as the main application container. The sidecar will be defined as a Kubernetes initCon tainer (*https://oreil.ly/80L5L*) inside the application deployment manifest. This type of container is guaranteed to run inside the pod it belongs to before the start of the other containers included in the pod.

Add this section to the *app-deployment.yaml* manifest file that was generated by the Kompose utility, and delete the *migrations-deployment.yaml* file:

```
        initContainers:
        - args:
          - manage.py
          - db
          - upgrade
          env:
```

```
      - name: APP_SETTINGS
        value: config.ProductionConfig
      - name: DATABASE_URL
        value: postgresql://wordcount_dbadmin:@db/wordcount
      image: griggheo/flask-by-example:v1
      name: migrations
      resources: {}

$ rm migrations-deployment.yaml
```

Reuse the fbe-secret Secret object created for the worker deployment in the application deployment manifest:

```
$ cat app-deployment.yaml
apiVersion: extensions/v1beta1
kind: Deployment
metadata:
  annotations:
    kompose.cmd: kompose convert
    kompose.version: 1.16.0 (0c01309)
  creationTimestamp: null
  labels:
    io.kompose.service: app
  name: app
spec:
  replicas: 1
  strategy: {}
  template:
    metadata:
      creationTimestamp: null
      labels:
        io.kompose.service: app
    spec:
      initContainers:
      - args:
        - manage.py
        - db
        - upgrade
        env:
        - name: APP_SETTINGS
          value: config.ProductionConfig
        - name: DBPASS
          valueFrom:
            secretKeyRef:
              name: fbe-secret
              key: dbpass
        - name: DATABASE_URL
          value: postgresql://wordcount_dbadmin:${DBPASS}@db/wordcount
        image: griggheo/flask-by-example:v1
        name: migrations
        resources: {}
      containers:
      - args:
```

```
        - manage.py
        - runserver
        - --host=0.0.0.0
        env:
        - name: APP_SETTINGS
          value: config.ProductionConfig
        - name: DBPASS
          valueFrom:
            secretKeyRef:
              name: fbe-secret
              key: dbpass
        - name: DATABASE_URL
          value: postgresql://wordcount_dbadmin:${DBPASS}@db/wordcount
        - name: REDISTOGO_URL
          value: redis://redis:6379
        image: griggheo/flask-by-example:v1
        name: app
        ports:
        - containerPort: 5000
        resources: {}
      restartPolicy: Always
  status: {}
```

Create the application deployment with kubectl create -f, then list the pods and describe the application pod:

```
$ kubectl create -f app-deployment.yaml
deployment.extensions/app created

$ kubectl get pods
NAME                     READY   STATUS    RESTARTS   AGE
app-c845d8969-l8nhg      1/1     Running   0          7s
db-67659d85bf-vrnw7      1/1     Running   1          22h
redis-c6476fbff-8kpqz    1/1     Running   1          21h
worker-7dbf5ff56c-vgs42  1/1     Running   0          4m53s
```

The last piece in the deployment of the application to minikube is to ensure that a Kubernetes service is created for the application and that it is declared as type LoadBalancer, so it can be accessed from outside the cluster:

```
$ cat app-service.yaml
apiVersion: v1
kind: Service
metadata:
  annotations:
    kompose.cmd: kompose convert
    kompose.version: 1.16.0 (0c01309)
  creationTimestamp: null
  labels:
    io.kompose.service: app
  name: app
spec:
  ports:
```

```
    - name: "5000"
      port: 5000
      targetPort: 5000
    type: LoadBalancer
    selector:
      io.kompose.service: app
status:
  loadBalancer: {}
```

 Similar to the db service, the app service is tied to the app deployment through a label declaration that exists in both the deployment
and the service manifest for the application:

```
        labels:
          io.kompose.service: app
```

Create the service with kubectl create:

```
$ kubectl create -f app-service.yaml
service/app created

$ kubectl get services
NAME         TYPE           CLUSTER-IP       EXTERNAL-IP   PORT(S)          AGE
app          LoadBalancer   10.99.55.191     <pending>     5000:30097/TCP   2s
db           ClusterIP      10.110.108.96    <none>        5432/TCP         21h
kubernetes   ClusterIP      10.96.0.1        <none>        443/TCP          26h
redis        ClusterIP      10.106.44.183    <none>        6379/TCP         21h
```

Next, run:

```
$ minikube service app
```

This command opens the default browser with the URL *http://192.168.99.100:30097/*
and shows the home page of the Flask site.

In our next section, we will take the same Kubernetes manifest files for our application and deploy them to a Kubernetes cluster that will be provisioned with Pulumi in
the Google Cloud Platform (GCP).

Launching a GKE Kubernetes Cluster in GCP with Pulumi

In this section, we'll make use of the Pulumi GKE example (*https://oreil.ly/VGBfF*)
and also of the GCP setup documentation (*https://oreil.ly/kRsFA*), so use these links
to obtain the necessary documents before proceeding.

Start by creating a new directory:

```
$ mkdir pulumi_gke
$ cd pulumi_gke
```

Set up the Google Cloud SDK using the macOS instructions (*https://oreil.ly/f4pPs*).

Initialize the GCP environment using the gcloud init command. Create a new configuration and a new project named *pythonfordevops-gke-pulumi*:

```
$ gcloud init
Welcome! This command will take you through the configuration of gcloud.

Settings from your current configuration [default] are:
core:
  account: grig.gheorghiu@gmail.com
  disable_usage_reporting: 'True'
  project: pulumi-gke-testing

Pick configuration to use:
 [1] Re-initialize this configuration [default] with new settings
 [2] Create a new configuration
Please enter your numeric choice:  2

Enter configuration name. Names start with a lower case letter and
contain only lower case letters a-z, digits 0-9, and hyphens '-':
pythonfordevops-gke-pulumi
Your current configuration has been set to: [pythonfordevops-gke-pulumi]

Pick cloud project to use:
 [1] pulumi-gke-testing
 [2] Create a new project
Please enter numeric choice or text value (must exactly match list
item):  2

Enter a Project ID. pythonfordevops-gke-pulumi
Your current project has been set to: [pythonfordevops-gke-pulumi].
```

Log in to the GCP account:

```
$ gcloud auth login
```

Log in to the default application, which is pythonfordevops-gke-pulumi:

```
$ gcloud auth application-default login
```

Create a new Pulumi project by running the pulumi new command, specifying *gcp-python* as your template and *pythonfordevops-gke-pulumi* as the name of the project:

```
$ pulumi new
Please choose a template: gcp-python
A minimal Google Cloud Python Pulumi program
This command will walk you through creating a new Pulumi project.

Enter a value or leave blank to accept the (default), and press <ENTER>.
Press ^C at any time to quit.

project name: (pulumi_gke_py) pythonfordevops-gke-pulumi
project description: (A minimal Google Cloud Python Pulumi program)
Created project 'pythonfordevops-gke-pulumi'
```

```
stack name: (dev)
Created stack 'dev'

gcp:project: The Google Cloud project to deploy into: pythonfordevops-gke-pulumi
Saved config

Your new project is ready to go!

To perform an initial deployment, run the following commands:

    1. virtualenv -p python3 venv
    2. source venv/bin/activate
    3. pip3 install -r requirements.txt

Then, run 'pulumi up'.
```

The following files were created by the `pulumi new` command:

```
$ ls -la
ls -la
total 40
drwxr-xr-x  7 ggheo  staff  224 Jul 16 15:08 .
drwxr-xr-x  6 ggheo  staff  192 Jul 16 15:06 ..
-rw-------  1 ggheo  staff   12 Jul 16 15:07 .gitignore
-rw-r--r--  1 ggheo  staff   50 Jul 16 15:08 Pulumi.dev.yaml
-rw-------  1 ggheo  staff  107 Jul 16 15:07 Pulumi.yaml
-rw-------  1 ggheo  staff  203 Jul 16 15:07 __main__.py
-rw-------  1 ggheo  staff   34 Jul 16 15:07 requirements.txt
```

We are going to make use of the `gcp-py-gke` example from the Pulumi examples (*https://oreil.ly/SIT-v*) GitHub repository.

Copy **.py* and *requirements.txt* from *examples/gcp-py-gke* to our current directory:

```
$ cp ~/pulumi-examples/gcp-py-gke/*.py .
$ cp ~/pulumi-examples/gcp-py-gke/requirements.txt .
```

Configure GCP-related variables needed for Pulumi to operate in GCP:

```
$ pulumi config set gcp:project pythonfordevops-gke-pulumi
$ pulumi config set gcp:zone us-west1-a
$ pulumi config set password --secret PASS_FOR_KUBE_CLUSTER
```

Create and use a Python `virtualenv`, install the dependencies declared in *requirements.txt*, and then bring up the GKE cluster defined in *mainpy* by running the `pulumi up` command:

```
$ virtualenv -p python3 venv
$ source venv/bin/activate
$ pip3 install -r requirements.txt
$ pulumi up
```

Make sure you enable the Kubernetes Engine API by associating it with a Google billing account in the GCP web console.

The GKE cluster can now be seen in the GCP console (*https://oreil.ly/Su5FZ*).

To interact with the newly provisioned GKE cluster, generate the proper `kubectl` configuration and use it. Handily, the `kubectl` configuration is being exported as out put by the Pulumi program:

```
$ pulumi stack output kubeconfig > kubeconfig.yaml
$ export KUBECONFIG=./kubeconfig.yaml
```

List the nodes comprising the GKE cluster:

```
$ kubectl get nodes
NAME                                               STATUS  ROLES    AGE
    VERSION
gke-gke-cluster-ea17e87-default-pool-fd130152-30p3 Ready   <none>   4m29s
    v1.13.7-gke.8
gke-gke-cluster-ea17e87-default-pool-fd130152-kf9k Ready   <none>   4m29s
    v1.13.7-gke.8
gke-gke-cluster-ea17e87-default-pool-fd130152-x9dx Ready   <none>   4m27s
    v1.13.7-gke.8
```

Deploying the Flask Example Application to GKE

Take the same Kubernetes manifests used in the `minikube` example and deploy them to the Kubernetes cluster in GKE, via the `kubectl` command. Start by creating the `redis` deployment and service:

```
$ kubectl create -f redis-deployment.yaml
deployment.extensions/redis created

$ kubectl get pods
NAME                             READY  STATUS   RESTARTS  AGE
canary-aqw8jtfo-f54b9749-q5wqj   1/1    Running  0         5m57s
redis-9946db5cc-8g6zz            1/1    Running  0         20s

$ kubectl create -f redis-service.yaml
service/redis created

$ kubectl get service redis
NAME    TYPE       CLUSTER-IP     EXTERNAL-IP  PORT(S)    AGE
redis   ClusterIP  10.59.245.221  <none>       6379/TCP   18s
```

Create a PersistentVolumeClaim to be used as the data volume for the PostgreSQL database:

```
$ kubectl create -f dbdata-persistentvolumeclaim.yaml
persistentvolumeclaim/dbdata created

$ kubectl get pvc
NAME     STATUS   VOLUME                                      CAPACITY
dbdata   Bound    pvc-00c8156c-b618-11e9-9e84-42010a8a006f    1Gi
  ACCESS MODES   STORAGECLASS   AGE
  RWO            standard       12s
```

Create the db deployment:

```
$ kubectl create -f db-deployment.yaml
deployment.extensions/db created

$ kubectl get pods
NAME                          READY   STATUS             RESTARTS   AGE
canary-aqw8jtfo-f54b9749-q5wqj  1/1   Running            0          8m52s
db-6b4fbb57d9-cjjxx            0/1     CrashLoopBackOff   1          38s
redis-9946db5cc-8g6zz         1/1     Running            0          3m15s

$ kubectl logs db-6b4fbb57d9-cjjxx

initdb: directory "/var/lib/postgresql/data" exists but is not empty
It contains a lost+found directory, perhaps due to it being a mount point.
Using a mount point directly as the data directory is not recommended.
Create a subdirectory under the mount point.
```

We hit a snag when trying to create the db deployment. GKE provisioned a persistent volume that was mounted as */var/lib/postgresql/data*, and according to the error message above, was not empty.

Delete the failed db deployment:

```
$ kubectl delete -f db-deployment.yaml
deployment.extensions "db" deleted
```

Create a new temporary pod used to mount the same dbdata PersistentVolumeClaim as */data* inside the pod, so its filesystem can be inspected. Launching this type of temporary pod for troubleshooting purposes is a useful technique to know about:

```
$ cat pvc-inspect.yaml
kind: Pod
apiVersion: v1
metadata:
  name: pvc-inspect
spec:
  volumes:
    - name: dbdata
      persistentVolumeClaim:
        claimName: dbdata
```

```
      containers:
        - name: debugger
          image: busybox
          command: ['sleep', '3600']
          volumeMounts:
            - mountPath: "/data"
              name: dbdata

$ kubectl create -f pvc-inspect.yaml
pod/pvc-inspect created

$ kubectl get pods
NAME                              READY   STATUS    RESTARTS   AGE
canary-aqw8jtfo-f54b9749-q5wqj    1/1     Running   0          20m
pvc-inspect                       1/1     Running   0          35s
redis-9946db5cc-8g6zz             1/1     Running   0          14m
```

Use kubectl exec to open a shell inside the pod so */data* can be inspected:

```
$ kubectl exec -it pvc-inspect -- sh
/ # cd /data
/data # ls -la
total 24
drwx------    3 999      root          4096 Aug  3 17:57 .
drwxr-xr-x    1 root     root          4096 Aug  3 18:08 ..
drwx------    2 999      root         16384 Aug  3 17:57 lost+found
/data # rm -rf lost\+found/
/data # exit
```

Note how */data* contained a directory called *lost+found* that needed to be removed.

Delete the temporary pod:

```
$ kubectl delete pod pvc-inspect
pod "pvc-inspect" deleted
```

Create the db deployment again, which completes successfully this time:

```
$ kubectl create -f db-deployment.yaml
deployment.extensions/db created

$ kubectl get pods
NAME                              READY   STATUS    RESTARTS   AGE
canary-aqw8jtfo-f54b9749-q5wqj    1/1     Running   0          23m
db-6b4fbb57d9-8h978               1/1     Running   0          19s
redis-9946db5cc-8g6zz             1/1     Running   0          17m

$ kubectl logs db-6b4fbb57d9-8h978
PostgreSQL init process complete; ready for start up.

2019-08-03 18:12:01.108 UTC [1]
LOG:  listening on IPv4 address "0.0.0.0", port 5432
2019-08-03 18:12:01.108 UTC [1]
LOG:  listening on IPv6 address "::", port 5432
```

```
2019-08-03 18:12:01.114 UTC [1]
LOG:  listening on Unix socket "/var/run/postgresql/.s.PGSQL.5432"
2019-08-03 18:12:01.135 UTC [50]
LOG:  database system was shut down at 2019-08-03 18:12:01 UTC
2019-08-03 18:12:01.141 UTC [1]
LOG:  database system is ready to accept connections
```

Create wordcount database and role:

```
$ kubectl exec -it db-6b4fbb57d9-8h978 -- psql -U postgres
psql (11.4 (Debian 11.4-1.pgdg90+1))
Type "help" for help.

postgres=# create database wordcount;
CREATE DATABASE
postgres=# \q

$ kubectl exec -it db-6b4fbb57d9-8h978 -- psql -U postgres wordcount
psql (11.4 (Debian 11.4-1.pgdg90+1))
Type "help" for help.

wordcount=# CREATE ROLE wordcount_dbadmin;
CREATE ROLE
wordcount=# ALTER ROLE wordcount_dbadmin LOGIN;
ALTER ROLE
wordcount=# ALTER USER wordcount_dbadmin PASSWORD 'MYNEWPASS';
ALTER ROLE
wordcount=# \q
```

Create the db service:

```
$ kubectl create -f db-service.yaml
service/db created

$ kubectl describe service db
Name:              db
Namespace:         default
Labels:            io.kompose.service=db
Annotations:       kompose.cmd: kompose convert
                   kompose.version: 1.16.0 (0c01309)
Selector:          io.kompose.service=db
Type:              ClusterIP
IP:                10.59.241.181
Port:              5432  5432/TCP
TargetPort:        5432/TCP
Endpoints:         10.56.2.5:5432
Session Affinity:  None
Events:            <none>
```

Create the Secret object based on the base64 value of the database password. The plain-text value for the password is stored in a file encrypted with sops:

```
$ echo MYNEWPASS | base64
MYNEWPASSBASE64
```

```
$ sops secrets.yaml.enc

apiVersion: v1
kind: Secret
metadata:
  name: fbe-secret
type: Opaque
data:
  dbpass: MYNEWPASSBASE64

$ sops -d secrets.yaml.enc | kubectl create -f -
secret/fbe-secret created

kubectl describe secret fbe-secret
Name:         fbe-secret
Namespace:    default
Labels:       <none>
Annotations:  <none>

Type:  Opaque

Data
===
dbpass:  21 bytes
```

Create another Secret object representing the Docker Hub credentials:

```
$ sops -d create_docker_credentials_secret.sh.enc | bash -
secret/myregistrykey created
```

Since the scenario under consideration is a production-type deployment of the appication to GKE, set replicas to 3 in *worker-deployment.yaml* to ensure that three worker pods are running at all times:

```
$ kubectl create -f worker-deployment.yaml
deployment.extensions/worker created
```

Make sure that three worker pods are running:

```
$ kubectl get pods
NAME                          READY   STATUS    RESTARTS   AGE
canary-aqw8jtfo-f54b9749-q5wqj  1/1   Running   0          39m
db-6b4fbb57d9-8h978           1/1     Running   0          16m
redis-9946db5cc-8g6zz         1/1     Running   0          34m
worker-8cf5dc699-98z99        1/1     Running   0          35s
worker-8cf5dc699-9s26v        1/1     Running   0          35s
worker-8cf5dc699-v6ckr        1/1     Running   0          35s

$ kubectl logs worker-8cf5dc699-98z99
18:28:08 RQ worker 'rq:worker:1355d2cad49646e4953c6b4d978571f1' started,
 version 1.0
18:28:08 *** Listening on default...
```

Similarly, set `replicas` to two in *app-deployment.yaml*:

```
$ kubectl create -f app-deployment.yaml
deployment.extensions/app created
```

Make sure that two app pods are running:

```
$ kubectl get pods
NAME                              READY   STATUS    RESTARTS   AGE
app-7964cff98f-5bx4s              1/1     Running   0          54s
app-7964cff98f-8n8hk              1/1     Running   0          54s
canary-aqw8jtfo-f54b9749-q5wqj    1/1     Running   0          41m
db-6b4fbb57d9-8h978               1/1     Running   0          19m
redis-9946db5cc-8g6zz             1/1     Running   0          36m
worker-8cf5dc699-98z99            1/1     Running   0          2m44s
worker-8cf5dc699-9s26v            1/1     Running   0          2m44s
worker-8cf5dc699-v6ckr            1/1     Running   0          2m44s
```

Create the app service:

```
$ kubectl create -f app-service.yaml
service/app created
```

Note that a service of type LoadBalancer was created:

```
$ kubectl describe service app
Name:                     app
Namespace:                default
Labels:                   io.kompose.service=app
Annotations:              kompose.cmd: kompose convert
                          kompose.version: 1.16.0 (0c01309)
Selector:                 io.kompose.service=app
Type:                     LoadBalancer
IP:                       10.59.255.31
LoadBalancer Ingress:     34.83.242.171
Port:                     5000  5000/TCP
TargetPort:               5000/TCP
NodePort:                 5000  31305/TCP
Endpoints:                10.56.1.6:5000,10.56.2.12:5000
Session Affinity:         None
External Traffic Policy:  Cluster
Events:
Type    Reason                Age   From                Message
----    ------                ----  ----                -------
Normal  EnsuringLoadBalancer  72s   service-controller  Ensuring load balancer
Normal  EnsuredLoadBalancer   33s   service-controller  Ensured load balancer
```

Test the application by accessing the endpoint URL based on the IP address corresponding to `LoadBalancer Ingress`: *http://34.83.242.171:5000*.

We have demonstrated how to create Kubernetes objects such as Deployments, Services, and Secrets from raw Kubernetes manifest files. As your application becomes more complicated, this approach will start showing its limitations, because it will get harder to customize these files per environment (for example, for staging versus integration versus production). Each environment will have its own set of environment values and secrets that you will need to keep track of. In general, it will become more and more complicated to keep track of which manifests have been installed at a given time. Many solutions to this problem exist in the Kubernetes ecosystem, and one of the most common ones is to use the Helm (*https://oreil.ly/duKVw*) package manager. Think of Helm as the Kubernetes equivalent of the yum and apt package managers.

The next section shows how to use Helm to install and customize Prometheus and Grafana inside the GKE cluster.

Installing Prometheus and Grafana Helm Charts

In its current version (v2 as of this writing), Helm has a server-side component called Tiller that needs certain permissions inside the Kubernetes cluster.

Create a new Kubernetes Service Account for Tiller and give it the proper permissions:

```
$ kubectl -n kube-system create sa tiller
```

```
$ kubectl create clusterrolebinding tiller \
  --clusterrole cluster-admin \
  --serviceaccount=kube-system:tiller
```

```
$ kubectl patch deploy --namespace kube-system \
  tiller-deploy -p  '{"spec":{"template":{"spec":{"serviceAccount":"tiller"}}}}'
```

Download and install the Helm binary for your operating system from the official Helm release (*https://oreil.ly/sPwDO*) page, and then install Tiller with the helm init command:

```
$ helm init
```

Create a namespace called monitoring:

```
$ kubectl create namespace monitoring
namespace/monitoring created
```

Install the Prometheus Helm chart (*https://oreil.ly/CSaSo*) in the monitoring namespace:

```
$ helm install --name prometheus --namespace monitoring stable/prometheus
NAME:   prometheus
LAST DEPLOYED: Tue Aug 27 12:59:40 2019
NAMESPACE: monitoring
STATUS: DEPLOYED
```

List pods, services, and configmaps in the `monitoring` namespace:

```
$ kubectl get pods -nmonitoring
NAME                                            READY  STATUS   RESTARTS AGE
prometheus-alertmanager-df57f6df6-4b8lv         2/2    Running  0        3m
prometheus-kube-state-metrics-564564f799-t6qdm  1/1    Running  0        3m
prometheus-node-exporter-b4sb9                  1/1    Running  0        3m
prometheus-node-exporter-n4z2g                  1/1    Running  0        3m
prometheus-node-exporter-w7hn7                  1/1    Running  0        3m
prometheus-pushgateway-56b65bcf5f-whx5t         1/1    Running  0        3m
prometheus-server-7555945646-d86gn              2/2    Running  0        3m

$ kubectl get services -nmonitoring
NAME                           TYPE       CLUSTER-IP    EXTERNAL-IP  PORT(S)
   AGE
prometheus-alertmanager        ClusterIP  10.0.6.98     <none>       80/TCP
   3m51s
prometheus-kube-state-metrics  ClusterIP  None          <none>       80/TCP
   3m51s
prometheus-node-exporter       ClusterIP  None          <none>       9100/TCP
   3m51s
prometheus-pushgateway         ClusterIP  10.0.13.216   <none>       9091/TCP
   3m51s
prometheus-server              ClusterIP  10.0.4.74     <none>       80/TCP
   3m51s

$ kubectl get configmaps -nmonitoring
NAME                     DATA   AGE
prometheus-alertmanager  1      3m58s
prometheus-server        3      3m58s
```

Connect to Prometheus UI via the `kubectl port-forward` command:

```
$ export PROMETHEUS_POD_NAME=$(kubectl get pods --namespace monitoring \
-l "app=prometheus,component=server" -o jsonpath="{.items[0].metadata.name}")

$ echo $PROMETHEUS_POD_NAME
prometheus-server-7555945646-d86gn

$ kubectl --namespace monitoring port-forward $PROMETHEUS_POD_NAME 9090
Forwarding from 127.0.0.1:9090 -> 9090
Forwarding from [::1]:9090 -> 9090
Handling connection for 9090
```

Go to localhost:9090 in a browser and see the Prometheus UI.

Install the Grafana Helm chart (*https://oreil.ly/--wEN*) in the `monitoring` namespace:

```
$ helm install --name grafana --namespace monitoring stable/grafana
NAME:   grafana
LAST DEPLOYED: Tue Aug 27 13:10:02 2019
NAMESPACE: monitoring
STATUS: DEPLOYED
```

List Grafana-related pods, services, configmaps, and secrets in the monitoring namespace:

```
$ kubectl get pods -nmonitoring | grep grafana
grafana-84b887cf4d-wplcr                              1/1      Running   0

$ kubectl get services -nmonitoring | grep grafana
grafana                        ClusterIP   10.0.5.154    <none>        80/TCP

$ kubectl get configmaps -nmonitoring | grep grafana
grafana               1        99s
grafana-test          1        99s

$ kubectl get secrets -nmonitoring | grep grafana
grafana                               Opaque
grafana-test-token-85x4x              kubernetes.io/service-account-token
grafana-token-jw2qg                   kubernetes.io/service-account-token
```

Retrieve the password for the admin user for the Grafana web UI:

```
$ kubectl get secret --namespace monitoring grafana \
-o jsonpath="{.data.admin-password}" | base64 --decode ; echo

SOMESECRETTEXT
```

Connect to the Grafana UI using the kubectl port-forward command:

```
$ export GRAFANA_POD_NAME=$(kubectl get pods --namespace monitoring \
-l "app=grafana,release=grafana" -o jsonpath="{.items[0].metadata.name}")

$ kubectl --namespace monitoring port-forward $GRAFANA_POD_NAME 3000
Forwarding from 127.0.0.1:3000 -> 3000
Forwarding from [::1]:3000 -> 3000
```

Go to localhost:3000 in a browser and see the Grafana UI. Log in as user admin with the password retrieved above.

List the charts currently installed with helm list. When a chart is installed, the current installation is called a "Helm release":

```
$ helm list
NAME         REVISION  UPDATED                STATUS    CHART
    APP VERSION NAMESPACE
grafana      1         Tue Aug 27 13:10:02 2019  DEPLOYED  grafana-3.8.3
    6.2.5       monitoring
prometheus. 1          Tue Aug 27 12:59:40 2019  DEPLOYED  prometheus-9.1.0
    2.11.1      monitoring
```

Most of the time you will need to customize a Helm chart. It is easier to do that if you download the chart and install it from the local filesystem with helm.

Get the latest stable Prometheus and Grafana Helm charts with the helm fetch command, which will download tgz archives of the charts:

```
$ mkdir charts
$ cd charts
$ helm fetch stable/prometheus
$ helm fetch stable/grafana
$ ls -la
total 80
drwxr-xr-x   4 ggheo  staff    128 Aug 27 13:59 .
drwxr-xr-x  15 ggheo  staff    480 Aug 27 13:55 ..
-rw-r--r--   1 ggheo  staff  16195 Aug 27 13:55 grafana-3.8.3.tgz
-rw-r--r--   1 ggheo  staff  23481 Aug 27 13:54 prometheus-9.1.0.tgz
```

Unarchive the `tgz` files, then remove them:

```
$ tar xfz prometheus-9.1.0.tgz; rm prometheus-9.1.0.tgz
$ tar xfz grafana-3.8.3.tgz; rm grafana-3.8.3.tgz
```

The templatized Kubernetes manifests are stored by default in a directory called *templates* under the chart directory, so in this case these locations would be *prometheus/templates* and *grafana/templates*. The configuration values for a given chart are declared in the *values.yaml* file in the chart directory.

As an example of a Helm chart customization, let's add a persistent volume to Grafana, so we don't lose the data when we restart the Grafana pods.

Modify the file *grafana/values.yaml* and set the the value of the `enabled` subkey under the `persistence` parent key to `true` (by default it is `false`) in this section:

```
## Enable persistence using Persistent Volume Claims
## ref: http://kubernetes.io/docs/user-guide/persistent-volumes/
##
persistence:
  enabled: true
  # storageClassName: default
  accessModes:
    - ReadWriteOnce
  size: 10Gi
  # annotations: {}
  finalizers:
    - kubernetes.io/pvc-protection
  # subPath: ""
  # existingClaim:
```

Upgrade the existing `grafana` Helm release with the `helm upgrade` command. The last argument of the command is the name of the local directory containing the chart. Run this command in the parent directory of the *grafana* chart directory:

```
$ helm upgrade grafana grafana/
Release "grafana" has been upgraded. Happy Helming!
```

Verify that a PVC has been created for Grafana in the `monitoring` namespace:

```
kubectl describe pvc grafana -nmonitoring
Name:        grafana
```

```
Namespace:     monitoring
StorageClass:standard
Status:        Bound
Volume:        pvc-31d47393-c910-11e9-87c5-42010a8a0021
Labels:        app=grafana
               chart=grafana-3.8.3
               heritage=Tiller
               release=grafana
Annotations: pv.kubernetes.io/bind-completed: yes
               pv.kubernetes.io/bound-by-controller: yes
               volume.beta.kubernetes.io/storage-provisioner:kubernetes.io/gce-pd
Finalizers:    [kubernetes.io/pvc-protection]
Capacity:      10Gi
Access Modes:RWO
Mounted By:    grafana-84f79d5c45-zlqz8
Events:
Type    Reason                    Age  From                     Message
----    ------                    ---- ----                     -------
Normal  ProvisioningSucceeded  88s  persistentvolume-controller  Successfully
provisioned volume pvc-31d47393-c910-11e9-87c5-42010a8a0021
using kubernetes.io/gce-pd
```

Another example of a Helm chart customization, this time for Prometheus, is modifying the default retention period of 15 days for the data stored in Prometheus.

Change the `retention` value in *prometheus/values.yaml* to 30 days:

```
## Prometheus data retention period (default if not specified is 15 days)
##
retention: "30d"
```

Upgrade the existing Prometheus Helm release by running `helm upgrade`. Run this command in the parent directory of the *prometheus* chart directory:

```
$ helm upgrade prometheus prometheus
Release "prometheus" has been upgraded. Happy Helming!
```

Verify that the retention period was changed to 30 days. Run `kubectl describe` against the running Prometheus pod in the `monitoring` namespace and look at the `Args` section of the output:

```
$ kubectl get pods -nmonitoring
NAME                                              READY  STATUS   RESTARTS  AGE
grafana-84f79d5c45-zlqz8                          1/1    Running  0         9m
prometheus-alertmanager-df57f6df6-4b8lv           2/2    Running  0         87m
prometheus-kube-state-metrics-564564f799-t6qdm    1/1    Running  0         87m
prometheus-node-exporter-b4sb9                    1/1    Running  0         87m
prometheus-node-exporter-n4z2g                    1/1    Running  0         87m
prometheus-node-exporter-w7hn7                    1/1    Running  0         87m
prometheus-pushgateway-56b65bcf5f-whx5t           1/1    Running  0         87m
prometheus-server-779ffd445f-4llqr                2/2    Running  0         3m

$ kubectl describe pod prometheus-server-779ffd445f-4llqr -nmonitoring
```

```
OUTPUT OMITTED
      Args:
      --storage.tsdb.retention.time=30d
      --config.file=/etc/config/prometheus.yml
      --storage.tsdb.path=/data
      --web.console.libraries=/etc/prometheus/console_libraries
      --web.console.templates=/etc/prometheus/consoles
      --web.enable-lifecycle
```

Destroying the GKE Cluster

It pays (literally) to remember to delete any cloud resources you've been using for
testing purposes if you do not need them anymore. Otherwise, you may have an
unpleasant surprise when you receive the billing statement from your cloud provider
at the end of the month.

Destroy the GKE cluster via `pulumi destroy`:

```
$ pulumi destroy

Previewing destroy (dev):

        Type                              Name                               Plan
    -   pulumi:pulumi:Stack               pythonfordevops-gke-pulumi-dev     delete
    -   ├─ kubernetes:core:Service        ingress                            delete
    -   ├─ kubernetes:apps:Deployment     canary                             delete
    -   ├─ pulumi:providers:kubernetes    gke_k8s                            delete
    -   ├─ gcp:container:Cluster          gke-cluster                        delete
    -   └─ random:index:RandomString      password                           delete

Resources:
    - 6 to delete

Do you want to perform this destroy? yes
Destroying (dev):

        Type                              Name                               Status
    -   pulumi:pulumi:Stack               pythonfordevops-gke-pulumi-dev     deleted
    -   ├─ kubernetes:core:Service        ingress                            deleted
    -   ├─ kubernetes:apps:Deployment     canary                             deleted
    -   ├─ pulumi:providers:kubernetes    gke_k8s                            deleted
    -   ├─ gcp:container:Cluster          gke-cluster                        deleted
    -   └─ random:index:RandomString      password                           deleted

Resources:
    - 6 deleted

Duration: 3m18s
```

Exercises

- Use Google Cloud SQL for PostgreSQL, instead of running PostgreSQL in a Docker container in GKE.

- Use the AWS Cloud Development Kit (*https://aws.amazon.com/cdk*) to launch an Amazon EKS cluster, and deploy the example application to that cluster.

- Use Amazon RDS PostgreSQL instead of running PostgreSQL in a Docker container in EKS.

- Experiment with Kustomize (*https://oreil.ly/ie9n6*) as an alternative to Helm for managing Kubernetes manifest YAML files.

## CHAPTER 13

Serverless Technologies

Serverless is a term that generates a lot of buzz in the IT industry these days. As often happens with these kinds of terms, people have different opinions about what they actually mean. At face value, *serverless* implies a world where you do not need to worry about managing servers anymore. To some extent, this is true, but only for the developers who are using the functionality offered by *serverless* technologies. This chapter shows there is a *lot* of work that needs to happen behind the scenes for this magical world of no servers to come into being.

Many people equate the term *serverless* with Function as a Service (FaaS). This is partially true, and it mostly came about when AWS launched the Lambda service in 2015. AWS Lambdas are functions that can be run in the cloud without deploying a traditional server to host the functions. Hence the word *serverless*.

However, FaaS is not the only service that can be dubbed serverless. These days the Big Three public cloud providers (Amazon, Microsoft, and Google) all offer Containers as a Service (CaaS), which allows you to deploy full-blown Docker containers to their clouds without provisioning servers to host those containers. These services can also be called serverless. Examples of such services are AWS Fargate, Microsoft Azure Container Instances, and Google Cloud Run.

What are some use cases for serverless technologies? For FaaS technologies such as AWS Lambda, especially due to the event-driven manner in which Lambda functions can be triggered by other cloud services, use cases include:

- Extract-Transform-Load (ETL) data processing, where, as an example, a file is uploaded to S3, which triggers the execution of a Lambda function that does ETL processing on the data and sends it to a queue or a backend database
- ETL processing on logs sent by other services to CloudWatch

- Scheduling tasks in a cron-like manner based on CloudWatch Events triggering Lambda functions
- Real-time notifications based on Amazon SNS triggering Lambda functions
- Email processing using Lambda and Amazon SES
- Serverless website hosting, with the static web resources such as Javascript, CSS, and HTML stored in S3 and fronted by the CloudFront CDN service, and a REST API handled by an API Gateway routing the API requests to Lambda functions, which communicate with a backend such as Amazon RDS or Amazon DynamoDB

Many serverless use cases are identified in each of the cloud service providers' online documentation. For example, in the Google Cloud serverless ecosystem, web applications are handled best by Google AppEngine, APIs are handled best by Google Functions, and CloudRun is preferred for running processes in Docker containers. For a concrete example, consider a service that needs to perform machine learning tasks such as object detection with the TensorFlow framework. Due to the compute, memory, and disk resource limitations of FaaS, combined with the limited availability of libraries in a FaaS setup, it is probably better to run such a service using a CaaS service such as Google Cloud Run, as opposed to a FaaS service such as Google Cloud Functions.

The Big Three cloud providers also offer a rich DevOps toolchain around their FaaS platforms. For example, when you use AWS Lambda, with little effort, you can also add these services from AWS:

- AWS X-Ray for tracing/observability
- Amazon CloudWatch for logging, alerting, and event scheduling
- AWS Step Functions for serverless workflow coordination
- AWS Cloud9 for an in-browser development environment

How do you choose between FaaS and CaaS? In one dimension, it depends on the unit of deployment. If you only care about short-lived functions, with few dependencies and small amounts of data processing, then FaaS can work for you. If, on the other hand, you have long-running processes with lots of dependencies and heavy computing power requirements, then you may be better off using CaaS. Most FaaS services have severe limits for running time (15 minutes maximum for Lambda), computing power, memory size, disk space, and HTTP request and response limits. The upside to FaaS' short execution times is that you only pay for the duration of the function.

If you remember the discussion at the beginning of Chapter 12 on pets versus cattle versus insects, functions can truly be considered ephemeral insects that briefly come into existence, perform some processing, and disappear. Because of their ephemeral nature, functions in FaaS are also stateless, which is an important fact to keep in mind as you architect your application.

Another dimension for choosing between FaaS and CaaS is the number and type of interactions that your service has with other services. For example, an AWS Lambda function can be triggered asynchronously by no less than eight other AWS services, including S3, Simple Notification Service (SNS), Simple Email Service (SES), and CloudWatch. This richness of interactions makes it easier to write functions that respond to events, so FaaS wins in this case.

As you'll see in this chapter, many FaaS services are actually based on Kubernetes, which these days is the de facto container orchestration standard. Even though your unit of deployment is a function, behind the scenes the FaaS tooling creates and pushes Docker containers to a Kubernetes cluster that you might or might not manage. OpenFaas and OpenWhisk are examples of such Kubernetes-based FaaS technologies. When you self-host these FaaS platforms, you very quickly become aware that *server* makes up most of the word serverless. All of a sudden you have to worry a lot about the care and feeding of your Kubernetes clusters.

When we split the word DevOps into its parts, Dev and Ops, serverless technologies are targeted more toward the Dev side. They help developers feel less friction when it comes to deploying their code. The burden, especially in a self-hosted scenario, is on Ops to provision the infrastructure (sometimes very complex) that will support the FaaS or CaaS platforms. However, even if the Dev side might feel there is little need for Ops when it comes to serverless (which happens, although by definition this split makes it a non-DevOps situation), there are still plenty of Ops-related issues to worry about when it comes to using a Serverless platform: security, scalability, resource limitations and capacity planning, monitoring, logging, and observability. These have traditionally been considered the domain of Ops, but in the brave new DevOps world we are talking about, they need to be tackled by both Dev and Ops in tandem and with cooperation. A Dev team should not feel that its task is done when it finishes writing the code. Instead, it should take ownership and yes, pride, in getting the service all the way to production, with good monitoring, logging, and tracing built in.

We start this chapter with examples of how to deploy the same Python function, representing a simple HTTP endpoint, to the Big Three cloud providers using their FaaS offerings.

 Some of the commands used in the following examples produce large amounts of output. Except for cases where it is critical to the understanding of the command, we will omit the majority of the output lines to save trees and enable the reader to focus better on the text.

Deploying the Same Python Function to the "Big Three" Cloud Providers

For AWS and Google, we use the Serverless platform, which simplifies these deployments by abstracting the creation of cloud resources that are involved in the FaaS runtime environments. The Serverless platform does not yet support Python functions for Microsoft Azure, so in that case we show how to use Azure-specific CLI tooling.

Installing Serverless Framework

The Serverless platform (*https://serverless.com*) is based on nodejs. To install it, use npm:

```
$ npm install -g serverless
```

Deploying Python Function to AWS Lambda

Start by cloning the Serverless platform examples GitHub repository:

```
$ git clone https://github.com/serverless/examples.git
$ cd aws-python-simple-http-endpoint
$ export AWS_PROFILE=gheorghiu-net
```

The Python HTTP endpoint is defined in the file *handler.py*:

```
$ cat handler.py
import json
import datetime

def endpoint(event, context):
    current_time = datetime.datetime.now().time()
    body = {
        "message": "Hello, the current time is " + str(current_time)
    }

    response = {
        "statusCode": 200,
        "body": json.dumps(body)
    }

    return response
```

The Serverless platform uses a declarative approach for specifying the resources it needs to create with a YAML file called *serverless.yaml*. Here is file that declares a function called currentTime, corresponding to the Python function endpoint from the handler module defined previously:

```
$ cat serverless.yml
service: aws-python-simple-http-endpoint
```

```
frameworkVersion: ">=1.2.0 <2.0.0"

provider:
  name: aws
  runtime: python2.7 # or python3.7, supported as of November 2018

functions:
  currentTime:
    handler: handler.endpoint
    events:
      - http:
          path: ping
          method: get
```

Modify the Python version to 3.7 in *serverless.yaml*:

```
provider:
  name: aws
  runtime: python3.7
```

Deploy the function to AWS Lambda by running the `serverless deploy` command:

```
$ serverless deploy
Serverless: Packaging service...
Serverless: Excluding development dependencies...
Serverless: Uploading CloudFormation file to S3...
Serverless: Uploading artifacts...
Serverless:
Uploading service aws-python-simple-http-endpoint.zip file to S3 (1.95 KB)...
Serverless: Validating template...
Serverless: Updating Stack...
Serverless: Checking Stack update progress...
.............
Serverless: Stack update finished...
Service Information
service: aws-python-simple-http-endpoint
stage: dev
region: us-east-1
stack: aws-python-simple-http-endpoint-dev
resources: 10
api keys:
  None
endpoints:
  GET - https://3a88jzlxm0.execute-api.us-east-1.amazonaws.com/dev/ping
functions:
  currentTime: aws-python-simple-http-endpoint-dev-currentTime
layers:
  None
Serverless:
Run the "serverless" command to setup monitoring, troubleshooting and testing.
```

Test the deployed AWS Lambda function by hitting its endpoint with `curl`:

```
$ curl https://3a88jzlxm0.execute-api.us-east-1.amazonaws.com/dev/ping
{"message": "Hello, the current time is 23:16:30.479690"}%
```

Invoke the Lambda function directly with the `serverless invoke` command:

```
$ serverless invoke --function currentTime
{
    "statusCode": 200,
    "body": "{\"message\": \"Hello, the current time is 23:18:38.101006\"}"
}
```

Invoke the Lambda function directly and inspect the log (which is sent to AWS CloudWatch Logs) at the same time:

```
$ serverless invoke --function currentTime --log
{
    "statusCode": 200,
    "body": "{\"message\": \"Hello, the current time is 23:17:11.182463\"}"
}
--------------------------------------------------------------------
START RequestId: 5ac3c9c8-f8ca-4029-84fa-fcf5157b1404 Version: $LATEST
END RequestId: 5ac3c9c8-f8ca-4029-84fa-fcf5157b1404
REPORT RequestId: 5ac3c9c8-f8ca-4029-84fa-fcf5157b1404
Duration: 1.68 ms Billed Duration: 100 ms    Memory Size: 1024 MB
Max Memory Used: 56 MB
```

Note how the `Billed Duration` in the preceding output is 100 ms. This shows one of the advantages of using FaaS—being billed in very short increments of time.

One other thing we want to draw your attention to is the heavy lifting behind the scenes by the Serverless platform in the creation of AWS resources that are part of the Lambda setup. Serverless creates a CloudFormation stack called, in this case, `aws-python-simple-http-endpoint-dev`. You can inspect it with the `aws` CLI tool:

```
$ aws cloudformation describe-stack-resources \
   --stack-name aws-python-simple-http-endpoint-dev
   --region us-east-1 | jq '.StackResources[].ResourceType'
"AWS::ApiGateway::Deployment"
"AWS::ApiGateway::Method"
"AWS::ApiGateway::Resource"
"AWS::ApiGateway::RestApi"
"AWS::Lambda::Function"
"AWS::Lambda::Permission"
"AWS::Lambda::Version"
"AWS::Logs::LogGroup"
"AWS::IAM::Role"
"AWS::S3::Bucket"
```

Note how this CloudFormation stack contains no less than 10 AWS resource types that you would have had to otherwise create or associate with one another manually.

Deploying Python Function to Google Cloud Functions

In this section, we will take as an example the code from the `google-python-simple-http-endpoint` directory from the Serverless platform examples GitHub repository:

```
$ gcloud projects list
PROJECT_ID                    NAME                         PROJECT_NUMBER
pulumi-gke-testing            Pulumi GKE Testing           705973980178
pythonfordevops-gke-pulumi    pythonfordevops-gke-pulumi   787934032650
```

Create a new GCP project:

```
$ gcloud projects create pythonfordevops-cloudfunction
```

Initialize the local `gcloud` environment:

```
$ gcloud init
Welcome! This command will take you through the configuration of gcloud.

Settings from your current configuration [pythonfordevops-gke-pulumi] are:
compute:
  region: us-west1
  zone: us-west1-c
core:
  account: grig.gheorghiu@gmail.com
  disable_usage_reporting: 'True'
  project: pythonfordevops-gke-pulumi

Pick configuration to use:
[1] Re-initialize this configuration with new settings
[2] Create a new configuration
[3] Switch to and re-initialize existing configuration: [default]
Please enter your numeric choice:  2

Enter configuration name. Names start with a lower case letter and
contain only lower case letters a-z, digits 0-9, and hyphens '-':
pythonfordevops-cloudfunction
Your current configuration has been set to: [pythonfordevops-cloudfunction]

Choose the account you would like to use to perform operations for
this configuration:
 [1] grig.gheorghiu@gmail.com
 [2] Log in with a new account
Please enter your numeric choice:  1

You are logged in as: [grig.gheorghiu@gmail.com].

Pick cloud project to use:
 [1] pulumi-gke-testing
 [2] pythonfordevops-cloudfunction
 [3] pythonfordevops-gke-pulumi
 [4] Create a new project
Please enter numeric choice or text value (must exactly match list
```

```
item):  2

    Your current project has been set to: [pythonfordevops-cloudfunction].
```

Authorize local shell with GCP:

```
$ gcloud auth login
```

Use the Serverless framework to deploy the same Python HTTP endpoint as in the
AWS Lambda example, but this time as a Google Cloud Function:

```
$ serverless deploy

  Serverless Error ---------------------------------------

  Serverless plugin "serverless-google-cloudfunctions"
  initialization errored: Cannot find module 'serverless-google-cloudfunctions'
  Require stack:
  - /usr/local/lib/node_modules/serverless/lib/classes/PluginManager.js
  - /usr/local/lib/node_modules/serverless/lib/Serverless.js
  - /usr/local/lib/node_modules/serverless/lib/utils/autocomplete.js
  - /usr/local/lib/node_modules/serverless/bin/serverless.js

     Get Support ------------------------------------------
        Docs:          docs.serverless.com
        Bugs:          github.com/serverless/serverless/issues
        Issues:        forum.serverless.com

  Your Environment Information --------------------------
        Operating System:       darwin
        Node Version:           12.9.0
        Framework Version:      1.50.0
        Plugin Version:         1.3.8
        SDK Version:            2.1.0
```

The error we just encountered is due to the fact that the dependencies specified in
package.json have not been installed yet:

```
$ cat package.json
{
  "name": "google-python-simple-http-endpoint",
  "version": "0.0.1",
  "description":
  "Example demonstrates how to setup a simple HTTP GET endpoint with python",
  "author": "Sebastian Borza <sebito91@gmail.com>",
  "license": "MIT",
  "main": "handler.py",
  "scripts": {
    "test": "echo \"Error: no test specified\" && exit 1"
  },
  "dependencies": {
    "serverless-google-cloudfunctions": "^2.1.0"
  }
}
```

The Serverless platform is written in node.js, so its packages need to be installed with `npm install`:

```
$ npm install
```

Try deploying again:

```
$ serverless deploy

  Error ---------------------------------------------------

  Error: ENOENT: no such file or directory,
  open '/Users/ggheo/.gcloud/keyfile.json'
```

To generate a credentials key, create a new service account named `sa` on the GCP IAM service account page. In this case, the email for the new service account was set to `sa-255@pythonfordevops-cloudfunction.iam.gserviceaccount.com`.

Create a credentials key and download it as `~/.gcloud/pythonfordevops-cloudfunction.json`.

Specify the project and the path to the key in *serverless.yml*:

```
$ cat serverless.yml

service: python-simple-http-endpoint

frameworkVersion: ">=1.2.0 <2.0.0"

package:
  exclude:
    - node_modules/**
    - .gitignore
    - .git/**

plugins:
  - serverless-google-cloudfunctions

provider:
  name: google
  runtime: python37
  project: pythonfordevops-cloudfunction
  credentials: ~/.gcloud/pythonfordevops-cloudfunction.json

functions:
  currentTime:
    handler: endpoint
    events:
      - http: path
```

Go to the GCP Deployment Manager page and enable the Cloud Deployment Manager API; then also enable billing for Google Cloud Storage.

Try deploying again:

```
$ serverless deploy
Serverless: Packaging service...
Serverless: Excluding development dependencies...
Serverless: Compiling function "currentTime"...
Serverless: Uploading artifacts...

  Error --------------------------------------------------

  Error: Not Found
  at createError
  (/Users/ggheo/code/mycode/examples/google-python-simple-http-endpoint/
  node_modules/axios/lib/core/createError.js:16:15)
  at settle (/Users/ggheo/code/mycode/examples/
  google-python-simple-http-endpoint/node_modules/axios/lib/
  core/settle.js:18:12)
  at IncomingMessage.handleStreamEnd
  (/Users/ggheo/code/mycode/examples/google-python-simple-http-endpoint/
  node_modules/axios/lib/adapters/http.js:202:11)
  at IncomingMessage.emit (events.js:214:15)
  at IncomingMessage.EventEmitter.emit (domain.js:476:20)
  at endReadableNT (_stream_readable.js:1178:12)
  at processTicksAndRejections (internal/process/task_queues.js:77:11)

  For debugging logs, run again after setting the "SLS_DEBUG=*"
  environment variable.
```

Read through the Serverless platform documentation on GCP credentials and roles (*https://oreil.ly/scsRg*).

The following roles need to be assigned to the service account used for the deployment:

- Deployment Manager Editor
- Storage Admin
- Logging Admin
- Cloud Functions Developer roles

Also read through the Serverless platform documentation on the GCP APIs that need to be enabled (*https://oreil.ly/rKiHg*).

The following APIs need to be enabled in the GCP console:

- Google Cloud Functions
- Google Cloud Deployment Manager
- Google Cloud Storage

- Stackdriver Logging

Go to Deployment Manager in the GCP console and the inspect error messages:

```
sls-python-simple-http-endpoint-dev failed to deploy

sls-python-simple-http-endpoint-dev has resource warnings
sls-python-simple-http-endpoint-dev-1566510445295:
{"ResourceType":"storage.v1.bucket",
"ResourceErrorCode":"403",
"ResourceErrorMessage":{"code":403,
"errors":[{"domain":"global","location":"Authorization",
"locationType":"header",
"message":"The project to be billed is associated
with an absent billing account.",
"reason":"accountDisabled"}],
"message":"The project to be billed is associated
 with an absent billing account.",
 "statusMessage":"Forbidden",
 "requestPath":"https://www.googleapis.com/storage/v1/b",
 "httpMethod":"POST"}}
```

Delete the `sls-python-simple-http-endpoint-dev` deployment in the GCP console and run `serverless deploy` again:

```
$ serverless deploy

Deployed functions
first
  https://us-central1-pythonfordevops-cloudfunction.cloudfunctions.net/http
```

The `serverless deploy` command kept failing because initially we did not enable billing for Google Cloud Storage. The deployment was marked as failed for the service specified in *serverless.yml*, and subsequent `serverless deploy` commands failed even after enabling Cloud Storage billing. Once the failed deployment was deleted in the GCP console, the `serverless deploy` command started to work.

Invoke the deployed Google Cloud Function directly:

```
$ serverless invoke --function currentTime
Serverless: v1os7ptg9o48 {
    "statusCode": 200,
    "body": {
        "message": "Received a POST request at 03:46:39.027230"
    }
}
```

Use the `serverless logs` command to inspect the logs:

```
$ serverless logs --function currentTime
Serverless: Displaying the 4 most recent log(s):

2019-08-23T03:35:12.419846316Z: Function execution took 20 ms,
```

```
finished with status code: 200
2019-08-23T03:35:12.400499207Z: Function execution started
2019-08-23T03:34:27.133107221Z: Function execution took 11 ms,
finished with status code: 200
2019-08-23T03:34:27.122244864Z: Function execution started
```

Test the function endpoint with `curl`:

```
$ curl \
https://undefined-pythonfordevops-cloudfunction.cloudfunctions.net/endpoint
<!DOCTYPE html>
<html lang=en>
  <p><b>404.</b> <ins>That's an error.</ins>
  <p>The requested URL was not found on this server.
  <ins>That's all we know.</ins>
```

Since we didn't define a region in *serverless.yml*, the endpoint URL starts with unde
fined and returns an error.

Set the region to `us-central1` in *serverless.yml*:

```
provider:
  name: google
  runtime: python37
  region: us-central1
  project: pythonfordevops-cloudfunction
  credentials: /Users/ggheo/.gcloud/pythonfordevops-cloudfunction.json
```

Deploy the new version with `serverless deploy` and test the function endpoint with
`curl`:

```
$ curl \
https://us-central1-pythonfordevops-cloudfunction.cloudfunctions.net/endpoint
{
    "statusCode": 200,
    "body": {
        "message": "Received a GET request at 03:51:02.560756"
    }
}%
```

Deploying Python Function to Azure

The Serverless platform does not yet support Azure Functions (*https://oreil.ly/
4WQKG*) based on Python. We will demonstrate how to deploy Azure Python Functions using Azure-native tools.

Sign up for a Microsoft Azure account and install the Azure Functions runtime for
your specific operating system, following the official Microsoft documentation
(*https://oreil.ly/GHS4c*). If you are on a macOS, use `brew`:

```
$ brew tap azure/functions
$ brew install azure-functions-core-tools
```

Create a new directory for the Python function code:

```
$ mkdir azure-functions-python
$ cd azure-functions-python
```

Install Python 3.6 because 3.7 is not supported by Azure Functions. Create and activate virtualenv:

```
$ brew unlink python
$ brew install \
https://raw.githubusercontent.com/Homebrew/homebrew-core/
f2a764ef944b1080be64bd88dca9a1d80130c558/Formula/python.rb \
--ignore-dependencies

$ python3 -V
Python 3.6.5

$ python3 -m venv .venv
$ source .venv/bin/activate
```

Using the Azure func utility, create a local Functions project called python-simple-http-endpoint:

```
$ func init python-simple-http-endpoint
Select a worker runtime:
1. dotnet
2. node
3. python
4. powershell (preview)
Choose option: 3
```

Change directories to the newly created *python-simple-http-endpoint* directory and create an Azure HTTP Trigger Function with the func new command:

```
$ cd python-simple-http-endpoint
$ func new
Select a template:
1. Azure Blob Storage trigger
2. Azure Cosmos DB trigger
3. Azure Event Grid trigger
4. Azure Event Hub trigger
5. HTTP trigger
6. Azure Queue Storage trigger
7. Azure Service Bus Queue trigger
8. Azure Service Bus Topic trigger
9. Timer trigger
Choose option: 5
HTTP trigger
Function name: [HttpTrigger] currentTime
Writing python-simple-http-endpoint/currentTime/__init__.py
Writing python-simple-http-endpoint/currentTime/function.json
The function "currentTime" was created successfully
from the "HTTP trigger" template.
```

Inspect the Python code created:

```
$ cat currentTime/__init__.py
import logging

import azure.functions as func

def main(req: func.HttpRequest) -> func.HttpResponse:
    logging.info('Python HTTP trigger function processed a request.')

    name = req.params.get('name')
    if not name:
        try:
            req_body = req.get_json()
        except ValueError:
            pass
        else:
            name = req_body.get('name')

    if name:
        return func.HttpResponse(f"Hello {name}!")
    else:
        return func.HttpResponse(
             "Please pass a name on the query string or in the request body",
             status_code=400
        )
```

Run the function locally:

```
$ func host start

[8/24/19 12:21:35 AM] Host initialized (299ms)
[8/24/19 12:21:35 AM] Host started (329ms)
[8/24/19 12:21:35 AM] Job host started
[8/24/19 12:21:35 AM]  INFO: Starting Azure Functions Python Worker.
[8/24/19 12:21:35 AM]  INFO: Worker ID: e49c429d-9486-4167-9165-9ecd1757a2b5,
Request ID: 2842271e-a8fe-4643-ab1a-f52381098ae6, Host Address: 127.0.0.1:53952
Hosting environment: Production
Content root path: python-simple-http-endpoint
Now listening on: http://0.0.0.0:7071
Application started. Press Ctrl+C to shut down.
[8/24/19 12:21:35 AM] INFO: Successfully opened gRPC channel to 127.0.0.1:53952

Http Functions:

    currentTime: [GET,POST] http://localhost:7071/api/currentTime
```

Test from another terminal:

```
$ curl http://127.0.0.1:7071/api/currentTime\?name\=joe
Hello joe!%
```

Change HTTP handler in *currentTime/init.py* to include the current time in its response:

```python
import datetime

def main(req: func.HttpRequest) -> func.HttpResponse:
    logging.info('Python HTTP trigger function processed a request.')

    name = req.params.get('name')
    if not name:
        try:
            req_body = req.get_json()
        except ValueError:
            pass
        else:
            name = req_body.get('name')

    current_time = datetime.datetime.now().time()
    if name:
        return func.HttpResponse(f"Hello {name},
        the current time is {current_time}!")
    else:
        return func.HttpResponse(
            "Please pass a name on the query string or in the request body",
            status_code=400
        )
```

Test the new function with `curl`:

```
$ curl http://127.0.0.1:7071/api/currentTime\?name\=joe
Hello joe, the current time is 17:26:54.256060!%
```

Install the Azure CLI with `pip`:

```
$ pip install azure.cli
```

Create an Azure Resource Group, Storage Account, and Function App using the `az` CLI utility in interactive mode. This mode places you in an interactive shell with auto-completion, command descriptions, and examples. Note that if you want to follow along, you will need to specify a different and unique `functionapp` name. You might also need to specify a different Azure region, such as `eastus`, that supports free trial accounts:

```
$ az interactive
az>> login
az>> az group create --name myResourceGroup --location westus2
az>> az storage account create --name griggheorghiustorage --location westus2 \
--resource-group myResourceGroup --sku Standard_LRS
az>> az functionapp create --resource-group myResourceGroup --os-type Linux \
--consumption-plan-location westus2 --runtime python \
--name pyazure-devops4all \
--storage-account griggheorghiustorage
az>> exit
```

Deploy the `functionapp` project to Azure using the `func` utility:

```
$ func azure functionapp publish pyazure-devops4all --build remote
Getting site publishing info...
Creating archive for current directory...
Perform remote build for functions project (--build remote).
Uploading 2.12 KB

OUTPUT OMITTED

Running post deployment command(s)...
Deployment successful.
App container will begin restart within 10 seconds.
Remote build succeeded!
Syncing triggers...
Functions in pyazure-devops4all:
    currentTime - [httpTrigger]
      Invoke url:
      https://pyazure-devops4all.azurewebsites.net/api/
      currenttime?code=b0rN93O04cGPcGFKyX7n9HgITTPnHZiGCmjJN/SRsPX7taM7axJbbw==
```

Test the deployed function in Azure by hitting its endpoint with `curl`:

```
$ curl "https://pyazure-devops4all.azurewebsites.net/api/currenttime\
?code\=b0rN93O04cGPcGFKyX7n9HgITTPnHZiGCmjJN/SRsPX7taM7axJbbw\=\=\&name\=joe"
Hello joe, the current time is 01:20:32.036097!%
```

It is always a good idea to remove any cloud resources you don't need anymore. In this case, you can run:

```
$ az group delete --name myResourceGroup
```

Deploying a Python Function to Self-Hosted FaaS Platforms

As mentioned earlier in this chapter, many FaaS platforms are running on top of Kubernetes clusters. One advantage of this approach is that the functions you deploy run as regular Docker containers inside Kubernetes, so you can use your existing Kubernetes tooling, especially when it comes to observability (monitoring, logging, and tracing). Another advantage is potential cost savings. By running your serverless functions as containers inside an existing Kubernetes cluster, you can use the existing capacity of the cluster and not pay per function call as you would if you deployed your functions to a third-party FaaS platform.

In this section, we consider one of these platforms: OpenFaaS (*https://www.open faas.com*). Some other examples of similar FaaS platforms running on Kubernetes include the following:

- Kubeless (*https://kubeless.io*)

- Fn Project (*https://fnproject.io*) (the underlying technology powering the Oracle FaaS offering called Oracle Functions)
- Fission (*https://fission.io*)
- Apache OpenWhisk (*https://openwhisk.apache.org*)

Deploying Python Function to OpenFaaS

For this example, we use a "Kubernetes-lite" distribution from Rancher called k3s. We use k3s instead of minikube to showcase the wide variety of tools available in the Kubernetes ecosystem.

Start by running the k3sup (*https://oreil.ly/qK0xJ*) utility to provision a k3s Kubernetes cluster on an Ubuntu EC2 instance.

Download and install k3sup:

```
$ curl -sLS https://get.k3sup.dev | sh
$ sudo cp k3sup-darwin /usr/local/bin/k3sup
```

Verify SSH connectivity into the remote EC2 instance:

```
$ ssh ubuntu@35.167.68.86 date
Sat Aug 24 21:38:57 UTC 2019
```

Install k3s via k3sup install:

```
$ k3sup install --ip 35.167.68.86 --user ubuntu
OUTPUT OMITTED
Saving file to: kubeconfig
```

Inspect the *kubeconfig* file:

```
$ cat kubeconfig
apiVersion: v1
clusters:
- cluster:
    certificate-authority-data: BASE64_FIELD
    server: https://35.167.68.86:6443
  name: default
contexts:
- context:
    cluster: default
    user: default
  name: default
current-context: default
kind: Config
preferences: {}
users:
- name: default
  user:
```

```
password: OBFUSCATED
username: admin
```

Point the `KUBECONFIG` environment variable to the local *kubeconfig* file and test `kubectl` commands against the remote k3s cluster:

```
$ export KUBECONFIG=./kubeconfig

$ kubectl cluster-info
Kubernetes master is running at https://35.167.68.86:6443
CoreDNS is running at
https://35.167.68.86:6443/api/v1/namespaces/kube-system/
services/kube-dns:dns/proxy

To further debug and diagnose cluster problems, use
'kubectl cluster-info dump'.

$ kubectl get nodes
NAME            STATUS   ROLES    AGE   VERSION
ip-10-0-0-185   Ready    master   10m   v1.14.6-k3s.1
```

The next step is to install the OpenFaas Serverless platform on the k3s Kubernetes cluster.

Install `faas-cli` on the local macOS:

```
$ brew install faas-cli
```

Create RBAC permissions for Tiller, which is the server component of Helm:

```
$ kubectl -n kube-system create sa tiller \
  && kubectl create clusterrolebinding tiller \
  --clusterrole cluster-admin \
  --serviceaccount=kube-system:tiller
serviceaccount/tiller created
clusterrolebinding.rbac.authorization.k8s.io/tiller created
```

Install Tiller via `helm init`:

```
$ helm init --skip-refresh --upgrade --service-account tiller
```

Download, configure, and install the Helm chart for OpenFaaS:

```
$ wget \
https://raw.githubusercontent.com/openfaas/faas-netes/master/namespaces.yml

$ cat namespaces.yml
apiVersion: v1
kind: Namespace
metadata:
  name: openfaas
  labels:
    role: openfaas-system
    access: openfaas-system
    istio-injection: enabled
```

```
---
apiVersion: v1
kind: Namespace
metadata:
  name: openfaas-fn
  labels:
    istio-injection: enabled
    role: openfaas-fn

$ kubectl apply -f namespaces.yml
namespace/openfaas created
namespace/openfaas-fn created

$ helm repo add openfaas https://openfaas.github.io/faas-netes/
"openfaas" has been added to your repositories
```

Generate a random password for basic authentication to the OpenFaaS gateway:

```
$ PASSWORD=$(head -c 12 /dev/urandom | shasum| cut -d' ' -f1)

$ kubectl -n openfaas create secret generic basic-auth \
--from-literal=basic-auth-user=admin \
--from-literal=basic-auth-password="$PASSWORD"
secret/basic-auth created
```

Deploy OpenFaaS by installing the Helm chart:

```
$ helm repo update \
 && helm upgrade openfaas --install openfaas/openfaas \
    --namespace openfaas  \
    --set basic_auth=true \
    --set serviceType=LoadBalancer \
    --set functionNamespace=openfaas-fn

OUTPUT OMITTED

NOTES:
To verify that openfaas has started, run:
kubectl --namespace=openfaas get deployments -l "release=openfaas,app=openfaas"
```

 The basic_auth setup used here without TLS should ONLY be used for experimenting/learning. Any environment of consquence should be configured to ensure that credentials are passed over a secure TLS connection.

Verify the services running in the openfaas namespace:

```
$ kubectl get service -nopenfaas
NAME                TYPE         CLUSTER-IP     EXTERNAL-IP   PORT(S)
alertmanager        ClusterIP    10.43.193.61   <none>        9093/TCP
basic-auth-plugin   ClusterIP    10.43.83.12    <none>        8080/TCP
gateway             ClusterIP    10.43.7.46     <none>        8080/TCP
```

```
gateway-external    LoadBalancer    10.43.91.91     10.0.0.185    8080:31408/TCP
nats                ClusterIP       10.43.33.153    <none>        4222/TCP
prometheus          ClusterIP       10.43.122.184   <none>        9090/TCP
```

Forward port 8080 from the remote instance to port 8080 locally:

```
$ kubectl port-forward -n openfaas svc/gateway 8080:8080 &
[1] 29183
Forwarding from 127.0.0.1:8080 -> 8080
```

Go to the OpenFaaS web UI at *http://localhost:8080* and log in using username admin and password $PASSWORD.

Continue by creating an OpenFaaS Python function. Use the faas-cli tool to create a new OpenFaaS function called hello-python:

```
$ faas-cli new --lang python hello-python
Folder: hello-python created.
Function created in folder: hello-python
Stack file written: hello-python.yml
```

Inspect the configuration file for the hello-python function:

```
$ cat hello-python.yml
version: 1.0
provider:
  name: openfaas
  gateway: http://127.0.0.1:8080
functions:
  hello-python:
    lang: python
    handler: ./hello-python
    image: hello-python:latest
```

Inspect the automatically created directory *hello-python*:

```
$ ls -la hello-python
total 8
drwx------   4 ggheo  staff   128 Aug 24 15:16 .
drwxr-xr-x   8 ggheo  staff   256 Aug 24 15:16 ..
-rw-r--r--   1 ggheo  staff   123 Aug 24 15:16 handler.py
-rw-r--r--   1 ggheo  staff     0 Aug 24 15:16 requirements.txt

$ cat hello-python/handler.py
def handle(req):
    """handle a request to the function
    Args:
        req (str): request body
    """

    return req
```

Edit *handler.py* and bring over the code that prints the current time from the Server-less platform's simple-http-example:

```
$ cat hello-python/handler.py
import json
import datetime

def handle(req):
    """handle a request to the function
    Args:
        req (str): request body
    """

    current_time = datetime.datetime.now().time()
    body = {
        "message": "Received a {} at {}".format(req, str(current_time))
    }

    response = {
        "statusCode": 200,
        "body": body
    }
    return json.dumps(response, indent=4)
```

The next step is to build the OpenFaaS Python function. Use the `faas-cli build` command, which will build a Docker image based on an autogenerated Dockerfile:

```
$ faas-cli build -f ./hello-python.yml
[0] > Building hello-python.
Clearing temporary build folder: ./build/hello-python/
Preparing ./hello-python/ ./build/hello-python//function
Building: hello-python:latest with python template. Please wait..
Sending build context to Docker daemon  8.192kB
Step 1/29 : FROM openfaas/classic-watchdog:0.15.4 as watchdog

DOCKER BUILD OUTPUT OMITTED

Successfully tagged hello-python:latest
Image: hello-python:latest built.
[0] < Building hello-python done.
[0] worker done.
```

Check that the Docker image is present locally:

```
$ docker images | grep hello-python
hello-python                        latest
05b2c37407e1        29 seconds ago      75.5MB
```

Tag and push the Docker image to Docker Hub registry so it can be used on the remote Kubernetes cluster:

```
$ docker tag hello-python:latest griggheo/hello-python:latest
```

Edit *hello-python.yml* and change:

```
image: griggheo/hello-python:latest
```

Use the `faas-cli` `push` command to push the image to Docker Hub:

```
$ faas-cli push -f ./hello-python.yml
[0] > Pushing hello-python [griggheo/hello-python:latest].
The push refers to repository [docker.io/griggheo/hello-python]
latest: digest:
sha256:27e1fbb7f68bb920a6ff8d3baf1fa3599ae92e0b3c607daac3f8e276aa7f3ae3
size: 4074
[0] < Pushing hello-python [griggheo/hello-python:latest] done.
[0] worker done.
```

Next, deploy the OpenFaaS Python function to the remote k3s cluster. Use the `faas-cli` `deploy` command to deploy the function:

```
$ faas-cli deploy -f ./hello-python.yml
Deploying: hello-python.
WARNING! Communication is not secure, please consider using HTTPS.
Letsencrypt.org offers free SSL/TLS certificates.
Handling connection for 8080

unauthorized access, run "faas-cli login"
to setup authentication for this server

Function 'hello-python' failed to deploy with status code: 401
```

Use the `faas-cli` `login` command to obtain authenication credentials:

```
$ echo -n $PASSWORD | faas-cli login -g http://localhost:8080 \
-u admin --password-stdin
Calling the OpenFaaS server to validate the credentials...
Handling connection for 8080
WARNING! Communication is not secure, please consider using HTTPS.
Letsencrypt.org offers free SSL/TLS certificates.
credentials saved for admin http://localhost:8080
```

Edit *hello-python.yml* and change:

```
gateway: http://localhost:8080
```

Because we are returning JSON from our handler, add these lines to *hello-python.yml*:

```
environment:
  content_type: application/json
```

Contents of *hello-python.yml*:

```
$ cat hello-python.yml
version: 1.0
provider:
  name: openfaas
  gateway: http://localhost:8080
functions:
  hello-python:
    lang: python
    handler: ./hello-python
    image: griggheo/hello-python:latest
    environment:
      content_type: application/json
```

Run the `faas-cli deploy` command again:

```
$ faas-cli deploy -f ./hello-python.yml
Deploying: hello-python.
WARNING! Communication is not secure, please consider using HTTPS.
Letsencrypt.org offers free SSL/TLS certificates.
Handling connection for 8080
Handling connection for 8080

Deployed. 202 Accepted.
URL: http://localhost:8080/function/hello-python
```

If a code change is needed, use the following commands to rebuild and redeploy the function. Note that the `faas-cli remove` command will delete the current version of the function:

```
$ faas-cli build -f ./hello-python.yml
$ faas-cli push -f ./hello-python.yml
$ faas-cli remove -f ./hello-python.yml
$ faas-cli deploy -f ./hello-python.yml
```

Now test the deployed function with `curl`:

```
$ curl localhost:8080/function/hello-python --data-binary 'hello'
Handling connection for 8080
{
    "body": {
        "message": "Received a hello at 22:55:05.225295"
    },
    "statusCode": 200
}
```

Test by invoking the function directly with `faas-cli`:

```
$ echo -n "hello" | faas-cli invoke hello-python
Handling connection for 8080
{
    "body": {
        "message": "Received a hello at 22:56:23.549509"
```

```
            },
        "statusCode": 200
    }
```

The next example will be more full featured. We will demonstrate how to use the AWS CDK to provision several Lambda functions behind an API Gateway for create/read/update/delete (CRUD) REST access to todo items stored in a DynamoDB table. We will also show how to load test our REST API with containers deployed in AWS Fargate and running the Locust load-testing tool against the API. The Fargate containers will also be provisioned with the AWS CDK.

Provisioning DynamoDB Table, Lambda Functions, and API Gateway Methods Using the AWS CDK

We briefly mentioned the AWS CDK in Chapter 10. AWS CDK is a product that allows you to define the desired state of the infrastructure using real code (currently supported languages are TypeScript and Python), as opposed to using a YAML definition file (as the Serverless platform does).

Install CDK CLI with npm at the global level (depending on your operating system, you may need to run the following command with sudo):

```
$ npm install cdk -g
```

Create a directory for the CDK application:

```
$ mkdir cdk-lambda-dynamodb-fargate
$ cd cdk-lambda-dynamodb-fargate
```

Create a sample Python application with cdk init:

```
$ cdk init app --language=python
Applying project template app for python
Executing Creating virtualenv...

# Welcome to your CDK Python project!

This is a blank project for Python development with CDK.
The `cdk.json` file tells the CDK Toolkit how to execute your app.
```

List the files created:

```
$ ls -la
total 40
drwxr-xr-x   9 ggheo  staff    288 Sep  2 10:10 .
drwxr-xr-x  12 ggheo  staff    384 Sep  2 10:10 ..
drwxr-xr-x   6 ggheo  staff    192 Sep  2 10:10 .env
-rw-r--r--   1 ggheo  staff   1651 Sep  2 10:10 README.md
-rw-r--r--   1 ggheo  staff    252 Sep  2 10:10 app.py
-rw-r--r--   1 ggheo  staff     32 Sep  2 10:10 cdk.json
drwxr-xr-x   4 ggheo  staff    128 Sep  2 10:10 cdk_lambda_dynamodb_fargate
```

```
-rw-r--r--   1 ggheo  staff      5 Sep  2 10:10 requirements.txt
-rw-r--r--   1 ggheo  staff   1080 Sep  2 10:10 setup.py
```

Inspect the main file *app.py*:

```
$ cat app.py
#!/usr/bin/env python3

from aws_cdk import core

from cdk_lambda_dynamodb_fargate.cdk_lambda_dynamodb_fargate_stack \
import CdkLambdaDynamodbFargateStack

app = core.App()
CdkLambdaDynamodbFargateStack(app, "cdk-lambda-dynamodb-fargate")

app.synth()
```

A CDK program is composed of an *app* that can contain one or more *stacks*. A stack corresponds to a CloudFormation stack object.

Inspect the module defining the CDK stack:

```
$ cat cdk_lambda_dynamodb_fargate/cdk_lambda_dynamodb_fargate_stack.py
from aws_cdk import core

class CdkLambdaDynamodbFargateStack(core.Stack):

    def __init__(self, scope: core.Construct, id: str, **kwargs) -> None:
        super().__init__(scope, id, **kwargs)

        # The code that defines your stack goes here
```

Because we are going to have two stacks, one for the DynamoDB/Lambda/API Gateway resources, and one for the Fargate resources, rename

cdk_lambda_dynamodb_fargate/cdk_lambda_dynamodb_fargate_stack.py

to *cdk_lambda_dynamodb_fargate/cdk_lambda_dynamodb_stack.py*

and the class CdkLambdaDynamodbFargateStack to CdkLambdaDynamodbStack.

Also change *app.py* to refer to the changed module and class names:

```
from cdk_lambda_dynamodb_fargate.cdk_lambda_dynamodb_stack \
import CdkLambdaDynamodbStack

CdkLambdaDynamodbStack(app, "cdk-lambda-dynamodb")
```

Activate virtualenv:

```
$ source .env/bin/activate
```

We are going to take the URL shortener CDK example (*https://oreil.ly/q2dDF*) and modify it with code from the Serverless platform AWS Python REST API example

---

(*https://oreil.ly/o_gxS*) to build a REST API for creating, listing, getting, updating, and deleting todo items. Amazon DynamoDB is used to store the data.

Inspect the *serverless.yml* file from *examples/aws-python-rest-api-with-dynamodb* and deploy it with the `serverless` command to see what AWS resources get created:

```
$ pwd
~/code/examples/aws-python-rest-api-with-dynamodb

$ serverless deploy
Serverless: Stack update finished...
Service Information
service: serverless-rest-api-with-dynamodb
stage: dev
region: us-east-1
stack: serverless-rest-api-with-dynamodb-dev
resources: 34
api keys:
  None
endpoints:
POST - https://tbst34m2b7.execute-api.us-east-1.amazonaws.com/dev/todos
GET - https://tbst34m2b7.execute-api.us-east-1.amazonaws.com/dev/todos
GET - https://tbst34m2b7.execute-api.us-east-1.amazonaws.com/dev/todos/{id}
PUT - https://tbst34m2b7.execute-api.us-east-1.amazonaws.com/dev/todos/{id}
DELETE - https://tbst34m2b7.execute-api.us-east-1.amazonaws.com/dev/todos/{id}
functions:
  create: serverless-rest-api-with-dynamodb-dev-create
  list: serverless-rest-api-with-dynamodb-dev-list
  get: serverless-rest-api-with-dynamodb-dev-get
  update: serverless-rest-api-with-dynamodb-dev-update
  delete: serverless-rest-api-with-dynamodb-dev-delete
layers:
  None
Serverless: Run the "serverless" command to setup monitoring, troubleshooting and
           testing.
```

The previous command created five Lambda functions, one API Gateway, and one DynamoDB table.

In the CDK directory, add a DynamoDB table to the stack we are building:

```
$ pwd
~/code/devops/serverless/cdk-lambda-dynamodb-fargate

$ cat cdk_lambda_dynamodb_fargate/cdk_lambda_dynamodb_stack.py
from aws_cdk import core
from aws_cdk import aws_dynamodb

class CdkLambdaDynamodbStack(core.Stack):

    def __init__(self, scope: core.Construct, id: str, **kwargs) -> None:
        super().__init__(scope, id, **kwargs)
```

```
# define the table stores Todo items
table = aws_dynamodb.Table(self, "Table",
                            partition_key=aws_dynamodb.Attribute(
                              name="id",
                              type=aws_dynamodb.AttributeType.STRING),
                            read_capacity=10,
                            write_capacity=5)
```

Install the required Python modules:

```
$ cat requirements.txt
-e .
aws-cdk.core
aws-cdk.aws-dynamodb

$ pip install -r requirements.txt
```

Inspect the CloudFormation stack that will be created by running cdk synth:

```
$ export AWS_PROFILE=gheorghiu-net
$ cdk synth
```

Pass a variable called variable containing the region value to the constructor CdkLambdaDynamodbStack in *app.py*:

```
app_env = {"region": "us-east-2"}
CdkLambdaDynamodbStack(app, "cdk-lambda-dynamodb", env=app_env)
```

Run cdk synth again:

```
$ cdk synth
Resources:
  TableCD117FA1:
    Type: AWS::DynamoDB::Table
    Properties:
      KeySchema:
        - AttributeName: id
          KeyType: HASH
      AttributeDefinitions:
        - AttributeName: id
          AttributeType: S
      ProvisionedThroughput:
        ReadCapacityUnits: 10
        WriteCapacityUnits: 5
    UpdateReplacePolicy: Retain
    DeletionPolicy: Retain
    Metadata:
      aws:cdk:path: cdk-lambda-dynamodb-fargate/Table/Resource
  CDKMetadata:
    Type: AWS::CDK::Metadata
    Properties:
      Modules: aws-cdk=1.6.1,
      @aws-cdk/aws-applicationautoscaling=1.6.1,
      @aws-cdk/aws-autoscaling-common=1.6.1,
```

```
@aws-cdk/aws-cloudwatch=1.6.1,
@aws-cdk/aws-dynamodb=1.6.1,
@aws-cdk/aws-iam=1.6.1,
@aws-cdk/core=1.6.1,
@aws-cdk/cx-api=1.6.1,@aws-cdk/region-info=1.6.1,
jsii-runtime=Python/3.7.4
```

Deploy the CDK stack by running cdk deploy:

```
$ cdk deploy
cdk-lambda-dynamodb-fargate: deploying...
cdk-lambda-dynamodb-fargate: creating CloudFormation changeset...
 0/3 | 11:12:25 AM | CREATE_IN_PROGRESS   | AWS::DynamoDB::Table |
 Table (TableCD117FA1)
 0/3 | 11:12:25 AM | CREATE_IN_PROGRESS   | AWS::CDK::Metadata   |
 CDKMetadata
 0/3 | 11:12:25 AM | CREATE_IN_PROGRESS   | AWS::DynamoDB::Table |
 Table (TableCD117FA1) Resource creation Initiated
 0/3 | 11:12:27 AM | CREATE_IN_PROGRESS   | AWS::CDK::Metadata   |
 CDKMetadata Resource creation Initiated
 1/3 | 11:12:27 AM | CREATE_COMPLETE      | AWS::CDK::Metadata   |
 CDKMetadata
 2/3 | 11:12:56 AM | CREATE_COMPLETE      | AWS::DynamoDB::Table |
 Table (TableCD117FA1)
 3/3 | 11:12:57 AM | CREATE_COMPLETE      | AWS::CloudFormation::Stack |
 cdk-lambda-dynamodb-fargate

Stack ARN:
arn:aws:cloudformation:us-east-2:200562098309:stack/
cdk-lambda-dynamodb/3236a8b0-cdad-11e9-934b-0a7dfa8cb208
```

The next step is to add Lambda functions and the API Gateway resource to the stack.

In the CDK code directory, create a *lambda* directory and copy the Python modules from the Serverless platform AWS Python REST API example (*https://oreil.ly/mRSjn*):

```
$ pwd
~/code/devops/serverless/cdk-lambda-dynamodb-fargate

$ mkdir lambda
$ cp ~/code/examples/aws-python-rest-api-with-dynamodb/todos/* lambda
$ ls -la lambda
total 48
drwxr-xr-x   9 ggheo  staff    288 Sep  2 10:41 .
drwxr-xr-x  10 ggheo  staff    320 Sep  2 10:19 ..
-rw-r--r--   1 ggheo  staff      0 Sep  2 10:41 __init__.py
-rw-r--r--   1 ggheo  staff    822 Sep  2 10:41 create.py
-rw-r--r--   1 ggheo  staff    288 Sep  2 10:41 decimalencoder.py
-rw-r--r--   1 ggheo  staff    386 Sep  2 10:41 delete.py
-rw-r--r--   1 ggheo  staff    535 Sep  2 10:41 get.py
-rw-r--r--   1 ggheo  staff    434 Sep  2 10:41 list.py
-rw-r--r--   1 ggheo  staff   1240 Sep  2 10:41 update.py
```

Add the required modules to *requirements.txt* and install them with pip:

```
$ cat requirements.txt
-e .
aws-cdk.core
aws-cdk.aws-dynamodb
aws-cdk.aws-lambda
aws-cdk.aws-apigateway

$ pip install -r requirements.txt
```

Create Lambda and API Gateway constructs in the stack module:

```
$ cat cdk_lambda_dynamodb_fargate/cdk_lambda_dynamodb_stack.py
from aws_cdk import core
from aws_cdk.core import App, Construct, Duration
from aws_cdk import aws_dynamodb, aws_lambda, aws_apigateway

class CdkLambdaDynamodbStack(core.Stack):

    def __init__(self, scope: core.Construct, id: str, **kwargs) -> None:
        super().__init__(scope, id, **kwargs)

        # define the table stores Todo todos
        table = aws_dynamodb.Table(self, "Table",
            partition_key=aws_dynamodb.Attribute(
                name="id",
                type=aws_dynamodb.AttributeType.STRING),
            read_capacity=10,
            write_capacity=5)

        # define the Lambda functions
        list_handler = aws_lambda.Function(self, "TodoListFunction",
            code=aws_lambda.Code.asset("./lambda"),
            handler="list.list",
            timeout=Duration.minutes(5),
            runtime=aws_lambda.Runtime.PYTHON_3_7)

        create_handler = aws_lambda.Function(self, "TodoCreateFunction",
            code=aws_lambda.Code.asset("./lambda"),
            handler="create.create",
            timeout=Duration.minutes(5),
            runtime=aws_lambda.Runtime.PYTHON_3_7)

        get_handler = aws_lambda.Function(self, "TodoGetFunction",
            code=aws_lambda.Code.asset("./lambda"),
            handler="get.get",
            timeout=Duration.minutes(5),
            runtime=aws_lambda.Runtime.PYTHON_3_7)

        update_handler = aws_lambda.Function(self, "TodoUpdateFunction",
            code=aws_lambda.Code.asset("./lambda"),
            handler="update.update",
```

```
        timeout=Duration.minutes(5),
        runtime=aws_lambda.Runtime.PYTHON_3_7)

    delete_handler = aws_lambda.Function(self, "TodoDeleteFunction",
        code=aws_lambda.Code.asset("./lambda"),
        handler="delete.delete",
        timeout=Duration.minutes(5),
        runtime=aws_lambda.Runtime.PYTHON_3_7)

    # pass the table name to each handler through an environment variable
    # and grant the handler read/write permissions on the table.
    handler_list = [
        list_handler,
        create_handler,
        get_handler,
        update_handler,
        delete_handler
    ]
    for handler in handler_list:
        handler.add_environment('DYNAMODB_TABLE', table.table_name)
        table.grant_read_write_data(handler)

    # define the API endpoint
    api = aws_apigateway.LambdaRestApi(self, "TodoApi",
        handler=list_handler,
        proxy=False)

    # define LambdaIntegrations
    list_lambda_integration = \
        aws_apigateway.LambdaIntegration(list_handler)
    create_lambda_integration = \
        aws_apigateway.LambdaIntegration(create_handler)
    get_lambda_integration = \
        aws_apigateway.LambdaIntegration(get_handler)
    update_lambda_integration = \
        aws_apigateway.LambdaIntegration(update_handler)
    delete_lambda_integration = \
        aws_apigateway.LambdaIntegration(delete_handler)

    # define REST API model and associate methods with LambdaIntegrations
    api.root.add_method('ANY')

    todos = api.root.add_resource('todos')
    todos.add_method('GET', list_lambda_integration)
    todos.add_method('POST', create_lambda_integration)

    todo = todos.add_resource('{id}')
    todo.add_method('GET', get_lambda_integration)
    todo.add_method('PUT', update_lambda_integration)
    todo.add_method('DELETE', delete_lambda_integration)
```

It is worth noting several features of the code we just reviewed:

- We were able to use the add_environment method on each handler object to pass the environment variable DYNAMODB_TABLE used in the Python code for the Lambda functions and set it to table.table_name. The name of the DynamoDB table is not known at construction time, so the CDK will replace it with a token and will set the token to the correct name of the table when it deploys the stack (see the Tokens (*https://oreil.ly/XfdEU*) documentation for more details).

- We made full use of a simple programming language construct, the for loop, when we iterated over the list of all Lambda handlers. While this may seem natural, it is still worth pointing out because loops and variable passing are features that are awkwardly implemented, if at all, in YAML-based Infrastructure as Code tools such as Terraform.

- We defined the HTTP methods (GET, POST, PUT, DELETE) associated with various endpoints of the API Gateway and associated the correct Lambda function with each of them.

Deploy the stack with cdk deploy:

```
$ cdk deploy
cdk-lambda-dynamodb-fargate failed: Error:
This stack uses assets, so the toolkit stack must be deployed
to the environment
(Run "cdk bootstrap aws://unknown-account/us-east-2")
```

Fix by running cdk bootstrap:

```
$ cdk bootstrap
Bootstrapping environment aws://ACCOUNTID/us-east-2...
CDKToolkit: creating CloudFormation changeset...
Environment aws://ACCOUNTID/us-east-2 bootstrapped.
```

Deploy the CDK stack again:

```
$ cdk deploy
OUTPUT OMITTED

Outputs:
cdk-lambda-dynamodb.TodoApiEndpointC1E16B6C =
https://k6ygy4xw24.execute-api.us-east-2.amazonaws.com/prod/

Stack ARN:
arn:aws:cloudformation:us-east-2:ACCOUNTID:stack/cdk-lambda-dynamodb/
15a66bb0-cdba-11e9-aef9-0ab95d3a5528
```

The next step is to test the REST API with curl.

First create a new todo item:

```
$ curl -X \
POST https://k6ygy4xw24.execute-api.us-east-2.amazonaws.com/prod/todos \
--data '{ "text": "Learn CDK" }'
{"id": "19d55d5a-cdb4-11e9-9a8f-9ed29c44196e", "text": "Learn CDK",
"checked": false,
"createdAt": "1567450902.262834",
"updatedAt": "1567450902.262834"}%
```

Create a second todo item:

```
$ curl -X \
POST https://k6ygy4xw24.execute-api.us-east-2.amazonaws.com/prod/todos \
--data '{ "text": "Learn CDK with Python" }'
{"id": "58a992c6-cdb4-11e9-9a8f-9ed29c44196e", "text": "Learn CDK with Python",
"checked": false,
"createdAt": "1567451007.680936",
"updatedAt": "1567451007.680936"}%
```

Try getting the details for the item just created by specifying its ID:

```
$ curl \
https://k6ygy4xw24.execute-api.us-east-2.amazonaws.com/
prod/todos/58a992c6-cdb4-11e9-9a8f-9ed29c44196e
{"message": "Internal server error"}%
```

Investigate by inspecting the CloudWatch Logs for the Lambda function
TodoGetFunction:

```
[ERROR] Runtime.ImportModuleError:
Unable to import module 'get': No module named 'todos'
```

To fix, change the line in *lambda/get.py* from:

```
from todos import decimalencoder
```

to:

```
import decimalencoder
```

Redeploy the stack with cdk deploy.

Try getting the todo item details with curl again:

```
$ curl \
https://k6ygy4xw24.execute-api.us-east-2.amazonaws.com/
prod/todos/58a992c6-cdb4-11e9-9a8f-9ed29c44196e
{"checked": false, "createdAt": "1567451007.680936",
"text": "Learn CDK with Python",
"id": "58a992c6-cdb4-11e9-9a8f-9ed29c44196e",
"updatedAt": "1567451007.680936"}
```

Make the import decimalencoder change to all modules in the *lambda* directory
that need the decimalencoder module and redeploy with cdk deploy.

List all todos and format the output with the jq utility:

```
$ curl \
https://k6ygy4xw24.execute-api.us-east-2.amazonaws.com/prod/todos | jq
[
  {
    "checked": false,
    "createdAt": "1567450902.262834",
    "text": "Learn CDK",
    "id": "19d55d5a-cdb4-11e9-9a8f-9ed29c44196e",
    "updatedAt": "1567450902.262834"
  },
  {
    "checked": false,
    "createdAt": "1567451007.680936",
    "text": "Learn CDK with Python",
    "id": "58a992c6-cdb4-11e9-9a8f-9ed29c44196e",
    "updatedAt": "1567451007.680936"
  }
]
```

Delete a todo and verify that the list does not contain it anymore:

```
$ curl -X DELETE \
https://k6ygy4xw24.execute-api.us-east-2.amazonaws.com/prod/todos/
19d55d5a-cdb4-11e9-9a8f-9ed29c44196e

$ curl https://k6ygy4xw24.execute-api.us-east-2.amazonaws.com/prod/todos | jq
[
  {
    "checked": false,
    "createdAt": "1567451007.680936",
    "text": "Learn CDK with Python",
    "id": "58a992c6-cdb4-11e9-9a8f-9ed29c44196e",
    "updatedAt": "1567451007.680936"
  }
]
```

Now test updating an existing todo item with curl:

```
$ curl -X \
PUT https://k6ygy4xw24.execute-api.us-east-2.amazonaws.com/prod/todos/
58a992c6-cdb4-11e9-9a8f-9ed29c44196e \
--data '{ "text": "Learn CDK with Python by reading the PyForDevOps book" }'
{"message": "Internal server error"}%
```

Inspecting the CloudWatch logs for the Lambda function associated with this end-point shows:

```
[ERROR] Exception: Couldn't update the todo item.
Traceback (most recent call last):
  File "/var/task/update.py", line 15, in update
    raise Exception("Couldn't update the todo item.")
```

Change the validation test in *lambda/update.py* to:

```
data = json.loads(event['body'])
if 'text' not in data:
    logging.error("Validation Failed")
    raise Exception("Couldn't update the todo item.")
```

Also change the value for checked to True, since we have already seen a post that we are trying to update:

```
ExpressionAttributeValues={
        ':text': data['text'],
        ':checked': True,
        ':updatedAt': timestamp,
    },
```

Redeploy the stack with cdk deploy_.

Test updating the todo item with curl:

```
$ curl -X \
PUT https://k6ygy4xw24.execute-api.us-east-2.amazonaws.com/prod/todos/
58a992c6-cdb4-11e9-9a8f-9ed29c44196e \
--data '{ "text": "Learn CDK with Python by reading the PyForDevOps book"}'
{"checked": true, "createdAt": "1567451007.680936",
"text": "Learn CDK with Python by reading the PyForDevOps book",
"id": "58a992c6-cdb4-11e9-9a8f-9ed29c44196e", "updatedAt": 1567453288764}%
```

List the todo items to verify the update:

```
$ curl https://k6ygy4xw24.execute-api.us-east-2.amazonaws.com/prod/todos | jq
[
  {
    "checked": true,
    "createdAt": "1567451007.680936",
    "text": "Learn CDK with Python by reading the PyForDevOps book",
    "id": "58a992c6-cdb4-11e9-9a8f-9ed29c44196e",
    "updatedAt": 1567453288764
  }
]
```

The next step is to provision AWS Fargate containers that will run a load test against the REST API we just deployed. Each container will run a Docker image that uses the Taurus test automation framework (*https://gettaurus.org*) to run the Molotov load-testing tool (*https://oreil.ly/OGDne*). We introduced Molotov in Chapter 5 as a simple and very useful Python-based load-testing tool.

Start by creating a Dockerfile for running Taurus and Molotov in a directory called *loadtest*:

```
$ mkdir loadtest; cd loadtest
$ cat Dockerfile
FROM blazemeter/taurus
```

```
COPY scripts /scripts
COPY taurus.yaml /bzt-configs/

WORKDIR /bzt-configs
ENTRYPOINT ["sh", "-c", "bzt -l /tmp/artifacts/bzt.log /bzt-configs/taurus.yaml"]
```

The Dockerfile runs the Taurus `bzt` command line using the *taurus.yaml* configuration file:

```
$ cat taurus.yaml
execution:
- executor: molotov
  concurrency: 10  # number of Molotov workers
  iterations: 5  # iteration limit for the test
  ramp-up: 30s
  hold-for: 5m
  scenario:
    script: /scripts/loadtest.py  # has to be valid Molotov script
```

In this configuration file, the value for `concurrency` is set to 10, which means that we are simulating 10 concurrent users or virtual users (VUs). The `executor` is defined as a `molotov` test based on a script called *loadtest.py* in the *scripts* directory. Here is the script, which is a Python module:

```
$ cat scripts/loadtest.py
import os
import json
import random
import molotov
from molotov import global_setup, scenario

@global_setup()
def init_test(args):
    BASE_URL=os.getenv('BASE_URL', '')
    molotov.set_var('base_url', BASE_URL)

@scenario(weight=50)
async def _test_list_todos(session):
    base_url= molotov.get_var('base_url')
    async with session.get(base_url + '/todos') as resp:
        assert resp.status == 200, resp.status

@scenario(weight=30)
async def _test_create_todo(session):
    base_url= molotov.get_var('base_url')
    todo_data = json.dumps({'text':
      'Created new todo during Taurus/molotov load test'})
    async with session.post(base_url + '/todos',
      data=todo_data) as resp:
        assert resp.status == 200

@scenario(weight=10)
```

```python
async def _test_update_todo(session):
    base_url= molotov.get_var('base_url')
    # list all todos
    async with session.get(base_url + '/todos') as resp:
        res = await resp.json()
        assert resp.status == 200, resp.status
        # choose random todo and update it with PUT request
        todo_id = random.choice(res)['id']
        todo_data = json.dumps({'text':
          'Updated existing todo during Taurus/molotov load test'})
        async with session.put(base_url + '/todos/' + todo_id,
          data=todo_data) as resp:
            assert resp.status == 200

@scenario(weight=10)
async def _test_delete_todo(session):
    base_url= molotov.get_var('base_url')
    # list all todos
    async with session.get(base_url + '/todos') as resp:
        res = await resp.json()
        assert resp.status == 200, resp.status
        # choose random todo and delete it with DELETE request
        todo_id = random.choice(res)['id']
        async with session.delete(base_url + '/todos/' + todo_id) as resp:
            assert resp.status == 200
```

The script has four functions decorated as scenarios to be run by Molotov. They exercise various endpoints of the CRUD REST API. The weights indicate the approximate percentage of the time of the overall test duration that each scenario will be invoked. For example, the _test_list_todos function will be invoked in this example approximately 50% of the time, _test_create_todo will run approximately 30% of the time, and _test_update_todo and _test_delete_todo will each run approximately 10% of the time.

Build the local Docker image:

```
$ docker build -t cdk-loadtest .
```

Create the local *artifacts* directory:

```
$ mkdir artifacts
```

Run the local Docker image and mount the local *artifacts* directory as */tmp/artifacts* inside the Docker container:

```
$ docker run --rm -d \
--env BASE_URL=https://k6ygy4xw24.execute-api.us-east-2.amazonaws.com/prod \
-v `pwd`/artifacts:/tmp/artifacts cdk-loadtest
```

Debug the Molotov script by inspecting the *artifacts/molotov.out* file.

Taurus results can be inspected either with docker logs CONTAINER_ID or by inspecting the file *artifacts/bzt.log*.

Results obtained by inspecting the Docker logs:

```
$ docker logs -f a228f8f9a2bc
19:26:26 INFO: Taurus CLI Tool v1.13.8
19:26:26 INFO: Starting with configs: ['/bzt-configs/taurus.yaml']
19:26:26 INFO: Configuring...
19:26:26 INFO: Artifacts dir: /tmp/artifacts
19:26:26 INFO: Preparing...
19:26:27 INFO: Starting...
19:26:27 INFO: Waiting for results...
19:26:32 INFO: Changed data analysis delay to 3s
19:26:32 INFO: Current: 0 vu  1 succ  0 fail  0.546 avg rt  /
Cumulative: 0.546 avg rt, 0% failures
19:26:39 INFO: Current: 1 vu  1 succ  0 fail  1.357 avg rt  /
Cumulative: 0.904 avg rt, 0% failures
ETC
19:41:00 WARNING: Please wait for graceful shutdown...
19:41:00 INFO: Shutting down...
19:41:00 INFO: Post-processing...
19:41:03 INFO: Test duration: 0:14:33
19:41:03 INFO: Samples count: 1857, 0.00% failures
19:41:03 INFO: Average times: total 6.465, latency 0.000, connect 0.000
19:41:03 INFO: Percentiles:
+---------------+---------------+
| Percentile, % | Resp. Time, s |
+---------------+---------------+
|           0.0 |          0.13 |
|          50.0 |          1.66 |
|          90.0 |        14.384 |
|          95.0 |         26.88 |
|          99.0 |        27.168 |
|          99.9 |        27.584 |
|         100.0 |        27.792 |
+---------------+---------------+
```

Create CloudWatch dashboards for the Lambda duration (Figure 13-1) and DynamoDB provisioned and consumed read and write capacity units (Figure 13-2).

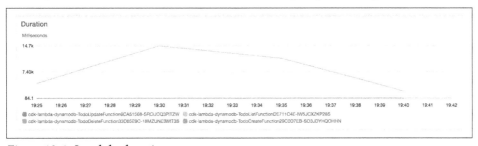

Figure 13-1. Lambda duration

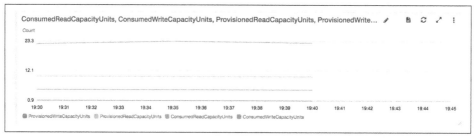

Figure 13-2. DynamoDB provisioned and consumed read and write capacity units

The DynamoDB metrics show that we underprovisioned the DynamoDB read capacity units. This introduced latency, especially for the List function (shown in the Lambda duration graph as the red line going to 14.7 seconds), which retrieves all todo items from the DynamoDB table, and thus is heavy on read operations. We set the value of the provisioned read capacity units to 10 when we created the DynamoDB table, and the CloudWatch graph shows it going to 25.

Let's change the DynamoDB table type from `PROVISIONED` to `PAY_PER_REQUEST`. Make the change in *cdk_lambda_dynamodb_fargate/cdk_lambda_dynamodb_stack.py*:

```
table = aws_dynamodb.Table(self, "Table",
    partition_key=aws_dynamodb.Attribute(
        name="id",
        type=aws_dynamodb.AttributeType.STRING),
    billing_mode = aws_dynamodb.BillingMode.PAY_PER_REQUEST)
```

Run cdk `deploy` and then run the local Docker load-testing container.

This time the results are much better:

```
+----------------+----------------+
| Percentile, % | Resp. Time, s |
+----------------+----------------+
|            0.0 |          0.136 |
|           50.0 |          0.505 |
|           90.0 |          1.296 |
|           95.0 |          1.444 |
|           99.0 |          1.806 |
|           99.9 |          2.226 |
|          100.0 |           2.86 |
+----------------+----------------+
```

The graphs for Lambda duration (Figure 13-3) and DynamoDB consumed read and write capacity units (Figure 13-4) look much better as well.

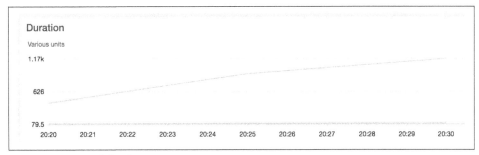

Figure 13-3. Lambda duration

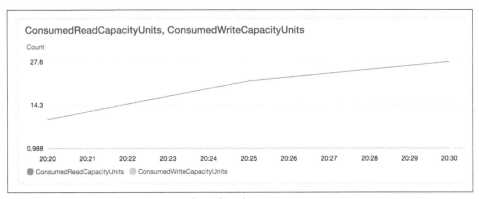

Figure 13-4. DynamoDB consumed read and write capacity units

Note that the DynamoDB consumed read capacity units are automatically allocated on demand by DynamoDB, and are scaling up to sustain the increased number of read requests from the Lambda functions. The function that contributes the most to the read requests is the List function that is called in the list, update, and delete scenarios in the Molotov *loadtest.py* script via `session.get(base_url + /todos)`.

Next, we will create a Fargate CDK stack that will run containers based on the Docker image created previously:

```
$ cat cdk_lambda_dynamodb_fargate/cdk_fargate_stack.py
from aws_cdk import core
from aws_cdk import aws_ecs, aws_ec2

class FargateStack(core.Stack):
    def __init__(self, scope: core.Construct, id: str, **kwargs) -> None:
        super().__init__(scope, id, **kwargs)

        vpc = aws_ec2.Vpc(
            self, "MyVpc",
            cidr= "10.0.0.0/16",
            max_azs=3
        )
```

```
# define an ECS cluster hosted within the requested VPC
cluster = aws_ecs.Cluster(self, 'cluster', vpc=vpc)

# define our task definition with a single container
# the image is built & published from a local asset directory
task_definition = aws_ecs.FargateTaskDefinition(self, 'LoadTestTask')
task_definition.add_container('TaurusLoadTest',
    image=aws_ecs.ContainerImage.from_asset("loadtest"),
    environment={'BASE_URL':
    "https://k6ygy4xw24.execute-api.us-east-2.amazonaws.com/prod/"})

# define our fargate service. TPS determines how many instances we
# want from our task (each task produces a single TPS)
aws_ecs.FargateService(self, 'service',
    cluster=cluster,
    task_definition=task_definition,
    desired_count=1)
```

A few things to note in the code for the `FargateStack` class:

- A new VPC is created by using the `aws_ec2.Vpc` CDK construct.
- An ECS cluster is created in the new VPC.
- A Fargate task definition is created based on the Dockerfile from the *loadtest* directory; the CDK is smart enough to build a Docker image based on this Dockerfile and then push it to the ECR Docker registry.
- An ECS service is created to run Fargate containers based on the image pushed to ECR; the `desired_count` parameter specifies how many containers we want to run.

Call the `FargateStack` constructor in *app.py*:

```
$ cat app.py
#!/usr/bin/env python3

from aws_cdk import core

from cdk_lambda_dynamodb_fargate.cdk_lambda_dynamodb_stack \
import CdkLambdaDynamodbStack
from cdk_lambda_dynamodb_fargate.cdk_fargate_stack import FargateStack

app = core.App()
app_env = {
    "region": "us-east-2",
}

CdkLambdaDynamodbStack(app, "cdk-lambda-dynamodb", env=app_env)
FargateStack(app, "cdk-fargate", env=app_env)

app.synth()
```

Deploy the `cdk-fargate` stack:

```
$ cdk deploy cdk-fargate
```

Go to the AWS console and inspect the ECS cluster with the running Fargate container (Figure 13-5).

Figure 13-5. ECS cluster with running Fargate container

Inspect the CloudWatch dashboards for Lambda duration (Figure 13-6) and DynamoDB consumed read and write capacity units (Figure 13-7), noting that latency looks good.

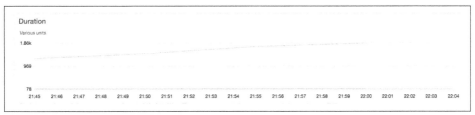

Figure 13-6. Lambda duration

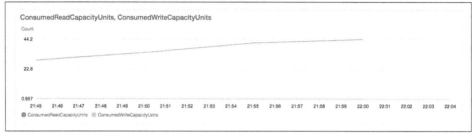

Figure 13-7. DynamoDB consumed read and write capacity units

Increase the Fargate container count to 5 in *cdk_lambda_dynamodb_fargate/cdk_fargate_stack.py*:

```
aws_ecs.FargateService(self, 'service',
    cluster=cluster,
    task_definition=task_definition,
    desired_count=5)
```

Redeploy the `cdk-fargate` stack:

```
$ cdk deploy cdk-fargate
```

Inspect the CloudWatch dashboards for Lambda duration (Figure 13-8) and DynamoDB consumed read and write capacity units (Figure 13-9).

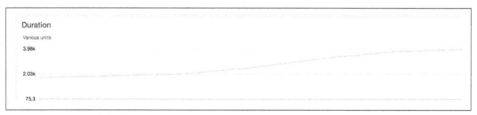

Figure 13-8. Lambda duration

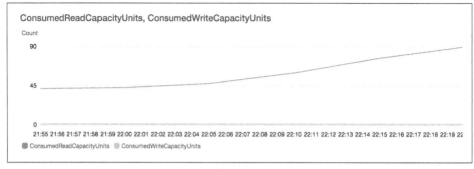

Figure 13-9. DynamoDB consumed read and write capacity units

Both DynamoDB read capacity units and Lambda duration metrics increased as expected because we are now simulating 5 × 10 = 50 concurrent users.

To simulate more users, we can both increase the `concurrency` value in the *taurus.yaml* configuration file, and increase the `desired_count` for the Fargate containers. Between these two values, we can easily increase the load on our REST API endpoints.

Delete the CDK stacks:

```
$ cdk destroy cdk-fargate
$ cdk destroy cdk-lambda-dynamodb
```

It is worth noting that the serverless architecture we deployed (API Gateway + five Lambda functions + DynamoDB table) turned out to be a good fit for our CRUD REST API application. We also followed best practices and defined all our infrastructure in Python code by using the AWS CDK.

Exercises

- Run a simple HTTP endpoint using Google's CaaS platform: Cloud Run (*https://cloud.google.com/run*).

- Run a simple HTTP endpoint on the other FaaS platforms we mentioned that are based on Kubernetes: Kubeless (*https://kubeless.io*), Fn Project (*https://fnproject.io*), and Fission (*https://fission.io*).

- Install and configure Apache OpenWhisk (*https://openwhisk.apache.org*) inside a production-grade Kubernetes cluster such as Amazon EKS, Google GKE, or Azure AKS.

- Port the AWS REST API example to GCP and Azure. GCP offers Cloud Endpoints (*https://cloud.google.com/endpoints*) to manage multiple APIs. Similarly, Azure offers API Management (*https://oreil.ly/tmDh7*).

## CHAPTER 14

MLOps and Machine learning Engineering

One of the hottest job titles in 2020 is machine learning engineer. Other hot job titles include data engineer, data scientist, and machine learning scientist. While you can be a DevOps specialist, DevOps is a behavior, and the principles of DevOps can be applied to any software project, including machine learning. Let's look at the some core DevOps best practices: Continuous Integration, Continuous Delivery, Microservices, Infrastructure as Code, Monitoring and Logging, and Communication and Collaboration. Which of these doesn't apply to machine learning?

The more complex a software engineering project is, and machine learning is complex, the more you need DevOps principles. Is there a better example of a Microservice than an API that does machine learning prediction? In this chapter, let's dive into the nitty-gritty of doing machine learning in a professional and repeatable way using a DevOps mindset.

What Is Machine Learning?

Machine learning is a method of using algorithms to automatically learn from data. There are four main types: supervised, semi-supervised, unsupervised, and reinforcement.

Supervised Machine Learning

In supervised machine learning, the correct answers are already known and labeled. For example, if you wanted to predict height from weight, you could collect examples of people's heights and weights. The height would be the target and the weight would be the feature.

Let's walk through what an example of supervised machine learning looks like:

- Original dataset (*https://oreil.ly/jzWmI*)
- 25,000 synthetic records of heights and weights of 18-year-old children

Ingest

In[0]:

```
import pandas as pd
```

In[7]:

```
df = pd.read_csv(
    "https://raw.githubusercontent.com/noahgift/\
    regression-concepts/master/\
    height-weight-25k.csv")
df.head()
```

Out[7]:

	Index	Height-Inches	Weight-Pounds
0	1	65.78331	112.9925
1	2	71.51521	136.4873
2	3	69.39874	153.0269
3	4	68.21660	142.3354
4	5	67.78781	144.2971

EDA

Let's look at the data and see what can be explored.

Scatterplot. In this example, seaborn, a popular plotting library in Python, is used to visualize the dataset. If you need to install it, you can always install with !pip install seaborn in your notebook. You can also install any other library in the section with the !pip install <name of package>. If you are using a Colab notebook, these libraries are installed for you. See the graph for the height/weight lm plot (Figure 14-1).

In[0]:

```
import seaborn as sns
import numpy as np
```

In[9]:

```
sns.lmplot("Height-Inches", "Weight-Pounds", data=df)
```

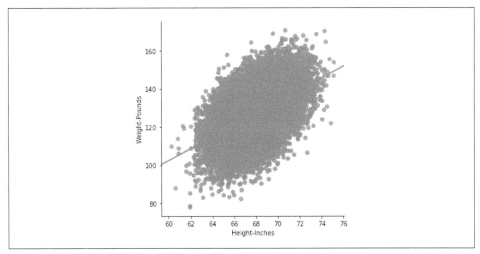

Figure 14-1. Height/weight lm plot

Descriptive Statistics

Next, some descriptive statistics can be generated.

In[10]:

```
df.describe()
```

Out[10]:

	Index	Height-Inches	Weight-Pounds
count	25000.000000	25000.000000	25000.000000
mean	12500.500000	67.993114	127.079421
std	7217.022701	1.901679	11.660898
min	1.000000	60.278360	78.014760
25%	6250.750000	66.704397	119.308675
50%	12500.500000	67.995700	127.157750
75%	18750.250000	69.272958	134.892850
max	25000.000000	75.152800	170.924000

Kernel Density Distribution

A distribution for the density plot (Figure 14-2) shows how the two variables relate to each other.

In[11]:

```
sns.jointplot("Height-Inches", "Weight-Pounds", data=df, kind="kde")
```

`Out[11]:`

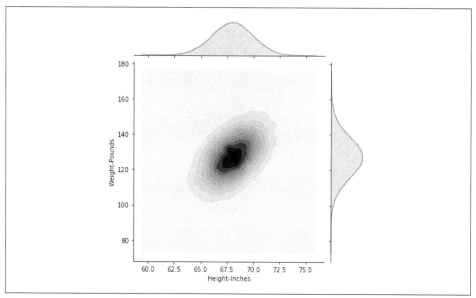

Figure 14-2. Density plot

Modeling

Now let's review modeling. Machine learning modeling is when an algorithm learns from the data. The general idea is to use previous data to predict future data.

Sklearn Regression Model

First the data is extracted into features and targets, and then it is split into a train and a test set. This allows the test set to be held aside to test the accuracy of the trained model.

`In[0]:`

```
from sklearn.model_selection import train_test_split
```

Extract and inspect feature and target.   It is a good idea to explicitly pull out the target and feature variables and reshape them in one cell. Afterwards you will want to check the shape to ensure it is the property dimension for doing machine learning with sklearn.

`In[0]:`

```
y = df['Weight-Pounds'].values #Target
y = y.reshape(-1, 1)
```

```
X = df['Height-Inches'].values #Feature(s)
X = X.reshape(-1, 1)
```

In[14]:

```
y.shape
```

Out[14]:

```
(25000, 1)
```

Split the data. The data is split into an 80%/20% split.

In[15]:

```
X_train, X_test, y_train, y_test = train_test_split(X, y, test_size=0.2)
print(X_train.shape, y_train.shape)
print(X_test.shape, y_test.shape)
```

Out[15]:

```
(20000, 1) (20000, 1)
(5000, 1) (5000, 1)
```

Fit the model. Now the model is fit using a LinearRegression algorithm imported via sklearn.

In[0]:

```
from sklearn.linear_model import LinearRegression
lm = LinearRegression()
model = lm.fit(X_train, y_train)
y_predicted = lm.predict(X_test)
```

Print accuracy of linear regression model. Now the trained model can show what the accuracy is in predicting new data. This is performed by asking for the RMSE or root mean squared error of the predicted and the test data.

In[18]:

```
from sklearn.metrics import mean_squared_error
from math import sqrt

#RMSE Root Mean Squared Error
rms = sqrt(mean_squared_error(y_predicted, y_test))
rms
```

Out[18]:

```
10.282608230082417
```

Plot predicted height versus actual height.   Now let's plot the predicted height versus actual height (Figure 14-3) to see how well this model performs at predictions.

In[19]:

```python
import matplotlib.pyplot as plt
_, ax = plt.subplots()

ax.scatter(x = range(0, y_test.size), y=y_test, c = 'blue', label = 'Actual',
  alpha = 0.5)
ax.scatter(x = range(0, y_predicted.size), y=y_predicted, c = 'red',
  label = 'Predicted', alpha = 0.5)

plt.title('Actual Height vs Predicted Height')
plt.xlabel('Weight')
plt.ylabel('Height')
plt.legend()
plt.show()
```

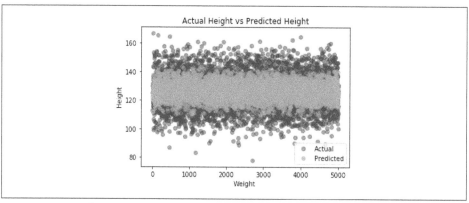

Figure 14-3. Predicted height versus actual height

This is a very simple yet powerful example of a realistic workflow for creating a machine learning model.

Python Machine learning Ecosystem

Let's take a quick look at the Python machine learning ecosystem (Figure 14-4).

There are really four main areas: deep learning, sklearn, AutoML, and Spark. In the area of deep learning, the most popular frameworks in order are: TensorFlow/Keras, PyTorch, and MXNet. Google is sponsoring TensorFlow, Facebook is sponsoring PyTorch, and MXNet comes from Amazon. You will see MXNet mentioned quite a bit by Amazon SageMaker. It is important to note that these deep learning frameworks target GPUs, giving them performance boosts over CPU targets of up to 50X.

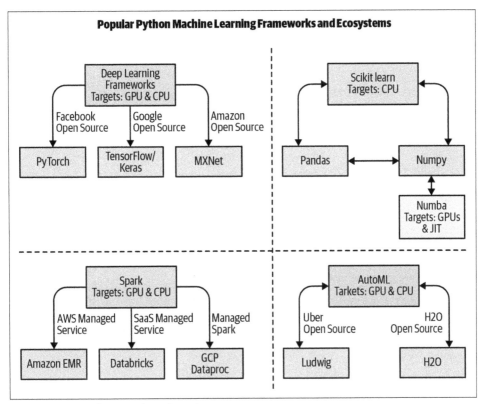

Figure 14-4. Python machine learning ecosystem

The sklearn ecosystem often has Pandas and Numpy in the same projects. Sklearn also intentionally does not target GPUs. However, there is a project called Numba that does specifically target the GPU (both NVIDIA and AMD).

In AutoML, two of the leaders are Uber with Ludwig and H20, with H20 AutoML. Both can save significant time developing machine learning models and can also potentially optimize existing machine learning models.

Finally, there is the Spark ecosystem, which builds on the legacy of Hadoop. Spark can target GPUs and CPUs and does so via many different platforms: Amazon EMR, Databricks, GCP Dataproc, and more.

Deep Learning with PyTorch

Now that the ecosystem for machine learning with Python has been defined, let's take a look at porting the simple linear regression example to PyTorch and run it on a CUDA GPU. One easy way to get access to an NVIDIA GPU is to use Colab notebooks. Colab notebooks are Google-hosted, Jupyter-compatible notebooks that give the user free access to both GPUs and tensor processing units (TPUs). You can run this code in a GPU (*https://oreil.ly/kQhKO*).

Regression with PyTorch

First, convert data to `float32`.

In[0]:

```
# Training Data
x_train = np.array(X_train, dtype=np.float32)
x_train = x_train.reshape(-1, 1)
y_train = np.array(y_train, dtype=np.float32)
y_train = y_train.reshape(-1, 1)

# Test Data
x_test = np.array(X_test, dtype=np.float32)
x_test = x_test.reshape(-1, 1)
y_test = np.array(y_test, dtype=np.float32)
y_test = y_test.reshape(-1, 1)
```

Note that if you are not using Colab notebooks, you may have to install PyTorch. Also, if you use Colab notebooks, you can have an NVIDIA GPU and run this code. If you are not using Colab, you will need to run on a platform that has a GPU.

In[0]:

```
import torch
from torch.autograd import Variable

class linearRegression(torch.nn.Module):
    def __init__(self, inputSize, outputSize):
        super(linearRegression, self).__init__()
        self.linear = torch.nn.Linear(inputSize, outputSize)

    def forward(self, x):
        out = self.linear(x)
        return out
```

Now create a model with CUDA enabled (assuming you are running in Colab or on a machine with an NVIDIA GPU).

In[0]:

```
inputDim = 1         # takes variable 'x'
outputDim = 1        # takes variable 'y'
learningRate = 0.0001
epochs = 1000

model = linearRegression(inputDim, outputDim)
model.cuda()
```

Out[0]:

```
linearRegression(
  (linear): Linear(in_features=1, out_features=1, bias=True)
)
```

Create the Stochastic Gradient Descent and Loss Function.

In[0]:

```
criterion = torch.nn.MSELoss()
optimizer = torch.optim.SGD(model.parameters(), lr=learningRate)
```

Now train the model.

In[0]:

```
for epoch in range(epochs):
    inputs = Variable(torch.from_numpy(x_train).cuda())
    labels = Variable(torch.from_numpy(y_train).cuda())
    optimizer.zero_grad()
    outputs = model(inputs)
    loss = criterion(outputs, labels)
    print(loss)
    # get gradients w.r.t to parameters
    loss.backward()
    # update parameters
    optimizer.step()
    print('epoch {}, loss {}'.format(epoch, loss.item()))
```

The output over 1,000 runs is supressed to save space.

Out[0]:

```
tensor(29221.6543, device='cuda:0', grad_fn=<MseLossBackward>)
epoch 0, loss 29221.654296875
tensor(266.7252, device='cuda:0', grad_fn=<MseLossBackward>)
epoch 1, loss 266.72515869140625
tensor(106.6842, device='cuda:0', grad_fn=<MseLossBackward>)
epoch 2, loss 106.6842269897461
....output suppressed....
epoch 998, loss 105.7930908203125
tensor(105.7931, device='cuda:0', grad_fn=<MseLossBackward>)
epoch 999, loss 105.7930908203125
```

Plot predicted height versus actual height. Now let's plot the predicted height versus actual height (Figure 14-5) as in the simple model.

In[0]:

```
with torch.no_grad():
    predicted = model(Variable(torch.from_numpy(x_test).cuda())).cpu().\
      data.numpy()
    print(predicted)

plt.clf()
plt.plot(x_test, y_test, 'go', label='Actual Height', alpha=0.5)
plt.plot(x_test, predicted, '--', label='Predicted Height', alpha=0.5)
plt.legend(loc='best')
plt.show()
```

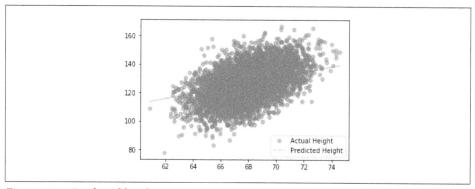

Figure 14-5. Predicted height versus actual height

Print RMSE. Finally, let's print out the RMSE and compare.

In[0]:

```
#RMSE Root Mean Squared Error
rms = sqrt(mean_squared_error(x_test, predicted))
rms
```

Out[0]:

```
59.19054613663507
```

It does take a little more code to do deep learning, but the concepts are the same from the sklearn model. The big takeaway here is that GPUs are becoming an integral part of production pipelines. Even if you aren't doing deep learning yourself, it is helpful to have a basic awareness of the process of building GPU-based machine learning models.

Cloud Machine learning Platforms

One aspect of machine learning that is becoming ubiquitious is cloud-based machine learning platforms. Google offers the GCP AI Platform (Figure 14-6).

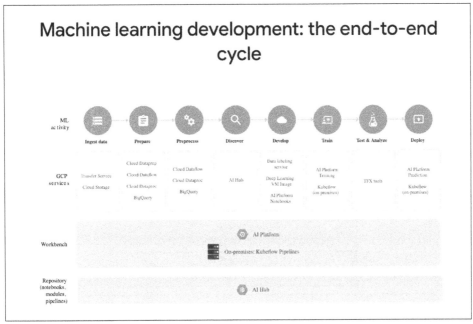

Figure 14-6. GCP AI platform

The GCP platform has many high-level automation components, from data preparation to data labeling. The AWS platform offers Amazon SageMaker (Figure 14-7).

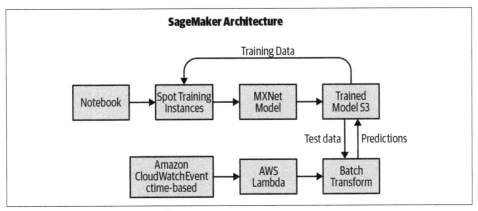

Figure 14-7. Amazon SageMaker

SageMaker also has many high-level components, including training on spot instances and elastic prediction endpoints.

Machine learning Maturity Model

One of the big challenges right now is a realization that transformational change is needed in companies that want to perform machine learning. The machine learning maturity model diagram (Figure 14-8) represents some challenges and opportunities.

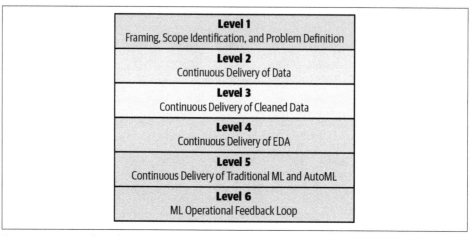

Figure 14-8. Machine learning maturity model

Machine Learning Key Terminology

Let's define some key machine learning terminology that will be helpful througout the rest of the chapter:

Machine learning
    A way of building mathmatical models based on sample or training data.

Model
    This is what the product is in a machine learning application. A simple example is a linear equation, i.e., a straight line that predicts the relationship between an X and a Y.

Feature
    A feature is a column in a spreadsheet that is used as a signal to create a machine learning model. A good example is points scored per game by an NBA team.

Target
    The target is the column in a spreadsheet you are trying to predict. A good example is how many games an NBA team wins in a season.

Supervised machine learning

This is a type of machine learning that predicts future values based on known correct historical values. A good example would be predicting the amount of NBA wins in a season by using the feature points per game.

Unsupervised machine learning

This is a type of machine learning that works with unlabeled data. Instead of predicting a future value, it finds hidden patterns by using tools such as clustering, which in turn could be used as labels. A good example would be to create clusters of NBA players that have similar points, rebounds, blocks, and assists. One cluster could be called "Tall, Top Players," and another cluster could be called "Point guards who score a lot of points."

Deep learning

This is a type of machine learning that uses artificial neural networks that can be used for supervised or unsupervised machine learning. The most popular framework for deep learning is TensorFlow from Google.

Scikit-learn

This is one of the most popular machine learning frameworks in Python.

Pandas

This is one of the most popular libraries for doing data manipulation and analysis. It works well with scikit-learn and Numpy.

Numpy

This is the predominant Python library for doing low-level scientific computing. It has support for a large, multidimensional array and has a large collection of high-level mathmatical functions. It is used extensively with scikit-learn, Pandas, and TensorFlow.

Level 1: Framing, Scope Identification, and Problem Definition

Let's look at the first layer. When implementing machine learning at a company, it is important to consider what problems need solving and how they can be framed. One of the key reasons for failure of machine learning projects is that organizations haven't first asked questions about what problems they need solved.

A good analogy to look at is building a mobile application for a restaurant chain in San Francisco. One naive approach would be to immediately start building a native iOS and a native Android app (using two development teams). A typical mobile team could be three full-time developers for each application. So this means hiring six developers at around two hundred thousand dollars each. The run rate for the project is about $1.2 million a year now. Will the mobile app deliver greater than $1.2 million in revenue each year? If not, is there an easier alternative? Perhaps a mobile-optimized web app that uses the existing web developers in the company is a better choice.

What about partnering with a company that specializes in food delivery and outsourcing this task completely? What are the pros and cons to this approach? The same type of thought process can and should be applied to machine learning and data science initiatives. For example, does your company need to hire six PhD-level machine learning researchers at, say, five hundred thousand dollars a year? What is the alternative? A little bit of scoping and problem definition goes a long way with machine learning and can ensure a higher chance of success.

Level 2: Continuous Delivery of Data

One of the fundamentals of civilization is running water. Roman aqueducts carried water for miles to provide crowded cities with water as early as 312 B.C. Running water enabled the infrastructure necessary for a large city to succeed. It is estimated by UNICEF that worldwide in 2018, women and girls spend an estimated two hundred million hours daily, collecting water. The opportunity cost is substantial; less time to spend learning, taking care of children, working, or relaxing.

A popular expression is that "software is eating the world." A corollary to that is that all software companies, which is every company in the future, need to have a machine learning and AI strategy. Part of that strategy is to think more seriously about continuous delivery of data. Just like running water, "running data" saves you hours per day. One potential solution is the concept of a *data lake*, as shown in Figure 14-9.

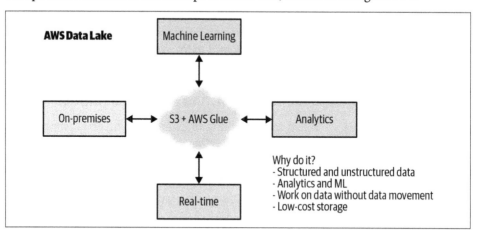

Figure 14-9. AWS data lake

At first glance, a data lake might seem like a solution in search of a problem, or too simple to do anything useful. Let's look at some of the problems it solves, though:

- You can process the data without moving it.
- It is cheap to store data.
- It is straightforward to create life cycle policies to archive the data.
- It is straightforward to create life cycle policies that secure and audit the data.
- The production systems are decoupled from data processing.
- It can have almost infinite and elastic storage and disk I/O.

The alternative to this architecture is often an ad hoc mess equivalent to walking four hours to a well and back simply to get some water. Security is also a major factor in a data lake architecture, just as security is in the water supply. By centralizing the architecture of data storage and delivery, preventing and monitoring data breaches becomes more straightforward. Here are a few ideas that may be helpful in preventing future data breaches:

- Is your data encrypted at rest? If so, who has the keys? Are decryption events logged and audited?
- Is your data moving out of your network logged and audited? For example, when is it ever a good idea for your entire customer database to move outside of your network? Why isn't this monitored and audited?
- Do you have periodic data security audits? Why not?
- Are you storing personally identifiable information (PII)? Why?
- You have monitoring for critical production events. Are you monitoring data security events? Why not?

Why would we ever let data flow outside of the internal network? What if we designed critical data to be a literal square peg that couldn't be transmitted outside of the host network without something like a nuclear launch code? Making it impossible to move data out of the environment does seem like a viable way to prevent these breaches. What if the external network itself could only transport "round peg" packets? Also, this could be a great "lock-in" feature for clouds providing this type of secure data lake.

Level 3: Continuous Delivery of Clean Data

Hopefully you are sold on the idea behind continuous delivery of data and how important it is to the success of a company's plans for doing machine learning. One huge improvement to continuous delivery of data is continuous delivery of clean data. Why go through all of the trouble of delivering data that is a mess? The recent problem of contaminated water in Flint, Michigan, comes to mind. Around 2014, Flint changed its water source from Lake Huron and the Detroit River to the Flint River. Officials failed to apply corrosion inhibitors, which allowed lead from aging pipes leak into the water supply. It is also possible that the water change caused an outbreak of Legionnaires' disease that killed 12 people and sickened another 87.

One of the earliest success stories of data science involves dirty water from 1849–1854. John Snow was able to use data visualization to identify clusters of cholera cases (Figure 14-10). This led to the discovery of the root cause of the outbreak. Sewage was being pumped directly into the drinking water supply!

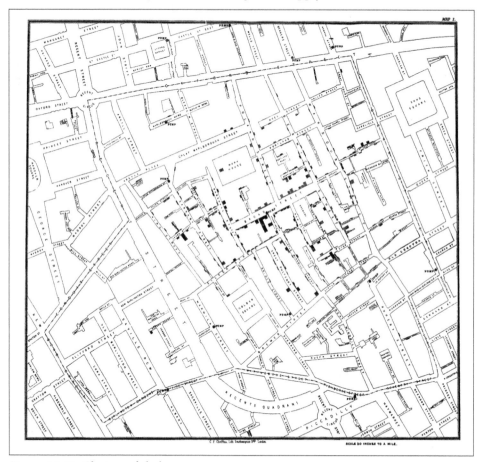

Figure 14-10. Clusters of cholera cases

Consider the following observations:

- Why isn't data automatically processed to "clean" it?
- Can you visualize parts of your data pipeline that have "sewage" in them?
- How much time is your company spending on data-cleaning tasks that are 100% automatible?

Level 4: Continuous Delivery of Exploratory Data Analysis

If your only view of data science is Kaggle projects, it may seem like the whole point of data science is to generate the most accurate prediction possible. There is more to data science and machine learning than just making predictions. Data science is a multidisciplinary field and there are a few ways to look at it. e One perspective is to focus on causality. What are the underlying features that drive the model? Can you explain how the model is coming to the prediction it has generated? Several Python libraries help in this regard: ELI5, SHAP, and LIME. They all work to help explain what machine learning models are really doing.

A prediction world view cares less about how you got to the answer, and more about whether the prediction is accurate. In a cloud-native, Big Data world, this approach has merits. Certain machine learning problems do very well with large quantities of data, such as image recognition using deep learning. The more data and the more computational power you have, the better your prediction accuracy will be.

Is what you created in production? Why not? If you are building machine learning models and they don't get used, then why are you building machine learning models?

What don't you know? What can you learn by looking at data? Often data science is more interested in the process than the outcome. If you are only looking for a prediction, then you may miss out on a completely different angle to the data.

Level 5: Continuous Delivery of Traditional ML and AutoML

Fighting automation is as old as human history. The Luddite movement was a secret organization of English textile workers who destroyed textile machinary as a form of protest from 1811 to 1816. Ultimately, protesters were shot, the rebellion was put down with legal and military might, and the path of progress kept going.

If you look at the history of humanity, tools that automate tasks that humans once did are constantly being developed. In technological unemployment, lower-skilled workers are displaced and higher-skilled workers get an increased salary. A case in point is the systems administrator versus the DevOps professional. Yes, some systems administrators lost their jobs, for example, workers focused on tasks such as changing hard drives out of data centers, but new, higher-paying jobs such as cloud architects appeared.

It isn't unusual to see job postings for machine learning and data science that command an annual salary of between three hundred thousand and one million dollars. Additionally these jobs often include many components that are essentially business rules: tweaking hyperparameters, removing null values, and distributing jobs to a cluster. The automator's law (something I came up with) says, "If you talk about something being automated, it will eventually be automated." There is a lot of talk around AutoML, so it is inevitable that large parts of machine learning will be automated.

This will mean that, just like other automation examples, the nature of jobs will change. Some jobs will become even more skilled (imagine a person who can train thousands of machine learning models a day), and some jobs will become automated because a machine can do them much better (jobs that involve tweaking values in a JSON data structure, i.e., tuning hyperparameters).

Level 6: ML Operational Feedback Loop

Why develop a mobile application? Presumably to have users on a mobile device use your application. What about machine learning? The point of machine learning, especially in comparison to data science or statistics, is to create a model and predict something. If the model isn't in production, then what is it doing?

Additionally, pushing the model to production is an opportunity to learn more. Does the model predict accurately when put into an environment where it gets new data? Does the model have the impact expected on the users: i.e., increasing purchases or staying on the site longer? These valuable insights can only be obtained when the model is actually deployed into a production environment.

Another important concern is scalability and repeatability. A truly technologically mature organization can deploy software, including machine learning models, on demand. The best practices of DevOps for ML models are required here as well: continuous deployment, microservices, monitoring, and instrumentation.

One easy way to inject more of this technological maturity into your organization is to apply the same logic as you do to choosing cloud computing over a physical data center. Rent the expertise of others and take advantage of economies of scale.

Sklearn Flask with Kubernetes and Docker

Let's walk through a real-world deployment of a sklearn-based machine learning model using Docker and Kubernetes.

Here is a Dockerfile. Note, that this serves out a Flask application. The Flask application will host the sklearn application. Note that you might want to install Hadolint, which allows you to lint a Dockerfile: *https://github.com/hadolint/hadolint*.

```
FROM python:3.7.3-stretch

# Working Directory
WORKDIR /app

# Copy source code to working directory
COPY . app.py /app/

# Install packages from requirements.txt
# hadolint ignore=DL3013
RUN pip install --upgrade pip &&\
    pip install --trusted-host pypi.python.org -r requirements.txt

# Expose port 80
EXPOSE 80

# Run app.py at container launch
CMD ["python", "app.py"]
```

This is the `Makefile` and it serves as a central point of the application runtime:

```
setup:
  python3 -m venv ~/.python-devops

install:
  pip install --upgrade pip &&\
    pip install -r requirements.txt

test:
  #python -m pytest -vv --cov=myrepolib tests/*.py
  #python -m pytest --nbval notebook.ipynb

lint:
  hadolint Dockerfile
  pylint --disable=R,C,W1203 app.py

all: install lint test
```

This is the *requirements.txt* file:

```
Flask==1.0.2
pandas==0.24.2
scikit-learn==0.20.3
```

This is the *app.py* file:

```python
from flask import Flask, request, jsonify
from flask.logging import create_logger
import logging

import pandas as pd
from sklearn.externals import joblib
from sklearn.preprocessing import StandardScaler

app = Flask(__name__)
LOG = create_logger(app)
LOG.setLevel(logging.INFO)

def scale(payload):
    """Scales Payload"""

    LOG.info(f"Scaling Payload: {payload}")
    scaler = StandardScaler().fit(payload)
    scaled_adhoc_predict = scaler.transform(payload)
    return scaled_adhoc_predict

@app.route("/")
def home():
    html = "<h3>Sklearn Prediction Home</h3>"
    return html.format(format)

# TO DO:  Log out the prediction value
@app.route("/predict", methods=['POST'])
def predict():
    """Performs an sklearn prediction

    input looks like:
            {
    "CHAS":{
      "0":0
    },
    "RM":{
      "0":6.575
    },
    "TAX":{
      "0":296.0
    },
    "PTRATIO":{
      "0":15.3
    },
    "B":{
      "0":396.9
    },
    "LSTAT":{
      "0":4.98
    }
```

```
    result looks like:
    { "prediction": [ 20.35373177134412 ] }

    """

    json_payload = request.json
    LOG.info(f"JSON payload: {json_payload}")
    inference_payload = pd.DataFrame(json_payload)
    LOG.info(f"inference payload DataFrame: {inference_payload}")
    scaled_payload = scale(inference_payload)
    prediction = list(clf.predict(scaled_payload))
    return jsonify({'prediction': prediction})

if __name__ == "__main__":
    clf = joblib.load("boston_housing_prediction.joblib")
    app.run(host='0.0.0.0', port=80, debug=True)
```

This is the *run_docker.sh* file:

```
#!/usr/bin/env bash

# Build image
docker build --tag=flasksklearn .

# List docker images
docker image ls

# Run flask app
docker run -p 8000:80 flasksklearn
```

This is the *run_kubernetes.sh* file:

```
#!/usr/bin/env bash

dockerpath="noahgift/flasksklearn"

# Run in Docker Hub container with kubernetes
kubectl run flaskskearlndemo\
    --generator=run-pod/v1\
    --image=$dockerpath\
    --port=80 --labels app=flaskskearlndemo

# List kubernetes pods
kubectl get pods

# Forward the container port to host
kubectl port-forward flaskskearlndemo 8000:80

#!/usr/bin/env bash
# This tags and uploads an image to Docker Hub

#Assumes this is built
#docker build --tag=flasksklearn .
```

```
dockerpath="noahgift/flasksklearn"

# Authenticate & Tag
echo "Docker ID and Image: $dockerpath"
docker login &&\
    docker image tag flasksklearn $dockerpath

# Push Image
docker image push $dockerpath
```

Sklearn Flask with Kubernetes and Docker

You may be asking yourself how the model got created and then "pickled" out. You can see the whole notebook here (*https://oreil.ly/_pHz-*).

First, import some libraries for machine learning:

```
import numpy
from numpy import arange
from matplotlib import pyplot
import seaborn as sns
import pandas as pd
from pandas import read_csv
from pandas import set_option
from sklearn.preprocessing import StandardScaler
from sklearn.model_selection import train_test_split
from sklearn.model_selection import KFold
from sklearn.model_selection import cross_val_score
from sklearn.model_selection import GridSearchCV
from sklearn.linear_model import LinearRegression
from sklearn.linear_model import Lasso
from sklearn.linear_model import ElasticNet
from sklearn.tree import DecisionTreeRegressor
from sklearn.neighbors import KNeighborsRegressor
from sklearn.svm import SVR
from sklearn.pipeline import Pipeline
from sklearn.ensemble import RandomForestRegressor
from sklearn.ensemble import GradientBoostingRegressor
from sklearn.ensemble import ExtraTreesRegressor
from sklearn.ensemble import AdaBoostRegressor
from sklearn.metrics import mean_squared_error
```

In[0]:

```
boston_housing = "https://raw.githubusercontent.com/\
noahgift/boston_housing_pickle/master/housing.csv"
names = ['CRIM', 'ZN', 'INDUS', 'CHAS',
'NOX', 'RM', 'AGE', 'DIS', 'RAD', 'TAX',
  'PTRATIO', 'B', 'LSTAT', 'MEDV']
df = read_csv(boston_housing,
  delim_whitespace=True, names=names)
```

In[0]:

    df.head()

Out[0]:

	CRIM	ZN	INDUS	CHAS	NOX	RM	AGE
0	0.00632	18.0	2.31	0	0.538	6.575	65.2
1	0.02731	0.0	7.07	0	0.469	6.421	78.9
2	0.02729	0.0	7.07	0	0.469	7.185	61.1
3	0.03237	0.0	2.18	0	0.458	6.998	45.8
4	0.06905	0.0	2.18	0	0.458	7.147	54.2

	DIS	RAD	TAX	PTRATIO	B	LSTAT	MEDV
0	4.0900	1	296.0	15.3	396.90	4.98	24.0
1	4.9671	2	242.0	17.8	396.90	9.14	21.6
2	4.9671	2	242.0	17.8	392.83	4.03	34.7
3	6.0622	3	222.0	18.7	394.63	2.94	33.4
4	6.0622	3	222.0	18.7	396.90	5.33	36.2

EDA

These are the features of the model:

CHAS
  Charles River dummy variable (1 if tract bounds river; 0 otherwise)

RM
  Average number of rooms per dwelling

TAX
  Full-value property tax rate per $10,000

PTRATIO
  Pupil-teacher ratio by town

Bk
  The proportion of black people by town

LSTAT
  % lower status of the population

MEDV
  Median value of owner-occupied homes in $1000s

```
prices = df['MEDV']
df = df.drop(['CRIM','ZN','INDUS','NOX','AGE','DIS','RAD'], axis = 1)
features = df.drop('MEDV', axis = 1)
df.head()
```

Out[0]:

	CHAS	RM	TAX	PTRATIO	B	LSTAT	MEDV
0	0	6.575	296.0	15.3	396.90	4.98	24.0
1	0	6.421	242.0	17.8	396.90	9.14	21.6
2	0	7.185	242.0	17.8	392.83	4.03	34.7
3	0	6.998	222.0	18.7	394.63	2.94	33.4
4	0	7.147	222.0	18.7	396.90	5.33	36.2

Modeling

This is where the modeling occurs in the notebook. One useful strategy is to always create four main sections of a notebook:

- Ingestion
- EDA
- Modeling
- Conclusion

In this modeling section, the data is extracted from the DataFrame and passed into the sklearn `train_test_split` module which does the heavy lifting of splitting the data into training and validation data.

Split Data

In[0]:

```
# Split-out validation dataset
array = df.values
X = array[:,0:6]
Y = array[:,6]
validation_size = 0.20
seed = 7
X_train, X_validation, Y_train, Y_validation = train_test_split(X, Y,
    test_size=validation_size, random_state=seed)
```

In[0]:

```
for sample in list(X_validation)[0:2]:
    print(f"X_validation {sample}")
```

```
Out[0]:

    X_validation [   1.      6.395 666.      20.2   391.34   13.27 ]
    X_validation [   0.      5.895 224.      20.2   394.81   10.56 ]
```

Tune Scaled GBM

This model uses several advanced techniques that you can reference in many success-ful Kaggle projects. These techniques include GridSearch which can help find the optimal hyperparameters. Note, too, that scaling of the data is peformed. Most machine learning algorithms expect some type of scaling to create accurate predictions.

In[0]:

```
# Test options and evaluation metric using Root Mean Square error method
num_folds = 10
seed = 7
RMS = 'neg_mean_squared_error'
scaler = StandardScaler().fit(X_train)
rescaledX = scaler.transform(X_train)
param_grid = dict(n_estimators=numpy.array([50,100,150,200,250,300,350,400]))
model = GradientBoostingRegressor(random_state=seed)
kfold = KFold(n_splits=num_folds, random_state=seed)
grid = GridSearchCV(estimator=model, param_grid=param_grid, scoring=RMS, cv=kfold)
grid_result = grid.fit(rescaledX, Y_train)

print("Best: %f using %s" % (grid_result.best_score_, grid_result.best_params_))
means = grid_result.cv_results_['mean_test_score']
stds = grid_result.cv_results_['std_test_score']
params = grid_result.cv_results_['params']
for mean, stdev, param in zip(means, stds, params):
    print("%f (%f) with: %r" % (mean, stdev, param))
```

Out[0]:

```
Best: -11.830068 using {'n_estimators': 200}
-12.479635 (6.348297) with: {'n_estimators': 50}
-12.102737 (6.441597) with: {'n_estimators': 100}
-11.843649 (6.631569) with: {'n_estimators': 150}
-11.830068 (6.559724) with: {'n_estimators': 200}
-11.879805 (6.512414) with: {'n_estimators': 250}
-11.895362 (6.487726) with: {'n_estimators': 300}
-12.008611 (6.468623) with: {'n_estimators': 350}
-12.053759 (6.453899) with: {'n_estimators': 400}

/usr/local/lib/python3.6/dist-packages/sklearn/model_selection/_search.py:841:
DeprecationWarning:
DeprecationWarning)
```

Fit Model

This model is fit using the GradientBoostingRegressor. The final step after training the model is to fit the model and check for error using the data that was set aside. This data is scaled and passed into the model, and the accuracy is evaluated using the metric "Mean Squared Error."

In[0]:

```
# prepare the model
scaler = StandardScaler().fit(X_train)
rescaledX = scaler.transform(X_train)
model = GradientBoostingRegressor(random_state=seed, n_estimators=400)
model.fit(rescaledX, Y_train)
# transform the validation dataset
rescaledValidationX = scaler.transform(X_validation)
predictions = model.predict(rescaledValidationX)
print("Mean Squared Error: \n")
print(mean_squared_error(Y_validation, predictions))
```

Out[0]:

```
Mean Squared Error:

26.326748591395717
```

Evaluate

One of the trickier aspects to machine learning is evaluating the model. This example shows how you can add predictions and the original home price to the same Data-Frame. That DataFrame can be used to substract the differences.

In[0]:

```
predictions=predictions.astype(int)
evaluate = pd.DataFrame({
        "Org House Price": Y_validation,
        "Pred House Price": predictions
    })
evaluate["difference"] = evaluate["Org House Price"]-evaluate["Pred House Price"]
evaluate.head()
```

The differences are shown here.

Out[0]:

	Org house price	Pred house price	Difference
0	21.7	21	0.7
1	18.5	19	-0.5
2	22.2	20	2.2

	Org house price	Pred house price	Difference
3	20.4	19	1.4
4	8.8	9	-0.2

Using the describe method on Pandas is a great way to see the distribution of the data.

In[0]:

```
evaluate.describe()
```

Out[0]:

	Org house price	Pred house price	Difference
count	102.000000	102.000000	102.000000
mean	22.573529	22.117647	0.455882
std	9.033622	8.758921	5.154438
min	6.300000	8.000000	-34.100000
25%	17.350000	17.000000	-0.800000
50%	21.800000	20.500000	0.600000
75%	24.800000	25.000000	2.200000
max	50.000000	56.000000	22.000000

adhoc_predict

Let's test this prediction model to see what the workflow would be after unpickling. When developing a web API for a machine learning model, it can be helpful to test out the sections of code that the API will perform in the notebook itself. It is much easier to debug and create functions inside the actual notebook than struggle to create the correct functions inside a web application.

In[0]:

```
actual_sample = df.head(1)
actual_sample
```

Out[0]:

	CHAS	RM	TAX	PTRATIO	B	LSTAT	MEDV
0	0	6.575	296.0	15.3	396.9	4.98	24.0

In[0]:

```
adhoc_predict = actual_sample[["CHAS", "RM", "TAX", "PTRATIO", "B", "LSTAT"]]
adhoc_predict.head()
```

Out[0]:

	CHAS	RM	TAX	PTRATIO	B	LSTAT
0	0	6.575	296.0	15.3	396.9	4.98

JSON Workflow

This is a section of the notebook that is useful for debugging Flask apps. As mentioned earlier, it is much more straightforward to develop the API code inside the machine learning project, make sure it works, then transport that code to a script. The alternative is trying to get the exact code syntax in a software project that doesn't have the same interactive tools that Jupyter provides.

In[0]:

```
json_payload = adhoc_predict.to_json()
json_payload
```

Out[0]:

```
{"CHAS":{"0":0},"RM":
{"0":6.575},"TAX":
{"0":296.0},"PTRATIO":
{"0":15.3},"B":{"0":396.9},"LSTAT":
{"0":4.98}}
```

Scale Input

The data has to be scaled back to be predicted. This workflow needed to be flushed out in the notebook instead of struggling to get it to work in a web application that will be much tougher to debug. The section below shows the code that solves that portion of the machine learning prediction pipeline. It can then be used to create a function in a Flask application.

In[0]:

```
scaler = StandardScaler().fit(adhoc_predict)
scaled_adhoc_predict = scaler.transform(adhoc_predict)
scaled_adhoc_predict
```

Out[0]:

```
array([[0., 0., 0., 0., 0., 0.]])
```

In[0]:

```
list(model.predict(scaled_adhoc_predict))
```

Out[0]:

```
[20.35373177134412]
```

Pickling sklearn

Next, let's export this model.

In[0]:

```
from sklearn.externals import joblib
```

In[0]:

```
joblib.dump(model, 'boston_housing_prediction.joblib')
```

Out[0]:

```
['boston_housing_prediction.joblib']
```

In[0]:

```
!ls -l
```

Out[0]:

```
total 672
-rw-r--r-- 1 root root 681425 May  5 00:35 boston_housing_prediction.joblib
drwxr-xr-x 1 root root   4096 Apr 29 16:32 sample_data
```

Unpickle and predict

In[0]:

```
clf = joblib.load('boston_housing_prediction.joblib')
```

adhoc_predict from Pickle

In[0]:

```
actual_sample2 = df.head(5)
actual_sample2
```

Out[0]:

	CHAS	RM	TAX	PTRATIO	B	LSTAT	MEDV
0	0	6.575	296.0	15.3	396.90	4.98	24.0
1	0	6.421	242.0	17.8	396.90	9.14	21.6
2	0	7.185	242.0	17.8	392.83	4.03	34.7
3	0	6.998	222.0	18.7	394.63	2.94	33.4
4	0	7.147	222.0	18.7	396.90	5.33	36.2

In[0]:

```
adhoc_predict2 = actual_sample[["CHAS", "RM", "TAX", "PTRATIO", "B", "LSTAT"]]
adhoc_predict2.head()
```

Out[0]:

	CHAS	RM	TAX	PTRATIO	B	LSTAT
0	0	6.575	296.0	15.3	396.9	4.98

Scale Input

In[0]:

```
scaler = StandardScaler().fit(adhoc_predict2)
scaled_adhoc_predict2 = scaler.transform(adhoc_predict2)
scaled_adhoc_predict2
```

Out[0]:

```
array([[0., 0., 0., 0., 0., 0.]])
```

In[0]:

```
# Use pickle loaded model
list(clf.predict(scaled_adhoc_predict2))
```

Out[0]:

```
[20.35373177134412]
```

Finally, the pickled model is loaded back in and tested against a real dataset.

Exercises

- What are some key differences between scikit-learn and PyTorch?
- What is AutoML and why would you use it?
- Change the scikit-learn model to use height to predict weight.
- Run the PyTorch example in Google Colab notebooks and toggle between CPU and GPU runtimes. Explain the performance difference if there is one.
- What is EDA and why is it so important in a data science project?

Case Study Question

- Go to the Kaggle website, take a popular notebook in Python, and convert it to a containerized Flask application that serves out predictions using the example shown in this chapter as a guide. Now deploy this to a cloud environment via a hosted Kubernetes service such as Amazon EKS.

Learning Assessments

- Explain the different types of machine learning frameworks and ecosystems.
- Run and debug a preexisting machine learning project in scikit-learn and PyTorch.
- Containerize a Flask scikit-learn model.
- Understand the production machine learning maturity model.

## CHAPTER 15

Data Engineering

Data science may be the sexiest job of the 21st century, but the field is evolving rapidly into different job titles. Data scientist has been too crude a description for a whole series of tasks. As of 2020, two jobs that can pay the same or more are data engineer and machine learning engineer.

Even more surprising is the vast number of data engineer roles needed to support a traditional data scientist. It is somewhere between three to five data engineers to one data scientist.

What is happening? Let's look at it from another angle. Let's pretend we are writing headlines for a newspaper and want to say something eye-catching. We could say, "CEO is the sexiest job for the rich." There are few CEOs, just like there are few NBA stars, just like there are few professional actors who are making a living. For every CEO, how many people are working to make that CEO successful? This last statement is content-free and meaningless, like "water is wet."

This statement isn't to say that you can't make a living as a data scientist; it is more a critique of the logistics behind the statement. There is a huge demand for skills in data, and they range from DevOps to machine learning to communication. The term data scientist is nebulous. Is it a job or a behavior? In a way, it is a lot like the word DevOps. Is DevOps a job, or is it a behavior?

In looking at job posting data and salary data, it appears the job market is saying there is an apparent demand for actual roles in data engineering and machine learning engineering. This is because those roles perform identifiable tasks. A data engineer task could be creating a pipeline in the cloud that collects both batch and streaming data and then creates APIs to access that data and schedule those jobs. This job is not a squishy task. It works, or it doesn't.

Likewise, a machine learning engineer builds machine learning models and deploys them in a way that they are maintainable. This job is also not squishy. An engineer can do data engineering or machine learning engineering though, and still exhibit behaviors attributed to data science and DevOps. Today is an exciting time to be involved in data, as there are some considerable opportunities to build complex and robust data pipelines that feed into other complex and powerful prediction systems. There is an expression that says, "you can never be too rich or too thin." Likewise, with data, you can never have too much DevOps or data science skills. Let's dive into some DevOps-flavored ideas for data engineering.

Small Data

Toolkits are an exciting concept. If you call a plumber to your house, they arrive with tools that help them be more effective than you could be at a task. If you hire a carpenter to build something at your house, they also have a unique set of tools that help them perform a task in a fraction of the time you could. Tools are essential to professionals, and DevOps is no exception.

In this section, the tools of data engineering outline themselves. These tools include small data tasks like reading and writing files, using `pickle`, using `JSON`, and writing and reading `YAML` files. Being able to master these formats is critical to be the type of automator who can tackle any task and turn it into a script. Tools for Big Data tasks are also covered later in the chapter. It discusses distinctly different tools than the tools used for small data.

What is Big Data and what is small data then? One easy way to figure the distinction out is the laptop test. Does it work on your laptop? If it doesn't, then it is Big Data. A good example is Pandas. Pandas require between 5 to 10 times the amount of RAM as the dataset. If you have a 2-GB file and you are using Pandas, most likely your laptop won't work.

Dealing with Small Data Files

If there was a single defining trait of Python, it would be a relentless pursuit of efficiency in the language. A typical Python programmer wants to write just enough code to get a task done but wants to stop at the point where the code becomes unreadable or terse. Also, a typical Python programmer will not want to write boilerplate code. This environment has led to a continuous evolution of useful patterns.

One example of an active pattern is using the `with` statement to read and write files. The `with` statement handles the boring boilerplate parts of closing a file handle after the work has completed. The `with` statement is also used in other parts of the Python language to make tedious tasks less annoying.

Write a File

This example shows that writing a file using the `with` statement automatically closes the file handle upon execution of a code block. This syntax prevents bugs that can occur quickly when the handle is accidentally not closed:

```
with open("containers.txt", "w") as file_to_write:
    file_to_write.write("Pod/n")
    file_to_write.write("Service/n")
    file_to_write.write("Volume/n")
    file_to_write.write("Namespace/n")
```

The output of the file reads like this:

```
cat containers.txt

Pod
Service
Volume
Namespace
```

Read a File

The `with` context also is the recommended way to read a file. Notice that using `read lines()` uses line breaks to return a lazily evaluated iterator:

```
with open("containers.txt") as file_to_read:
    lines = file_to_read.readlines()
    print(lines)
```

The output:

```
['Pod\n', 'Service\n', 'Volume\n', 'Namespace\n']
```

In practice, this means that you can handle large log files by using generator expressions and not worry about consuming all of the memory on your machine.

Generator Pipeline to Read and Process Lines

This code is a generator function that opens a file and returns a generator:

```
def process_file_lazily():
    """Uses generator to lazily process file"""

    with open("containers.txt") as file_to_read:
        for line in file_to_read.readlines():
            yield line
```

Next, this generator is used to create a pipeline to perform operations line by line. In this example, the line converts to a lowercase string. Many other actions could be chained together here, and it would be very efficient because it is only using the memory necessary to process a line at a time:

```
# Create generator object
pipeline = process_file_lazily()
# convert to lowercase
lowercase = (line.lower() for line in pipeline)
# print first processed line
print(next(lowercase))
```

This is the output of the pipeline:

```
pod
```

In practice, this means that files that are effectively infinite because they are so large could still be processed if the code works in a way that exits when it finds a condition. For example, perhaps you need to find a customer ID across terabytes of log data. A generator pipeline could look for this customer ID and then exit the processing at the first occurrence. In the world of Big Data, this is no longer a theoretical problem.

Using YAML

YAML is becoming an emerging standard for DevOps-related configuration files. It is a human-readable data serialization format that is a superset of JSON. It stands for "YAML Ain't Markup Language." You often see YAML in build systems such as AWS CodePipeline (*https://oreil.ly/WZnIl*), CircleCI (*https://oreil.ly/0r8cK*), or PaaS offerings such as Google App Engine (*https://oreil.ly/ny_TD*).

There is a reason YAML is so often used. There is a need for a configuration language that allows rapid iteration when interacting with highly automated systems. Both a nonprogrammer and a programmer can intuitively figure out how to edit these files. Here is an example:

```
import yaml

kubernetes_components = {
    "Pod": "Basic building block of Kubernetes.",
    "Service": "An abstraction for dealing with Pods.",
    "Volume": "A directory accessible to containers in a Pod.",
    "Namespaces": "A way to divide cluster resources between users."
}

with open("kubernetes_info.yaml", "w") as yaml_to_write:
    yaml.safe_dump(kubernetes_components, yaml_to_write, default_flow_style=False)
```

The output written to disk looks like this:

```
cat kubernetes_info.yaml

Namespaces: A way to divide cluster resources between users.
Pod: Basic building block of Kubernetes.
```

```
Service: An abstraction for dealing with Pods.
Volume: A directory accessible to containers in a Pod.
```

The takeway is that it makes it trivial to serialize a Python data structure into a format that is easy to edit and iterate on. Reading this file back is just two lines of code.

```
import yaml

with open("kubernetes_info.yaml", "rb") as yaml_to_read:
    result = yaml.safe_load(yaml_to_read)
```

The output then can be pretty printed:

```
import pprint
pp = pprint.PrettyPrinter(indent=4)
pp.pprint(result)
{   'Namespaces': 'A way to divide cluster resources between users.',
    'Pod': 'Basic building block of Kubernetes.',
    'Service': 'An abstraction for dealing with Pods.',
    'Volume': 'A directory accessible to containers in a Pod.'}
```

Big Data

Data has been growing at a rate faster than the growth of computer processing power. To make things even more interesting, Moore's Law, which states that speed and capability of computers can be expected to double every two years, effectively ceased to apply around 2015, according to Dr. David Patterson at UC Berkeley. CPU speed is only increasing around 3% per a year now.

New methods of dealing with Big Data are necessary. Some of the new methods, include using ASICs like GPUs, tensor processing units (TPUs), and as well as AI and data platforms provided by cloud vendors. On the chip level, this means that a GPU could be the ideal target for a complex IT process instead of a CPU. Often this GPU is paired together with a system that can deliver a distributed storage mechanism that allows both distributed computing and distributed disk I/O. An excellent example of this is Apache Spark, Amazon SageMaker, or the Google AI Platform. All of them can utilize ASICs (GPU, TPU, and more), plus distributed storage along with a management system. Another example that is more low level is Amazon Spot Instance deep learning AMIs with Amazon Elastic File System (EFS) mount points.

For a DevOps professional, this means a few things. First, it means that special care when delivering software to these systems makes sense. For example, does the target platform have the correct GPU drivers? Are you deploying via containers? Is this system going to use distributed GPU processing? Is the data mostly batch, or is it streaming? Thinking about these questions up front can go a long way to ensuring the correct architecture.

One problem with buzzwords like AI, Big Data, cloud, or data scientist is that they mean different things to different people. Take data scientist for example. In one company it could mean someone who generates business intelligence dashboards for the sales team, and in another company, it could mean someone who is developing self-driving car software. Big Data has a similar context issue; it can mean many different things depending on whom you meet. Here is one definition to consider. Do you need different software packages to handle data on your laptop than in production?

An excellent example of a "small data" tool is the Pandas package. According to the author of the Pandas package, it can take between 5 and 10 times the amount of RAM as the size of the file used. In practice, if your laptop has 16 GB of RAM and you open a 2-GB CSV file, it is now a Big Data problem because your laptop may not have enough RAM, 20 GB, to work with the file. Instead, you may need to rethink how to handle the problem. Perhaps you can open a sample of the data, or truncate the data to get around the problem initially.

Here is an example of this exact problem and a workaround. Let's say you are supporting data scientists that keep running into Pandas out-of-memory errors because they are using files too large for Pandas. One such example is the Open Food Facts dataset from Kaggle (*https://oreil.ly/w-tmA*). When uncompressed, the dataset is over 1 GB. This problem fits precisely into the sweet spot of where Pandas could struggle to process it. One thing you can do is use the Unix shuf command to create a shuffled sample:

```
time shuf -n 100000 en.openfoodfacts.org.products.tsv\
   > 10k.sample.en.openfoodfacts.org.products.tsv
   1.89s user 0.80s system 97% cpu 2.748 total
```

In a little under two seconds, the file can be cut down to a manageable size. This approach is preferable to simply using heads or tails, because the samples are randomly selected. This problem is significant for a data science workflow. Also, you can inspect the lines of the file to see what you are dealing with first:

```
wc -l en.openfoodfacts.org.products.tsv
   356002 en.openfoodfacts.org.products.tsv
```

The source file is about 350,000 lines, so grabbing 100,000 shuffled lines is approximately a third of the data. This task can be confirmed by looking at the transformed file. It shows 272 MB, around one-third of the size of the original 1-GB file:

```
du -sh 10k.sample.en.openfoodfacts.org.products.tsv
272M    10k.sample.en.openfoodfacts.org.products.tsv
```

This size is more much manageable by Pandas, and this process could then be turned into an automation workflow that creates randomized sample files for Big Data sources. This type of process is just one of many particular workflows that Big Data demands.

Another definition of Big Data is by McKinsey, who defined Big Data in 2011 as "datasets whose size is beyond the ability of typical database software tools to capture, store, manage, and analyze." This definition is reasonable as well, with the slight modification that it isn't just database software tools; it is any tool that touches data. When a tool that works well on a laptop, such as Pandas, Python, MySQL, deep learning/machine learning, Bash, and more, fails to perform conventionally due to the size or velocity (rate of change) of the data, it is now a Big Data problem. Big Data problems require specialized tools, and the next section dives into this requirement.

Big Data Tools, Components, and Platforms

Another way to discuss Big Data is to break it down into tools and platforms. Figure 15-1 shows a typical Big Data architecture life cycle.

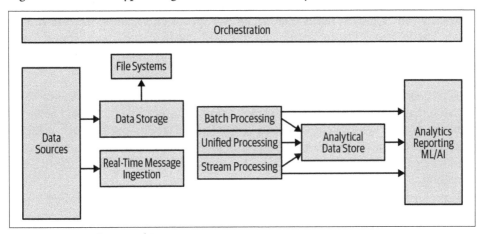

Figure 15-1. Big Data architecture

Let's discuss a few key components.

Data Sources

Some of the familiar sources of Big Data include social networks and digital transactions. As people have migrated more of their conversations and their business transactions online, it has led to an explosion of data. Additionally, mobile technology such as tablets, phones, and laptops that record audio and video, exponentially create sources of data.

Other data sources include the Internet of Things (IoT), which includes sensors, lightweight chips, and devices. All of this leads to an unstoppable proliferation of data that needs to be stored somewhere. The tools involved in Data Sources could range from IoT client/server systems such as AWS IoT Greengrass, to object storage systems such as Amazon S3 or Google Cloud Storage.

Filesystems

Filesystems have played a huge role in computing. Their implementation, though, is continuously evolving. In dealing with Big Data, one issue is having enough disk I/O, to handle distributed operations.

One modern tool that deals with this is the Hadoop Distributed File System (HDFS). It works by clustering many servers together, allowing aggregated CPU, disk I/O, and storage. In practice, this makes HDFS a fundamental technology for dealing with Big Data. It can migrate large volumes of data or filesystems for distributed computing jobs. It is also the backbone of Spark, which can do both stream- and batch-based machine learning.

Other types of filesystems include object storage filesystems such as Amazon S3 filesystem and Google Cloud Platform storage. They allow for huge files to be stored in a distributed and highly available manner, or more precisely, 99.999999999% reliability. There are Python APIs and command-line tools available that communicate with these filesystems, enabling easy automation. These cloud APIs are covered in more detail in Chapter 10.

Finally, another type of filesystem to be aware of is a traditional network filesystem, or NFS, made available as a managed cloud service. An excellent example of this is Amazon Elastic File System (Amazon EFS). For a DevOps professional, a highly available and elastic NFS filesystem can be an incredibly versatile tool, especially coupled with containers technology. Figure 15-2 shows an example of mounting EFS in a container.

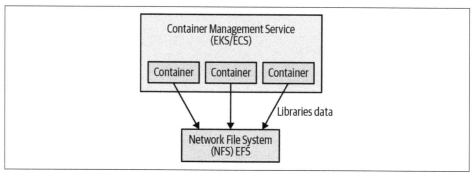

Figure 15-2. Mounting EFS in a container

One powerful automation workflow is to programmatically create Docker containers through a build system such as AWS CodePipeline or Google Cloud Build. Those containers then get registered in the cloud container registry, for example, Amazon ECR. Next, a container management system such as Kubernetes spawns containers that mount the NFS. This allows both the power of immutable container images that spawn quickly, and access to centralized source code libraries and data. This type of workflow could be ideal for an organization looking to optimize machine learning operations.

Data Storage

Ultimately the data needs to live somewhere, and this creates some exciting opportunities and challenges. One emerging trend is to utilize the concept of a data lake. Why do you care about a data lake? A data lake allows for data processing in the same location as storage. As a result, many data lakes need to have infinite storage and provide infinite computing (i.e., be on the cloud). Amazon S3 is often a common choice for a data lake.

The data lake constructed in this manner can also be utilized by a machine learning pipeline that may depend on the training data living in the lake, as well as the trained models. The trained models could then always be A/B tested to ensure the latest model is improving the production prediction (inference) system, as shown in Figure 15-3.

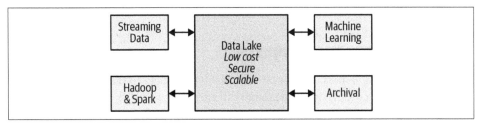

Figure 15-3. Data lake

Other forms of storage will be very familiar to traditional software developers. These storage systems include relational databases, key/value databases, search engines like Elasticsearch, and graph databases. In a Big Data architecture, each type of storage system may play a more specific role. In a small-scale system, a relational database may be a jack of all trades, but in a Big Data architecture, there is less room for tolerance of a mismatch of the storage system.

An excellent example of mismatch in storage choice is using a relational database as a search engine by enabling full-text search capabilities instead of using a specialized solution, like Elasticsearch. Elasticsearch is designed to create a scalable search solution, while a relational database is designed to provide referential integrity and transactions. The CTO of Amazon, Werner Vogel, makes this point very well by stating that a "one size database doesn't fit anyone." This problem is illustrated in Figure 15-4, which shows that each type of database has a specific purpose.

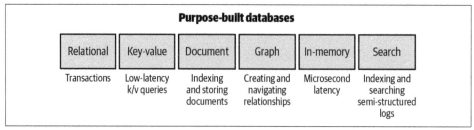

Figure 15-4. Amazon databases

Picking the correct storage solutions, including which combination of databases to use, is a crucial skill for any type of data architect to ensure that a system works at optimal efficiency. In thinking through the design of a system that is fully automated and efficient, maintenance should be a consideration. If a particular technology choice is being abused, such as using a relational database for a highly available messaging queue, then maintenance costs could explode, which in turn creates more automation work. So another component to consider is how much automation work it takes to maintain a solution.

Real-Time Streaming Ingestion

Real-time streaming data is a particularly tricky type of data to deal with. The stream itself increases the complexity of dealing with the data, and it is possible the stream needs to route to yet another part of the system that intends to process the data in a streaming fashion. One example of a cloud-based streaming ingestion solution is Amazon Kinesis Data Firehose. See Figure 15-5.

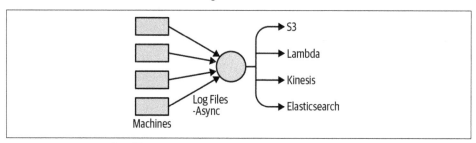

Figure 15-5. Kinesis log files

Here is an example of code that would do that. Notice that Python's `asyncio` module allows for highly concurrent network operations that are single threaded. Nodes could emit this in a job farm, and it could be metrics or error logs:

```python
import asyncio

def send_async_firehose_events(count=100):
    """Async sends events to firehose"""
```

```
start = time.time()
client = firehose_client()
extra_msg = {"aws_service": "firehose"}
loop = asyncio.get_event_loop()
tasks = []
LOG.info(f"sending aysnc events TOTAL {count}",extra=extra_msg)
num = 0
for _ in range(count):
    tasks.append(asyncio.ensure_future(put_record(gen_uuid_events(),
                                        client)))
    LOG.info(f"sending aysnc events: COUNT {num}/{count}")
    num +=1
loop.run_until_complete(asyncio.wait(tasks))
loop.close()
end = time.time()
LOG.info("Total time: {}".format(end - start))
```

Kinesis Data Firehose works by accepting capture data and routing it continuously to any number of destinations: Amazon S3, Amazon Redshift, Amazon Elasticsearch Service, or some third-party service like Splunk. An open source alternative to using a managed service like Kinesis is to use Apache Kafka. Apache Kafka has similar principles in that it works as a pub/sub architecture.

Case Study: Building a Homegrown Data Pipeline

In the early days of Noah's work as CTO and General Manager at a startup in the early 2000s, one problem that cropped up was how to build the company's first machine learning pipeline and data pipeline. A rough sketch of what that looked like is in the following diagram of a Jenkins data pipeline (Figure 15-6).

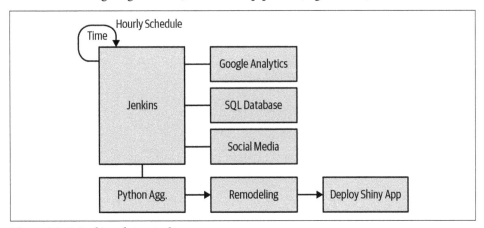

Figure 15-6. Jenkins data pipeline

The inputs to the data pipeline are any data source needed for business analytics or machine learning predictions. These sources included a relational database, Google Analytics, and social media metrics, to a name a few. The collection jobs ran every hour and generated CSV files that were available internally by Apache web service. This solution was a compelling and straightforward process.

The jobs themselves were Jenkins jobs that were Python scripts that ran. If something needed to be changed, it was fairly straightforward to change a Python script for a particular job. An added benefit to this system was that it was straightforward to debug. If a job had a failure, the jobs showed up as failed, and it was straightforward to look at the output of the job and see what happened.

The final stage of the pipeline then created machine learning predictions and an analytics dashboard that served out dashboards via an R-based Shiny application. The simplicity of the approach is the most influential factor in this type of architecture, and as a bonus it leverages existing DevOps skills.

Serverless Data Engineering

Another emerging pattern is serverless data engineering. Figure 15-7 is a high-level architectural diagram of what a serverless data pipeline is.

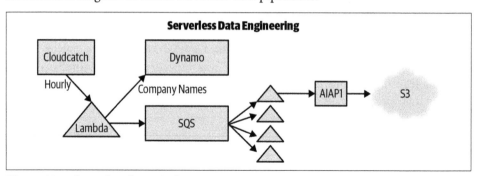

Figure 15-7. Serverless data pipeline

Next, let's look at what a timed lambda does.

Using AWS Lambda with CloudWatch Events

You can create a CloudWatch timer to call the lambda using the AWS Lambda console and to set up a trigger, as shown in Figure 15-8.

Figure 15-8. CloudWatch Lambda timer

Using Amazon CloudWatch Logging with AWS Lambda

Using CloudWatch logging is an essential step for Lambda development. Figure 15-9 is an example of a CloudWatch event log.

Figure 15-9. CloudWatch event log

Using AWS Lambda to Populate Amazon Simple Queue Service

Next, you want to do the following locally in AWS Cloud9:

1. Create a new Lambda with Serverless Wizard.

2. cd into lambda and install packages one level up.

```
pip3 install boto3 --target ../
pip3 install python-json-logger --target ../
```

Next, you can test local and deploy this code:

```
'''
Dynamo to SQS
'''

import boto3
import json
import sys
import os

DYNAMODB = boto3.resource('dynamodb')
TABLE = "fang"
QUEUE = "producer"
SQS = boto3.client("sqs")

#SETUP LOGGING
import logging
from pythonjsonlogger import jsonlogger

LOG = logging.getLogger()
LOG.setLevel(logging.INFO)
logHandler = logging.StreamHandler()
formatter = jsonlogger.JsonFormatter()
logHandler.setFormatter(formatter)
LOG.addHandler(logHandler)

def scan_table(table):
    '''Scans table and return results'''

    LOG.info(f"Scanning Table {table}")
    producer_table = DYNAMODB.Table(table)
    response = producer_table.scan()
    items = response['Items']
    LOG.info(f"Found {len(items)} Items")
    return items

def send_sqs_msg(msg, queue_name, delay=0):
    '''Send SQS Message

    Expects an SQS queue_name and msg in a dictionary format.
    Returns a response dictionary.
```

```
    '''

    queue_url = SQS.get_queue_url(QueueName=queue_name)["QueueUrl"]
    queue_send_log_msg = "Send message to queue url: %s, with body: %s" %\
        (queue_url, msg)
    LOG.info(queue_send_log_msg)
    json_msg = json.dumps(msg)
    response = SQS.send_message(
        QueueUrl=queue_url,
        MessageBody=json_msg,
        DelaySeconds=delay)
    queue_send_log_msg_resp = "Message Response: %s for queue url: %s" %\
        (response, queue_url)
    LOG.info(queue_send_log_msg_resp)
    return response

def send_emissions(table, queue_name):
    '''Send Emissions'''

    items = scan_table(table=table)
    for item in items:
        LOG.info(f"Sending item {item} to queue: {queue_name}")
        response = send_sqs_msg(item, queue_name=queue_name)
        LOG.debug(response)

def lambda_handler(event, context):
    '''
    Lambda entrypoint
    '''

    extra_logging = {"table": TABLE, "queue": QUEUE}
    LOG.info(f"event {event}, context {context}", extra=extra_logging)
    send_emissions(table=TABLE, queue_name=QUEUE)

```

This code does the following:

1. Grabs company names from Amazon DynamoDB.

2. Puts the names into Amazon SQS.

To test it, you can do a local test in Cloud9 (Figure 15-10).

Figure 15-10. Local test in Cloud9

Next you can verify messages in SQS, as shown in Figure 15-11.

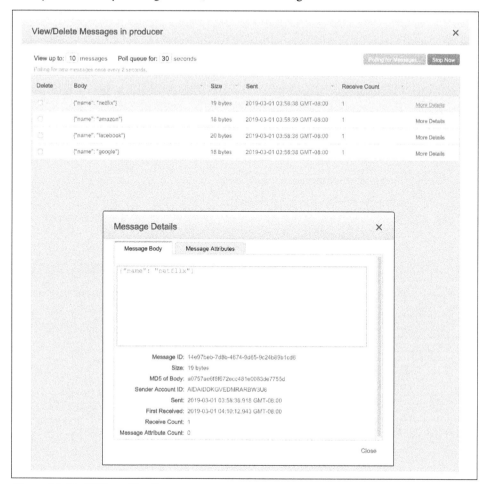

Figure 15-11. SQS verification

Don't forget to set the correct IAM role! You need to assign the lambda an IAM role that can write messages to SQS, as shown in Figure 15-12.

Figure 15-12. Permission error

Wiring Up CloudWatch Event Trigger

The final step to enable CloudWatch trigger does the following: enable timed execution of producer, and verify that messages flow into SQS, as shown in Figure 15-13.

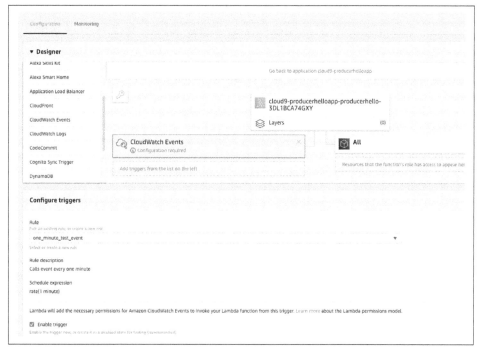

Figure 15-13. Configure timer

You can now see messages in the SQS queue (Figure 15-14).

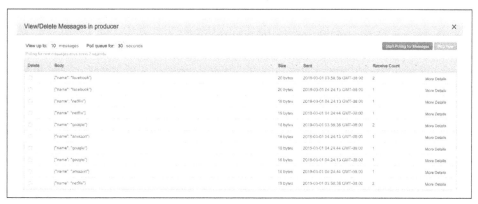

Figure 15-14. SQS queue

Creating Event-Driven Lambdas

With the producer lambda out of the way, next up is to create an event-driven lambda that fires asynchronously upon every message in SQS (the consumer). The Lambda function can now fire in response to every SQS message (Figure 15-15).

Figure 15-15. Fire on SQS event

Reading Amazon SQS Events from AWS Lambda

The only task left is to write the code to consume the messages from SQS, process them using our API, and then write the results to S3:

```
import json

import boto3
import botocore
#import pandas as pd
import pandas as pd
import wikipedia
import boto3
from io import StringIO

#SETUP LOGGING
import logging
from pythonjsonlogger import jsonlogger

LOG = logging.getLogger()
```

```python
LOG.setLevel(logging.DEBUG)
logHandler = logging.StreamHandler()
formatter = jsonlogger.JsonFormatter()
logHandler.setFormatter(formatter)
LOG.addHandler(logHandler)

#S3 BUCKET
REGION = "us-east-1"

### SQS Utils###
def sqs_queue_resource(queue_name):
    """Returns an SQS queue resource connection

    Usage example:
    In [2]: queue = sqs_queue_resource("dev-job-24910")
    In [4]: queue.attributes
    Out[4]:
    {'ApproximateNumberOfMessages': '0',
     'ApproximateNumberOfMessagesDelayed': '0',
     'ApproximateNumberOfMessagesNotVisible': '0',
     'CreatedTimestamp': '1476240132',
     'DelaySeconds': '0',
     'LastModifiedTimestamp': '1476240132',
     'MaximumMessageSize': '262144',
     'MessageRetentionPeriod': '345600',
     'QueueArn': 'arn:aws:sqs:us-west-2:414930948375:dev-job-24910',
     'ReceiveMessageWaitTimeSeconds': '0',
     'VisibilityTimeout': '120'}

    """

    sqs_resource = boto3.resource('sqs', region_name=REGION)
    log_sqs_resource_msg =\
      "Creating SQS resource conn with qname: [%s] in region: [%s]" %\
    (queue_name, REGION)
    LOG.info(log_sqs_resource_msg)
    queue = sqs_resource.get_queue_by_name(QueueName=queue_name)
    return queue

def sqs_connection():
    """Creates an SQS Connection which defaults to global var REGION"""

    sqs_client = boto3.client("sqs", region_name=REGION)
    log_sqs_client_msg = "Creating SQS connection in Region: [%s]" % REGION
    LOG.info(log_sqs_client_msg)
    return sqs_client

def sqs_approximate_count(queue_name):
    """Return an approximate count of messages left in queue"""

    queue = sqs_queue_resource(queue_name)
    attr = queue.attributes
```

```
        num_message = int(attr['ApproximateNumberOfMessages'])
        num_message_not_visible = int(attr['ApproximateNumberOfMessagesNotVisible'])
        queue_value = sum([num_message, num_message_not_visible])
        sum_msg = """'ApproximateNumberOfMessages' and\
    'ApproximateNumberOfMessagesNotVisible' =\
      *** [%s] *** for QUEUE NAME: [%s]""" %\
          (queue_value, queue_name)
        LOG.info(sum_msg)
        return queue_value

    def delete_sqs_msg(queue_name, receipt_handle):

        sqs_client = sqs_connection()
        try:
            queue_url = sqs_client.get_queue_url(QueueName=queue_name)["QueueUrl"]
            delete_log_msg = "Deleting msg with ReceiptHandle %s" % receipt_handle
            LOG.info(delete_log_msg)
            response = sqs_client.delete_message(QueueUrl=queue_url,
              ReceiptHandle=receipt_handle)
        except botocore.exceptions.ClientError as error:
            exception_msg =\
              "FAILURE TO DELETE SQS MSG: Queue Name [%s] with error: [%s]" %\
                (queue_name, error)
            LOG.exception(exception_msg)
            return None

        delete_log_msg_resp = "Response from delete from queue: %s" % response
        LOG.info(delete_log_msg_resp)
        return response

    def names_to_wikipedia(names):

        wikipedia_snippit = []
        for name in names:
            wikipedia_snippit.append(wikipedia.summary(name, sentences=1))
        df = pd.DataFrame(
            {
                'names':names,
                'wikipedia_snippit': wikipedia_snippit
            }
        )
        return df

    def create_sentiment(row):
        """Uses AWS Comprehend to Create Sentiments on a DataFrame"""

        LOG.info(f"Processing {row}")
        comprehend = boto3.client(service_name='comprehend')
        payload = comprehend.detect_sentiment(Text=row, LanguageCode='en')
        LOG.debug(f"Found Sentiment: {payload}")
        sentiment = payload['Sentiment']
        return sentiment
```

```python
def apply_sentiment(df, column="wikipedia_snippit"):
    """Uses Pandas Apply to Create Sentiment Analysis"""

    df['Sentiment'] = df[column].apply(create_sentiment)
    return df

### S3 ###

def write_s3(df, bucket):
    """Write S3 Bucket"""

    csv_buffer = StringIO()
    df.to_csv(csv_buffer)
    s3_resource = boto3.resource('s3')
    res = s3_resource.Object(bucket, 'fang_sentiment.csv').\
        put(Body=csv_buffer.getvalue())
    LOG.info(f"result of write to bucket: {bucket} with:\n {res}")

def lambda_handler(event, context):
    """Entry Point for Lambda"""

    LOG.info(f"SURVEYJOB LAMBDA, event {event}, context {context}")
    receipt_handle  = event['Records'][0]['receiptHandle'] #sqs message
    #'eventSourceARN': 'arn:aws:sqs:us-east-1:561744971673:producer'
    event_source_arn = event['Records'][0]['eventSourceARN']

    names = [] #Captured from Queue

    # Process Queue
    for record in event['Records']:
        body = json.loads(record['body'])
        company_name = body['name']

        #Capture for processing
        names.append(company_name)

        extra_logging = {"body": body, "company_name":company_name}
        LOG.info(f"SQS CONSUMER LAMBDA, splitting arn: {event_source_arn}",
          extra=extra_logging)
        qname = event_source_arn.split(":")[-1]
        extra_logging["queue"] = qname
        LOG.info(f"Attempting Delete SQS {receipt_handle} {qname}",
          extra=extra_logging)
        res = delete_sqs_msg(queue_name=qname, receipt_handle=receipt_handle)
        LOG.info(f"Deleted SQS receipt_handle {receipt_handle} with res {res}",
          extra=extra_logging)

    # Make Pandas dataframe with wikipedia snippts
    LOG.info(f"Creating dataframe with values: {names}")
    df = names_to_wikipedia(names)
```

```
# Perform Sentiment Analysis
df = apply_sentiment(df)
LOG.info(f"Sentiment from FANG companies: {df.to_dict()}")

# Write result to S3
write_s3(df=df, bucket="fangsentiment")
```

You can see that one easy way to download the files is to use the AWS CLI:

```
noah:/tmp $ aws s3 cp --recursive s3://fangsentiment/ .
download: s3://fangsentiment/netflix_sentiment.csv to ./netflix_sentiment.csv
download: s3://fangsentiment/google_sentiment.csv to ./google_sentiment.csv
download: s3://fangsentiment/facebook_sentiment.csv to ./facebook_sentiment.csv
```

OK, so what did we accomplish? Figure 15-16 shows our serverless AI data engineering pipeline.

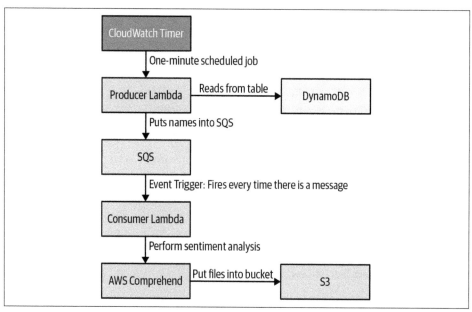

Figure 15-16. Serverless AI data engineering pipeline

Conclusion

Data engineering is an evolving job title, and it benefits greatly from strong DevOps skills. The DevOps best practices of Microservices, Continous Delivery, Infrastructure as Code, and Monitoring and Logging play a tremendous role in this category. Often by leveraging cloud-native technologies, it makes hard problems possible, and simple problems effortless.

Here are some next steps to continue on a journey of mastery with data engineering. Learn serverless technology. It doesn't matter what the cloud is, learn it! This environment is the future, and data engineering, in particular, is well suited to capitalize on this trend.

Exercises

- Explain what Big Data is and what its key characteristics are.
- Use small data tools in Python to solve common problems.
- Explain what a data lake is and how it is used.
- Explain the appropriate use cases for different types of purpose-built databases.
- Build a serverless data engineering pipeline in Python.

Case Study Question

- Using the same architecture shown in this chapter, build an end-to-end serverless data engineering pipeline that scrapes a website using Scrapy, Beautiful Soup, or a similar library, and sends image files to Amazon Rekognition to be analyzed. Store the results of the Rekognition API call in Amazon DynamoDB. Run this job on a timer once a day.

## CHAPTER 16

DevOps War Stories and Interviews

Author: Noah

When I was finishing my last year of college at Cal Poly San Louis Obispo, I needed to take Organic Chemistry over the summer to graduate on time. Unfortunately, there was no financial aid over the summer, so I had to rent a house and get a full-time job. I was able to get a part-time job at the library for minimum wage, but it still wasn't enough money. I scoured the help wanted ads and the only job popping up was for a bouncer at a vast country-western nightclub.

At my job interview, the manager who interviewed me was about six feet tall, close to three hundred pounds of mostly muscle. He also had a huge black eye. He told me that the previous weekend a large pack of people had beat up all the bouncers, including him. He told me it was between me and a shot-putter on the track team. To help decide between me and the shot-putter, he asked me if I would run in the middle of a similar fight. I told him that I wouldn't run from a brawl and I got the job.

Later I started to realize that I may have been a little bit naive in estimating my courage and my abilities. There were some massive wrestlers and football players that would regularly come in and get into fights, and they were terrifying people. At one concert, they called in for backup because they were expecting trouble. A new bouncer with a mohawk and Chinese writing tattooed on his skull was my coworker for that event. Several years later I saw him on TV winning the UFC Heavyweight Championship and put a name to a face, Chuck Liddel. Bouncing was a dangerous job. This fact became evident one day when I tried to break up a fight in which a drunk 250-pound football player was pummeling a victim in the face. I wanted to pull him off but instead I was thrown several feet back, as if the man was effortlessly punching a pillow across the room. It dawned on me at that moment that I wasn't invincible, and my martial arts skills were nonexistent. I never forgot that lesson.

One way of describing this overconfidence is the Dunning-Kruger effect. The Dunning-Kruger effect is a cognitive bias where people mistakenly assess their cognitive ability as more significant than it is. You can see this effect in practice on the yearly StackOverflow survey. In 2019, 70% of developers considered themselves above average, while 10% considered themselves below average. What is the takeaway here? Don't trust human cognition! Trust automation instead. "Trust me," "I am the boss," "I have been doing this for X years," and other statements of confidence are nonsense in comparison to the brutal efficiency of automation done correctly. The belief that automation is greater than hierarchy is what DevOps is all about.

This chapter links everything in the book about automation together by using real people and real case studies to explore the DevOps best practices of:

- Continuous Integration
- Continuous Delivery
- Microservices
- Infrastructure as Code
- Monitoring and Logging
- Communication and Collaboration

Film Studio Can't Make Film

After living in New Zealand for a year working on the movie *Avatar*, I was in a very peaceful frame of mind. I lived on the North Island in a town called Miramar, which was a stunningly beautiful peninsula. I would step outside my door onto the beach for my daily 14-kilometer daily run. Eventually, the contract ended, and I had to get a new job. I accepted a position in the Bay Area at a major film studio that employed hundreds of people and was located at a facility covered over a hundred thousand square feet. Hundreds of millions of dollars had been invested in this company, and it seemed like a cool place to work. I flew in over the weekend and arrived on a Sunday (the day before work).

My first day at work was quite shocking. It snapped me right out of my paradise mindset. The entire studio was down for the count, and hundreds of employees couldn't work because the central software system, an asset management system, wouldn't work. Out of panic and desperation, I was brought into the secret war room and shown the extent of the problem. I could tell my peaceful days of running casually along the beach were over. I had entered a war zone. Yikes!

As I learned more about this crisis, it became apparent that it had been a slow-burning fire for quite some time. Regular all-day outages and severe technical problems were the norm. The list of issues was as follows:

- The system was developed in isolation without code review.
- There was no version control.
- There was no build system.
- There were no tests.
- There were functions over a thousand lines long.
- It was sometimes hard to get a hold of key people responsible for the project.
- Outages were costly because highly paid personnel couldn't work.
- Film encourages reckless software development because they "are not a software company."
- Remote locations had mysterious connections issues.
- There was no real monitoring.
- Many departments had implemented ad hoc solutions and patches for problems.

The only fix to this standard set of problems is to start doing one right thing at a time. The new team formed to solve this problem did precisely that. One of the first steps to address the challenge was to set up continuous integration and automated load-testing in a staging environment. It is incredible how much a simple action like this can lead to considerable gains in understanding.

One of the last and more interesting problems we resolved surfaced in our monitoring system. After the system performance had stabilized and software engineering best practices were applied, we discovered a surprising bug. We had the system perform a daily check-in of assets as a basic health check. Several days later, we began experiencing severe performance issues daily. When we looked at the spikes in CPU on the database, they correlated to the basic health check. Digging further, it became apparent that the check-in code (a homegrown ORM, or object-relational mapper) was exponentially generating SQL queries. Most workflow processes only involved two or three versions of an asset, and our health check monitoring had discovered a critical flaw. One more reason for automated health checking.

When we ran the load test, we discovered a whole host of issues. One issue we found immediately was that after a small amount of concurrent traffic, the MySQL database would flatline. We found that the exact version of MySQL we were using had some severe performance problems. Switching to the latest version dramatically improved performance. With that performance issue solved and a way to automatically test whether we were making the problem better, we quickly iterated dramatic fixes.

Next, we got source code into version control, creating a branch-based deployment strategy and then running linting and testing, along with code review, on each check-in. This action also dramatically improved visibility into our performance issues and presented self-evident solutions. In an industrial crisis, automation and standards of excellence are two of the essential tools you can deploy.

One final issue we had to resolve was that our remote film studio location was having severe reliability problems. Staff at the remote location was sure the issue was performance issues related to our API. The crisis was urgent enough that the top executives at the company had me and another engineer fly down to the location to troubleshoot the problem. When we got there, we called our central office and had them look only at requests from that IP range. When we launched their application, there was no network traffic observed.

We checked the network infrastructure at the remote location and verified we could send traffic between the client machine and the central office. On a hunch, we decided to look at both local and network performance on the Windows machine using specialized diagnostic software. We then observed thousands of socket connections launched over 2 to 3 seconds. After digging into the issue a bit, we discovered that the Windows operating system would temporarily shut down the entire network stack. If too many network connections spawn within a short window, the OS protects itself. The client application was attempting to launch thousands of network connections in a for loop and eventually shut off its network stack. We went into the code and limited the machine so it could only make one network connection, and suddenly, things worked.

Later we ran pylint on the source code of the client software and discovered approximately one-third of the system was not executable. The key issue wasn't a performance problem, but a lack of software engineering and DevOps best practices. A few simple modifications to the workflow, such as continuous integration, monitoring, and automated load testing, could have flushed this problem out in under a week.

Game Studio Can't Ship Game

When I first joined an established game company, they were undergoing a transformational change. The existing product was extremely innovative when it first launched, but by the time I joined, they had decided they needed to invest in new products. The current culture of the company was a very data center-centric culture with substantial change management at every step. Many of the tools developed were logical extensions of the desire to maintain uptime for a highly successful, but dying, game. The introduction of new people, new departments, and new products led to inevitable, consistent conflict and also a crisis.

The initial depth of the crisis became known to me early, even though I was working on the legacy product. As I was walking by the new products team on the way to another meeting, I heard an interesting conversation. A Spanish developer on the flagship new product caught my ear when he said during an Agile standup, "It no worketh…" This statement alone was quite shocking, but I was even more shocked to hear the response, "Luigi, that is *tech talk*; this is not the forum for that."

I knew at that point there was, in fact, something wrong. Later, many people on the project quit, and I took over a project that was over a year late and was on rewrite number three in language number three. One of the key findings was that this "canary in the coal mine" developer was precisely correct. Nothing worked! On my first day on the project, I checked out the source code on my laptop and tried to run the web application. It completely locked up my computer on a few refreshes of Chrome. Uh-oh, here I was again.

After digging into the project a bit, I realized there were a few critical issues. The first was that the core technical crisis needed addressing. There was a "cargo cult" Agile process that was very good at creating and closing tickets, but that built something that didn't function. One of the first things I did was isolate the core engineers from this project management process, and we designed a fix for the core solutions without the overhead of "Agile." Next, when the core engine issue resolved, we created an automated deployment and custom load-testing process.

Because this was the top priority for the company, we reprioritized the work of members of some of the other teams working on the core product to build a custom load test and custom instrumentation. This initiative was also met with substantial pushback because it meant that product managers who were working with these resources would be standing idly by. It was an essential point in the project because it forced management to decide whether launching this first new product was a top priority to the company or not.

The final big hurdle in launching the product was the creation of a continuous delivery system. On average, it took around one week to make even a small change like changing HTML. The deployment process that worked reasonably well for a C++ game that had hundreds of thousands of paying customers did not work for a modern web application. The legacy game ran out of a traditional data center. It was very different than what was ideal for creating a web-based game in the cloud.

One of the things cloud computing also exposes is lack of automation. The very nature of cloud computing demands a higher level of DevOps skills and automation. Things are not elastic if it requires a human to be involved in scaling up and scaling down servers. Continuous delivery means that software runs continuously, delivered to environments where it can be deployed quickly as a final step. A "release manager" who is involved in a week-long deployment process with many manual steps is in direct opposition to DevOps.

Python Scripts Take 60 Seconds to Launch

Working at one of the top film studios in the world, with one of the largest supercomputers in the world, is a great way to see what happens at scale. One of the critical issues with open source software is that it may be built on a laptop in isolation from the needs of a large company. A developer is trying to solve a particular problem. On the one hand, the solution is elegant, but on another hand, it creates a problem.

One of these problems in Python surfaced at this film studio because they had to deal with petabytes of data on a centralized file server. Python scripts were the currency of the company, and they ran just about everywhere. Unfortunately, they took around 60 seconds to launch. A few of us got together to solve the issue, and we used one of our favorite tools, strace:

```
root@f1bfc615a58e:/app# strace -c -e stat64,open python -c 'import click'
% time     seconds  usecs/call     calls    errors syscall
------ ----------- ----------- --------- --------- ----------------
  0.00    0.000000           0        97         4 open
------ ----------- ----------- --------- --------- ----------------
100.00    0.000000                     97         4 total
```

The Python 2 is O(nlogn) or "Super Linear time" for module lookup. The number of directories in your path would at least linearly increase the time it took to launch the script. This performance penalty became a real problem at the film studio because this often meant more than one hundred thousand calls to the filesystem to launch a Python script. This process was not only slow but incrementally destructive to the performance of the file server. Eventually, this started to crush the centralized multi-million dollar file server completely.

The solution was a combination of doing a deep dive with strace, i.e., using the right tool for the job, and also hacking Python to stop looking up imports by using paths. Later versions of Python have addressed this issue through caching lookups, but it pays to learn tools that enable you to do a deep dive on performance. A final touch is to always run profiling as a part of the continuous integration process to catch these types of performance bugs.

Two other situations at film studios involving bad UX design combined with lousy architecture come to mind. One day an animator came over to the main engineering section and asked for advice on solving a problem with a Filemaker Pro database that had been set up. The Filemaker Pro database that kept track of shots for the animation department kept getting deleted. When I asked to look at the database, there was a UI with two buttons next to each other. One was a medium-sized green button that said "Save Entry," and another was a large red button that said, "Delete Database."

At a completely different company, we noticed that one particular IP address was sending a tremendous amount of load toward the production MySQL database. When we tracked down the developer, they seemed a bit hesitant to talk to us. We asked if their department was doing anything special. They said they had a PyQt GUI that performed automation tasks. When we looked at the GUI, there were several buttons of normal size, and then a large button labeled "GO." We asked what the "GO" button did, and the developer sheepishly said that everyone knows you don't press that button. I opened up an SSH connection to our database and ran top on the MySQL server. Next, I did press that button, despite his protests not to. Sure enough, the database immediately went to 100% CPU sustained for several minutes.

Putting Out a Fire with a Cache and Intelligent Instrumentation

At a Sports Social network where I was CTO, we were experiencing substantial problems with the performance from our relational database. We started to reach the limits of vertical scaling. We were running the biggest version of SQL Server that Amazon RDS (Amazon's managed relational database service) provided. To make things worse, we couldn't easily switch to horizontal scaling because, at that time, SQL Server didn't integrate read slaves into RDS.

There are many ways to solve a crisis like this. One method could have involved rewriting key queries, but we were experiencing so much traffic and a shortage of engineers that we had to get creative. One of our DevOps-centric engineers came up with a critical solution by doing the following:

- Added more instrumentation via an APM that traced the time SQL calls took and mapped those to routes

- Added Ngnix as a cache to read-only routes

- Load-tested this solution in a dedicated staging environment

This engineer saved our bacon, and he implemented the solution through minimal modifications to the application. It dramatically increased our performance and allowed us to eventually scale to millions of monthly users, becoming one of the largest sports sites in the world. DevOps principles aren't just important in the abstract; they can figurately saving you from drowning in a sea of deliberate technical debt.

You'll Automate Yourself Out of a Job!

In my early twenties, I got a job at one of the top film studios in the world and was pretty excited to use my combination of skills in video, film, programming, and IT. It was also a union job, which I had never experienced before working in technology. The upside of a union job was that it had incredible benefits and pay, but I later discovered that there were some downsides involving automation.

After working there for a couple of months, I realized that one of my tasks was pretty silly. I would walk around the film studio on a Saturday (for overtime pay), place a CD into high-end editing systems, and "do maintenance." The general premise was a good one; do weekly preventative maintenance so that these expensive machines would have minimal downtime during the week. The implementation was flawed, though. Why would I do anything manually if I could automate it? After all, it was a computer.

After my second Saturday "doing maintenance," I constructed a secret plan to automate my job. Because it was a union job, I had to be a bit careful, though, and keep it a secret until I had validated that it would work. If I asked for permission, you could forget about it. I first wrote down a series of steps that were necessary to automate this:

1. Connect the OS X machines to the company LDAP servers. This step would allow multiple users and allow me to mount NFS home directories.

2. Reverse engineer the editing software to let multiple users access the software. I had applied group-level permissions to several lists to hack it, allowing various users to use the same machine.

3. Create an image of the software in the state I would want it to install.

4. Write a script to "NetBoot," i.e., boot the machine from a networking operating system and then reimage the machines.

Once I got this sorted out, I was able to walk over to any machine, reboot it, and hold down the "N" key. It then wholly reimaged the software (and still preserved user data because it was on the network). It took 3.5 to 5 minutes to completely reinstall the entire machine because of the fast system and because I was doing block-level copying.

In my first test run, I was able to complete my "maintenance" in 30 minutes. The only bottleneck was walking over to the machines and rebooting them while holding down the "N" key. Additionally, I then told the film editors first to try restoring their machines by resetting them and holding the "N" key, and this eliminated support calls dramatically. Yikes, my job and my whole department's job got way more manageable. This automation wasn't entirely good at the union shop.

Soon an older union worker pulled me into a surprise meeting with my boss. He was unhappy with what I did. The meeting ended with him screaming at me while pointing a finger at me and saying, "You will script yourself out of a job, kid!" The boss's boss was also unhappy. He had advocated to management for months to get a maintenance team approved, and then I wrote a script that eliminated much of what our department did. He also yelled at me profusely.

The word spread, and everyone liked the new automated process, including the stars and the film editors. I did not get fired because of this. Later, word spread about what I was doing, and I did script myself out of a job. I got recruited to work at Sony Imageworks and was hired to do what I almost got fired for doing. It was a fun job, too. I got to play basketball at lunch with Adam Sandler and the cast of his movies quite frequently. So, yes, you can script yourself out of a job and right into a better one!

DevOps Antipatterns

Let's dive into some clear examples of what not to do. It is often much easier to learn from mistakes than to learn from perfection. This section dives into many horror stories and antipatterns to avoid.

No Automated Build Server Antipattern

It never ceased to amaze me how many troubled projects or companies had no build server. This fact is perhaps the most significant red flag that exists for a software company. If your software isn't put through a build server, you can pretty much guarantee minimal other forms of automation are occurring. This problem is a canary in the coal mine. Build servers are a foundational piece that must be in place to ensure you can reliably deliver software. Often, the first thing I would do in a crisis would be to immediately set up a build server. Just running code through pylint makes things better quickly.

Somewhat related to this is the "almost working" build server. It is shocking how some organizations do the same thing they do with DevOps and say, "that isn't my job...that is the build engineer." This dismissive attitude, just like the attitude of "this is not my job; this is DevOps," is cancer. Every job in automation is your job if you work in a software company. There is no more critical or virtuous task than making sure things are automated. It is frankly ridiculous to say automation tasks are not your job. Shame on anyone who says this.

Flying Blind

Are you logging your code? If you are not, why? Do you drive your car without headlights, too? Application visibility is another problem that is quite easy to remedy. For production software, it is technically possible to have too much logging, but more often than not in a troubled project, there is zero! For distributed systems, it is critical to have it logged. No matter how skilled the developers, no matter how simple the problem, no matter how good the operations team, you need logging. If you don't include logging in your application, your project is dead on arrival.

Difficulties in Coordination as an Ongoing Accomplishment

One of the difficulties in working in DevOps teams is the status differences among the cofounder/CTO, the cofounder/CEO, and other members of the group. This conflict causes coordination difficulties in getting: a more reliable infrastructure, better instrumentation, proper backups, testing and QA, and ultimate resolution of any ongoing stability crisis.

Another ordinary organization dynamic that erodes the integrating conditions and causes coordination breakdowns is status differences in groups, because high-status groups may feel no need to recognize the task contributions of members of low-status groups. For instance, Metiu shows how, in software production, high-status programmers refuse to read the notes and comments that low-status programmers provide to document the progress of work. Because accountability requires an acknowledgment of mutual responsibilities, status differences that prevent such acknowledgment limit the development of liability.[1]

In situations where substantial status differences exist, members of groups may not be able to trust one another. When working interdependently, low-status individuals in these situations will ask fewer questions and give less feedback, for fear of offending others and possible repercussions. Such a situation leads to less sharing of knowledge, limiting common understanding in the group."

In organizational behavior, there is a concept called "closure." Closure is defined as the act of monopolizing goods or opportunities based on status. According to Metiu, a typical high-status group of software developers will use the following techniques to practice closure:

---

1 Anca Metiu, "Owning the Code: Status Closure in Distributed Groups," *Organization Science*, (Jul-Aug. 2006).

- Lack of interaction
- Use of geographical distance or proximity (in the case of an office)
- Nonuse of work
- Criticism
- Code-ownership transfer

Having observed interactions inside companies, my belief is that executive management often engages in closure for projects they work on with staff. For example, even though a CTO may ask a DevOps engineer to work on an instrumentation task, the CTO may then refuse to use it. By not using it, it infers the DevOps engineer could never be in the same high-status group as the CTO. This behavior is textbook "closure" according to research in software development teams by Metiu.[2]

This behavior is one of the most substantial challenges to overcome in fixing pervasive problems within engineering in organizations. When a high-status individual "owned" a component, it has historically not worked until several "low status" team members got involved and took joint responsibility. These projects included UI, logging, data-center migration, infrastructure, and more. Admittedly this is a complex problem and not the only factor, but it is a factor with some unknown, yet significant, weight.

If the leadership in an organization "is better" than other people, you will never implement true DevOps principles. You will be applying Highest Paid Person's Opinon (HIPO) principles. While DevOps can quite literally save lives and save your company, HIPOs are ferocious animals that can and do kill everything in their path.

No Teamwork

It is ubiquitous at martial arts studios to have the students help mop the floor. There are a lot of obvious reasons for doing this. It shows respect to the instructor and teaches students self-discipline. However, there are also some more subtle reasons as well.

There is a game theory problem at work here. Being exposed to a staph infection can cause serious health concerns. If you are offered an opportunity to mop the floor at the gym you train at, think very carefully about how you respond. People will watch how well you clean the floor, and if you do it well, they will do it well because they respect you. If you treat the task as something "beneath you" and don't perform it well, you could cause two problems. One, you have not cleaned the floor well, which could cause other members of the gym to get sick. Two, you have "infected" the

---

2 Anca Metiu, "Owning the Code: Status Closure in Distributed Groups," *Organization Science*, (Jul-Aug. 2006).

mindset of others, who will in turn not clean the floor. Your actions have actions in the present and the future.

So by "winning" and not mopping the floor correctly, you actually "lose" because you have played a part in encouraging unsanitary conditions that can be life-threatening. What is the moral of the story? If you train at a martial arts gym regularly and are asked to mop the floor, make sure you do an incredible job with a happy face. Your life could depend on it.

Let's look at the same situation at a software company. Many critical tasks fit this same profile: adding proper logging, creating a continuous deployment of your project, load testing your project, linting your code, or doing a code review. If you show a poor attitude or don't complete these tasks, your company may get a life-threating disease, just like staph. Approach and completion both are important. What is the message you are sending to your coworkers?

There is an excellent book on teamwork by Larson and LaFast[3] that covers a comprehensive and scientific study of teams. There are eight characteristics they identified that explain how and why effective teams develop:

- A clear, elevating goal
- A results-driven structure
- Competent team members
- Unified commitment
- A collaborative climate
- Standards of excellence
- External support and recognition
- Principled leadership

Let's review some examples of how these have worked or not worked in organizations.

A clear, elevating goal

If your organization doesn't have a clear, elevating goal, you're in trouble, full stop! As an engineer, I wanted the goal to be to make excellent, reliable software that worked. At troubled companies, though, I was told about many goals: going after whales, letting Amazon "burn down" while we moved to a data center, getting the company sold to "X" or "Y."

---

3 Larson, C. E., & LaFasto, F. M. J. (1989). *Sage series in interpersonal communication, Vol. 10. Teamwork: What must go right/what can go wrong.* Thousand Oaks, CA, US: Sage Publications, Inc.

A results-driven structure

Is your organization a R.O.W.E, or results-only work experience? Many of the tools and processes used in companies are questionable if they are not directly attributable to results: Skype, email, extremely long meetings, working "late." Ultimately, none of this helps the company by itself. More of a focus on results, versus "face time" or a "quick response on Skype" or email could be a breakout change in an organization. What about "fake Agile"? Is your company doing a cargo-cult agile? Does this process accomplish nothing but burn hours of developers' time in meetings while you talk about burndown charts, story points, and use lots of other process buzzwords?

Competent team members

It should go without saying that you need competent team members at your organization to be successful. Competency doesn't mean "elite" schooling or "leet code," though, it means the ability and desire to perform tasks as part of a team.

Unified commitment

Do you have self-serving people on your team? Are they looking out only for themselves? Do they push a last-minute change to the database, then walk out the door without testing because it was 4:35? They need to catch the bus (not caring if they burned down production). This behavior is cancer that destroys your team quicker than anything else. You cannot have self-serving people in a high-performing team; they will ruin it.

A collaborative climate

Is there an appropriate level of task conflict? Everyone cannot merely agree with each other, because you won't catch mistakes. At the same time, you cannot have people yelling at each other. It needs to be a respectful environment where people are open and expect feedback. If the scale falls too far in either direction, you're doomed. Achieving this balance is easier said than done.

Another example is the hiring process. Many companies complain about the inability to hire, hire for diversity, and generally get good candidates. The real issue is that their hiring process is "fugly:"

1. First, the company FLATTERs candidates to apply.
2. Next, they WASTE their time with bespoke irrelevant tests.
3. Then they HAZE them with a round of interviews that have worse predictive value than random.
4. Then they GHOST the candidate and don't give them any feedback.
5. They LIE and say they are trying to hire people when they have a broken process.

6. They then YELL on social media about how hard it is to engage diverse, or any, candidate.

The reason you cannot hire is your process is FUGLY! Treat people with respect, and you will get respect. The connection will manifest itself in being able to retain many great employees who have been needlessly disregarded by a hiring practice that optimizes for the wrong thing.

Standards of excellence

This step is a significant challenge for organizations. Most IT professionals work very hard but could improve their standards of excellence and craftsmanship. One other way of stating this is to say that a higher degree of self-discipline is required. Higher standards for writing software, testing, and deploying are necessary. More stringent measures are required for reading the documentation on new technologies before they deploy.

One example is the software life cycle. At every stage, Higher standards are necessary. Write a technical overview and create a diagram before work starts. It is important to never release code that hasn't been through a proper DevOps life cycle.

In terms of infrastructure, best practices need to be followed at many steps, whether a zookeeper configuration, EC2 storage configuration, or mongo or serverless. Every single component in the technology stack needs to be revisited and looked at for best-practice compliance. Many situations exist where documentation stated a proper way to configure an element, but it was never read! It would be safe to assume over 50% of the technology stacks at many companies are still improperly configured, despite significant technology improvements.

Please note that I am making a clear distinction between working "long hours, nights, and weekends," versus being highly disciplined at work and following standards of excellence. There are too many nights and weekends worked, and not enough discipline, by an order of magnitude in the software industry. It would be a grave mistake to underestimate how significant the lack of standards and controls is versus merely telling someone to work longer and harder.

Finally, there needs to be a higher standard for gathering quantitative data when recommending strategic directions for many companies. The lack of any real quantitative analysis of "migrating to a new data center" or "pursuing whales," speaks to a lack of discipline and process for many in management. It simply isn't good enough to have an opinion, often stated as a fact by a member of a management team, without having the data to back it up. Management needs high standards. Everyone in the company can see when data, not opinion, hierarchy, aggression, or a desire for a commission, is used to make decisions.

External support and recognition

Historically, there have been some real issues with external support and recognition for DevOps professionals. A readily evident example is being on call. Things have improved dramatically in the tech world. But even today, many people on pager duty are not recognized for how hard they work and how challenging it is to be on call.

At many organizations, there appears to be no tangible reward for working hard, such as volunteering to be on call. If anything, there is a clear precedent that shirking your duty could get you promoted because you were crafty enough to get out of lower-status work. In the case of one employee I worked with, he said it "wasn't smart" (his words) to agree to be on call. He refused to go on call when he was in engineering. Shirking his duty then led to a promotion. It is challenging to ask for extraordinary contributions when leaders show below average commitment and below average integrity.

Another example of a lack of external support is when one department drops the hard tasks on another. They commonly say, "This is DevOps; this isn't my job." I have seen sales engineering teams set up many environments: a data center environment, a Rackspace environment, AWS environment. They continuously paged the people on call, even though they hadn't set these environments up. When the sales engineer confronts this problem, he mentions he is in sales, and this "wasn't his job." Engineering didn't have access to the machines he had set up. They were misconfigured and paging people. The clear message here is "don't be a sucker" and get stuck on call. The "smart" people shirk this responsibility and delegate it to the lower status "suckers."

Yet another example of a lack of external support is when I was working at a company where customer data was deleted accidentally. A sales engineer initially misconfigured the machine without enough storage to support the customer's desired retention period. The responsibility, though, of continually cleaning up the data was in the hands of DevOps, the "suckers."

The maintenance of the machine required running dangerous Unix commands multiple times a day, and often in the middle of the night. Unsurprisingly, one member of the DevOps team mistyped one of the commands and deleted the customer data. The sales engineer got angry and refused to let the customer know; instead, he attempted to force the DevOps engineer to call the customer and perform a "mea culpa." It is problematic that companies have weak external support, and management has allowed individuals to behave in a way that is not supportive. This behavior sends a clear message that the administration will not tackle the "tough" problems like addressing immature or unprincipled behavior and instead will shift it to DevOps.

Principled leadership

There have been some great examples of principled leadership at companies I have worked at, as well as some unfortunate cases. Larson and LaFasto mention that a transformative leader, "establishes trust through positioning—assuring that the leader's behavior exemplifies the ideals and course of the vision." A CTO, for example, was on call for months during a crisis to show solidarity with everyone. This situation is an example of not asking someone to do something you wouldn't do yourself. Responsibility occurs when it is a personal sacrifice and inconvenient.

Another excellent example of principled leadership was with a product manager and the front-end team. She "required" that the front-end team use the ticket system and led by example, actively working with the queue and culling it. As a result, UX engineers learn this skill and how important it was for planning. She could have just said, "use the system," but instead used it herself. This situation has led to a real success that can be measured quantitatively. The ticket turnover rate, which the product manager closely monitored, improved.

On the other hand, some of the practices that startup CEOs promoted were unprincipled. Some would frequently send emails out about people needing to "work late," then go home at 4 P.M. Teams pick up on this behavior, and some of these repercussions remain forever. Another way to phrase this would be to call this "inauthentic leadership."

I have seen situations where a DevOps team was harassed and it was quite damaging. This harassment was created by saying the team didn't work hard, or was incompetent. This can be particularly damaging if it comes from someone who often leaves early and refuses to do challenging engineering tasks. Harassment is terrible enough, but when it comes from a legitimate slacker who is allowed to terrorize people, it becomes insufferable.

Larson and LaFasto also mention that any team that rated itself as low performing in these three categories didn't last long::

- Clear, elevating goal
- Competent team members
- Standards of excellence

Interviews

Glenn Solomon

What are some brief pieces of wisdom you can offer to Python and DevOps folks?

All companies will become software companies. There will be four or five companies that will be fundamental in this growth. DevOps is a critical aspect of this evolution. The velocity of change is important. New and different jobs will be created.

Personal website

https://goinglongblog.com

Company website

https://www.ggvc.com

Public contact information

https://www.linkedin.com/in/glennsolomon

Andrew Nguyen

Where do you work and what do you do there?

I am the Program Director of Health Informatics and the Chair of the Department of Health Professions at the University of San Francisco. My research interests involve the application of machine/deep learning to healthcare data with a specific focus on unstructured data. This includes text using NLP as well as sensor data using signal processing and analysis, both of which highly benefit from advances in deep learning. I am also the founder and CTO of qlaro, Inc., a digital health startup focused on using machine learning and NLP to empower cancer patients from diagnosis through survival. We help patients prioritize what they need to do next and how best to ask questions of their physicians and care team.

What is your favorite cloud and why?

While I started exploring cloud services (primarily from the perspective of IaaS) using AWS, I'd most recently been using GCP for my work. I made the switch early on purely due to the cost saving when deploying a HIPAA-compliant solution. Since then, I've been using GCP out of convenience since it's what I have the most experience with. However, where possible, I do my work using platform-agnostic tools to minimize impact, should I need to make the change.

From a machine learning perspective, I'm much more agnostic and happy to use either AWS or GCP, depending on the particulars of the machine learning project. That said, for my next project (which will involve collecting, storing, and processing a significant amount of data), I am planning on using GCP given the ease of developing and running Apache Beam jobs on various runners, including Google Dataflow.

When did you start using Python?

I started using Python about 15 years ago as a web development language when Django was first released. Since then, I've used it as a general-purpose programming/scripting language as well as a data science language.

What is your favorite thing about Python?

My favorite thing is that it's a ubiquitous, interpretable, object-oriented language. It runs on pretty much any system and provides the power of OOP with the simplicity of an interpreted scripting language.

What is your least favorite thing about Python?

Whitespace. I understand the reasoning behind using whitespace the way Python does. However, it gets annoying when trying to determine the scope of a function that spans more than the screen can display.

What is the software industry going to look like in 10 years?

I think we will see more and more people doing "software development" without writing as much code. Similar to how Word and Google Docs make it easy for anyone to format a document without manual word processing, I think folks will be able to write small functions or use GUIs to take care of simple business logic. In some sense, as tools like AWS Lambda and Google Cloud Functions become the norm, we'll see an increasing amount of turnkey functions that don't require formal computer science training to use effectively.

What technology would you short?

I would short MLaaS (machine learning as a service) companies—that is, companies that focus purely on machine learning algorithms. Just as we don't see companies that provide word processing services, tools and platforms such as AutoML or SageMaker will make it easy enough for most companies to bring the ML capability in-house. While we can't solve all ML problems using such tools, we can probably solve 80 to 90% of them. So, there will still be companies creating new ML approaches or providing ML as a service, but we'll see immense consolidation around major cloud providers (versus the endless stream of companies "doing machine learning" that we see today).

What is the most important skill you would recommend someone interested in Python DevOps learn?

Learn the concepts, not just the tools and tooling. New paradigms will come and go; but for every paradigm, we'll see dozens of competing tools and libraries. If you're only learning the specific tool or library, you'll quickly fall behind as a new paradigm starts to materialize and take over.

What is the most important skill you would recommend someone learn?

Learn how to learn. Figure out how you learn and how you can learn quickly. As with Moore's Law, where we saw the doubling of processor speeds with each generation, we are seeing accelerating growth of DevOps tools. Some build on existing approaches, while others attempt to supplant them. In any case, you'll need to know how you learn so that you can quickly and efficiently learn about the ever-increasing number of tools out there—and then quickly decide if it's worth pursuing.

Tell the readers something cool about you.

I enjoy hiking, backpacking, and generally being outside. In my free time, I also volunteer with the search and rescue team of my local Sheriff's Office, usually searching for missing people in the woods, but also during disasters such as the Camp Fire that hit Paradise, California.

Gabriella Roman

What is your name and current profession?

Hello! My name is Gabriella Roman, and I'm currently an undergraduate student studying computer science at Boston University.

Where do you work and what do you do there?

I'm an intern at Red Hat, Inc., where I work on the Ceph team. I mainly work with ceph-medic, a python tool that performs checks against Ceph clusters, either by fixing bugs in old checks or resolving issues with new checks. I also work with the DocUBetter team to update Ceph's documentation.

What is your favorite cloud and why?

Though I've only ever really used Google Cloud Storage, I can't really make a point as to why it's my favorite. I just happened to try it out and without much reason to dislike it, I have stayed loyal to it for the past 10 years. I do like its simple interface, and as someone who does not like to keep much digital clutter, the 15-GB limit does not bother me.

When did you start using Python?

I first learned Python in an introductory computer science course I took in the second half of my sophomore year.

What is your favorite thing about Python?

Its readability. Python's syntax is among the simplest of the programming languages, making it a great choice for beginners.

What is your least favorite thing about Python?

I don't have enough experience with other programming languages yet for comparison.

What is the software industry going to look like in 10 years?

It's nearly impossible to know what the future will hold, especially in a field that is constantly changing. All I can say is that I hope the software industry continues to evolve in a positive direction, and that software is not used wrongfully.

What is the most important skill you would recommend to someone interested in learning Python?

Practicing good code style, especially when working with a team, helps avoid a lot of unnecessary headache. As a Python newbie myself, I find it especially helpful when I read through code that is well organized and has detailed documentation.

What is the most important skill you would recommend someone learn?

This one isn't exactly a skill, but more of a state of mind: be willing to learn new things! We're constantly learning, even when we least expect it, so keep an open mind and allow others to share their knowledge with you!

Tell the readers something cool about you.

I really enjoy playing video games! Some of my favorites are *The Last of Us*, *Hollow Knight*, and *League of Legends*.

Professional website

https://www.linkedin.com/in/gabriellasroman

Rigoberto Roche

Where do you work and what do you do there?

I work at NASA Glenn Research Center as Lead Engineer for the Meachine Learning and Smart Algorithms Team. My job is to develop decision-making algorithms to controll all aspects of space communication and navigation.

What is your favorite cloud and why?

Amazon Web Services, because it is the one I have the most experience with due to its availability in my work flow.

When did you start using Python?

2014

What is your favorite thing about Python?

Easy-to-read code and quick development time.

What is your least favorite thing about Python?

Whitespace delineation.

What is the software industry going to look like in 10 years?

It is hard to tell. It seems there is a drive to cloud computing and decentralized programming that will drive developers to work as independent contractors for everything. It'll be a gig economy, not a large business industry. The biggest shift will be the use of automatic coding tools to separate the creative development from the syntax learning tasks. This can open the door to more creative professionals to develop new things and new systems.

What technology would you short?

Uber and Lyft. Anything that has manual labor that can be automated by narrow AI: driving, warehousing, paralegal work. Problems that can be solved by deep learning.

What is the most important skill you would recommend someone interested in Python DevOps learn?

The ability to learn quickly, with a benchmark of "Can you be dangerous in one month or less?" Another is the ability to understand and build from basic principles "like a physicist," by doing the actual work yourself and understanding more than the theory.

What is the most important skill you would recommend someone learn?

Brain hooks (memory palace), the pomodoro technique, and spaced recall self-testing for content absorption.

Tell the readers something cool about you.

I love combat training systems like Rickson Gracie's style JiuJitsu and Mussad Krav Maga (not the sport one). My passion in this world is to build a truly thinking machine.

Personal website

Just google my name.

Personal Blog

Don't have one.

Company website

www.nasa.gov (*https://www.nasa.gov*)

Public contact information

rigo.j.roche@gmail.com

Jonathan LaCour

Where do you work and what do you do there?

I am the CTO for Mission, a cloud consulting and managed service provider focused on AWS. At Mission, I direct the creation and definition of our service offerings and lead our platform team, which focuses on driving efficiency and quality via automation.

What is your favorite cloud and why?

I have deep roots in public cloud, both as a consumer and a builder of public cloud services. That experience has led me to understand that AWS provides the deepest, broadest, and most widespread public cloud available. Because AWS is the clear market leader, they also have the largest community of open source tools, frameworks, and projects.

When did you start using Python?

I first started programming in Python in late 1996 around the release of Python 1.4. At the time, I was in high school, but was working in my spare time as a programmer for an enterprise healthcare company. Python instantly felt like "home," and I have been using Python as my language of choice ever since.

What is your favorite thing about Python?

Python is a very low-friction language that happily fades into the background, allowing the developer to focus on solving problems rather than fighting with unnecessary complexity. Python is just so much fun to use as a result!

What is your least favorite thing about Python?

Python applications can be more difficult to deploy and distribute than I'd like. With languages like Go, applications can be built into portable binaries that are easy to distribute, whereas Python programs require significantly more effort.

What is the software industry going to look like in 10 years?

The last 10 years have been about the rise of public cloud services, with a focus on infrastructure as code, and infrastructure automation. I believe that the next 10 years will be about the rise of serverless architectures and managed services. Applications will no longer be built around the concept of "servers," and will instead be built around services and functions. Many will transition off of servers into container orchestration platforms like Kubernetes, while others will make the leap directly to serverless.

What technology would you short?

Blockchain. While an interesting technology, the overreach of its applicability is astounding, and the space is filled with hucksters and snake oil salesmen peddling blockchain as the solution to all problems.

What is the most important skill you would recommend someone interested in Python DevOps learn?

Since I first started using Python in 1996, I've found that the most important driver for learning has been curiosity and the drive to automate. Python is an incredible tool for automation, and a curious mind can constantly find new ways to automate every-thing from our business systems to our homes. I'd encourage anyone getting started with Python to look for opportunities to "scratch your own itches" by solving real problems with Python.

What is the most important skill you would recommend someone learn?

Empathy. Too often, technologists embrace technology without considering the impact on humanity and on each other. Empathy is a personal core value for me, and it helps me to be a better technologist, manager, leader, and human.

Tell the readers something cool about yourself.

I have spent the last three years resurrecting my personal website, pulling in content from as far back as 2002. Now, my website is my personal archive of memories, pho-tos, writing, and more.

Personal website

https://cleverdevil.io

Personal blog

https://cleverdevil.io

Company website

https://www.missioncloud.com

Public contact information

https://cleverdevil.io

Ville Tuulos

Where do you work and what do you do there?

I work at Netflix where I lead our machine learning infrastructure team. Our job is to provide a platform for data scientists that allows them to prototype end-to-end ML workflows quickly and deploy them to production confidently.

What is your favorite cloud and why?

I am a shameless fan of AWS. I have been using AWS since the EC2 beta in 2006. AWS continues to impress me both technically and as a business. Their core pieces of infrastructure, like S3, scale and perform extremely well, and they are very robust. From a business point of view they have done two things right. They have embraced open source technologies, which has made adoption easier in many cases, and they are very sensitive to customer feedback.

When did you start using Python?

I started using Python around 2001. I remember being very excited about the release of generators and generator expressions soon after I had started using Python.

What is your favorite thing about Python?

I am fascinated by programming languages in general. Not only technically, but also as a medium of human communication and as a culture. Python is an extremely well-balanced language. In many ways it is a simple and easily approachable language, but at the same time expressive enough to handle even complex applications. It is not a high-performance language, but in most cases it is performant enough, especially when it comes to I/O. Many other languages are better optimized for particular use cases, but only a few are as well-rounded as Python.

Also, the CPython implementation is a straightforward piece of C code and much simpler than JVM, V8, or the Go runtime, which makes it easy to debug and extend when needed.

What is your least favorite thing about Python?

The other side of being a well-rounded generalist language is that Python is not an optimal language for any particular use case. I miss C when I work on anything performance-critical. I miss Erlang when I am building anything requiring concurrency. And when hacking algorithms, I miss the type inference of OCaml. Paradoxically, when using any of these languages, I miss the generality, pragmatism, and the community of Python.

What is the software industry going to look like in 10 years?

The trend is clear if you look at the past 50 years of computing. Software is eating the world and the software industry keeps moving upward in the tech stack. Relatively speaking, we have fewer people focusing on hardware, operating systems, and low-level coding than ever before. Correspondingly, we have an increasing number of people writing software who don't have much experience or knowledge of the lower levels of the stack, which is OK. I think this trend has massively contributed to the success of Python this far. I predict that we will see more and more human-centered solutions like Python in the future, so we can empower an ever-increasing group of people to build software.

What technology would you short?

I tend to short technologies that assume that technical factors trump human factors. The history is littered with technologies that were technically brilliant but failed to appreciate the actual needs of their users. Taking this stance is not always easy, since it is a natural engineering instinct to feel that technically elegant solutions should deserve to win.

What is the most important skill you would recommend someone interested in Python DevOps learn?

I would recommend anyone serious about Python, DevOps in particular, to learn a bit about functional programming. Nothing hardcore, just the mindset around idempotency, function composition, and the benefits of immutability. I think the functional mindset is very useful for large-scale DevOps: how to think about immutable infrastructure, packaging, etc.

What is the most important skill you would recommend someone learn?

Learning to identify what problems are worth solving is critical. So many times I have observed software projects where an almost infinite amount of resources has been put into solving problems that ultimately don't matter. I have found Python to be a good way to hone this skill, since it allows you to quickly prototype fully functional solutions that can help you see what is relevant.

Tell the readers something cool about you.

With a friend of mine, I hacked an urban game that was played in NYC. Players took photos with their phones that were projected on a giant billboard in the Times Square in real time. A nerdy cool thing about this is that the whole game, including the client running on the phones, was written in Python. What's even cooler is that the game took place in 2006, in the Jurassic era of smartphones, predating the iPhone.

Personal website

https://www.linkedin.com/in/villetuulos

Company website

https://research.netflix.com

Public contact information

@vtuulos on Twitter

Joseph Reis

Where do you work and what do you do there?

I'm the cofounder of Ternary Data. Mostly I work in sales, marketing, and product development.

What is your favorite cloud and why?

It's a toss up between AWS and Google Cloud. I find AWS better for apps, but Google Cloud superior for data and ML/AI.

When did you start using Python?

2009

What is your favorite thing about Python?

There's (usually) one way to do things, so that cuts down on the mental overhead needed to figure out the best solution to the problem at hand. Just do it the Python way and move on.

What is your least favorite thing about Python?

The GIL is my least favorite thing. Though thankfully, the world seems to be moving toward a resolution of the GIL.

What is the software industry going to look like in 10 years?

Probably much like it does now, though with faster iteration cycles of best practices and new tools. What's old is new again, and what's new is old. The thing that doesn't change is people.

What technology would you short?

I'd short AI in the short term, but very long AI over the coming decades. A lot of hype around AI poses a risk of some broken hearts in the short term.

What is the most important skill you would recommend someone interested in Python DevOps learn?

Automate EVERYTHING possible. Python is an awesome language for simplifying your life, and your company's processes. Definitely take advantage of this great power.

What is the most important skill you would recommend someone learn?

Learn to have a growth mindset. Being flexible, adaptable, and able to learn new things will keep you relevant for a very long time. With the hyper-fast changes in tech —and the world in general—there will be endless opportunities to learn…mostly because you'll have to :).

Tell the readers something cool about you.

I'm a former rock climbing bum, club DJ, and adventurer. Now I'm a rock climber with a job, I still DJ, and I go on as many adventures as possible. So, not much has changed, but the itch to explore and do dangerous things still continues.

Personal website and blog

https://josephreis.com

Company website

https://ternarydata.com

Public contact information

josephreis@gmail.com

Teijo Holzer

Where do you work and what do you do there?

I have been working as a Senior Software Engineer at Weta Digital, New Zealand, for 12 years. My responsibilities include software development (mainly Python and C++), but I also occasionally perform System Engineering and DevOps tasks.

What is your favorite cloud and why?

It has to be AWS.

One of the main features they offer is the support for continous integration and delivery. In software engineering, you want to automate as many mundane tasks as possible so you can concentrate on the fun parts of innovative software development.

Things that you usually don't want to think about are code builds, running existing automated tests, releasing and deploying new versions, restarting services, etc. So you want to rely on tools like Ansible, Puppet, Jenkins, etc., to perform these tasks automatically at certain defined points (e.g., when you merge a new feature branch into master).

Another big plus is the amount of available support in online forums like Stack Overflow, etc. Being the current market leader in the cloud platform space naturally leads to a larger user base asking questions and solving problems.

When did you start using Python?

I started using Python more than 15 years ago and have more than 12 years of professional Python experience.

What is your favorite thing about Python?

That there is no need to reformat your source code, ever. The choice to have white-space carry syntactical/grammatical meaning means that other people's Python code immediately has a very high readability score. I also like the Python license, which led to a huge uptake of Python as a scripting language in many third-party commercial applications.

What is your least favorite thing about Python?

The difficulty of performing highly concurrent tasks in a reliable and effective fashion. In Python, efficient and reliable threading and multiprocessing are still difficult to achieve in complex environments.

What is the software industry going to look like in 10 years?

In my opinion, more emphasis will be placed on being able to integrate and deliver customer-centric solutions based on existing infrastructure and tooling within an aggressive time frame. There is no need to constantly reinvent the same wheel. So system engineering and DevOps skills will become more important in the software industry. You need to be able to scale fast if required.

What technology would you short?

Any system that has a single point of failure. Building robust systems requires you to acknowledge that all systems will eventually fail, so you need to cater for that at every level. That starts by not using assert statements in your code, and goes all the way up to providing high-availability, multimaster DB servers. Building fault-tolerant systems is especially important when there are many users relying on your systems 24/7. Even AWS only offers 99.95% uptime.

What is the most important skill you would recommend someone interested in Python DevOps learn?

Speedy automation. Every time you find yourself repeating the same tasks over and over, or you find yourself again waiting for a long-running task to complete, ask yourself: How can I automate and speed up those tasks ? Having a quick turnaround time is essential for effective DevOps work.

What is the most important skill you would recommend someone learn?

Speedy automation, as discussed above.

Tell the readers something cool about you.

I like presenting at Python conferences. Look for my most recent talk about Python, Threading and Qt at the Kiwi PyCon X.

Recent talk:

https://python.nz/kiwipycon.talk.teijoholzer

Company website

http://www.wetafx.co.nz

Matt Harrison

Where do you work and what do you do there?

I work at a company I created called MetaSnake. It provides corporate training and consulting in Python and data science. I spend about half of my time teaching engineers how to be productive with Python or how to do data science. The other half is consulting and helping companies leverage these technologies.

What is your favorite cloud and why?

I've used both Google and AWS in the past. They (and others) have excellent Python support, which I love. I don't know that I have a favorite, but I'm glad there are multiple clouds, as I believe competition gives us better products.

When did you start using Python?

I started using Python in 2000, when working at a small startup doing search. A colleague and I needed to build a small prototype. I was pushing for using Perl and he wanted to use TCL. Python was a compromise, as neither of us wanted to use the other's preferred technology. I believe both of us promptly forgot what we were using before and have leveraged Python since.

What is your favorite thing about Python?

Python fits my brain. It is easy to start from something simple to build an MVP and then productionize it. I'm really enjoying using notebook environments like Jupyter and Colab. They make data analysis really interactive.

What is your least favorite thing about Python?

The built-in docstrings for the classes, such as lists and dictionaries, need some cleanup. They are hard for newcomers to understand.

What is the software industry going to look like in 10 years?

I don't have a crystal ball. For me, the main difference between now and 10 years ago is leveraging the cloud. Otherwise, I use many of the same tools. I expect programming in the next 10 years to be very similar, off-by-one errors will still pop up, CSS will still be hard, maybe deployment might be slightly easier.

What technology would you short?

I imagine that proprietary tools for data analysis will go the way of the dinosaur. There might be an effort to save them by open sourcing them, but it will be too little, too late.

What is the most important skill you would recommend someone interested in Python DevOps learn?

I think curiosity and a willingness to learn are very important, especially as many of these tools are fast-moving targets. There seems to always be a new offering or new software.

What is the most important skill you would recommend someone learn?

I have two. One, learning how you learn. People learn in different ways. Find what way works for you.

The other skill is not technical. It is learning how to network. This doesn't have to be a dirty word and is very useful for people in tech. Most of my jobs and work have come from networking. This will pay huge dividends.

Tell the readers something cool about you.

I like to get outside. That might be running, ultimate hiking, or skiing.

Personal website/blog

https://hairysun.com

Company website

https://www.metasnake.com

Public contact information

matt@metasnake.com

Michael Foord

Where do you work and what do you do there?

My last two jobs have been working on DevOps tools, which has led to a reluctant passion for the topic on my part. Reluctant because I was long skeptical of the DevOps movement, thinking that it was mostly managers wanting developers to do sysadmin work as well. I've come to see that the part of DevOps I really care about is the systems-level thinking and having development processes be fully aware of that.

I worked for three years on Juju for Canonical, an interesting foray into programming with Go, and then for a year for Red Hat building a test automation system for Ansible Tower. Since then I've been self-employed with a mixture of training, team coaching, and contracting, including an AI project I'm working on now.

I'm my copious spare time I work on Python itself as part of the Python Core Dev team.

What is your favorite cloud and why?

I'm going to throw this question sideways a little. My favorite cloud is all of them, or at least not having to care (too much) which cloud I'm on.

The Juju model describes your system in a backend agnostic way. It provides a modelling language for describing your services and the relationships between them, which can then be deployed to any cloud.

This allows you to start on, say, AWS or Azure, and for cost or data security reasons migrate to an on-prem private cloud like Kubernetes or OpenStack without having to change your tooling.

I like to control my major dependencies, so I prefer to work with something like OpenStack than a public cloud. I'm also a fan of Canonical's MaaS (Metal As A Service), which is a bare-metal provisioner. It started life as a fork of Cobbler, I believe. You can use it directly, or as a substrate for managing the hardware with a private cloud. I wrote the Juju code to connect to the MaaS 2 API, and I was very impressed with it.

I'm much more of a fan of LXC/LXD or KVM virtualization than I am of Docker (virtually heresy these days), so Kubernetes or OpenShift wouldn't be my first port of call.

For commercial projects I sometimes recommend VMware cloud solutions, simply because of the availability of sysadmins used to running these systems.

When did you start using Python?

I started programming with Python as a hobby in about 2002. I enjoyed it so much that I started full-time programming around 2006. I was lucky enough to get a job with a London fintech startup where I really learned the craft of software engineering.

What is your favorite thing about Python?

It's pragmatism. Python is enormously practical, which makes it useful for real world tasks. This stretches right into the object system that strives to make the theory match the practice.

This is why I love teaching Python. For the most part, the theory is the same as the practice, so you get to teach them in the same breath.

What is your least favorite thing about Python?

Python is old, and if you include the standard library, big. Python has quite a few warts, such as the lack of symmetry in the descriptor protocol, meaning you can't write a setter for a class descriptor. Those are largely minor.

The big wart for me, which many will agree with, is the lack of true free-threading. In a multicore world, this has been getting more and more important, and the Python community was in denial about it for years. Thankfully we're now seeing the core-devs make practical steps to fix this. Subinterpreter support has several PEPs and is actively being worked on. There are also people looking at [possibly] moving away from reference counting for garbage collection, which will make free-threading much easier. In fact, most of the work has already been done by Larry Hastings in his Gilectomy experiment, but it's still hampered by reference counting.

What is the software industry going to look like in 10 years?

I think we're in the early part of an AI gold rush. That's going to spawn thousands of short-lived and useless products, but also completely change the industry. AI will be a standard part of most large-scale systems.

In addition, DevOps is providing a way for us to think about system development, deployment, and maintenance. We've already seen the effects of that in microservices and polyglot environments. I think we'll see a rise of a new generation of DevOps tooling that democratises system-level thinking, making it much easier to build and maintain larger-scale systems. These will become more "solved problems," and the frontiers will expand into new challenges that haven't yet been described.

What technology would you short?

Ooh, a challenging question. I'm going to say the current generation of DevOps tooling.

The genius of DevOps is codifying arcane deployment and configuration knowledge; for example, playbooks with Ansible, and Charms for Juju.

The ideal DevOps tooling would allow you to describe and then orchestrate your system, in a backend agnostic way, but also incorporate monitoring and an awareness of the system state. This would make deployment, testing, reconfiguring, scaling, and self healing straightforward and standard features.

Perhaps we need an App Store for the cloud. I think a lot of people are trying to get there.

What is the most important skill you would recommend someone interested in Python DevOps learn?

I tend to learn by doing, so I resent being told what to learn. I've definitely taken jobs just to learn new skills. When I started with Canonical, it was because I wanted to learn web development.

So practical experience trumps learning. Having said that, virtual machines and containers are likely to remain the base unit of system design and deployment. Being comfortable slinging containers around is really powerful.

Networking is hard, important, and a very valuable skill. Combine that with containers through software-defined networking layers, and it makes a potent combination.

What is the most important skill you would recommend someone learn?

You'll never know enough, so the most important skill is to be able to learn and to change. If you can change, you're never stuck. Being stuck is the worst thing in the world.

Tell the readers something cool about you.

I dropped out of Cambridge University, I've been homeless, I've lived in a community for a number of years, I sold bricks for 10 years, and I taught myself to program. Now I'm on the Python core development team and have the privilege of traveling the world to speak about and teach Python.

Personal website/blog

http://www.voidspace.org.uk

Public contact information

michael@voidspace.org.uk

Recommendations

"All models are wrong…but some are useful," certainly applies to any general piece of advice on DevOps. Some elements of my analysis will be absolutely wrong, but some of it will be useful. It is impossible that my own personal bias doesn't play a role in my analysis. Despite being potentially wrong in some of my analysis and being very biased, there are clearly some urgent issues to fix in the management of most companies. Some of the highest priority issues are:

1. Status differences have lead to accountability problems, with software stability being a highly visible example. Engineering managers (especially startup founders), in particular, need to acknowledge how informal status closure affected software quality and fix it.

2. There is a culture of meaningless risk (firing silver bullets versus fixing broken windows) at many organizations.

3. There are ineffective or meaningless standards of excellence, and there is a general lack of discipline in engineering at many organizations.

4. Culturally, data has not been used to make decisions. The highest paid person's opinion (HIPO), status, aggression, intuition, and possibly even the roll of the dice have been the reasons for a decision.

5. True understanding of the concept of "opportunity cost" eludes executive management. This lack of understanding then trickles down the ranks.

6. The need to increase focus on meritocracy over "snake oil and bullshit," as senior data scientist Jeremy Howard at Kaggle says.

The "right" things can be put in place in a few months in engineering: a ticket system, code review, testing, planning, scheduling, and more. Executive leadership in companies can agree these are the right things to do, but their actions must match their words. Instead of focusing on execution, consistency and accountability, executive leadership is often focused on firing silver bullets from a high-powered elephant gun. Unfortunately, they often miss every elephant they shoot at. Executive teams would be wise to learn from these mistakes and avoid the negative culture around these mistakes.

Exercises

- What are the core components necessary for a capable team?
- Describe three areas you could improve as a team member.
- Describe three areas you excel at as a team member.
- What is right about all companies in the future?
- Why does DevOps need external support and recognition?

Challenges

- Create a detailed analysis of your current team using the teamwork framework by Larson and LaFast.
- Have everyone on your team fill out anonymous index cards that have three positive things and three valuable feedback items for each member of your small group (must have negative and positive issues). Get into a room and have each

person read the index cards from their teammates. (*Yes, this does work and can be a life-changing experience for individuals in your team.*)

Capstone Project

Now that you have reached the end of this book, there is a Capstone Project that you can build that demonstrates mastery of the concepts covered:

- Using the ideas explored in the book, create a scikit-learn, PyTorch, or Tensor-Flow application that servers out predictions via Flask. Deploy this project to a primary cloud provider while completing all of these tasks:
  - Endpoint and health-check monitoring
  - Continuous delivery to multiple environments
  - Logging to a cloud-based service such as Amazon CloudWatch
  - Load-test the performance and create a scalability plan

Index

About the Authors

Noah Gift is a lecturer at the Duke MIDS and the Northwestern Graduate Data Science, UC Berkeley Graduate Data Science, and UC Davis Graduate School of Management in the MSBA programs. Professionally, Noah has approximately 20 years of experience programming in Python and is a Python Software Foundation Fellow. He has worked for a variety of companies in roles ranging from CTO, general manager, consulting CTO, and cloud architect. Currently, he is consulting startups and other companies on machine learning and cloud architecture, and is doing CTO-level consulting as the founder of Pragmatic AI Labs (*https://paiml.com*).

He has published over one hundred technical publications, including two books, on subjects ranging from cloud machine learning to DevOps, for publications including O'Reilly, Pearson, DataCamp, and Udacity. He is also a certified AWS Solutions Architect. Noah has an MBA from the University of California, Davis; an MS in computer information systems from California State University, Los Angeles; and a BS in nutritional science from Cal Poly, San Luis Obispo. You can find more about Noah by following him on Github (*https://github.com/noahgift*), visiting his personal website (*https://noahgift.com*), or connecting with him on LinkedIn (*https://www.linkedin.com/in/noahgift*).

Kennedy Behrman is a veteran consultant specializing in architecting and implementing cloud solutions for early-stage startups. He has both undergraduate and graduate degrees from the University of Pennsylvania, including an MS in Computer Information Technology and postgraduate work in the Computer Graphics and Game Programming program.

He is experienced in data engineering, data science, AWS solutions, and engineering management, and has acted as a technical editor on a number of Python and data science-related publications. As a data scientist, he helped develop a proprietary growth hacking machine-learning algorithm for a startup that led to the exponential growth of the platform. Afterward, he then hired and managed a data science team that supported this technology. In addition to that experience, he has been active in the Python language for close to 15 years, giving talks at user groups, writing articles, and serving as a technical editor to many publications.

Alfredo Deza is a passionate software engineer, avid open source developer, Vim plug-in author, photographer, and former Olympic athlete. He has given several lectures around the world about open source software, personal development, and professional sports. He has rebuilt company infrastructure, designed shared storage, and replaced complex build systems, always in search of efficient and resilient environments. With a strong belief in testing and documentation, he continues to drive robust development practices wherever he is.

As a knowledge-craving developer, Alfredo can be found giving presentations in local groups about Python, filesystems and storage, system administration, and professional sports.

Grig Gheorghiu has more than 25 years of industry experience working in diverse roles such as programmer, test engineer, research lab manager, system/network/security/cloud architect, and DevOps lead. For the past 20 years, Grig has been architecting and building the infrastructure for large consumer-facing and ecommerce websites such as Evite and NastyGal, as well as leading technical operations and engineering teams. Grig has a BSc degree in CS from the University of Bucharest, Romania, and a MSc degree in CS from USC in Los Angeles.

Grig blogs on programming, cloud computing, system administration, data analytics, and automated testing tools and techniques on Medium (*https://medium.com/@grig gheo*), and likes to believe that a fortune cookie he once got is right: his mind is creative, original, and alert.

Colophon

The animal on the cover of *Python for DevOps* is a carpet python (*Morelia spilota*), a nonvenomous constricting snake native primarily to Australia and the neighboring Solomon Islands and New Guinea. As one of the most widespread pythons on the Australian continent, they have been spotted anywhere from the tropical rainforests of Queensland in the Northeast to the Mediterranean woodlands of the Southwest. It is not uncommon to find carpet pythons slithering through garden beds, coiling up attic rafters, or even residing as household pets.

Most carpet pythons are olive green with dark-edged cream-colored blotches. Notably, the jungle carpet python (*Morelia spilota cheynei*) has bright yellow and black skin, making it a popular specimen among snake owners. Adults measure an average of 6.6 feet in length, with some reaching a reported 13 feet.

The carpet python is a nocturnal hunter and uses thermoreceptive labial pits that line the sides of their mouth to detect the body heat of birds, lizards, and small mammals. During the day, they will wrap themselves up in a tree or search for an open field to bask in. Females in particular will bask in the morning sun and transfer the heat to their eggs when they return to their nests. Additionally, they will contract their muscles to generate heat for the 10–47 eggs they lay every summer.

While the carpet python has a conservation status of Least Concern, many of the animals on O'Reilly covers are endangered; all of them are important to the world.

The cover illustration is by Jose Marzan, based on a black and white engraving from Georges Cuvier's *The Animal Kingdom*. The cover fonts are Gilroy Semibold and Guardian Sans. The text font is Adobe Minion Pro; the heading font is Adobe Myriad Condensed; and the code font is Dalton Maag's Ubuntu Mono.

O'REILLY®

There's much more where this came from.

Experience books, videos, live online training courses, and more from O'Reilly and our 200+ partners—all in one place.

Learn more at oreilly.com/online-learning

Milton Keynes UK
Ingram Content Group UK Ltd.
UKHW032052291123
433505UK00002B/7

9 781492 057697